The Professional Development Early Years Educators

This book provides a critical insight into comparative approaches to the professional learning and development of early years educators – taken to include all those working in a professional capacity with young children in educative settings, including home-based care and education. It also analyses leadership development for the early years workforce, and the evaluation of the success or otherwise of professional development initiatives involving early years educators. The book includes perspectives on relevant policy development at local and national levels and critical consideration of research literature on the effectiveness of professional development programmes for early years educators.

The book is essential reading for professionals working in early years settings, for those engaged with the professional learning of early years educators, and for academics researching professionalism in early years education. It provides international perspectives on the professional learning and development of those working in early years education.

This book was originally published as a special issue of *Professional Development in Education*.

Jane Waters is Associate Professor and Assistant Dean (Research) in the Faculty of Education and Communities, University of Wales Trinity Saint David, UK. Her research interests lie in adult-child interactions in early years education, child participation and the interplay of space and culture in shaping educational experiences of young children.

Jane Payler is Professor of Education (Early Years), Deputy Associate Dean (Scholarship) and Co-Director of the Children's Research Centre at the Open University, UK. Her research centres on early years professional and workforce development, interprofessional practice in the early years and children's participatory learning processes.

Ken Jones is Managing Editor of *Professional Development in Education* and an Education Consultant working internationally in the fields of professional learning and development and school leadership. He is Professor Emeritus at the University of Wales Trinity Saint David, UK.

The Professional Development of Early Years Educators

Edited by
Jane Waters, Jane Payler and Ken Jones

LONDON AND NEW YORK

First published 2018 by Routledge

2 Park Square, Milton Park, Abingdon, Oxfordshire OX14 4RN
52 Vanderbilt Avenue, New York, NY 10017

Routledge is an imprint of the Taylor & Francis Group, an informa business

First issued in paperback 2019

Copyright © 2018 International Professional Development Association (IPDA)

All rights reserved. No part of this book may be reprinted or reproduced
or utilised in any form or by any electronic, mechanical, or other means,
now known or hereafter invented, including photocopying and recording,
or in any information storage or retrieval system, without permission in
writing from the publishers.

Notice:
Product or corporate names may be trademarks or registered trademarks,
and are used only for identification and explanation without intent to
infringe.

British Library Cataloguing in Publication Data
A catalogue record for this book is available from the British Library

ISBN 13: 978-1-138-55942-4 (hbk)
ISBN 13: 978-0-367-89210-4 (pbk)

Typeset in Times New Roman
by RefineCatch Limited, Bungay, Suffolk

Publisher's Note
The publisher accepts responsibility for any inconsistencies that may have
arisen during the conversion of this book from journal articles to book chapters,
namely the possible inclusion of journal terminology.

Disclaimer
Every effort has been made to contact copyright holders for their permission to
reprint material in this book. The publishers would be grateful to hear from any
copyright holder who is not here acknowledged and will undertake to rectify
any errors or omissions in future editions of this book.

Contents

Citation Information	vii
Notes on Contributors	xi

Foreword   1
Ken Jones

Introduction: The professional development of early years educators – achieving systematic, sustainable and transformative change   3
Jane Waters and Jane Payler

1. Professional development of the early childhood education teaching workforce in the United States: an overview   11
Rebecca E. Gomez, Sharon Lynn Kagan and Emily A. Fox

2. Contemporary practice in professional learning and development of early childhood educators in Australia: reflections on what works and why   29
Fay Hadley, Manjula Waniganayake and Wendy Shepherd

3. Implementing curriculum reform: insights into how Australian early childhood directors view professional development and learning   45
Kaye Colmer, Manjula Waniganayake and Laurie Field

4. The role of motive objects in early childhood teacher development concerning children's digital play and play-based learning in early childhood curricula   64
Joce Nuttall, Susan Edwards, Ana Mantilla, Sue Grieshaber and Elizabeth Wood

5. Preschool teachers' informal online professional development in relation to educational use of tablets in Swedish preschools   78
Leif Marklund

6. Reflecting on reflection: improving teachers' readiness to facilitate participatory learning with young children   96
Naomi McLeod

7. Do reflections on personal autobiography as captured in narrated life-stories illuminate leadership development in the field of early childhood?   115
Sara Layen

CONTENTS

8. Preschool teachers' insights about web-based self-coaching versus on-site expert coaching   132
Darbianne Shannon, Patricia Snyder and Tara McLaughlin

9. The nature of professional learning communities in New Zealand early childhood education: an exploratory study   152
Sue Cherrington and Kate Thornton

10. 'Accept the change and enjoy the range': applications of the Circles of Change methodology with professionals who support early childhood educators   171
Kym Macfarlane, Ali Lakhani, Jennifer Cartmel, Marilyn Casley and Kerry Smith

11. Head Start classroom teachers' and assistant teachers' perceptions of professional development using a LEARN framework   186
Ilham Nasser, Julie K. Kidd, M. Susan Burns and Trina Campbell

12. Educators' expectations and aspirations around young children's mathematical knowledge   208
Bob Perry and Amy MacDonald

13. 'The exchange of ideas was mutual, I have to say': negotiating researcher and teacher 'roles' in an early years educators' professional development programme on inquiry-based mathematics and science learning   224
Stavroula Philippou, Chrystalla Papademetri-Kachrimani and Loucas Louca

14. The professional identity of early years educators in England: implications for a transformative approach to continuing professional development   243
Sarah Lightfoot and David Frost

15. Evaluative decision-making for high-quality professional development: cultivating an evaluative stance   261
Jennifer Sumsion, Joanne Lunn Brownlee, Sharon Ryan, Kerryann Walsh, Ann Farrell, Susan Irvine, Gerry Mulhearn and Donna Berthelsen

Index   275

Citation Information

The chapters in this book were originally published in *Professional Development in Education*, volume 41, issue 2 (April 2015). When citing this material, please use the original page numbering for each article, as follows:

Foreword

Foreword
Ken Jones
Professional Development in Education, volume 41, issue 2 (April 2015),
pp. 159–160

Editorial

The professional development of early years educators – achieving systematic, sustainable and transformative change
Jane Waters and Jane Payler
Professional Development in Education, volume 41, issue 2 (April 2015),
pp. 161–168

Chapter 1

Professional development of the early childhood education teaching workforce in the United States: an overview
Rebecca E. Gomez, Sharon Lynn Kagan and Emily A. Fox
Professional Development in Education, volume 41, issue 2 (April 2015),
pp. 169–186

Chapter 2

Contemporary practice in professional learning and development of early childhood educators in Australia: reflections on what works and why
Fay Hadley, Manjula Waniganayake and Wendy Shepherd
Professional Development in Education, volume 41, issue 2 (April 2015),
pp. 187–202

Chapter 3

Implementing curriculum reform: insights into how Australian early childhood directors view professional development and learning
Kaye Colmer, Manjula Waniganayake and Laurie Field
Professional Development in Education, volume 41, issue 2 (April 2015),
pp. 203–221

CITATION INFORMATION

Chapter 4
The role of motive objects in early childhood teacher development concerning children's digital play and play-based learning in early childhood curricula
Joce Nuttall, Susan Edwards, Ana Mantilla, Sue Grieshaber and Elizabeth Wood
Professional Development in Education, volume 41, issue 2 (April 2015), pp. 222–235

Chapter 5
Preschool teachers' informal online professional development in relation to educational use of tablets in Swedish preschools
Leif Marklund
Professional Development in Education, volume 41, issue 2 (April 2015), pp. 236–253

Chapter 6
Reflecting on reflection: improving teachers' readiness to facilitate participatory learning with young children
Naomi McLeod
Professional Development in Education, volume 41, issue 2 (April 2015), pp. 254–272

Chapter 7
Do reflections on personal autobiography as captured in narrated life-stories illuminate leadership development in the field of early childhood?
Sara Layen
Professional Development in Education, volume 41, issue 2 (April 2015), pp. 273–289

Chapter 8
Preschool teachers' insights about web-based self-coaching versus on-site expert coaching
Darbianne Shannon, Patricia Snyder and Tara McLaughlin
Professional Development in Education, volume 41, issue 2 (April 2015), pp. 290–309

Chapter 9
The nature of professional learning communities in New Zealand early childhood education: an exploratory study
Sue Cherrington and Kate Thornton
Professional Development in Education, volume 41, issue 2 (April 2015), pp. 310–328

Chapter 10
'Accept the change and enjoy the range': applications of the Circles of Change methodology with professionals who support early childhood educators
Kym Macfarlane, Ali Lakhani, Jennifer Cartmel, Marilyn Casley and Kerry Smith
Professional Development in Education, volume 41, issue 2 (April 2015), pp. 329–343

CITATION INFORMATION

Chapter 11

Head Start classroom teachers' and assistant teachers' perceptions of professional development using a LEARN framework
Ilham Nasser, Julie K. Kidd, M. Susan Burns and Trina Campbell
Professional Development in Education, volume 41, issue 2 (April 2015), pp. 344–365

Chapter 12

Educators' expectations and aspirations around young children's mathematical knowledge
Bob Perry and Amy MacDonald
Professional Development in Education, volume 41, issue 2 (April 2015), pp. 366–381

Chapter 13

'The exchange of ideas was mutual, I have to say': negotiating researcher and teacher 'roles' in an early years educators' professional development programme on inquiry-based mathematics and science learning
Stavroula Philippou, Chrystalla Papademetri-Kachrimani and Loucas Louca
Professional Development in Education, volume 41, issue 2 (April 2015), pp. 382–400

Chapter 14

The professional identity of early years educators in England: implications for a transformative approach to continuing professional development
Sarah Lightfoot and David Frost
Professional Development in Education, volume 41, issue 2 (April 2015), pp. 401–418

Chapter 15

Evaluative decision-making for high-quality professional development: cultivating an evaluative stance
Jennifer Sumsion, Joanne Lunn Brownlee, Sharon Ryan, Kerryann Walsh, Ann Farrell, Susan Irvine, Gerry Mulhearn and Donna Berthelsen
Professional Development in Education, volume 41, issue 2 (April 2015), pp. 419–432

For any permission-related enquiries please visit:
http://www.tandfonline.com/page/help/permissions

Notes on Contributors

Donna Berthelsen is Adjunct Professor in the School of Early Childhood, Queensland University of Technology, Australia. She is a developmental psychologist engaged in research that focuses on child outcomes in relation to: family environments, early childhood education programs, early intervention and the transition to school.

M. Susan Burns is Professor of Early Childhood Education at George Mason University, USA. Her research centres on the development and learning of young children (preschool through Grade 3).

Trina Campbell is Adjunct Instructor for Maths at Germanna Community College, USA.

Jennifer Cartmel is Senior Lecturer in the School of Human Services and Social Work, Griffith University, Australia. Her research interests include the role of critical reflection in the development of professional competencies, the interaction between educators and children in group settings and the many facets of outside school hours care services.

Marilyn Casley is Associate Lecturer at the School of Human Services and Social Work, Griffith University, Australia.

Sue Cherrington is Associate Dean of the School of Education, Victoria University of Wellington, New Zealand. She teaches specifically around professional learning communities and pedagogical practices.

Kaye Colmer is the Executive Director of Gowrie SA, Australia. She is interested in early childhood curriculum and the development of early childhood centres that provide safe, and challenging places where children can experience secure relationships and learn and where their families get the support they need.

Susan Edwards is Professor of Education in the Learning Sciences Institute of Australia, Australian Catholic University, where she directs the Early Childhood Futures research program. Her research investigates the role of play-based learning in the early childhood curriculum for the 21st century.

Ann Farrell is Professor and Head of the School of Early Childhood and Inclusive Education, Faculty of Education, Queensland University of Technology, Australia.

Laurie Field is Senior Lecturer at the School of Education, Macquarie University, Australia. His academic interests and expertise relate to human resource management, training and learning (both individual and organisational) and workplace change.

NOTES ON CONTRIBUTORS

Emily A. Fox is a Clinical Research Associate at Seattle Children's Autism Center, University of Washington, USA.

David Frost is Senior Lecturer in the Faculty of Education and a member of the 'Leadership for Learning' academic group. He is the Programmes Director for the HertsCam Network which supports around 500 teachers who lead innovation in Hertfordshire schools.

Rebecca E. Gomez is a Program Officer for the Education program at the Heising-Simons Foundation, USA.

Sue Grieshaber is Professor in the Faculty of Education at Monash University, Australia. Her research interests include early childhood curriculum, policy, pedagogies and families, with a focus on social justice and equity.

Fay Hadley is Senior Lecturer at the Institute of Early Childhood, Macquarie University, Australia. Her main areas of teaching include professional experience, working with families and leadership.

Susan Irvine is Senior Lecturer in the School of Early Childhood, Queensland University of Technology, Australia.

Ken Jones is Managing Editor of *Professional Development in Education* and an Education Consultant working internationally in the fields of professional learning and development and school leadership. He is Professor Emeritus at the University of Wales Trinity Saint David, UK.

Sharon Lynn Kagan is the Virginia and Leonard Marx Professor of Early Childhood and Family Policy, Co-Director of the National Center for Children and Families, and Associate Dean for Policy at Teachers College, Columbia University, USA. Her research focuses on the institutions that impact child and family life.

Julie K. Kidd is Professor of Education in the College of Education and Human Development at George Mason University, USA. Her research is focused on developing the cognitive, literacy and numeracy abilities of children from diverse cultural, linguistic and socio-economic backgrounds as well as on the professional development of preservice and inservice teachers.

Ali Lakhani is a Post-Doctorate Fellow with Menzies Health Institute Queensland, Griffith University, Australia and Synapse, and his research focuses on self-directed policy for persons with disability, integrated practice for early child development and care, and culturally appropriate research methods.

Sara Layen is Senior Lecturer at the Institute for Education, Bath Spa University, UK. Her teaching specialism covers early childhood pedagogy and leadership.

Sarah Lightfoot is a Doctoral Student at the School of Education, University of Cambridge, UK.

Loucas Louca is Associate Professor of Science Education, the Department of Education Sciences, the European University Cyprus.

Joanne Lunn Brownlee is Professor in the School of Early Childhood at the Queensland University of Technology, Australia. Her current research investigates early childhood professionals' personal epistemology and the impact of such beliefs on early childhood practice.

NOTES ON CONTRIBUTORS

Amy MacDonald is Senior Lecturer in Early Childhood Mathematics Education at Charles Sturt University, Australia. Her current research focuses on the mathematics experiences and education of infants, toddlers, preschoolers and children in the early years of primary school.

Kym Macfarlane is Associate Professor at the School of Human Services and Social Work, Griffith University, Australia. Her research expertise includes working with children in Early Childhood settings, reconceptualising Early Childhood Education, designing innovative programs for students involved in flexible learning and post-structuralist research.

Ana Mantilla is Senior Research Assistant for the Learning Sciences Institute Australia, Faculty of Education and Arts, Australian Catholic University.

Leif Marklund is a postgraduate student at the Department of Applied Educational Science, Umeå Universtiy, Sweden.

Tara McLaughlin is Senior Lecturer in Early Years at the Institute of Education, Massey University of New Zealand. Her research interests include promotion of children's social-emotional development, inclusive education and early intervention.

Naomi McLeod teaches Early Childhood and Education Studies, Liverpool John Moores University, UK. She also leads the MA in International Approaches to Early Childhood Education.

Gerry Mulhearn is currently completing a Doctor of Education at Charles Sturt University, Australia. Her research and practice interests are early childhood policy, pedagogy and curriculum, with a particular focus on social justice, equity and working with families.

Ilham Nasser is Associate Professor of Early Childhood Education at George Mason University, USA.

Joce Nuttall is Director of the Teacher Education Research Concentration in the Learning Sciences Institute Australia at Australian Catholic University. Her research describes, implements and theorises effective interventions in professional learning in schools and early childhood settings, particularly in childcare.

Chrystalla Papademetri-Kachrimani is Assistant Professor at the Department of Education Sciences, European University Cyprus. Her research interests include creative learning and play in early childhood education, teacher education/in-service education and action research, and modelling-based learning in Early Childhood Mathematics Education.

Jane Payler is Professor of Education (Early Years), Deputy Associate Dean (Scholarship) and Co-Director of the Children's Research Centre at the Open University, UK. Her research centres on early years professional and workforce development, interprofessional practice in the early years and children's participatory learning processes.

Bob Perry is Emeritus Professor at the School of Education, Charles Sturt University, Australia. He has particular expertise in the mathematics education of young children and educational transitions.

Stavroula Philippou is Assistant Professor in Curriculum and Teaching at the Department of Education, University of Cyprus.

NOTES ON CONTRIBUTORS

Sharon Ryan is Professor at the Graduate School of Education, Rutgers University, USA. Her research centres around how early childhood educators might improve their practices to achieve educational equity for all students in their classrooms.

Darbianne Shannon is working as a Research Assistant in the Center for Excellence in Early Childhood Studies, University of Florida, USA. Her research interests include teacher learning; training, and technical assistance; instructional coaching; early intervention; socio-emotional development; literacy; and children and families with multiple risk factors.

Wendy Shepherd is the Director of Mia Mia Child and Family Study Centre and an academic in the Institute of Early Childhood Teacher Education Program, Macquarie University, Australia.

Kerry Smith is Associate Lecturer at the School of Human Services and Social Work, Griffith University, Australia.

Patricia Snyder is Director at the Anita Zucker Center for Excellence in Early Childhood Studies, University of Florida, USA. She studies the developmental impacts of early experiences and learning, social-emotional foundations of early learning, and how families and practitioners support young children's development and learning.

Jennifer Sumsion is Foundation Professor of Early Childhood Education at Charles Sturt University, Australia.

Kate Thornton is Senior Lecturer at the School of Education, Victoria University of Wellington, New Zealand. Her research interests include educational leadership and leadership development, blended learning, mentoring and coaching, and professional learning communities.

Kerryann Walsh is Associate Professor in the School of Early Childhood, Queensland University of Technology, Australia. She is a pre-eminent scholar in the interdisciplinary field of child maltreatment prevention and has researched in the areas of child protection policy, school-based child sexual abuse prevention programs, professionals' reporting of child abuse and neglect and training interventions for mandatory reporters.

Manjula Waniganayake is Professor at the Institute of Early Childhood, Macquarie University, Australia. She has a strong knowledge base in early childhood policy and practice built through teaching, research and active involvement in the early childhood sector in a voluntary capacity.

Jane Waters is Associate Professor and Assistant Dean (Research) in the Faculty of Education and Communities, University of Wales Trinity Saint David, UK. Her research interests lie in adult-child interactions in early years education, child participation and the interplay of space and culture in shaping educational experiences of young children.

Elizabeth Wood is Professor of Education at the University of Sheffield, UK. Her fields of research and teaching include early childhood and primary education.

Foreword

Routeways to professional learning may appear as a series of furrows in a ploughed field. Psychologists, engineers, medics, lawyers, political scientists, educators and others are likely to follow the routes defined or prescribed by the professional communities to which they belong. Often, due to the desire to enhance specific professional skills and knowledge, or simply due to the constraints of time and the pragmatism of needing to focus on current priorities, we become deeply entrenched in specific and specialised aspects of our own professional furrow. There are many advantages to specialising in a particular area of study and to deepening expertise in that area. There is also much to be lost by failing to look outside the furrow at the ways in which other professionals, within or beyond our own areas of focus, engage in professional learning. Within the field of education, specialisms occur in a multitude of sub-fields including curriculum studies, leadership, policy, pedagogy and age-related practice. It is easy to ignore or be unaware of ideas because they exist in a different specialist area, and a practitioner in the field of adult learning, school leadership or the teaching of mathematics might ignore literature relating to early childhood education. There is even a danger that in adding the qualification 'Early Years Educators' to a publication such as this, the readership is likely to be immediately limited to those practising or researching within this sector of education.

We hope that this will not be the case because to ignore the contributions within this issue would be to miss exposure to a rich seam of educational research. By looking at the keywords provided with each article, rather than at the title of the article, the diversity of perspectives taken by the contributing authors is highlighted: phenomenology; autobiography; curriculum reform; critical practice; mathematics and scientific literacy; professional learning communities; professional identity; leadership; digital technologies; cultural–historical activity theory; mentoring and coaching; and so forth. The generic issues relating to professional learning and development reflected in the articles reproduced here are universally valuable and their contextualisation within early childhood education enhances rather than reduces their applicability to other sectors of education. They stimulate us to look critically at our own sector by peering over the furrow at practice within another sector or culture. In doing this, we are moved to look critically at professional identity; at individual and collaborative approaches to professional learning; at policy that has an expectation of measurable impact; and, through these, at the definition, process and practice of professional learning and development itself.

The call for articles for this special issue exceeded expectations. It prompted a wide range of submissions that focused on the policy, practice and professional implications of Early Years Education. The 15 articles selected, underpinned by their research, provide differing perspectives on the literature and on the theory and practice of professional learning and development. Some emerge from a strong cultural context; others implicitly or explicitly demonstrate that the key principles of professional learning and development are often cross-cultural.

The two Guest Editors of this special issue, Jane Waters and Jane Payler, have done a remarkable job in selecting and compiling the final publication. Their ability to craft a coherent and academically rigorous publication has been impressive and *Professional Development in Education* owes them a great deal of thanks.

The articles selected for this issue do not present solutions. Frequently they present challenges for policy-makers and practitioners. We would prefer to see this special issue as *invitational*. We invite professionals from sectors in education outside the early childhood area to comment on the strategies and processes raised here; we invite academics and practitioners to delve into the diverse range of literature referenced in the articles; we invite policy-makers to engage with the ideas and examples of practice that are shown to make a difference; we invite Early Years Educators themselves to reflect on the models and practices discussed and apply them critically within their own areas of work.

Finally, although the articles published here emanate from a range of countries and continents, it is significant that African, Asian and emerging nations (educationally and economically) are under-represented. This is both ironic and of concern when we note that the highest birth rates and percentages of the world's children under five years old are found in such countries. We must therefore issue one further invitation: and that is for academics, practitioners and researchers in the field of early childhood education and care in emerging settings to engage with the articles in this special issue and contribute to the literature on the professional learning and development of the Early Years Educators who will provide the foundation for the futures of these young children.

Ken Jones

INTRODUCTION

The professional development of early years educators – achieving systematic, sustainable and transformative change

Within this special issue on professional learning and development (PLD) in the early years sector, we aim to do three things: to highlight the state of play in PLD in early years internationally; to challenge all involved to consider carefully how scarce resources are used, review the PLD on offer and demand what is most effective; and to move the field forward with regard to developing and evaluating effective PLD. This editorial begins by addressing the question of what is distinctive about PLD in the early years and the contexts within which it takes place. We then outline what is current in early years PLD and discuss the themes addressed in the papers presented. While authors of the chapters have adopted local terminology to describe those who work in the early years sector, we have taken the term 'early years educator' to include all those adults who are charged, as part of their professional role, with the care and education of young children. The age range spanned by the term 'early years' varies between countries from birth to five, from birth to six or seven, or from three to six or seven, depending on specific curricula, nature of provision and funding arrangements. Nonetheless, there is widespread agreement that whatever the policy determinants, 'early years' encompasses education and care of children from birth to seven years, wherever that may be located.

Early childhood education and care (ECEC) has come somewhat later than other sectors of education to what Ball (2013) refers to as a global project to ensure economic productivity and competitiveness. Increasingly, early years has been brought into this discernible 'global policy' discourse that sets out to plan for a particular vision of productive and competitive nations. With it have come distinct ideas about the purpose of early years education and care and the form it should take, not least that it should provide childcare for an increase in the (female) workforce in the short term, ensure a cost-effective means of ensuring a productive and competitive workforce in the long term and reduce inequality by improving outcomes for children from disadvantaged circumstances (UNESCO 2000, 2006, Barnett and Masse 2007, Field 2010, Allen 2011, Barnett and Nores 2012, Heckman and Kautz 2012). Since one of the key factors considered to contribute to the quality of early years education is the quality of its workforce, including levels of qualification and training (Siraj-Blatchford *et al.* 2006, Australian Children's Education and Care Quality Authority 2012), there are clear implications of this global project for the initial training and PLD of early years educators to enable them to deliver the desirable results, most often measured by children's learning and developmental outcomes.

The question is therefore raised about the distinctive nature of the context for professional learning and development in ECEC. The following examples give a flavour of this distinctiveness. Historically, England's ECEC sector, as in many countries, has been staffed primarily by educators who were vocationally qualified, as well as by unqualified educators. While England's current statutory framework, revised in

2014 (Department for Education 2014), still allows for up to 50% of educators to be unqualified and the highest level of qualification required to lead ECEC provision remains a one-year or two-year college vocational qualification, there has been a concerted, government-funded effort, particularly since 2006, to improve qualification levels. In particular, the drive has been to encourage graduate leadership, initially through early years professionals and more recently through early years teachers (Children's Workforce Development Council 2006, Teaching Agency 2012, National College for Teaching and Leadership 2013). Qualification levels have subsequently increased in England, with 42% of ECEC providers now employing a graduate educator, up from 32% in 2009 (Taylor 2014). In Australia since January 2014, there has been a requirement as part of the National Quality Framework (Australian Children's Education and Care Quality Authority 2012) for all educators working in early childhood settings to have a qualification of some kind from a specified range and that there must be a 'teacher' in every early childhood setting.[1] Recent developments in the USA to improve access to high-quality funded pre-school provision during 2015, signalled by the Child Care and Development Block Grant Act of 2014, are similarly tied to drives for provision led by qualified staff (see, for example, National Centre for Infants, Toddlers and Families 2014, US Department of Education 2014).

Much of the international project to increase the quality of the ECEC workforce has meant experienced, vocationally qualified practitioners undertaking further study, often part-time while retaining their role as practitioners, to obtain graduate-level qualifications, creating a blurring of lines between initial teacher education and PLD. Vocationally qualified educators have undertaken professional learning and development designed to enhance their professionalism and to achieve appropriate and approved graduate status. While qualification levels in the sector have risen, it is still nonetheless the case that a sizeable proportion, often still the majority, of early years educators in many countries are not graduate teachers. Professional learning and development in ECEC therefore needs to encompass educators from a range of qualification levels. An additional feature of the context of ECEC PLD in several countries, such as the United Kingdom, Australia and the USA, is that a large proportion of provision falls within the private, voluntary and independent sector, particularly with regard to provision for babies and children younger than two or three years of age (see, for example, Lewis 2003, Department for Education 2010). Professional learning and development therefore takes place in systems of care and education with a large variety of provider-types, bringing challenges in terms of costs, regulatory systems and organisational networks, all of which frame PLD.

Professional learning and development is in part driven by regulation and government imperatives, but the ways in which it is enacted in ECEC across countries and internationally show a wide range of localised variation. Although writing about educational policy in general, Ball's explanation of the nuances of the development and enactment of policy could be applied specifically to policy and enactment of PLD. He explains that:

> ... we must recognize policy [on PLD] as a composite of (1) regulation and imperatives, (2) principles and (3) multi-level and collective efforts of interpretation and translation (creative enactment) and that policies [on PLD] are enacted in material conditions, with varying resources, in relation to particular 'problems' that are constructed nationally and locally. They are also set against existing commitments, values and forms of experience. [...] In this way policies are almost always localized and customized. (Ball 2013, p. 11)

This special issue provides an opportunity to obtain an overview of the current approaches to PLD in the early years sector, which include specific stand-alone training courses, development of online PLD courses, fostering of learning communities, reflective techniques and coaching or mentoring, and the issues encountered in PLD in ECEC, framed by consideration of contexts, policy drivers, costs and effectiveness.

In considering how best we might present the articles in the special issue we have attempted to group them loosely as outlined below; however, the reader will find many resonances between articles throughout the issue. A reoccurring theme throughout is the recognition that in the field of ECEC there is a real need to consider mechanisms of PLD that support systematic, sustainable and transformative change. These three words – systematic, sustainable and transformative – encompass a vision that is well articulated by all of the authors in this special issue; they reiterate the vision in different ways across their international contexts but the common theme is persistent. This vision is challenging, it is complex and requires deep understanding of the nature of professional learning and refuses to accept the *status quo*. The challenge is serious and demands attention; as the editors of this issue, we hope that this challenge is accepted by those who plan for the professional learning of others as well as by those who undertake professional learning themselves. In ECEC it is time for approaches to PLD to come of age.

The first and second articles in this special issue help us to frame our field of consideration and provide an overview of the national context of two countries with regards to the professional learning and development of those working in the ECEC sector. In the first article, Gomez, Kagan and Fox describe the 'state of the nation' of ECEC professionals working in the USA. This article, along with the next, contains much that will resonate with all those involved with ECEC whether working in contexts within the USA or elsewhere. The authors clearly and critically articulate the challenges of a fragmented policy landscape, uneven investment in ECEC, varied qualification frameworks for those working in the sector and the persistent issues related to low status and low pay. They sum up the situation that many will recognise in the ECEC sector: 'a lack of quality, equity and sustainability' (p. 169). However, although these challenges are deeply embedded, they offer examples of a constructive way in which policy-makers and those working in the field may respond to them; adopting a framework of systems thinking can support the development of high-quality, sustainable and accessible PLD for the ECEC workforce. The article, while acknowledging the obstacles that are yet to be faced, is therefore an optimistic and constructive lens through which the issues inherent to the ECEC sector can be viewed. As such this article sets us up for the wealth of innovation that exists in the international arena of PLD in ECEC, some of which is exemplified in the subsequent chapters.

In the second article, Hadley, Waniganayake and Shepherd provide a detailed consideration of the approaches taken to PLD for the ECEC sector in Australia and offer an evaluation of which approaches appear to be most successful in supporting sustained change and why. Again, all those working in the field will recognise the variety of approaches to PLD described here, although of course these will have been experienced differently in different cultural contexts. Adopting a contextual theory of leadership, the authors highlight that a strategic approach to the development of both organisations and individuals is important. They emphasise the notion of alignment in the success or otherwise of PLD initiatives; that is, the match of the PLD strategy to the educator's qualification and experience as well as the match of the structure of the PLD experience to the intended outcomes of the initiative. This last point is particularly relevant when the aims for PLD move beyond compliance matters into the development of pedagogic practice, especially if a critical, reflective pedagogic approach is the intention.

There then follows a series of articles in which authors exemplify particular approaches to PLD in ECEC and offer insight and critical evaluation of these approaches. The maturity of the discussion in these articles challenges us to think deeply and honestly about the forms of PLD offered to the ECEC workforce, the mechanisms that are in place to embed new learning in practice and the depth to which we submit our PLD events to scrutiny about their longer-term impact in relation to benefits for children's experiences and outcomes. Colmer, Waniganayake and Field comment on a study focusing on leaders of ECEC centres in Australia. These leaders, while reporting a commitment to collaborative professional learning for their staff and recognising the benefits of such approaches to PLD, tended to offer other models of PLD that are less associated with effective longer-term change. The authors explore why this might be the case and explain the architecture of the critical role that the centre leader plays in establishing the organisational attitude to PLD. The delineated architecture allows policy-makers and centre leaders alike to consider critically how to support an environment that is conducive to sustainable and transformative PLD.

In an article that tackles an often divisive issue, Nuttall *et al.* address the issue of professional development of ECEC staff working with digital technologies in ECEC settings. The authors challenge the ECEC community to re-conceptualise this 'problem' and consider, rather, the way in which young children engage and play with digital technologies. The 'problem' of early years teacher uptake and use of digital technology is re-framed as an enquiry into young children's digital play. Nuttall *et al.* adopt cultural–historical activity theory to understand the nature of early years professionals' motive objects in relation to their work, and demonstrate how re-framing issues related to the use of digital technologies in ECEC may support transformative professional engagement.

The following article by Marklund considers the informal methods that ECEC staff adopt to develop their knowledge related to use of mobile technology in the form of tablets in ECEC settings in Sweden. In an analysis of the content of two online blogs, Marklund identifies the technological, pedagogical and content knowledge sought by those using the blogs. In terms of PLD the article demonstrates how the Internet has provided new opportunities for teachers to create their own online environments for collegial communication that has the advantage of being immediate and responsive to specific need. However, the marketisation of this online community is an aspect about which those driving forward innovation in PLD may wish to be mindful.

The next two articles relate to approaches to PLD in ECEC that aim to deepen reflective capacities. In the first, McLeod focuses on how a practical tool to facilitate deep self-awareness and critical reflection, devised in England, supported early years teachers to change their pedagogic approaches and become better at participatory teaching. In the second article, Layen draws on leadership theory and explores the potential for biographical story-telling, re-telling and reflection to support increased self-awareness and confidence in ECEC leaders and those who may aspire to leadership. The importance of genuine, meaningful, personal engagement in reflection to support sustainable and transformative change is emphasised by these authors.

Shannon, Snyder and McLaughlin consider the efficacy of PLD that is characterised by training followed by coaching in order to embed new practices. They report and discuss the feedback from participants who undertook the PLD activity through one of two modes of delivery and follow up: a web-based mode or a face-to-face mode. The authors have identified characteristics of the PLD delivery model that transcended the mode of delivery and are associated with sustaining new learning and transforming pedagogy. These individual and environmental factors contribute to the evidence base for provision of transformative PLD and focus attention on the need to ensure that a network of support, and indeed accountability, is available. This is particularly pertinent when decisions about provision for PLD necessarily include consideration of financial management and web-based provision can appear a cost-effective option for policy-makers.

The last article in this section that exemplifies particular approaches to PLD is from Cherrington and Thornton and reports on work undertaken in New Zealand related to a professional learning community in a non-school-based ECEC setting. The development and maintenance of professional learning communities as a form of effective PLD has received academic attention with regard to school-based development, and the author here exemplifies how particular structural and relational conditions may similarly characterise an effective professional learning community within the ECEC sector. The contextual challenges for working in this way in New Zealand are outlined in this early stage of the development of this exciting project; these challenges will certainly be familiar across other contexts and so, as with all the articles in this section, we are all left with much to consider in terms of the form and structure of PLD for the ECEC workforce, not least of which is the impact upon children's experiences of ECEC.

The final section of the special issue is given over to context-specific and country-specific examples of PLD activity within specific ECEC settings. The theme that threads through each of these articles is the manner in which the specific event can contribute to our understanding of PLD provision that is systematic, sustainable and transformative.

The first article in this final section, from Lakhani *et al.*, exemplifies how adoption of a specific methodology, Circles of Change, encourages reflection, communication and transformational change in a group of professionals whose peripatetic support roles may mean that the demands of their professional lives can be particularly stressful. The author adopts a quasi-experimental approach to the evaluation of the impact of a Circles of Change intervention in the context of those working as Inclusion Support Facilitators in Australia. The practice of 'thinking otherwise' appears to have considerable potential, on the one hand, to enable these staff to reflect on their professional lives in a developmental manner, enabling transformative change to take place, and, on the other, to offer a sustainable toolkit for managing change in the future.

The second article is located within the context of Head Start teachers working in the USA, focusing on the development of intentional learning. Nasser *et al.* describe the use of a professional development framework to guide the intervention; this framework is delivered in three modes: one-on-one mentoring, onsite community/practice groups and through an online community of practice. Using a key-concepts analysis of post-intervention interviews, the authors highlight the value of the relationships developed during the professional development intervention that provided both a supportive network and a resource of 'usable knowledge'. These elements supported both satisfaction with the PLD intervention and sustainable transformation of pedagogic practice. One of the key messages emerging from this special issue is exemplified in both of these articles; that is, effective and transformational change through PLD programmes demands time commitment both from those providing the intervention and from those developing their practice.

The next article is a specific example of a particular programme of PLD that aimed to transform pedagogy related to children's experiences of mathematics in early years classrooms in Australia. Delivered in two modes, face to face and online, the coaching programme Let's Count seeks, in the eyes of the early years staff who work in ECEC settings, to construct the young child as a powerful mathematician. The programme appears to have been effective in both its modes of delivery because of the underpinning coaching elements. Perry and McDonald highlight the increased confidence of early years educators in relation to their pedagogical practice and their professional identity. Such reported changes indicate transformative learning has taken place, and indeed the impact evaluation in early years settings appears to support this. What is important to draw out, at this stage, is the connection of PLD to changes in professional identity that have been highlighted by this article; all of the exemplification articles in this special issue indicate that PLD that succeeds in being sustainable and transformative 'speaks' to the professional learner in a genuine manner that relates to the core of their professional persona.

In a reflective contribution that considers how the structure of a three-year PLD project transformed the roles of teacher and researcher, Philippou *et al.* exemplify the 'troubling' of traditional models of PLD in such a way that the lines between the 'expert' and the 'learner' become blurred. Set in the specific context of Cyprus, the project used an inquiry-based approach to mathematics and science education and involved participants as teacher-researchers and curriculum-makers in cycles of action research. The authors demonstrate how the project led to the development of a community of practice and a reconceptualisation of the 'practical'; they suggest that the epistemology-oriented approach adopted in mathematics and science education provided a particular context in which the blurring of lines between researcher and teacher was possible.

The last of our exemplification articles, from Lightfoot and Frost, considers the complexity of the professional identity of those who make up the early years workforce. An alternative approach to PLD is proposed as a result of detailed consideration of the professional–emotional needs of the diverse group of early years staff involved in the research, undertaken in an English context. The proposal involves 're-claiming' and 're-constructing' PLD in the early years sector that supports educators in being valued, having (professional) connections and making a difference. This article chimes with our concluding contribution in challenging us to consider, and re-consider, our approach to PLD provision, with a view to effecting sustainable change in working practices. Arguably this cannot take place without consideration of the construction of individual professional identity and motivation.

Finally, Sumsion *et al.* call for all those involved in early years PLD to consider an 'evaluative stance' when planning for the professional development of those who work in the early years sector. This powerful and compelling call to arms is located within the Australian context but provides a lens through which we can consider systematic change in ECEC. An 'evaluative stance' refers to a mindset and a skill set geared towards analysis of evidence, and is asked of all those involved in planning for the professional development of those working in ECEC; from senior bureaucrats who consider and allocate funding for national and regional PLD programmes, to individuals working with early years children making decisions about their own – or their colleagues' – professional learning. The authors put forward a conceptual framework based on three bodies of literature that have previously been largely absent from consideration with regard to professional development in the early years workforce, in order to support systemic change within ECEC organisations. Consideration of evaluation capacity-building, personal epistemology and co-production allows Sumsion *et al.* to re-imagine how we might plan for PLD by adopting an 'evaluative stance' to guide decision-making as well as to facilitate sustainable and transformative change in practice.

Concluding remarks

We would like readers to take from the special issue a call to re-imagine PLD in early years education and care, reflecting critically on whether the way in which resources for PLD are used matches the research evidence on what is most effective; to re-imagine how we research and evaluate effectiveness in PLD at the level of the individual professional as well as at the regional and national levels. This special issue provides evidence that should encourage those working in the early years sector to be confident in their demands for effective forms of PLD which support systemic, sustainable transformation of professional practice. We hope you agree.

Note

1. Variations apply depending on the size of the setting.

References

Allen, G., 2011. *Early intervention: the next steps, an independent report to Her Majesty's government by Graham Allen MP*. London: The Stationery Office.

Australian Children's Education and Care Quality Authority (ACECQA), 2012. *The National Quality Framework for education and care across long day care, family day care, pre-school/kindergarten, and outside school hours care* [online]. Available from: http://www.acecqa.gov.au/national-quality-framework [Accessed 4 September 2014].

Ball, S.J., 2013. *The education debate*. 2nd ed. Bristol: The Policy Press.

Barnett, W.S. and Masse, L.N., 2007. Early childhood program design and economic returns: comparative benefit-cost analysis of the Abecedarian program and policy implications [online]. *Economics of education review*, 26 (1), 113–125. Available from: http://nieer.org/sites/nieer/files/BenefitCostAbecedarian.pdf [Accessed 26 November 2014].

Barnett, W.S. and Nores, M., 2012. Estimated participation and hours in early care and education by type of arrangement and income at ages 2 to 4 in 2010 [online]. *National Institute for Early Educational Research*, 1–19. Available from: http://www.nieer.org/sites/nieer/files/ECE%20Participation%20Estimations.pdf [Accessed 26 November 2014].

Children's Workforce Development Council (CWDC), 2006. *Guidance to the standards for the award of Early Years Professional Status*. Leeds: CWDC.

Department for Education (DfE), 2010. *Childcare and early years providers survey: research brief* [online]. Available from: http://www.education.gov.uk/rsgateway/DB/STR/d001024/index.shtml [Accessed 10 May 2012].

Department for Education (DfE), 2014. *Statutory framework for the Early Years Foundation Stage* [online]. Available from: https://www.gov.uk/government/uploads/system/uploads/attachment_data/file/335504/EYFS_framework_from_1_September_2014__with_clarification_note.pdf [Accessed 12 December 2014].

Field, F., 2010. *The foundation years: preventing poor children becoming poor adults*. London: The Stationery Office.

Heckman, J.J. and Kautz, T.D., 2012. *Hard evidence on soft skills* [online]. National Bureau of Economic Research. Working Paper 18121. Available from: http://www.nber.org/papers/w18121 [Accessed 27 November 2014].

Lewis, J., 2003. Developing early years childcare in England, 1997–2002: the choices for (working) mothers. *Social policy & administration*, 37 (3), 219–238.

National Centre for Infants, Toddlers and Families, 2014. *Zero to three* [online]. Available from: http://www.zerotothree.org/policy/docs/ehs-child-care-partnerships-fact-sheet-ztt-04-04-2014.pdf [Accessed 25 November 2014].

National College for Teaching and Leadership, 2013. *Teaching standards (Early Years)* [online]. London: NCTL. Available from: https://www.gov.uk/government/publications/early-years-teachers-standards [Accessed 13 November 2014].

Siraj-Blatchford, I., *et al.*, 2006. *Monitoring and Evaluation of the Effective Implementation of the Foundation Phase (MEEIFP) project across Wales*. Cardiff: WAG.

Taylor, C., 2014. *Early years teachers: what do they offer?* [online]. Nursery World Business Summit, 12 November, London. Available from: https://www.gov.uk/government/speeches/early-years-teachers-what-do-they-offer. [Accessed 25 November 2014].

Teaching Agency, 2012. *Review of the Early Years professional status standards* [online]. Available from: https://www.gov.uk/government/uploads/system/uploads/attachment_data/file/180957/TA-00084-2012.pdf [Accessed 13 November 2014].

UNESCO (United Nations Educational, Scientific and Cultural Organisation), 2000. *The Dakar Framework for Action: Education for All – meeting our collective commitments*. Paris: UNESCO.

UNESCO (United Nations Educational, Scientific and Cultural Organisation), 2006. *Strong foundations: early childhood education and care*. EFA Global Monitoring Report. Paris: UNESCO.

US Department of Education, 2014. *Early learning: America's middle class promise begins early* [online]. Available from: http://www.ed.gov/early-learning [Accessed 26 November 2014].

Jane Waters
Jane Payler

Professional development of the early childhood education teaching workforce in the United States: an overview

Rebecca E. Gomez, Sharon Lynn Kagan and Emily A. Fox

Resulting from a fragmented landscape of policies for and uneven investments in the early childhood education (ECE) field in the United States, the qualifications of the ECE teaching workforce are typically quite low. This article first reviews the history and status of the ECE teaching workforce in the United States, focusing on the evolution of the field, current demographic characteristics of the teaching workforce and the pathways to professional development and professional preparation of the teaching workforce. The authors then discuss the legacies of this history and policy landscape: a lack of quality, equity and sustainability. Offering a re-conceptualization of professional development within the context of systems thinking, the article concludes with a discussion of innovations and challenges with which the field contends relative to workforce development.

Introduction

This article reviews the professional development (PD) and workforce supports available for those who are a part of the early childhood education (ECE) teaching workforce in the United States. Although ECE is conventionally defined as embracing children from birth through age eight, this article focuses on the adults who work directly with children from birth to age five. Our reasons for doing so are multiple: in the United States, individuals teaching children ages six through eight fall within the purview of the country's public education system; as such, the requirements for their PD are quite consistent and differ markedly from the requirements for individuals who work with children birth to age five. Moreover, our focus is grounded in the fact that the minimum qualifications for the birth to five segment of the ECE teaching workforce and requirements for PD are highly idiosyncratic, quite complex and tightly coupled with the evolution of the ECE field.

As is the case globally, contemporary ECE is contextually situated and is derived from a country's ideas, values and governmental structures. Because context and history also shape ECE PD policies and programs, we begin our review with a brief history of the field and its teaching workforce in the United States. We then turn to an examination of the various professional preparation and PD pathways that are available to the ECE teaching workforce, the process of creating systemic approaches to PD, teaching workforce trends and challenges with which the field is contending presently. In so doing, we aim to provide an overview of the ECE teaching workforce past, present and future.

Professional preparation for ECE teachers in the United States: understanding the context

Early childhood education in the United States: a market-driven, mixed-delivery sector

Stemming from the values espoused by the founders of the United States, policy-makers have long sought to limit the reach of government intervention in the lives of young children, holding the primacy of the family in making decisions about a child's health, education and care during the first five years of life in high regard. Given this ethos, government-funded programs have targeted children and families who demonstrate a need for assistance in accessing basic health, education and welfare services (Lombardi 2003). Despite this deeply embedded governmental stance, at times of national crises (e.g. World Wars I and II and the War on Poverty), the federal government funded massive efforts for young children, often with the purpose of enabling parents to work and/or to improve their economic situation (Lombardi 2003, Kagan 2009). These intermittent federal efforts, however successful, were abolished once these crises abated, and ECE provision was relegated to the private sector, individual states and/or to localities.

In the 1960s, as women surged into the workforce and the needs of at-risk children mounted, the importance of early childhood development and education began to be recognized, with enhanced commitments following (Kagan 1996, Lombardi 2003, Polakow 2004). Given the need for non-maternal care, public and private commitments to ECE grew. Simultaneously, parents from more affluent socioeconomic backgrounds wanted experiences that would enhance their children's development and socialization, giving rise to a surge in private nursery schools, which provided a developmental orientation and educational enrichment (Lombardi 2003). Entwined, these multiple purposes created a wide array of services in the public and private sectors, with some programs focusing on the children (e.g. childcare, Head Start, pre-kindergarten, family childcare) and others focusing on parenting supports and education. Diverse as the programs are in intent, they also vary in how they are funded (e.g. vouchers, contracts, direct program funding), in how they are regulated and monitored, and in how they are held accountable. Complicating matters, given that education is a state responsibility in the United States, many states and some municipalities have invested heavily in ECE, creating even more funding streams. These varied state, local and federal programs and funding streams have resulted in a patchwork landscape of ECE programs and services among and within US states.

The ECE teaching workforce in the United States

Just as the landscape of ECE service provision is complicated, the nature of the US ECE teaching workforce is complicated, as are the approaches to teachers' professional preparation and PD. One thing that does not vary, however, is the clear relationship between the importance of high-quality teaching and the outcomes realized by young children. Many studies, both experimental and quasi-experimental, have found 'teachers to be at the fulcrum of both ECE quality and children's lifelong development' (Schweinhart *et al.* 1993 cited in Kagan *et al.* 2008, p. 5). Teachers' education and training play a huge role in the quality of children's ECE experiences (Shonkoff and Phillips 2000, Ackerman and Barnett 2006, National Academy of Sciences 2012). For example, ECE programs that achieve the largest long-term economic gains and impacts on children's development/outcomes largely employ teachers that have specialized training in early childhood (Early *et al.* 2005, Neuman and Kamil 2010, Connors-Tadros and Horwitz 2014, Ginsburg *et al.* 2014, Zaslow 2014). Despite this agreement, the research is somewhat mixed regarding the specific nature and dosage of the specialized training that is needed to become a 'high-quality' teacher (indeed, the definition of 'high-quality teaching' is still up for debate) – whether it should consist of a college degree (either an associate or bachelor's degree) in ECE, a credential, field/clinical experiences or a combination of these modalities (Fukkink and Lont 2007, Kagan and Gomez 2011, 2014).

Complicating matters, there is tremendous variation in attitudes about and attributes of the ECE teaching workforce. In some cases, this workforce is unfortunately and inappropriately regarded as 'babysitters' (Kagan *et al.* 2008). Moreover, the ECE teaching workforce suffers from high rates of employee turnover, low compensation, low and inconsistent entry requirements, and uncertain opportunities for PD. Combined, these factors make recruiting new teachers and sustaining a quality teaching workforce very challenging.

Having noted these challenges, we turn now to a discussion of the demographics and characteristics of the ECE teaching workforce. Resulting from the mixed delivery system, the diversity of state commitments and program diversity, the ECE teaching workforce is composed of diverse types of professionals with varying levels of education and experience. The US Bureau of Labor Statistics (BLS), for example, divides the ECE workforce into 'child care workers' and 'preschool teachers.' Childcare workers, according to the US BLS (2014), are those individuals typically working in privately owned childcare programs who care for children ages birth to five years when their family is not available. Preschool teachers are defined as those individuals who both care for and educate children prior to their entry to kindergarten (US BLS 2014) – this term refers to individuals working with children ages three to five in either publicly funded pre-kindergarten programs or privately owned programs. This paper regards both categories as a part of the 'ECE teaching workforce.'

In some ways, the US ECE teaching workforce is quite homogeneous. First, it is composed of mostly women; as of 2013, according to the US BLS, 94.8% of childcare workers and 97.8% of preschool/kindergarten teachers were women. Second, the majority of the ECE teaching workforce is Caucasian (70.5% of preschool/kindergarten teachers and 61% of childcare workers). Hispanics make up the next largest portion of the childcare workforce at 22.4%, followed by black/African American workers (13.2%) and Asian workers (3.4%) (US BLS 2014). As for preschool/kindergarten teachers, 12.9% are Hispanic, 12.1% are black/African American and 4.5% are Asian (US BLS 2014).

Despite the uniformity in the ECE teaching workforce's gender and race, their levels of experience and education vary significantly. Maroto and Brandon (2012) estimate that about 7–12% of teachers classified as childcare workers have their associate (AA) degree, 11–17% their bachelor's (BA) degree and 2–4% have an advanced degree (master's/professional). Preschool teachers demonstrate higher levels of education, with 28–73% having at least a bachelor's degree (Maroto and

Brandon 2012). Entry requirements for ECE teachers differ within and among US states. Forty-five states require lead teachers working in state-funded pre-kindergarten programs to have some type of 'specialized early education training' (Barnett *et al.* 2013, p. 7); within these 45 states, 30 states require ECE teachers to have a BA degree in ECE, and 16 require teachers to attain state certification/licensure (Gilliam and Marchesseault 2005, Barnett *et al.* 2013). Fifteen states require assistant teachers working in state-funded pre-kindergarten programs to obtain a Child Development Associate (CDA) credential, and 42 states require all teachers to participate in ongoing (in-service) professional development each year. Requirements for teachers working in other ECE settings are lower: more than 30 states have no requirements for entry-level teachers working in privately owned childcare programs (Whitebook *et al.* 2012). Only two states require teachers to have some type of ECE credential; four states require an ECE credential and experience; two states require that teachers complete a vocational childcare program; and, finally, four states require some combination of education, training and experience (LeMoine and Azer 2006 cited in Kagan *et al.* 2008).

Overall, compensation for the ECE workforce is very low in comparison with that of the US workforce as a whole and in comparison with teachers working in elementary and secondary schools (US BLS 2014). Within this context, compensation is highly idiosyncratic, with much of it predicated on the individual's education and the setting in which she/he works. Compensation for the ECE teaching workforce varies from state to state, with some states paying teachers less than $18,000 per year and others paying as much as $44,000 per year, depending on education, experience and ECE program type (US BLS 2014). It also varies by classification. As of 2013, individuals classified as childcare workers earned a mean annual wage of $21,490. Preschool teachers fared somewhat better, making an average of $31,420 (US BLS 2014). Preschool teachers earn the most when working in state-funded pre-kindergarten programs ($44,760) and the least in privately owned programs ($27,070) (US BLS 2014). Compensation is generally higher for those with more education. For instance, the median hourly wage of childcare center teachers with a BA or graduate degree is $11.90 versus $9.00/hour for those who have only an AA degree (National Survey of Early Care and Education Project Team 2013). Similar to wages, benefits available to ECE teachers are generally low and vary considerably; one study estimates that only one-third of childcare workers receive paid benefits/sick leave (Whitebook *et al.* 2010 cited in Institute of Medicine and National Research Council 2012). The combination of minimal compensation and benefits contribute to the high rates of teacher turnover: both preschool teachers and childcare workers leave their jobs at high rates (15% and 29% turnover, respectively); and among the childcare workers who leave their jobs, 21% leave the ECE field completely (Whitebook *et al.* 2001, Whitebook *et al.* 2010 cited in Institute of Medicine and National Research Council 2012).

Defining and distinguishing professional preparation and professional development activities for the ECE workforce

Despite these unfavorable working conditions and compensation limitations, many elect to enter the ECE field and experience two broad types, or temporal categories, of education and training activities: pre-service and in-service. Pre-service training refers to the range of activities in which individuals engage prior to entering the workforce; it is truly preparation. In-service training, or ongoing PD, refers to the range of learning activities and supports that take place once an individual is working in an early childhood setting. In the United States, some individuals enter the ECE teaching workforce with no or very limited pre-service training, making the focus on in-service PD critical.

Professional preparation: 'pre-service'

Activities that occur before an individual enters the ECE workforce are an important component of professional preparation. Education and training subsumed under the auspices of professional preparation can also be called pre-service PD. Within the pre-service category, PD may take place in a higher education institution or via the completion of a certification process for teachers who have completed a degree but who have not yet entered the workforce.

Professional development: 'in-service'

The second type of PD, in-service PD, is intended for early childhood practitioners who are already employed in an early childhood program, with the precise goal of enhancing their knowledge and expertise in working with young children and their families. In-service PD can include working to achieve a credential or certification, personalized PD plans or workshops that bolster an individual's understanding of a particular domain or issue related to his/her current work.

Pathways to accessing professional development in the United States

Given the diversity inherent in the ECE workforce demographics, compensation and state requirements for teacher preparation and PD, it is not surprising that the pathways available to the ECE workforce for accessing PD and for meeting qualification requirements are equally diverse. We iterate here three common pathways available to the workforce in the United States. These pathways are not mutually exclusive and may overlap, or they may be accessed by teachers at different times in their careers.

Pathway 1: higher education

The low and inconsistent requirements for ECE teachers mean that, historically, teachers have not had to obtain higher education (BA, BS, AA or AS) degrees to work in the field. As the press for ECE grows, the minimum qualifications for the ECE workforce are increasing. Given this, there is an increased demand for degree programs at the associate (AA), bachelor's (BA) and graduate levels (MA, MEd, PhD or EdD) that focus specifically on early childhood.

Offered at two-year colleges, associate degree (AA or AS) programs in ECE provide an entry-point into higher education for many in the field of ECE. Evolving from the need for vocational education in the United States, two-year colleges offer degrees whose content relies heavily on the skills that students will need for direct practice. In the case of ECE associate degrees, coursework offers the opportunity for students to engage in practica, and to learn about theories of child development, curriculum and instructional practice (Maxwell *et al.* 2006). While in some states having an associate degree qualifies an individual to be a lead teacher or a program director, states are beginning to raise the minimum qualifications for these positions so that associate degrees are increasingly being reserved for teacher assistant positions.

Bachelor's degrees in ECE, offered at four-year colleges and universities, are increasingly becoming the baseline requirement for head teachers in state-funded pre-kindergarten programs and Head Start programs, and for program administrators. These degrees traditionally focus on theory as well as practice. Bachelor's degree programs in ECE are frequently located within the college's school of education, which often conceptualize early childhood as including the period from birth to age eight, and which tend to focus more on children in primary school (kindergarten through Grade 3) than on the birth to five age range (Barnett and Whitebook 2011). This is changing somewhat, as states exert pressure on degree-granting programs to be more inclusive of content related to child development and to community/family partnerships. The challenge arising, however, from the focus on the kindergarten to Grade 3 range is that these programs often overlook content related to working with infants and toddlers (Barnett and Whitebook 2011).

Graduate degrees in ECE are also offered at many four-year institutions. These degrees are pursued by individuals who wish to take on leadership roles, such as working in the policy arena, serving as PD instructors and as college faculty, and the like. A major challenge in the field is that there are not enough of these programs to satisfy the increasing demand for graduate degrees (National Association for the Education of Young Children [NAEYC] 2011, National Academy of Sciences 2012). As early childhood policy becomes more important, there is a lack of programs to train leaders for leadership, policy and research roles as well. Complicating matters, a recent study of ECE graduate degree programs offered across the United States revealed the fact that there is a shortage of qualified faculty at the associate, bachelor's and graduate levels (Pianta 2007) to train those who might be interested in more advanced ECE skills and competencies.

Pathway 2: competency-based credentials

Almost always voluntary in nature, the competency-based credential pathway requires that individuals demonstrate their competence in planning for and working directly with young children. Competency-based credentials are awarded when an individual has fulfilled a set of competencies that demonstrate his or her knowledge and skill set. Individuals seeking a credential prepare materials illustrating how she/he is a candidate for the credential, engage in self-study and evaluation, and then submit this information for review to a credentialing body, often a membership organization or a professional association, which is then responsible for awarding the credential. In addition, candidates must also perform their work in ways that demonstrate their abilities in front of a seasoned professional who judges their competence according to a set of pre-determined criteria.

For the purpose of illustrating the nature of competency-based credentials, we describe two exemplars in ECE: the CDA Credential and the National Board of Professional Teaching Standards (NBPTS) Credential for Early Childhood. These credentials are considered 'national' credentials. That is, they are offered by two national organizations, and they are recognized by all 50 states as a valid type of credential for ECE educators, and, as such, they are a professional qualification that is portable from state to state.

The Child Development Associate credential

The CDA credential is perhaps the most well-known credential in ECE. Offered by the Council for Professional Recognition (CPR), the CDA is considered an entry-level credential. For many individuals, the CDA is a stepping-stone to entry into a formal degree program (CPR 2011); for some ECE teachers, the CDA is a precursor to entry into the workforce (i.e. pre-service preparation); and for others, a CDA is obtained during their tenure as a classroom teacher (i.e. in-service PD).

Each individual applying for the CDA credential must meet six goals related to the health, development, care and education of young children (CPR 2013). CDA candidates must complete 120 hours of PD related to these six goals, and they must document 480 hours of experience working directly with young children (CPR 2013). There is a great deal of flexibility with regard to the process by which an individual demonstrates how each of the six goals has been met, reflected in the fact that individuals develop a professional portfolio illustrating how her/his work and educational experiences have enabled her/him to meet these goals. The candidate also receives an evaluation visit from a CDA assessor, who observes the applicant in the classroom, evaluating his/her teaching skills using a standardized assessment. Once these tasks are complete, the portfolio is submitted to the CPR, who will grant the credential. The CDA is good for three years, and must be renewed thereafter (CPR 2013).

The CDA is highly regarded as a pathway to professional preparation; indeed, many states support the CDA financially. Examples of such support include the provision of scholarships to candidates to cover assessment fees, and financial incentives to institutions of higher education that create classes which help candidates meet the 120 hours of PD.

The National Board of Professional Teaching Standards credential

The mission of the NBPTS is to improve the quality of education, from pre-primary through secondary grades; as such, the NBPTS offers a suite of credentials that apply to various elements of the education workforce. The NBPTS has created a credential that is specifically geared towards educators working with children ages three to eight, called the early childhood generalist credential (NBPTS 2012). In contrast to the CDA, the NBPTS credential is offered to individuals who have already completed a bachelor's degree, who have obtained state licensure (if required by the state for ECE teachers) and who have been teaching for at least three years (as such, it is considered to be a form of in-service PD). The NBPTS awards credentials to teachers who demonstrate competency in five core areas (called core propositions): a commitment to student learning; knowledge of the subjects they choose to teach; appropriate management of student learning; dedication to systematic and reflective practice; and participation in learning communities (NBPTS 2012). Candidates must complete a series of 10 assessments, and demonstrate competency in additional standards to achieve the credential germane to the age group with whom they work. The ECE generalist credential assesses teaching practices via standards that address child development and diversity, developmentally appropriate assessment, integrated curriculum, and family and community partnerships (NBPTS 2012). Rigorous in its process, the NBPTS credential produces clear results. Research has shown that students taught by teachers who have an NBPTS credential in ECE had greater gains on achievement tests than students taught by teachers without this credential (Hakel *et al.* 2008). As such, it is a widely respected credential and is considered to be a viable pathway through which to obtain additional teaching qualifications.

Pathway 3: ongoing/experience-based professional development

Similarly to many other professions, ECE educators have the need for and the opportunity to engage in PD and growth opportunities throughout their career. Almost all US states (48 out of 50) require ECE teachers to participate in PD each year, though the requirements for what constitutes this vary dramatically (National Child Care Information Center 2010).

There are four modalities of ongoing PD in which the ECE workforce typically participates: workshop-based instruction, during which individuals learn about a specific topic in a classroom-like learning setting for a set number of hours; communities of practice, in which ECE professionals come together as a group over an extended period of time to engage in a shared inquiry (Iilari 2010); individualized or on-site PD, sometimes called 'coaching,' 'mentoring' or 'technical assistance,' during which a teacher has a content expert or more seasoned individual come into his/her classroom to observe and render advice on how to improve teaching practices (Buysse and Wesley 2009, Skiffington *et al.* 2011, NAEYC 2012); and credit for prior learning and experience, where states set up a process through which teachers who have been in the field for a number of years can create a portfolio that demonstrates their experience in a particular topic area and receive college credit (Kagan and Gomez 2011).

While each of these types of PD offers important in-service PD experiences, they alone are insufficient preparation for working with young children. Yet in some states this is the only type of PD available to ECE educators. For many ECE educators, a combination of the three pathways we have discussed here is needed to ensure that they are armed with the knowledge and skills necessary to work with young children and their families.

Professional development legacies: the quest for quality, equity and sustainability

The legacies of the mixed delivery system for ECE in the United States, the variability in the baseline requirements for ECE teachers, the lack of adequate compensation and the multiple preparation and development pathways utilized by ECE teachers are that ECE teachers are underserved and under-supported. The reality is that the US context for ECE has resulted in a lack of quality in its delivery, a lack of equitably distributed services and a lack of sustainability in its funding and implementation.

While the pathways articulated above offer multiple avenues to improving the teaching workforce, quality remains poor. As we have noted, states' requirements for teaching in ECE settings are also quite low. While institutions of higher education and the organizations that offer the CDA and NBPTS credentials do have mechanisms in place to ensure the quality of the PD that they offer, a large segment of the PD offered to the ECE workforce has not been subject to quality assurance protocols or to oversight by an entity that has the authority to ensure that PD content meets a particular set of standards. Moreover, few states have mechanisms in place to monitor the content and the quality of PD offered by community-based organizations; thus, they have no way of knowing, for instance, whether PD delivered on a particular topic is delivered consistently over time. Additionally, a common implementation challenge is that the content of PD offered in states often duplicates and/or does not match the core knowledge areas set forth in a state's requirements for teachers' annual in-service PD (National Child Care Information Center 2010). The result is that teachers either participate in content that does not fulfill their requirements, or they seek PD from other – usually costly – venues.

From the equity perspective, many teachers lack equitable access to PD and preparation opportunities. As research emerges to support the need for additional qualifications for ECE teachers, and as the demand for ECE grows, so does the need for more equitably distributed PD. States now find themselves struggling to increase the capacity of institutions of higher education to offer degree programs in ECE, to support teachers to go back to school and/or obtain credentials, and to develop avenues for teachers to physically access PD (Professional Development Systems and Workforce Initiatives Center 2014). The demand for and supply of both in-service and pre-service PD have been driven by states' somewhat inconsistent response to enhanced requirements for PD (Kagan *et al.* 2008, Kagan and Gomez 2011).

The third lack, resulting from inconsistent PD policies, is PD and professional preparation practices that are not sustainable. States' provisions for PD have been idiosyncratic, with PD opportunities often being provided either for participants in a particular program or funding stream (e.g. PD provided for teachers working in state-funded pre-kindergarten programs) or via an allotment of funding for in-service PD that is insufficient to meet the needs of the entire teaching workforce in that state.

Shifting our conceptualization of professional preparation: systemic approaches to improving the status of the ECE teaching workforce

Recently in the United States, major conceptual shifts have repositioned ECE, moving it from a programmatic focus to one that is far more systemic. This shift, taking place gradually but consistently, draws its momentum from the realization that, overall, current ECE quality is poor (Burchinal *et al.* 2008, Justice *et al.* 2008, Zaslow *et al.* 2009). As the ECE field becomes more normative, it will not be able to produce the kinds of results expected from model programs for all children unless the supports available to these programs are systematically available to all programs on a sustained basis. In other words, as ECE has evolved, it has outgrown its conventional programmatic *modus operandi*, delineated earlier in this chapter; new demands and new opportunities must be matched by systemic thinking.

While there is conventional understanding of what constitutes an ECE program, the elements that constitute the ECE system are less clear. After reviewing research on systemic thinking and systems development, one national effort discerned that in order for programs to be successful, they needed to be undergirded by a supportive infrastructure (Kagan and Cohen 1996). The elements deemed essential, with each one evoking its own sub-system, include: a functioning governance mechanism, replete with well delineated functions, structures and tools; a financing scheme that is capable of generating and distributing resources consistently and equitably; PD mechanisms that produce high-quality personnel capable of adapting to the changing ECE world; quality enhancement strategies/tools, including standards, curricula, accreditation and quality rating efforts that seek to improve program quality; data and assessment systems that provide ongoing performance feedback, essential to thoughtful improvement and policy; family and community engagement that recognizes the unique and fundamental role families play in ECE, and, reciprocally, ECE's obligation to families and communities as conveyers of culture; and linkages with institutions serving young children so as to foster youngsters' holistic development. Not separate entities, each element of the infrastructure is linked with all other elements in ways that are specified and that capitalize on synergies.

While much has been written about each of these subsystems (Gomez 2014, Kagan and Kauerz 2008, 2012), the focus in this chapter is on the PD subsystem, its properties and the ways in which it links with other infrastructural elements. The PD subsystem is composed of standards that specify what quality educators need to know and be able to do, mechanisms for inculcating the skills, competencies and values attendant to the standards, and vehicles/tools to credential and account for how well such standards are being met. In addition, a functional PD subsystem must have a governance structure that makes its work transparent and coordinated, as well as the resources to render its work sustainable.

Within ECE, standards for PD vary and often are not linked to the standards that have been developed for children. Far more attention needs to be accorded standards' specification that respects changing pedagogies, enhanced research and diversified cultures and languages. Armed with a codified conceptual framework regarding what individuals working with young children need to know and be able to do, the mechanisms for inculcating skills and competencies can be varied. Moreover, they should be encouraged to employ different techniques, and to accommodate diverse needs, learning styles and teaching modalities. Having underscored a call for diverse mechanisms, efforts to achieve economic efficiencies and to avoid service redundancies for some and service paucities for others need to be mounted. Developing clear accountability mechanisms has long been a part of ECE. Replete with inspectorates, regulations and monitoring tools, ECE does a solid job of collecting data on individual programs. Less clear, however, are the ways in which data are used to inform decisions. Recent efforts to create mechanisms to rate and improve programs have taken hold with much success.

Systemically, governing and financing ECE PD have improved. Given the centrality of personnel competence to the overall quality of ECE programs, much energy has recently been expended to develop workforce and leadership training programs. At the federal level, new technical assistance centers have emerged (see discussion below), and a plethora of webinars, conferences and materials are being produced to support those engaged in PD. Increasingly, federal programs are allowing 'set-asides' to be used for PD and salary enhancements. States, too, are increasing their commitment to PD; for example, where state ECE offices exist, they often have personnel devoted to advancing PD.

Looking forward

The evolution of systems thinking serves to advance the quality, accessibility and sustainability of PD for the ECE teaching workforce. This section highlights some of the most recent innovations in PD and explicates some of the major challenges the field is currently facing.

Innovations in systems development

While all states have at least one element of a PD subsystem, there is no state that – at present – has a fully articulated PD subsystem for ECE (LeMoine and National Governor's Association Center for Best Practices 2010). There are, however, a number of innovations taking place within states, nationally, and at the federal level that further the progress of PD subsystems.

Innovation at the state level

The most widely proliferated systemic innovation occurring at the state level, presently, is the implementation of Quality Rating and Improvement Systems (QRIS), which are mechanisms created to rate and improve the quality of ECE programs. Similar in intent to rating systems for hotels and restaurants, QRIS evaluate ECE programs on a variety of programmatic indicators and assign them a star rating. Largely voluntary, QRIS typically evaluate programs on the dimensions of program governance, standards, financing, communication, accountability and the workforce (Mitchell 2009). Although QRIS are distinct from PD subsystems, they are often the driver for investments in PD subsystems because each ascending star level sets forth increasing requisite minimum qualifications for staff members. As such, the QRIS efforts are designed to be elixirs of PD; PD is regarded as a critical driver of quality improvement. So strong is the commitment to encouraging PD as a part of the QRIS efforts that many states offer diverse incentives to support the achievement of additional education levels for those working in the field. For instance, several states offer scholarships, stipends or other forms of financial assistance to teachers who are willing to return to school to obtain a degree, or to complete the requirements for a CDA or other credential if the program in which these teachers are employed participates in the QRIS.

Innovation at the federal level

To incentivize states to further develop PD subsystems, the federal government has developed three mechanisms through which to assist states in their work.

The first of these mechanisms is a source of funding targeted to support investments in PD systems. In 2011, the Administration for Children and Families implemented a competitive grant program to specifically incentivize the development of ECE systems (US Department of Education 2011, Administration for Children and Families 2013). These grants, called the Race to the Top – Early Learning Challenge Fund, have been awarded to a total of 20 states, constituting a total investment of over US$1 billion (US Department of Education 2013). The Race to the Top – Early Learning Challenge Fund is unique in that it represents a departure from programmatic approaches to funding, and signals a shift towards investing in infrastructure and systems development. Included in the goals for the Race to the Top – Early Learning Challenge Fund are three priorities related to PD: developing workforce knowledge and competencies; supporting the ECE workforce in developing its knowledge, skills and abilities; and partnering with institutions of higher education and other PD organizations to develop effective ECE educators (US Department of Education 2013). States that are awarded grant funding are expected to make significant strides towards developing these and other aspects of their ECE system, and are provided with technical assistance in order to ensure that adequate progress occurs.

A second mechanism to support the development of state PD subsystems is the 2012 creation of the PDW Center. Funded by the US Department of Health and Human Services, the PDW Center provides technical assistance to all states to improve the supports available to the ECE workforce via the creation of PD subsystems. Specifically, the focus of the PDW Center is on supporting states to resolve the major issues discussed in this article – the lack of access to sequential, high-quality PD opportunities (i.e. professional preparation pathways), financing for PD, the need for quality assurance mechanisms through which to monitor PD, and issues related to compensation for the ECE workforce (Professional Development Systems and Workforce Initiatives Center 2014).

In September 2014, the US Congress voted to reauthorize the Child Care and Development Fund Block Grant legislation, a major federal funding stream designated to support parents in accessing and paying for ECE services and to assist states in improving the quality of ECE programs via a variety of strategies (e.g. standards, QRIS, PD). The Child Care and Development Fund Block Grant is the third mechanism through which the federal government provides assistance to states to improve the supports for the ECE teaching workforce. A sustainable funding stream, the new legislation requires that, within five years of enactment of the legislation, states dedicate a minimum of 9% of their Child Care and Development Fund Block Grant funds to quality activities (Child Care Aware 2014). While states have a choice of what these activities could be, PD is considered – under the regulations – to be an acceptable designee for these quality set-aside funds. Prior to reauthorization, the minimum quality set-aside was 4%, so the current legislation represents a sizeable increase in the federal government's commitment to improving quality for the ECE field and, in turn, the ECE teaching workforce.

Innovative professional development tools

While we have argued in favor of efforts to create a PD subsystem as a part of a broader infrastructure for ECE, there is still a place for program-level interventions – practical tools for supporting and improving classroom teaching. Here, we highlight two of those tools.

One such tool is designed to examine the influence of the environment on teaching. Entitled the Supportive Environmental Quality Underlying Adult Learning (SEQUAL) and developed by the Center for the Study of Child Care Employment at the University of California at Berkeley, the tool is currently being piloted with several US states. Supportive Environmental Quality Underlying Adult Learning is a research-based measure that examines the influence of the work environment (i.e. the childcare program) on teacher practice and adult learning (Whitebook and Ryan 2013). This tool examines the environment across five dimensions: teaching supports; learning community; job crafting; adult well-being; and program leadership. The first of its kind, the findings from the pilots of SEQUAL fill a gap in the research regarding the ways in which the program environment serves as an infrastructure for reflective practice, adult learning and targeted individual learning.

Another tool gaining traction in the field is individualized PD, often referred to as coaching, mentoring or technical assistance (NAEYC 2012, Kagan *et al.* 2014). Some organizations, for example, are now offering PD workshops on a particular topic of interest/need to ECE teachers, and follow those sessions up with one-on-one coaching in the classroom. This approach to PD actively supports the teacher by combining different pedagogical strategies for the purpose of developing a practice-based, reflective and intensive experience (Buysse and Wesley 2009, Office of Child Development and Early Learning 2012).

The use of technology

Not unique to the US context, advances in technology have rendered a host of new modalities for delivering PD, enabling greater access to the existing pathways for professional preparation and development. In the past decade, there has been a proliferation of online degrees, many of which are now available to ECE educators at the associate, bachelor's and graduate levels. The CDA and NBPTS credentials offer candidates online resources, including the opportunity to submit certain application materials online (NBPTS 2012, CPR 2013). Many professional associations and community-based organizations are now offering workshops and conferences online via webinars and other interactive platforms (e.g. NAEYC now offers members the opportunity to purchase and 'live stream' segments of its annual conference). Citing a challenge to using technology to increase the availability of PD for ECE teachers, some scholars note that many PD instructors and ECE teachers feel that they need assistance in developing competence at using technology (Byington and Tannock 2011, NAEYC 2012). Overall, however, technology is a promising and practical tool through which to enhance access to and quality of supports available to ECE teachers.

Challenges

As promising as the above innovations are, significant hurdles remain; a few of these are presented below.

Lack of data

To date, much of ECE data collection has focused on program data, and on the degree to which programs meet specific requirements for licensure. Information on the workforce is sometimes collected, but more often than not, critical information about the workforce is absent. More precisely, we lack a solid database that documents the demographics and characteristics of the ECE workforce, including how and where they are prepared and the settings in which they are employed. We also have limited knowledge regarding how PD supports vary by state. This limitation prevents us from effectively discerning the impact of state policies and context on the nature and quality of the workforce. To alleviate this problem, a national database should be established to provide information on the workforce and on the PD taking place in the field as a whole, rather than just collecting data on individual ECE programs.

Lack of an adequate research base

In addition to a marked lack of data, there is also little research that has been conducted on ECE PD in the United States. To date, much of our knowledge regarding 'what works' with regard to PD has come from small-scale studies, often conducted in only a handful of states or from analyses of specific interventions (National

Academy of Sciences 2012). Ideally, a research agenda devoted to the teaching workforce would include the implementation of large-scale experimental and quasi-experimental studies on effective PD practices, as well as qualitative studies that examine the nature of PD and its influence on the workforce. This endeavor necessitates significant investments both intellectually and fiscally in order to build a research base on what actually constitutes 'effective' PD for the ECE workforce.

Lack of durable professional development systems

While current efforts to develop PD subsystems bode well for the short term, the sustainability of such efforts is not clear. While the increased federal investments we have discussed here can bolster the status of PD for ECE, the United States is a federalist democracy. States, being the entity with constitutional authority over the provision of education, will probably bear the financial burden of investing in the workforce. As such, there are important steps that states can take to foster durability of PD subsystems. First, line items in state ECE budgets should be systematically devoted to PD, with PD deemed as essential to the infrastructure, in addition to facilities and materials. Second, to ensure more coordinated long-range planning, states should have dedicated PD plans that assess potential needs, determine potential deliverers and instantiate the mechanisms to ensure that PD achieves its rightful place in the early childhood infrastructure.

Lack of articulation

Currently, the United States has no universal method for determining which courses, credits or degrees acquired from one institution of higher education can be transferred to another institution. This lack of articulation from one institution to another often results in students having to repeat courses already taken, and means that they have to bear the financial burden of taking extra courses. In some states with more advanced PD subsystems, inroads have been made – particularly between public two-year and four-year institutions – and 'articulation agreements' have been developed. These agreements benefit both the student and the institution in that they expedite a student's progress in working towards their degree, while reducing the administrative time needed to review a student's transcript and adjudicating disagreements about what should 'count' as coursework.

Lack of reciprocity

A point of pride among many in the United States is the fact that each state has its own unique context and culture. To wit, presidential candidates often talk about needing to develop a '50-state strategy,' recognizing that each state must be courted and considered according to its unique needs and character. While this diversity is, in many ways, a blessing, it can also hamper efficient PD delivery. The myriad requirements for the ECE workforce mean that teachers who have obtained a degree, credential or certification in one state may not be able to have those achievements transferred to another state. This challenge is commonly termed a lack of 'reciprocity' (Professional Development Systems and Workforce Initiatives Center 2014). Reciprocity is the concept that credentials, certifications and other PD are 'portable' from state to state (National Academy of Sciences 2012). Since there is a high degree of mobility among ECE practitioners (resulting from both the lack of stability in the field and the geographic and cultural composition of the United States), a lack of reciprocity is an important challenge to overcome.

Conclusions

The realities and challenges of PD for ECE discussed in this analysis represent some – although not all – of the major issues with which ECE policy-makers, scholars and practitioners must contend in the contemporary US context. Stemming from fragmentation and a lack of sustainable resources, the challenges we have articulated throughout this article pose major barriers that have caused some teachers to leave the field of ECE entirely. Not without hope, however, the work on ECE systems happening in US states and the increasing federal investments present exciting opportunities for increasing the quality of ECE PD in all 50 US states. Although the experiences are unique to the United States, they may have some applicability to other countries with highly decentralized governance approaches and/or to those seeking some innovations in PD.

References

Ackerman, D.J. and Barnett, W.S., 2006. *Increasing the effectiveness of preschool programs*. Preschool policy brief, issue 11. New Brunswick, NJ: National Institute of Early Education Research.

Administration for Children and Families, 2013. *2014–2015 child care and development fund plan*. Washington, DC: US Department of Health and Human Services.

Barnett, W.S. and Whitebook, M., 2011. *Degrees in context: asking the right questions about preparing skilled and effective teachers of young children*. New Brunswick, NJ: National Institute for Early Education Research.

Barnett, W.S., *et al.*, 2013. *The state of preschool 2013: state preschool yearbook*. New Brunswick, NJ: National Institute for Early Education Research.

Burchinal, M.R., *et al.*, 2008. Predicting child outcomes at the end of kindergarten from the quality of pre-kindergarten teacher–child interactions and instruction. *Applied developmental science*, 12 (3), 140–153.

Bureau of Labor Statistics, US Department of Labor. 2014. *Occupational outlook handbook, 2014-2015 edition* [online]. Childcare Workers. Available from: http://www.bls.gov/ooh/personal-care-and-service/childcare-workers.htm#tab-5 [Accessed 11 February 2015].

Buysse, V. and Wesley, P.W., 2009. *Consultation in early childhood settings*. Baltimore, MD: Paul H. Brookes.

Byington, T.A. and Tannock, M.T., 2011. Professional development needs and interests of early childhood education trainers [online]. *Early childhood research and practice*, 13 (2), 1. Available from: http://ecrp.uiuc.edu/v13n2/byington.html [Accessed 11 February 2015].

Child Care Aware, 2014. *S. 1086 the child care and development block grant amended version: summary of bi-partisan, bicameral agreement by House and Senate negotiators, reintroduced September 12, 2014*. Washington, DC: CCA.

Connors-Tadros, L. and Hororwitz, M., 2014. *How are early childhood teachers faring in state teacher evaluation systems? (CEELO policy report)*. New Brunswick, NJ: Center on Enhancing Early Learning Outcomes.

Council for Professional Recognition (CPR), 2011. *How to earn your CDA*. Washington, DC: CPR.

Council for Professional Recognition (CPR), 2013. *CDA renewal: updated summer 2013* [online]. Washington, DC: Author. Available from: http://www.cdacouncil.org/the-cda-credential/how-to-renew-your-cda [Accessed 11 February 2015].

Early, D.M., *et al.*, 2005. *Pre-kindergarten in eleven states: NCEDL's multi-state study of pre-kindergarten and study of state-wide early education programs (SWEEP)*. Chapel Hill, NC: University of North Carolina.

Fukkink, R.G. and Lont, A., 2007. Does training matter? A meta-analysis and review of caregiver training studies. *Early childhood research quarterly*, 22 (3), 294–311.

Gilliam, W.S. and Marchesseault, C.M., 2005. *From capitols to classrooms, policies to practice: state-funded prekindergarten at the classroom level: part 1. Who's teaching our youngest students? Teacher education and training, experience, compensation and benefits, and assistant teachers.* New Haven, CT: Yale University, Yale Child Study Center.

Ginsburg, H.P., Hyson, M., and Woods, T.A., eds., 2014. *Preparing early childhood educators to teach math: professional development that works.* Baltimore, MD: Paul H. Brookes.

Gomez, R.E., 2014. *Exploring the potential of consolidated approaches to governance for bringing coherence to early childhood systems.* New York, NY: Columbia University, UMI 3621772.

Hakel, M.D., Koenig, J.A., and Elliot, S., eds., 2008. *Assessing accomplished teaching: advanced-level certification programs.* Washington, DC: National Research Council of the National Academies Press.

Ilari, B., 2010. A community of practice in music teacher training: the case of Musicalização Infantil. *Research studies in music education*, 32 (1), 42–60.

Institute of Medicine (IOM) and National Research Council (NRC), 2012. *The early childhood care and education workforce: challenges and opportunities: a workshop report.* Washington, DC: The National Academies Press.

Justice, L.M., *et al.*, 2008. Experimental evaluation of a preschool language curriculum: influence on children's expressive language skills. *Journal of speech, language, and hearing research*, 51 (4), 983–1001.

Kagan, S.L., 1996. America's family support movement: a moment of change. *In*: E. Zigler, S.L. Kagan, and N. Hall, eds. *Children, families, and government: preparing for the 21st century.* New York, NY: Cambridge University Press, 156–170.

Kagan, S.L., 2009. *American early childhood education: preventing or perpetuating inequality?* New York: Teachers College Campaign for Educational Equity.

Kagan, S.L. and Cohen, N.E., 1996. A vision for a quality early care and education system: quality programs and a quality infrastructure. *In*: S.L. Kagan and N.E. Cohen, eds. *Reinventing early care and education.* San Francisco, CA: Jossey-Bass, 309–332.

Kagan, S.L. and Gomez, R.E., 2011. BA plus: reconciling reality and reach. *In*: E. Zigler, W.S. Gilliam, and W.S. Barnett, eds. *The pre-k debates: current controversies and issues.* Baltimore, MD: Brookes, 68–73.

Kagan, S.L. and Gomez, R.E., 2014. One two buckle my shoe: early mathematics education and teacher professional development. *In*: H. Ginsburg, M. Hyson, and T. Woods, eds. *Helping early childhood educators teach math.* Baltimore, MD: Paul H. Brookes, 1–28.

Kagan, S.L., Gomez, R.E., and Friedlander, J., 2014. The status of early care and education: teacher preparation in the United States. *In*: W.E. Fthenakis, ed. *Natur-wissen Schaffen*, Bremen, Germany: University of Bremen, 1–44.

Kagan, S.L. and Kauerz, K., 2008. Governing American early care and education: shifting from government to governance and from form to function. *In*: S. Feeney, A. Galper, and C. Seefeldt, eds. *Continuing issues in early childhood education.* 3rd ed. Columbus, OH: Pearson Merrill Prentice Hall, 12–32.

Kagan, S.L. and Kauerz, K., eds., 2012. *Early childhood systems: transforming early learning.* New York, NY: Teachers College Press.

Kagan, S.L., Kauerz, K., and Tarrant, K., 2008. *Early care and education teaching workforce at the fulcrum: an agenda for reform.* New York, NY: Teachers College Press.

LeMoine, S. and Azer, S.L., 2006. *Center child care licensing requirements (October 2006): minimum early childhood education (ECE) preservice qualifications and annual ongoing training hours for teachers and master teachers* [online]. Available from: http://www.nccic.org/pubs/cclicensingreq/cclr-teachers.html

LeMoine, S. and National Governors' Association Center for Best Practices, 2010. *Issue brief: building an early childhood professional development system.* Washington, DC: National Governors' Association Center for Best Practices.

Lombardi, J., 2003. *A time to care: redesigning child care to promote education, support families, and build communities.* Philadelphia, PA: Temple University Press.

Maroto, M. and Brandon, R.N., 2012. Summary of background data on the ECCE workforce. *In*: Institute of Medicine and National Research Council, eds. *The early childhood care and education workforce: challenges and opportunities. A workshop report*. Washington, DC: The National Academies Press, 141–210.

Maxwell, K., Lim, C.I., and Early, D.M., 2006. *Early childhood teacher preparation programs in the United States: national report*. Chapel Hill, NC: University of North Carolina, Frank Porter Graham Institute.

Mitchell, A., 2009. *Quality rating and improvement systems as the framework for early care and education system reform* [online]. Available from: www.buildinitiative.org [Accessed 10 February 2015].

National Academy of Sciences, 2012. *The early childhood care and education workforce: challenges and opportunities. A workshop report*. Washington, DC: The National Academies Press.

National Association for the Education of Young Children (NAEYC), 2011. *2010 NAEYC standards for initial and advanced early childhood professional preparation programs*. Washington, DC: NAEYC.

National Association for the Education of Young Children (NAEYC), 2012. *Technology and interactive media as tools in early childhood programs serving children from birth to age eight*. Washington, DC: NAEYC.

National Board for Professional Teaching Standards (NPBTS), 2012. *Early childhood/generalist standards, third edition: for teachers of students ages 3 to 8*. Arlington, VA: NBPTS.

National Child Care Information Center, 2010. *Minimum requirements for preservice qualifications and annual ongoing training hours for center teaching roles in 2008* [online]. Available from: http://nccic.acf.hhs.gov/pubs/cclicensingreq/cclr-teachers.html

National Survey of Early Care and Education Project Team, 2013. *Number and characteristics of early care and education (ECE) teachers and caregivers: initial findings from the National Survey of Early Care and Education (NSECE)*. Office of Planning, Research and Evaluation (OPRE) Report #2013-38. Washington, DC: Office of Planning, Research and Evaluation, Administration for Children and Families, US Department of Health and Human Services.

Neuman, S.B. and Kamil, M.L., 2010. *Preparing teachers for the early childhood classroom: proven models and key principles*. Baltimore, MD: Brookes.

Office of Child Development and Early Learning, 2012. *Pennsylvania professional development system framework for early care and education*. Harrisburg, PA: OCDEL.

Pianta, R., 2007. Preschool is school, sometimes. *Education next*, 1, 44–49.

Polakow, V., 2004. *Who cares for our children: the child care crisis in the other America*. New York, NY: Teachers College Press.

Professional Development Systems and Workforce Initiatives Center, 2014. *Professional development systems and workforce initiatives resources* [online]. Washington, DC: PDW Center. Available from: https://childcareta.acf.hhs.gov/professional-development-systems-and-workforce-initiatives [Accessed 11 February 2015].

Schweinhart, L.J., Barnes, H.V., and Weikert, D.P., 1993. *Significant benefits: the High/Scope Perry Preschool study through age 27*. Ypsilanti, MI: High/Scope Press.

Shonkoff, J.P. and Phillips, D.A., eds., 2000. *From neurons to neighborhoods: the science of early childhood development*. National Research Council and Institute of Medicine, Committee on Integrating the Science of Early Childhood Development. Washington, DC: National Academies Press.

Skiffington, S., Washburn, S., and Elliot, K., 2011. Instructional coaching: helping preschool teachers reach their full potential. *Young children*, 66 (3), 12–19.

US Department of Education, 2011. *Partnering with postsecondary institutions and other professional development providers in developing effective early childhood educators* [online]. Washington, DC: US Department of Education. Available from: http://www.ed.gov/early-learning/elc-draft-summary/selection-criteria-d3 [Accessed 10 February 2015].

US Department of Education, 2013. *Race to the Top – Early Learning Challenge awards* [online]. Washington, DC: US Department of Education. Available from: http://www2.ed.gov/programs/racetothetop-earlylearningchallenge/awards.html [Accessed 10 February 2015].

Whitebook, M., *et al.*, 2001. *Then & now: changes in child care staffing, 1994-2000. Technical report.* Washington, DC: Center for the Child Care Workforce.

Whitebook, M. and Ryan, S., 2013. *Supportive environmental quality underlying adult learning (SEQUAL): early childhood workforce data systems meeting.* Berkeley, CA: Center for the Study of Child Care Employment, University of California at Berkeley.

Whitebook, M., Sakai, L., and Kipnis, F., 2010. *Beyond homes and centers: the workforce in three California early childhood infrastructure organizations.* Berkeley, CA: Center for the Study of Child Care Employment, University of California, Berkeley.

Whitebook, M., *et al.*, 2012. *By default or by design? Variations in higher education programs for early care and education teachers and their implications for research methodology, policy, and practice.* Berkeley, CA: Center for the Study of Child Care Employment, University of California at Berkeley.

Zaslow, M., 2014. General features of effective professional development: implications for preparing early educators to teach mathematics. *In*: H. Ginsburg, M. Hyson, and T. Woods, eds. *Helping early childhood educators teach math.* Baltimore, MD: Paul H. Brookes, 97–116.

Zaslow, M., *et al.*, 2009. *Multiple purposes for measuring quality in early childhood settings: implications for collecting and communicating information on quality.* OPRE Issue Brief. Washington, DC: Office of Planning, Research and Evaluation, Administration for Children and Families, US Department of Health and Human Services.

Contemporary practice in professional learning and development of early childhood educators in Australia: reflections on what works and why

Fay Hadley, Manjula Waniganayake and Wendy Shepherd

Continuous professional learning and development (PLD) is an essential component of effective practice in any profession. PLD as a professional responsibility and workplace requirement in early childhood (EC) settings is now embedded in Australian national policy. What PLD looks like and how it happens in EC settings is a hot topic both locally and internationally. Much of this discussion is associated with major reforms in the EC policy landscape. Increasingly, approaches to PLD are being documented as research inquiry in EC journals. Traditional forms of professional development delivered collectively to educators from diverse backgrounds are being questioned in terms of influencing changes in practice. This article will unpack current thinking on PLD of EC educators using research conducted in EC settings in Sydney. The article will outline what strategies were successful, and how and why these strategies enhanced practice. Adopting Hujala's contextual theory of leadership, examples illustrate how the organisational context and the integration of individual capabilities of educators align in promoting sustained professional growth. Findings highlight the importance of adopting a strategic approach to both organisational improvement and professional advancement of educators at different stages of their careers.

Introduction

For the purposes of this paper, given the centrality of 'learning' in relation to professional growth and development, we use the short-hand term 'professional learning and development' (PLD). This is based on the conceptual model incorporating three spheres of learning as proposed by Waniganayake *et al.* (2012, pp. 236–238) and incorporates self-directed learning, guided learning with a critical friend and collective learning in small groups. In selecting appropriate learning strategies, it is further asserted that options must be 'relevant, properly costed and evaluated against individual staff development plans and organisational goals' (2012, p. 237). Australian government policy reforms in the past six years have had a powerful impact on the access, availability and affordability of PLD in this country. The aim of this paper is to unpack the nature of PLD employed within prior-to-school settings in Australia as a way of considering challenges encountered in delivering effective PLD in the early childhood (EC) sector.

This exploration will be contextualised within global and national understandings on PLD. Adopting an approach reflective of Hujala's (2013) contextual theory of leadership, we will discuss how the integration of the organisational context with individual capabilities aligns in promoting the professional growth of EC educators. Two studies illustrate the type of professional learning that occurs within Australian contexts, what is valued by educators and what supports are necessary to enact innovation and change within EC settings. Challenges of implementation are outlined from the perspectives of these educators. In conclusion, we argue that a systematic approach is crucial in achieving sustainable PLD that can be impactful in enhancing the quality of EC programmes.

Orientation to the Australian landscape

During 2007–2013, the political landscape in EC education reflected major changes in national policy impacting on the professionalisation of the EC workforce (Productivity Commission 2011, Waniganayake *et al.* 2012, Productivity Commission 2014). Captured under the National Quality Framework (NQF),[1] those working in diverse prior-to-school settings were all brought under a single national policy framework for the first time. The NQF comprises the Early Years Learning Framework (EYLF), the National Quality Standard and the Education and Care Services National Law and Regulations (Australian Children's Education and Care Quality Authority [ACECQA] 2011). Within Australia, prior-to-school settings usually include children from birth to six years only. Government funding of these services is subject to compliance and accreditation of quality under the NQF, and this work includes a commitment to PLD by both educators and service providers (ACECQA 2011).

The development of the EC workforce strategy begun during the Australian Labor Government's term of office was not completed when they lost the national elections in 2013. The status of government support for PLD is once again on the margins, as the current government's review of EC policies appears to lack a sound focus on this area. For instance, the *Childcare and Early Childhood Learning* draft report recommends that by simplifying the National Quality Standard there will be a, 'reduction in the volume and complexity of professional development, training and guidance materials for providers, educators and state and territory regulatory staff' (Productivity Commission 2014, p. 271). This report goes on to argue that removing restrictions on maintaining staff:child ratios would also release educators to complete short courses and training. These records reflect an inadequate consideration of the implications stemming from the absence of regular staff involved in PLD. For instance, who will replace staff attending training? How will this impact on the consistency of programme delivery and relationships with children and families? Given the low levels of staff wages, who will pay for the actual cost of PLD, including the hiring of relief staff? The proposed policy changes based on a narrow conceptualisation of training provision have the potential to undermine programme quality.

The National Quality Standard assesses EC settings in Australia under seven Quality Areas. Within Quality Area 4, which focuses on staffing arrangements, the introductory comments refer to continuous PLD as follows:

Updating and maintaining educators' knowledge is a joint responsibility of educators, co-ordinators, the nominated supervisor and the approved provider, and includes a range of professional development strategies that challenge and extend current thinking. (ACECQA 2011, p. 111)

The responsibility for PLD is buttressed further in Quality Area 7.1, which states: 'Effective leadership promotes a positive organisational culture and builds a professional learning community' (ACECQA 2011, p. 173). Whilst inclusion of PLD is a pleasing development in the EC national policy framework, it has limited traction without adequate infrastructure support, funding and pedagogical leadership at the organisational setting.

In Australia, the EC workforce comprises educators without any EC qualifications as well as those with an EC qualification ranging from a basic entry-level vocational certificate, to a diploma, to a bachelor's and/or master's degree. Regardless of the type of qualification, all EC educators are expected to implement the NQF. A pre-requisite in implementing these policies is a sound knowledge base and professional confidence acquired through adequate formal training and preparation as educators as well as continuous PLD 'to remain up-to-date with evolving developments in the field' (Waniganayake *et al.* 2008, p. 118). There has been an increasing demand to have well-qualified EC educators with the necessary expertise and dispositions to implement the new national policies (Productivity Commission 2011). These reforms continue to influence educators to re-examine their approaches to programme planning and pedagogical practice. The proliferation of professional learning opportunities in the sector in recent years is reflective of both the availability of government funding for PLD and the increasing professionalisation of the EC sector.

Professional Support Coordinators are funded by the Australian government to provide subsidised, affordable professional learning to educators employed in approved EC services. The Professional Support Coordinators provide a suite of PLD programmes with various registered training organisations in each state and territory consisting of mandatory training to satisfy legislative responsibilities, including first aid, asthma management, anaphylaxis and child protection. It also includes specialist programmes about EC pedagogy, programme planning and leadership preparation, either as groups from different services or as individually tailored sessions delivered to staff in particular centres. Today, there is a wide variety of professional learning and support strategies (Waniganayake *et al.* 2012). These are highly variable in terms of content, structure, cost, delivery method and duration. The target participants can also vary from educators to cooks, and administrative staff, as well as centre directors, owners and management committee members. There is, however, limited published information about exactly how PLD providers or participants identify and target professional learning in terms of their needs, interests and abilities as well as learning styles.

Current understandings on professional learning and development

Research on PLD shows clearly the benefits of engaging in continuous learning for the educator as well as children, families and the organisation that employs the educator (Elliott 2006, Organisation for Economic Co-operation and Development [OECD] 2012, Snell *et al.* 2013). Nationwide studies carried out in countries such as Australia (for example, Waniganayake *et al.* 2008) and New Zealand

(Cherrington and Wansbrough 2007) demonstrate the variable nature of PLD sessions, strategies and programmes. The large number and spread of topics on offer and the challenges of gaining access to any systematic evaluations make it difficult to generalise about the quality of the professional learning available and its impact on children's learning outcomes, let alone the professionalisation of individual educators, their organisations or the sector as a whole. Moreover, the necessity to target differing contextual factors such as programme type, location, centre size as well as age, ethnicity, learning styles, experience and qualifications of the participants adds to the complexity of making overall conclusions. As such, the OECD (2012, p. 148) declares: 'in general, there is little clarity about what forms of professional development are MOST effective'.

Approaches to professional learning are increasingly being examined and researched within diverse contexts. Traditional forms of professional development (e.g. attending a one-off workshop on music) are being questioned in terms of effecting changes in practice (Webster-Wright 2009). Others have found that models of professional learning which include academics, experts or consultants have had positive effects on teacher practice (Evans *et al.* 2000, Hahs-Vaughn and Yanowitz 2009, Degotardi *et al.* 2012, Hadley 2012). When teachers are provided with release time to participate in professional learning with mentors or coaches, they are more likely to undertake action research in their classrooms (Hahs-Vaughn and Yanowitz 2009). Walter and Briggs (2012) analysed 35 school studies and found that the types of professional learning that impacted on teacher practice included the following: being classroom based; expertise brought from outside; teachers chose areas to focus on; teachers worked collaboratively with colleagues; and mentoring and coaching was provided, was sustained over a period of time and was supported by the leadership team. Likewise, implemented over two years, a government-funded mentoring programme conducted in Australia revealed that new and isolated EC teachers overwhelmingly called out for continuous 'support from more experienced teacher colleagues with whom they can talk and work through the issues and challenges they face on a day-to-day basis' (Nolan *et al.* 2013, p. 169).

In 2013, the *Early Years* journal published seven papers on professional development based on research conducted in Australia, Canada, England, Italy, New Zealand and the USA. In writing the editorial for this issue, Oberhuemer (2013) noted three themes: funding of diverse professional learning as an entitlement to ensure access; facilitation of 'active engagement and critical reflection' (2013, p. 105); and the placement of professional learning within a system-wide framework. Research published elsewhere also reinforces these themes. For instance, when reporting on a research-driven state-wide professional learning programme, Carter and Fewster (2013) emphasised that it was not just the participation in the sessions that made the difference; rather, it was the support provided by the facilitators in scaffolding the educators' learnings that led to major changes in increasing self-confidence and improved practice. These changes were visible in terms of 'new and modified practices, processes and strategies implemented within their work contexts' (Carter and Fewster 2013, p. 80). Importantly, this professional learning programme was government funded, facilitated by experts and systematically coordinated and evaluated, making it possible to assess achievements of a planned PLD programme.

Likewise, in the USA, continuous evaluation of a master teacher professional development programme conducted by Crawford *et al.* (2010, p. 36) revealed that participants completed the programme having acquired 'a greater sense of confidence, courage, collaboration and empowerment' as professionals. Adoption of a systemic approach reflected widespread commitment to support the programme and guaranteed time and funding for professional learning over three years. Likewise, having a systematic approach to PLD also means monitoring changes in practice that occur after educators return to their workplaces. As Brown and Inglis (2013) note, centre-based pedagogical leadership can make a difference in creating in-centre support mechanisms to build capacity from a long-term perspective.

Commitment by key stakeholders can be a key driver in facilitating and maintaining active engagement in PLD. It is also evident that educators who work with infants and toddlers may benefit from participating in 'specialised and practical training' as this 'seems to be more strongly associated with pedagogical quality and cognitive and social outcomes' (OECD 2012, p. 148). As such, it is necessary to examine the impact of PLD programmes with care, regardless of the duration as a one-off offering for instance. Likewise, research also affirms the key role played by EC centre directors, managers and educational leaders by allocating funding, motivating and supporting staff in their professional growth (Ackerman 2006, Sylva *et al*. 2010, Colmer 2013).

Global trends in professional development within OECD (2012, pp. 173–174) countries reflect the following:

- Funding of professional development may involve governments, employers or educators either in partnership or as the sole provider.
- The nature of PLD accessed may differ according to educator qualifications, experience and type of employment role performed as a teacher, manager, leader.
- The range of incentives available included full or partial payment of training costs, study leave, promotion and further study options.

It appears that governments in countries such as Finland, the Netherlands and Slovenia offered the biggest range of incentives for engagement in PLD, whereas opportunities in countries like Australia were limited to financial support for training (OECD 2012, p. 175). Government-funded PLD may also be used for specific purposes. For example, Spain guarantees 'attention to minorities' (2012, pp. 204–205), and in Sweden the government has been aiming to increase the number of preschool staff with postgraduate qualifications.

The OECD (2012, pp. 144–145) has identified professional qualifications, education and training as a key policy lever impacting the delivery of high-quality EC education and care programmes. Whilst acknowledging the importance of initial professional preparation, the OECD reinforces the importance of PLD throughout the career of an EC educator by declaring, 'ongoing professional development should not only be available, but it should be a requirement to stay and grow in the profession' (2012, p. 149). Likewise, in benchmarking early education across 45 countries, the Economist Intelligence Unit (2012, p. 25) declared that 'overall a well trained workforce was the most important determinant of quality' as reflected in the Nordic countries, which have a high bar for professional preparation including postgraduate qualifications. Professional learning is therefore a central aspect of an educator's engagement in the profession as well as in everyday practice as teachers of young children.

Guiding professional learning through contextual leadership

Contextually defined leadership (Hujala 2013) can assist in examining the placement and significance of professional learning within prior-to-school settings. According to Hujala, the pioneer of contextual leadership theorising within EC education, leadership enactment is both situational and socially constructed: 'The situational system means that leadership is influenced by social situations and by the operational environment as well as by expectations and traditions of the society' (2013, p. 54). Likewise, the visionary nature of leadership also means that children, staff and families are all connected with the core tasks of quality EC education and care. Referring to leadership studies carried out by various Finnish researchers, Hujala (2013) asserts further that the culture of leadership created within an organisation can 'determine what the development work based on that should be' (p. 56) for everyone involved in that setting. This includes the provision of PLD to engage staff actively in contributing to the mission of pursuing quality outcomes for children. By adopting a contextual theory of leadership (Hujala 2013), we explore examples from research carried out in Australia to illustrate how the integration of the organisational context with staff capabilities aligns in promoting professional growth.

In discussing the two studies used in this paper we outline the research design, data analysis and key findings of each study in terms of what educators value by way of support that is necessary to enact innovation and change within prior-to-school settings.

Research design

The two studies were conducted at the beginning of the major EC national policy reforms introduced in 2009. Ethical approval was obtained for both research studies. Both studies were conducted with ethical approval from the Macquarie University Human Sciences and Humanities Committee. A brief design of each study is outlined next.

Study 1 (2009–2011)

This research project provided professional learning support to the teachers (both in groups and individually) to support their engagement with the EYLF, including decision-making on curriculum and pedagogy. In five centres an academic expert (first author) was employed as a consultant directly with educators and directors of these organisations. The consultancy period varied between 3 and 18 months with each organisation. The consultancies also varied in how professional learning was undertaken in each organisation. For instance, within Organisation 1 there was in-house training across 18 months with the educators, as well as meeting individually with the educators and directors to guide programme development in terms of implementing the EYLF (for a detailed disussion of the project, see Hadley 2012). In Organisation 2 the consultancy was for three months, to meet with the room leaders and directors (job share position) regularly to examine the EYLF and how it could be implemented effectively into their planning and programming. For Organisation 3 the consultancy involved working with the whole staff team for six months. This involved monthly learning circles, where each room developed a practitioner inquiry question to focus on in regard to working with their families. Email and telephone contact also occurred outside these monthly sessions.

As a requirement of the University's Faculty of Human Sciences Human Research Ethics Committee, a research assistant was employed to conduct all of the follow-up interviews to increase impartiality of participants' responses. Twenty educators across three organisations participated in the interviews. This included nine from Organisation 1 (a not-for-profit organisation with three childcare centres), four from Organisation 2 (a stand-alone childcare centre) and seven from Organisation 3 (a workplace childcare centre). Interviews ranged from 14 to 48 minutes with an average of 33 minutes overall. These semi-structured interviews included questions on demographic data, professional learning opportunities, familiarisation and confidence with the EYLF, leading the team (pedagogical leadership), the role of the director/management in professional learning and the role of the external consultant.

Study 2 (2012–2013)

In four childcare centres the same academic consultant conducted research with five EC teachers on developing partnerships with families utilising a practitioner inquiry approach. One of the centres was from Organisation 1, and the other four centres were from two new organisations: Organisation 4 was a not-for-profit organisation based at a university campus with two centres and Organisation 5 was a not-for-profit organisation with a multi-disciplinary integrated services approach. The aim of this research study was to investigate the perceptions of teachers and culturally diverse families about what partnerships in prior-to-school settings meant for them. A practitioner inquiry approach was used in the study and data about this process were collected through interviews with the EC teachers. The data that related to professional learning, what was valued and why have now been brought together with Study 1 data, for the purposes of discussing PLD matters in this paper.

Participants' demographics

The 25 participants (see Table 1) varied in qualifications and experience across the 5 organisations. This included 3 educators with a master's degree, 13 educators with an EC bachelor's degree (three- to four-year university qualification), 7 educators with a diploma (two-year technical college or vocational qualification) and 2 educators with a certificate III (10-week vocational qualification). Not surprisingly, only a small number of educators ($n = 9$) had been teaching in the prior-to-school sector for more than 10 years. The majority of the participants ($n = 16$) had taught in EC settings for less than 10 years, including two who had less than 4 years' experience.

To some extent these participants' experience in the sector is representative of the EC workforce (The Social Research Centre 2014). The small number of

Table 1. Participants of both studies.

	Organisation 1	Organisation 2	Organisation 3	Organisation 4	Organisation 5
Study 1	9	4	7	0	0
Study 2	1	0	0	3	1
Total	10	4	7	3	1

participants in each study, however, sets limits in terms of wider applications of the findings. Nevertheless, the key findings can be used to illustrate emerging trends in professional learning in the sector that require further exploration and discussion.

The time the educators had been at their current centre was also representative of the EC workforce participation in Australia and illustrated one of the difficulties faced in the EC sector in terms of retaining educators (The Social Research Centre 2014). In this group of 25 educators, the majority ($n = 14$) have been at their current workplace for less than four years regardless of their level of qualification. Only two had been at their current workplace for more than 10 years.

Data analysis and key findings of the two studies

Data from the interviews were analysed into themes with the assistance of QSR NVivo 10 (a qualitative software program). During the interviews, participants were asked to identify the types of professional learning that they valued. The data were coded into themes on professional learning and the findings are discussed in terms of what is valued (see Figure 1) and how these assessments varied according to the participants' EC qualifications (see Figure 2).

As can be seen in Figure 1, practitioner inquiry was valued by a majority of participants ($n = 18$) in contrast to professional readings, which was selected by less than one-quarter of the participants ($n = 6$). Importantly the analyses of these data also showed that not a single participant identified mandatory training required by government. Mentoring and networking was only valued by approximately one-half of the participants ($n = 13$). Those who mentioned other types of learning were each less than one-half. This included in-house training ($n = 12$), maintaining a reflective journal ($n = 12$), attending seminars ($n = 10$) and undertaking formal qualifications ($n = 9$). Interestingly, the three most popular PLD strategies identified in this research were practitioner inquiry, mentoring/networking and in-house training, and all of these comprised learning with others. In contrast, the less valued strategies comprising formal studies and reading professional publications demanded self-motivation, self-reflection and perseverance to stay on task.

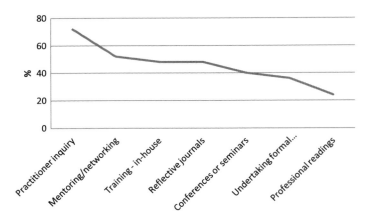

Figure 1. Valuing professional learning: educator perspectives.

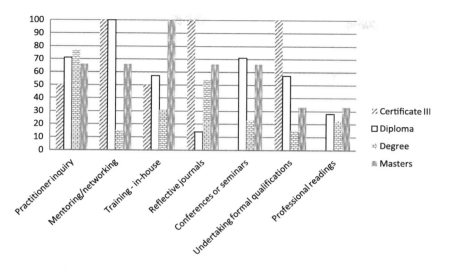

Figure 2. Types of professional learning valued by qualifications.

The analysis of these data in terms of the participants' qualifications gave a different picture on what was valued (see Figure 2), and potential reasons for this variation are discussed next.

Practitioner inquiry

Although in Study 1 participation in professional inquiry projects was a requirement by the employers, during the interviews diploma-trained and degree-trained participants stated that they valued this type of professional learning over other strategies. This was illustrated in comments such as the following:

> The practitioner inquiry that we did with Fay was fantastic. We gained so much from that and it's actually the first one that I've ever been involved in and I would recommend it to anybody. I thought it really worked well, the staff were so enthusiastic. They were so into getting their information and doing all their groundwork and all that kind of stuff. It's the first one I've ever really been involved in but it's definitely something that I would look at doing again, for staff and for myself. (Study 1, Organisation 3, diploma, assistant director)

> I think it's because you get that chance to go back into your workplace, reflect on what you're doing, maybe make some changes and then you go back to a group of people who've been doing the same thing. Bounce off ideas, what worked, what didn't work, what you struggled with and also have somebody in a facilitating role who can keep that together and maybe provide more resources or send people back out again. (Study 1, Organisation 3, degree, director)

These educators also recognised that although practitioner inquiry can give them a specific focus for learning, it may not always evolve the way it was originally planned. For example:

> I've achieved some good partnerships with parents not as much as with the bigger group that I would have liked to. I think I feel like I achieved more with the learning of children, learning development of children and the centre itself more than actual parents. So I kind of feel like it has gone away from the question. But whatever happened, it happened really. (Study 2, Organisation 4, degree)

Participants in both studies, however, reinforced the use of practitioner inquiry approaches as a way of providing sustained engagement in PLD consistently, over a period of time. For instance, in the words of one director: 'I really think, for me, things work best when I do get to speak to other people and unpack things. So key learning circles work really well where I can get ideas' (Study 1, Organisation 1, master's degree, director).

Mentoring and networking

Mentoring and networking was highly valued by all of the certificate III-trained and diploma-trained participants ($n = 9$). When discussing mentoring, they referred to the informal mentoring that occurred amongst peers in their centres, although they recognised this could occur either within or outside their centre. When discussing mentoring occurring within their centre, they saw this in a hierarchical way. For example, being mentored by their room leader or centre director. When they discussed mentoring that took place externally, it was in relation to obtaining support from a consultant or expert. Therefore, mentoring was perceived as a traditional expert as mentor and mentee as novice model, as reflected in the following comment:

> Directing my learning. So I think if your director or room leader can help you, give you some books and give you ideas, you can improve very fast. It will mean you come back to the work and do the program, that's very easy for [whole room] program, even for centre's program. Because you've got – I think all of you got the same direction. (Study 1, Organisation 1, diploma)

In-house training

All participants with master's degrees ($n = 3$) highly valued in-house training sessions, and they were usually the director at their centre. As one director stated: 'Internal is quite effective, just because everyone's there. If you want some change to occur then that's the way forward, I think' (Study 1, Organisation 1, master's degree, director). The value of in-house training was linked to having a holistic team approach to training as everyone could participate in the training together. For instance:

> If they're only getting little bits every now and again, it's not that helpful. As I said, it depends what it is – what training it is. For deeper thinking ... when they really do have to reflect on their thinking, it needs to be more sustained. (Study 1, Organisation 1, degree, director)

It is unclear whether this approach enacts effective change over time, especially if the educators who work directly with children did not value this type of learning. Given that this is a hot topic within the research literature, further investigation is warranted to ascertain its value for both the educators and their employers.

Reflective journals

All participants with a vocational certificate ($n = 2$) felt that keeping reflective journals and engaging in formal studies was important for their continuing development as educators. Both of these participants were currently enrolled in diploma-level studies. This was not surprising given that undertaking formal studies was initiated by individual educators and it was supported by their employers. Importantly, a culture of learning was valued and encouraged in all the organisations involved in these two studies.

The other participants gave mixed feedback about the process of writing in a reflective journal regularly. Some did value it, but they also acknowledged that they kept journals in their personal life (i.e. they liked to keep a private diary to write about life events). For example:

> I've always been a kind of journal diary kind of person. Ok. Keep a daily dairy of my personal life. Not like a daily diary. But just a sentence of what happened that day. This journal itself (page turning) I just find, I just wrote how I wanted to, I just, just babbled really. That's what I do normally when it comes to writing. I don't really read what I write but I don't change anything, much or at all. (Study 2, Organisation 4, degree)

> I've been over the last couple of years I've just been trying to be really, really reflective. And I think that just kind of helped me to do that in a more structured way I suppose. Because it's usually just something else to do and it can get lost in there sometimes. So I think whilst I certainly didn't do a lot of journaling, the journaling that I did was really helpful, because I've looked back on that and thought about where I was then and where I am now. (Study 2, Organisation 5, degree)

Even though just over one-half of the participants ($n = 13$) did not value the process of journaling, they did acknowledge that it was important for them to reflect with others in their team or centre. For instance, there were comments such as:

> Probably it's helpful. I'm not very good at this and again it's my learning style. I don't write at all. I prefer to talk and I prefer having conversation and even when I was doing this project, I was having a lot of conversations with the staff about what they were doing with the families but I never documented it. (Study 2, Organisation 4, master's degree, director)

> I like to talk. Yes, so for me personally I probably … I don't really tend to write things much in my daily life. (Study 2, Organisation 4, degree)

Critical reflection can occur as an individual or collective process. The literature (Stremmel 2002, Perry 2004) acknowledges the importance of educators being critically reflective practitioners; but how can this occur effectively if the staff within a centre have different perspectives about this? This is illustrated poignantly by one of the degree-qualified participants when she said: 'I guess I really enjoy the whole social connection between the staff and the way staff can work together as a team and staff development' (Study 1, Organisation 3, degree).

Undertaking formal qualifications

When commenting about the value of formal qualifications, those with a vocational certificate ($n = 2$) noted that this was important to them. Just over one-half ($n = 4$) of diploma participants described their studies as valuable professional learning. For instance, one of the diploma participants who had begun a bachelor's degree said:

> I started last year, mid-year. So this will be my second semester and I kind of expected it to be – with all the work that they give you with readings and that – I was expecting all that. So that's why it took me quite a few years to actually prepare myself. I always said I will go to study further, university as an adult, not when I came straight out of high school. (Study 1, Organisation 1, diploma)

Undertaking formal qualifications was only mentioned by two of the degree-qualified and one of the master's-qualified participants. These three participants commented on this being valuable for other educators whom they worked with, not for their own learning. Comments included:

> It's really good because they – I think they just need that encouragement. They could work in childcare for so many years and their experiences are great, but having that formal qualification is different. (Study 1, Organisation 2, degree, director)

Importantly, these participants all acknowledged the support received from their employers, which enabled the pursuit of formal studies.

Conferences

Attendance at conferences was valued more by participants with either a diploma ($n = 5$) or a master's degree ($n = 2$). Issues of access were highlighted as some participants were unable to attend due to factors such as costs, geographical distance and lack of replacement staff. For example, one of the assistant directors from Organisation 1 stated:

> I went to this amazing indigenous conference, it was just a seminar, really. I learnt so much from it. But no-one else was with me. Although we're trying to bring in more representation of people and cultures within our centre, I haven't really done much with it and it has gone in my folder. I feel very disappointed in myself that I haven't done anything with that. But being an acting director in the centre and having a lot of other initiatives that we're working on at the moment, it's very hard to bring that in. I did present it to everyone in our staff meeting to follow up. But we haven't really done much with it – so that's an example of where it has just gone on the shelf and where it hasn't really been that effective. (Study 1, Organisation 1, master's degree, assistant director)

Others also noted that only the director went and then reported back to the team due to the expensive nature of this training. Another participant commented that as only one or two people from the centre could afford to go to a conference, this made it difficult to implement any learning across the centre because it was difficult to convince others, who did not attend, of the potential benefits.

Professional readings

This involved forming a reading circle to maintain a regular commitment to reading professional publications, including book chapters and peer-reviewed journals. This type of learning was the least valued by those participating in this research and was not even discussed by those with certificate-level qualifications. Lack of time was the primary constraint, as well as difficulties in accessing readings that were relevant and available. This is another area for further investigation in terms of looking at the types of readings available, what audience the reading is pitched at and how this is built into the workload of the educators.

Discussion

Findings from these two studies and the research literature on professional learning reflect the contextual nature of how and why engagement in PLD strategies is valued by educators. This research also highlights the importance of adopting a strategic approach by organisations and their leaders to ensure improvement of teaching practices and professional advancement of educators at different stages of their career. The two Australian studies targeted for reporting in this paper also serve to illustrate several key challenges pertinent to those with shared interests in exploring the professional learning of educators within their own countries. These include the following:

(1) Alignment of PLD strategies to match educators' qualifications and experience in the sector.
(2) Mapping, monitoring and measuring the effectiveness and impact of professional learning on quality programme delivery, particularly from the perspective of outcomes for children.
(3) Identification of the focus and objectives of the PLD programmes to ensure coverage of topics beyond mere compliance matters and incorporating pedagogy and curriculum.
(4) Allocation of adequate funding and infrastructure support to access relevant PLD.
(5) Importance of follow-up and scaffolded learning to continue beyond the formal presentations to ensure better take-up of knowledge and skills acquired through everyday practice within their own workplaces.

If the focus of learning is simply on compliance matters (such as health and safety, child protection and behaviour management), when and where do educators get access to engage in critical pedagogical thinking? For instance, one of the participants commented: 'Challenge is a good thing. If you're [not] challenged you just feel every day is the same. No challenge – and if you're getting used to no challenge you will lose yourself' (Study 1, Organisation 1, diploma). As such, without a planned approach to professional learning, as this educator noted, complacency can set in and without intervention this can become patterned behaviour halting creativity, innovation and change in practice. In this scenario, leadership for learning is essential to motivate and mentor these practitioners to break out of their professional isolation through engagement in attractive professional experiences that resonate with their individual needs, interests and abilities to work effectively with young children and their families. As McCormack *et al.* so eloquently stated:

> ... if professional growth is to occur teachers need to have sustained and substantive learning opportunities involving serious ongoing discussions with critical colleagues such as mentors and continued reflection on all aspects of their practice and beliefs to enhance their knowledge of teaching. (2004, p. 3)

Of particular concern in Australia is the absence of systematic assessment of the quality of professional learning providers and the programmes they provide. Competition for government funding for professional learning has seen an increase in registered training organisations offering workshops and conferences on the implementation of the NQF. It is not, however, clear how the take up of this funding will be audited to ensure high-quality delivery and enable the evaluation and measurement of the impact of the PLD sessions. For instance, issues such as the facilitator's skills in adult training require exploration. Likewise, a focus on compliance, standardisation and accountability could impact the way skills and knowledge acquired are put into practice by PLD participants.

The cyclic nature of learning also underscores the long-term outcomes of PLD. Engagement in reflective practice can take different forms, as shown in our studies. Targeted reflective work against set readings appears to be valued by those with degree qualifications, perhaps because of first-hand experience through their university studies. Documenting reflections in isolation was less valued. This pattern, however, raises questions about engagement in reflective practice in different ways according to one's background, qualifications and experience in the sector. Future research could investigate whether collaborative reflective processes involving a critical friend with expert knowledge may be more effective and sustainable than critical reflection by yourself. For instance, the degree-qualified director in Organisation 3 noted the importance of ongoing reflection:

> So there's a bit of a reflection going on between sessions so that you're actually – I think the learning is deeper because you've had the opportunity to think about how you're implementing it in your own space. You're reading in between so you've got more time to absorb the information that you might have received. Whereas if it's just one session, a lot of that – if you're doing it afterwards – you've got nobody to go back to and bounce ideas off or ask questions of. (Study 1, Organisation 3, degree, director)

These comments reinforce the approach adopted by Raban *et al.* (2007) to include guided reflection for both novice and experienced practitioners. Educators employed within schools have mandated four to five pupil-free days built into their annual training calendar. This contrasts with PLD options available to those who are employed in prior-to-school settings. Typically they work longer days (seven to eight hours per day), without school holidays and with little or no respite from children to undertake professional learning regularly. Without adequate funding, achieving parity with school educators is impossible for time-poor EC educators. Within Australia, this situation is also exacerbated due to perceived division between education (or preschool) and childcare services. It highlights structural impediments facing EC educators nationwide and the misalignment between individual educators' needs and interests in PLD, government policy and the objectives of their employing organisation to build professional capacity within the EC sector.

Conclusion

To enhance our understanding about concepts such as critical reflection and the development of cultures of learning within EC organisations requires investigations into pedagogical leadership within prior-to-school settings. Due to the turnover rates in the sector there is also a continuous need for professional learning for both new and experienced educators. Emerging evidence from the two studies conducted in Australia is supported by other research, which suggests that collaboration by academic experts and practitioner leaders can have a long-lasting impact on professionalisation and quality improvement. While the small scale of these studies means that the evidence base requires consolidation through replication and longitudinal research, we see potential for this model to be used in the future with teachers to ensure engagement with contemporary practices and for academics to also maintain connections with the sector. In this way, we can ensure that PLD offered is relevant, based on research and evaluated to assess quality learning.

THE PROFESSIONAL DEVELOPMENT OF EARLY YEARS EDUCATORS

Disclosure statement

No potential conflict of interest was reported by the authors.

Funding

This work was supported by the Macquarie University New Staff Grant Scheme 2012.

Note

1. See: http://www.acecqa.gov.au/national-quality-framework/introducing-the-national-quality-framework.

References

Ackerman, D.J., 2006. The costs of being a childcare teacher: revisiting the problem of low wages. *Educational policy*, 20 (1), 85–112.

Australian Children's Education and Care Quality Authority (ACECQA), 2011. *Guide to the national quality standard* [online]. Available from: http://www.acecqa.gov.au/storage/1% 20Guide%20to%20the%20NQF.pdf

Brown, A. and Inglis, S., 2013. So what happens after the event? Exploring the realisation of professional development with early childhood educators. *Australasian journal of early childhood*, 38 (1), 11–15.

Carter, M.A. and Fewster, C., 2013. Diversifying early years professional learning – one size no longer fits all. *Australasian journal of early childhood*, 38 (1), 73–80.

Cherrington, S. and Wansbrough, D., 2007. *An evaluation of Ministry of Education funded early childhood education professional development programs*. Victoria: University of Wellington.

Colmer, K., 2013. Leadership for professional development and learning. *Research symposium on leadership perspectives from near and far: from Australia and Europe*, Wesley Conference Centre, Sydney, December.

Crawford, P.A., Roberts, S.K., and Hickmann, R., 2010. Nurturing early childhood teachers as leaders: long-term professional development. *Dimensions of early childhood*, 38 (3), 31–37.

Degotardi, S., Semann, A., and Shepherd, W., 2012. Using practitioner inquiry to promote reflexivity and change in infant-toddler early childhood programs. *In*: P. Whiteman and K. De Gioia, eds. *Children and childhoods 1: perspectives, places and practices*. Newcastle upon Tyne: Cambridge Scholars, 36–57.

Economist Intelligence Unit, 2012. *Starting well: benchmarking early education across the world*. London: EIU.

Elliott, A., 2006. Early childhood education: pathways to quality and equity for all children. *In*: C. Glascodine, ed. *Australian education review, No 50*. Melbourne, VIC: Australian Council of Educational Research (ACER) Press, 1–75.

Evans, M., Lomax, P., and Morgan, H., 2000. Closing the circle: action research partnerships towards better learning and teaching in schools. *Cambridge journal of teacher education*, 30 (3), 405–419.

Hadley, F., 2012. Rethinking pedagogical practices. How can teachers in early childhood settings be supported professionally to examine their practices? *In*: P. Whiteman and K. De Gioia, eds. *Children and childhoods 1: perspectives, places and practices*. Newcastle upon Tyne: Cambridge Scholars, 16–35.

Hahs-Vaughn, D. and Yanowitz, K., 2009. Who is conducting teacher research? *Journal of educational research*, 102 (6), 415–426.

Hujala, E., 2013. Contextually defined leadership. *In*: E. Hujala, M. Waniganayake, and J. Rodd, eds. *Researching leadership in early childhood education*. Tampere: Tampere University Press, 47–60.

McCormack, A., Gore, J., and Thomas, K., 2004. Learning to teach: narratives from early career teachers. *Paper presented at the Australian Association for Research in Education*, University of Melbourne, Melbourne, November.

Nolan, A., Morrissey, A., and Dumenden, I., 2013. Expectations of mentoring in a time of change: views of new and professionally isolated early childhood teachers in Victoria, Australia. *Early years*, 33 (2), 161–171.

Oberhuemer, P., 2013. Continuing professional development and the early years workforce. *Early years*, 33 (2), 103–105.

Organsation for Economic Co-operation and Development (OECD), 2012. *Starting strong III: a quality toolbox for early childhood education and care*. Paris: OECD.

Perry, R., 2004. *Teaching practice for early childhood: a guide for students*. London: Routledge Falmer.

Productivity Commission, 2011. *Early childhood devlopment workforce*. Research report. Canberra, ACT: Commonwealth of Australia.

Productivity Commission, 2014. *Childcare and early childhood learning*. Productivity Commission draft report. Canberra, ACT: Commonwealth of Australia.

Raban, B., *et al.*, 2007. *Building capacity: strategic professional development for early childhood practitioners*. Melbourne: Thomson Social Science Press.

Snell, M.E., *et al.*, 2013. A review of 20 years of research on professional development interventions for preschool teachers and staff. *Early child development and care*, 183, 857–873.

Stremmel, A.J., 2002. Nurturing professional and personal growth through inquiry. *Young children*, September, 62–70.

Sylva, K., *et al.*, eds., 2010. *Early childhood matters: evidence from the effective pre-school and primary education project*. London: Routledge.

The Social Research Centre, 2014. *2013 national early childhood education and care workforce census*. North Melbourne, VIC: The Social Research Centre.

Walter, C. and Briggs, J., 2012. *What professional development makes the difference to teachers?* Oxford: Oxford University Press.

Waniganayake, M., *et al.*, 2008. *Practice potentials: impact of participation in professional development and support in quality outcomes for children in childcare centres* [online]. Canberra Professional Support Coordinators Alliance, ACCESS Macquarie and Department of Education, Employment and Workplace Relations. Available from: http://pscalliance.org.au/wp-content/uploads/PDResearchReportMac08.pdf [Accessed 10 February 2015].

Waniganayake, M., *et al.*, 2012. *Leadership. Contexts and complexities in early childhood education*. Melbourne: Oxford University Press.

Webster-Wright, A., 2009. Reframing professional development through understanding authentic professional learning. *Review of educational research*, 79 (2), 702–739.

Implementing curriculum reform: insights into how Australian early childhood directors view professional development and learning

Kaye Colmer, Manjula Waniganayake and Laurie Field

A range of studies has demonstrated that collaborative professional development and learning (PD&L) is effective in implementing curriculum reform. PD&L that is contextualised within a specific setting enables educators to explore new theoretical perspectives, review existing knowledge and beliefs, and examine their current practice. This article reports on an investigation of how Australian early childhood centre directors understand and lead PD&L during a major reform of curriculum. Qualitative analysis was undertaken drawing on orienting concepts from the literature. Analysis of data collected from two focus groups of early childhood centre directors shows the importance of the director as overall educational leader but suggests that distributing leadership supports PD&L. Although directors articulated belief in the value of collaborative professional learning, individualised, one-off, external professional development events remained a common strategy. Directors' perceptions about managing curriculum reform, their understanding of leadership and PD&L, together with considerations of broader social and system influences such as organisational culture and structural arrangements are factors that contribute to professional learning. A model for a centre-based professional learning system is proposed.

Introduction

In 2009, the Early Years Learning Framework (EYLF) was launched by the Australian Department of Education, Employment and Workplace Relations (ADEEWR 2009) with expectations for implementation in early childhood settings nationwide by 2011 (Council of Australian Governments 2008). The EYLF defines early childhood curriculum as 'the interactions, experiences, activities, routines and events, planned and unplanned that occur in an environment designed to foster children's learning and development' (ADEEWR 2009, p. 9). This definition reveals the nature of the EYLF as a framework for guiding educators' teaching and learning practices and for developing curriculum at a local level (ADEEWR 2010). Pedagogy as reflected in the EYLF encompasses professional practice including the complexity of relationships that nurture young children, intentional teaching and critical reflection (Sumsion *et al.* 2009, p. 10), as well as the use of diverse theories in analysis of learning and teaching (Fleet *et al.* 2011). In reflecting contemporary research and theoretical understandings of early education, the EYLF challenges traditional understandings about teaching and learning in early childhood (Ortlipp *et al.* 2011) and can be expected to represent significant educational change for educators.

Nationally, the Australian government funded EYLF professional development (PD) workshops that were delivered primarily as one-off events. This pattern reveals assumptions often employed in national curriculum initiatives that transmission of information to large audiences is cost-effective and efficient (Dadds 2014). A problem inherent in transmission models, however, is an underlying assumption that educational reform is dependent on the technical skills of individual educators (Dadds 2014). A review of the early childhood education (ECE) workforce reflects a narrow understanding of PD as transmission of knowledge and skills to augment qualifications (Productivity Commission 2011). This finding reflects widespread views of educators that PD means 'going on a course' (Keay and Lloyd 2011b, p. 15). Typically, PD involves one-off sessions that are delivered by experts who disseminate information to a (more or less) passive participant with little account of existing knowledge or local context (Burgess *et al.* 2010).

Research is ambiguous about the benefits of one-off PD. A recent review of literature suggested that short courses can achieve outcomes for individuals in education and human services (Lauer *et al.* 2014). Conversely, when examining educational change and curriculum development, research suggests that collaborative follow-up activities are essential for achieving change (Timperley *et al.* 2007, Brown and Inglis 2013). Research has also revealed that transmissive and individualised approaches to PD are unsuitable for achieving complex educational reform (Fleet *et al.* 2009, Nuttall 2013).

Transmissive models of PD perpetuate an understanding that educational change is a logical and linear process simply requiring implementation rather than interpretation (Oberhuemer 2005). Furthermore, transmissive modes of PD may result in superficial adoption of new curriculum with little or no change in existing practices (Burgess *et al.* 2010, Nuttall 2013), such as the use of the language and structure of a new curriculum without adopting new pedagogical practices (Winter 2003) or through interpreting frameworks as prescriptive (Ortlipp *et al.* 2011, Pirard 2011).

Professional development and learning: prerequisites for curriculum change

In education and early childhood contexts, contemporary understandings of PD embed professional learning (PL) as an essential component of PD (Buysse *et al.* 2009, Keay and Lloyd 2011a). Indeed, Rinaldi (2012) defines PD as integrating educator learning with their pedagogical practice, which occurs collaboratively during day-to-day work. Educators focus on curriculum and pedagogical impacts on children's learning (Rinaldi 2012) through examining the gap between what children are expected to learn and their actual performance (Fleming and Kleinhenz 2007). Professional development and learning (PD&L) therefore comprises activities designed to improve children's learning, achieved through adjusting pedagogical practice. Perhaps a defining feature of PD&L is encouraging educators to participate in critical reflection to undertake 'intentional investigation' of their practice (Cochran-Smith and Lytle 2001 cited Cardno 2008, p. 90).

PL occurs through praxis, which is the synthesis of theory and practice to produce new contextualised knowledge (Campbell and McNamara 2010). PL involves multiple processes as educators access new theoretical concepts, develop understanding of the implications of new theories and critically examine new curriculum through deconstructing their existing theoretical beliefs and practices (Timperley *et al.* 2007, Pirard 2011). Adult learning principles provide insights into how educators develop new conceptual knowledge where learning is contextualised to the specific setting, related to the educator's practice and can include peer support (Fleet *et al.* 2009). Processes that engage educators in collaborative work enable new knowledge and learning to be integrated and embedded as new professional practice (Groundwater-Smith and Campbell 2010). These complex processes overlap and are undertaken in dynamic environments where educators' interactions with colleagues can influence their PL. Educators may bring knowledge gained from many different sources that is processed collaboratively to build new contextual knowledge and understanding which is generated socially and constructed within a group of educators (Hord 2009). These constructivist educational theories reflect the situated nature of educator PL (Cherrington and Thornton 2013) and are particularly important in early childhood contexts where educators teach interdependently in team situations.

Early childhood researchers have recognised PL as a prerequisite for curriculum change (Muijs *et al.* 2004, Clarkin-Phillips 2007, Thornton 2009). For practice to change, educators need access to information about new curriculum theories and pedagogical approaches (Muijs *et al.* 2004, Siraj-Blatchford and Manni 2007), which can be obtained through transmission modes of PD. PL, however, encompasses transformative processes through which educators re-examine their existing beliefs, leading to cognitive and behavioural changes in practice (Zwart *et al.* 2007 cited Nabhani *et al.* 2014, p. 230). Transformative learning theory (Mezirow 1991, 1996 cited Shields 2010, p. 565) emphasises the importance of processes that bring about change in people's frame of reference or their unexamined assumptions and beliefs about the world. The concept of 'creating dissonance' with existing values of educators is considered fundamental in educational change (Timperley *et al.* 2007, p. xv). PD&L for curriculum reform therefore involves a complex mix of transmissive and transformative learning activities (Keay and Lloyd 2011a). In this paper, the term PD will be used in relation to events that are predominantly transmissive in nature, such as one-off events (workshop, conference, etc.), whereas the term PD&L will be used where processes are available for examining prior knowledge, integrating new information and skills into existing belief systems and exploring possibilities for new practice (Timperley *et al.* 2007). The area of formal study undertaken to obtain professional qualifications is outside the scope of this paper.

Understanding professional learning

Transformative PL is considered to be predominantly a collaborative undertaking because of the complexity inherent in processes. Learning is aligned to the assessment of children's learning rather than to individual fulfilment (Rinaldi 2012). While recognising that an individual educator may undertake transformative learning, the impact on educational outcomes throughout an institution may be significantly less than efforts achieved by groups of educators. The intrinsic nature of collective teaching in early childhood means that teaching and therefore PL occurs within a collective of professionals, is contextual, occurs during everyday practice and focuses on improving and developing practice (Rinaldi 2006).

Within educational literature, systems that encompass PD&L have been termed PL communities, which are characterised by shared purpose, collaborative work and collective responsibility (Stoll *et al.* 2006), with the goal of PL to interpret and assimilate new theories into everyday practice (Groundwater-Smith and Campbell 2010). The synthesis of theory and practice necessitates critical reflection and informed action with transformative intent (Freire 2000 cited Petrarca and Bullock 2014, p. 268). Therefore, to formulate new curriculum practice, educators need opportunities to participate in critical reflection and professional dialogue about their curriculum and pedagogy (Cardno 2008, Ortlipp *et al.* 2011).

Critical reflection and professional dialogue are dispositions that enable educators to look beyond routine decisions to analyse the impact of their pedagogical decisions on children's learning and well-being and to consider alternate possible practices that are based on research and theoretical evidence (Miller 2011). While these dispositions are considered as ongoing professional practice to achieve quality curriculum (Siraj-Blatchford and Manni 2007), professional dialogue can be challenging. Dispositions for critical reflection and professional dialogue necessitate the development of sophisticated professional skills, including sensitivity to enable educators to discuss different pedagogical and ethical viewpoints (Oberhuemer 2005) and resilience in educators to manage their own emotional responses as familiar ways of thinking and acting may be challenged (Beatty 2007). Urban *et al.* (2011) proposed that PL activities which bring all staff in an organisation together are effective because learning occurs through participation in pedagogical reflection where staff with different qualifications and knowledge share intellectual exchanges, building on existing knowledge and generating new knowledge. Such learning is iterative and intensive, building over extended periods of time (Buysse *et al.* 2009), as educators work collaboratively, participating in formal and informal interactions to interpret new theories for their specific context (Nuttall 2013, Oberhuemer 2005).

Leading professional development and learning

Research has commonly identified early childhood centre directors as holding responsibilities for pedagogical leadership (Stamopoulos 2012), assuming pedagogical, curriculum and assessment knowledge (Fasoli *et al.* 2007). Furthermore, pedagogical leadership encompasses learning of both children and their educators, with ongoing educator PL considered a core function of early education (Rinaldi 2012). Such responsibilities are reflected in the Australian system, with directors seen as responsible for building educator knowledge and understanding of child development (Productivity Commission 2011).

Within school-based research, effective educational leadership assumes an ability to make administrative decisions necessary to support PL processes (Robinson and Timperley 2007), including the power to allocate resources and develop and plan structures to support implementation of change (Leithwood *et al.* 2006). Leaders have therefore been integrally linked to achievements of educational reform. Leadership models proposed as supportive of complex PD&L and educational change combine positional leadership with shared leadership (Leithwood *et al.* 2006). While sharing leadership has been found to support PL in groups (Hord 2009, Maloney and Konza 2011), distributed leadership approaches specifically promote participatory cultures through emphasising collective rather than individual PL (Oberhuemer 2005, Thornton 2010). Distributed leadership provides an enabling environment for PD&L (Thortnon 2009). This occurs because collaboration provides opportunities to develop professional relationships among educators, which nurtures interdependence and promotes valuing of diverse capacities of educators (Heikka *et al.* 2013). Furthermore, collegial work promotes support and trust throughout a team (Aubrey *et al.* 2013).

Distributed leadership approaches enable formal positional leaders to recognise the leadership of educators who are not in formal leadership positions (Harris 2004). Through combinations of distributed and positional leadership, specialist knowledge and dispositions for PL are nurtured, resulting in multiple leaders exerting influence throughout an organisation, which builds organisational culture (Lewis and Murphy 2008).

Achieving the conditions for leadership distribution and PL requires both pedagogical and organisational leadership. Pedagogical leadership involves a complex interplay of knowledge of pedagogy, curriculum and assessment but also organisational leadership to make the administrative decisions required to support pedagogy and PL (Robinson *et al.* 2009).

Despite extensive school-based educational research about the conditions for PD&L to achieve educational change, little is known about how educators in early childhood centres learn to change their pedagogy and improve curriculum. Whether the Australian reforms will result in improved child learning outcomes remains to be seen. The Educators' Guide to the EYLF proposes that PL is collaborative and contextual, where educators learn together with colleagues building professional knowledge through 'questioning, planning, acting and reflecting' (ADEEWR 2010, p. 6). However, little research has been undertaken to investigate how this might occur or be organised in early childhood centres. This lack of knowledge represents a significant gap and a risk to Australia's early childhood national reform agenda. It is argued that research is specifically required to determine how early childhood educators can be supported to participate in collaborative, collective and situated processes of PD&L (Nuttall 2013) essential for improving their practice.

Methods and participants

This research aimed to explore how early childhood centre directors understand and lead PD&L during a major reform of curriculum. As early childhood directors appear to be primarily responsible for organising PD in their centres, two focus groups with 12 centre directors were conducted as the first stage of a larger research study. A second stage included case studies undertaken in two early childhood centres. Focus groups have been recommended for exploratory stages of research (Johnson and Christensen 2004) and provide an efficient way to gather data from diverse participants. A purposive sample of directors (see Table 1) was recruited by invitation through existing PD organisations.

The focus groups sought to gain insights into how early childhood directors lead curriculum change, their choices regarding PD and the rationale underpinning their decisions about processes for PD&L. The researcher aimed to facilitate an open and interactive conversation among the participants about how curriculum changes

THE PROFESSIONAL DEVELOPMENT OF EARLY YEARS EDUCATORS

Table 1. Profiles of participants.

Participant	Age	Qualification	Years in early childhood	Years in current centre	Type of centre	Number of child places
1.1	45+	B ECE	16+	6–10	Community – group of centres	80
1.2	35–44	B ECE	11–15	1–5	Community – group of centres	80
1.3	25–34	B ECE	6–10	1–5	Community – group of centres	55
1.4	45+	B ECE	16+	6–10	Community – group of centres	40–45
1.5	35–44	Other bachelor	6–10	6–10	For-profit, group of centres	90
1.6	25–34	B ECE	6–10	1–5	Community – group of centres	40–45
1.7	45+	B ECE	16+	6–10	Community – group of centres	40–45
2.1	35–44	B ECE	16+	1–5	Community – integrated (State and Federal funding)	70
2.2	45+	B ECE	16+	11–15	Community – integrated (State and Federal funding)	40–45
2.3	45+	B ECE	16+	15+	Community – stand-alone	100
2.4	35–44	B ECE	16+	6–10	Community – stand-alone	40–45
2.5	45+	Other bachelor	16+	11–15	Community – stand-alone	80

Note: B ECE, Bachelor of Early Childhood Education.

occur. The researcher's non-verbal language encouraged participant contributions and where necessary direct invitations were made to individuals to gain their perspectives. Discussion began with an invitation to talk about experiences of PD initiatives undertaken within centres to improve curriculum. Unexpectedly, each focus group began with a participant offering an account of experience deemed to be unsuccessful. These contributions supported the development of trust within the groups and dialogue was free flowing. Participants took turns and all participants contributed with diverse experiences of curriculum change and processes used to learn about the EYLF (ADEEWR 2009). The researcher's professional role in early childhood may have been a contributing factor in promoting trust and candid accounts. In both groups, participants commented that the professional conversation had been enjoyable. Each focus group was of 90 minutes' duration, recorded digitally and subsequently transcribed. Data collation and analysis began using qualitative software (Nvivo).

The overall analysis of data was located within an 'adaptive' approach (Layder 1998) that advocates using orienting concepts drawn from the literature to assist in the development of a preliminary coding structure for data analysis, enabling matching of concepts with empirical data (Layder 2013).

An iterative process of data review was undertaken with continual assessment of the data to determine the extent to which codes matched the data and whether modification or elaboration was required (Layder 2013). For example, initial coding resulted in multiple descriptions of forms of PD such as one-off events, external workshops, courses or information sessions, full-day and short forms, through to examples of in-centre PD such as staff meeting discussions, presentations, small group work and various projects. These were later categorised based on the nature of activities involved, examining for passive versus interactive forms of PD with a final category of 'collaborative' or 'individualised'. In this way, explanations for directors' rationale for PD became apparent. In adaptive research, orienting concepts are used to examine relationships between groups of codes in order to identify core concepts emerging from the data (Layder 2013).

Focus group data analysis continued concurrently with collection and analysis of incoming data gathered in the second stage of the research (Layder 2013). Through each round of analysis, patterns and commonalities in participants' responses were identified and emergent themes were documented. A research journal that included a record of decisions and justifications for coding and categorisation, observations and queries arising from the analysis assisted the researcher to review coding decisions and maintain consistency in categorising data. The journal assisted in keeping track of developing ideas and emerging theoretical insights.

Results and discussion

This paper reports on the findings from the focus groups. Orienting concepts drawn from educational research point to a link between leadership and PL in educational reform. In this research, data analysis suggests that leadership is indeed a factor in early childhood curriculum reform but indicates that other influences are involved in PD&L. The findings and discussion are organised into four key themes:

(1) Leading professional development, learning and change.
(2) Collaborative versus individualised approaches.
(3) Conceptualisation of professional development and learning as a continuum.
(4) Organisational structures.

The discussion includes a diagram illustrating a continuum of PD&L and concludes with a model illustrating the collaborative processes that educators may undertake during centre-based PL.

Leading professional development, learning and change

As expected from orienting concepts, early childhood centre directors positioned themselves as the educational leaders of their centres, accepting primary responsibility for planning PD&L and monitoring improvements to curriculum and pedagogical practice (Siraj-Blatchford and Manni 2007). Data revealed that each participant believed their role as director encompassed responsibility and authority to lead change. As explained by one participant: 'You are the person with that positional authority to be able to make changes.' The director's role included power in exercising overall decision-making about PD&L strategies and the focus of change initiatives at the centre, as explained by another participant: '… no matter how much talking you get from the staff team … if you don't want it, more than 9 times out of 10 it's probably not going to happen.' Another participant also captured the director's leadership role in motivating educators' learning: '… they can't do that without a leader who is empowering them …' Yet another participant observed the director's responsibility for leading curriculum initiatives: '… I was also aware that the staff were looking at direction on how to do that.'

These directors embraced their responsibilities as leaders of curriculum change, demonstrating understanding that leaders are critical to achieving educational reforms (Stamopoulos 2012) and recognising their significant decision-making powers relating to staff PD&L (Siraj-Blatchford and Manni 2007). In this study, directors were highly influential (Siraj-Blatchford and Manni 2007), determining the focus of PD&L (Buysse *et al.* 2009), selecting external PD for educators, organising subsequent follow-up work (or not) and making arrangements regarding the extent of collaboration among educators (Waniganayake *et al.* 2008).

Although the majority of directors participating in this study were qualified ECE teachers, it was noteworthy that two directors who were not ECE teachers also positioned themselves as the educational leader of their centre. This finding raises questions about the importance of the director's knowledge and understanding of early childhood curriculum and pedagogy (Fasoli *et al.* 2007, Clarkin-Phillips 2011) for leading PD&L.

Data across both focus groups indicated that participants sought to share leadership through involving their positional leaders comprising assistant directors and room leaders to support educators' learning (Aubrey *et al.* 2013). One participant explained that 'room leaders pass on their learning to their staff', suggesting an understanding that PL may occur informally in day-to-day work (Fleet *et al.* 2009, Rinaldi 2012). Participants expected their positional leaders to assist through leading PD&L with their room staff, suggesting that early childhood leadership is distributed within a centre (Siraj-Blatchford and Manni 2007), at least amongst the formal leaders.

For several participants, however, there was a gap in their positional leaders' capacity to lead PL. One participant described an unsuccessful inquiry project: '… the reason it was a disaster was that there wasn't a leader leading it.' From this experience she had decided that as director she was responsible for pedagogical leadership (Hujala 2004), as well as monitoring and guiding centre-based projects. Another participant described her difficulties in distributing leadership: '… we deliberately did it [the project] in groups in the rooms but we found that we could tell (who were?) the leaders and the not leaders [*sic*]'. This comment 'elicited spontaneous laughter with all participants smiling and nodding agreement' (researcher field notes), suggesting that participants were familiar with situations where leadership was not enacted.

When distributing leadership to their positional leaders, participants found it necessary to relax control, relinquishing power to enable positional leaders autonomy to lead work within their teams (Bennett *et al.* 2003). One participant had recognised the importance of trust in this relationship and had allowed room leaders to explore a pathway in their learning despite her own concerns about their direction: 'I had to let them go there to start with ….' This account revealed the contradictions and complexities of leading collaborative PL and the subtle demands on the director in distributing leadership. It also suggests that directors undertake a rebalancing of power and must know when to take charge and when to step back.

An important component in building a safe environment for critical reflection and professional dialogue during collaborative PD&L is respectful communication. This allows different perspectives and dissenting views to be heard (Thornton 2010), essential for learning but also for developing trust and recognition of existing knowledge within a group (Clarkin-Phillips 2011). Several participants elaborated views respecting educators' knowledge. As one participant observed: 'much of it is just coming back to empowering them really … and believing that they have got something that is worthwhile.' In contrast, four participants expressed their frustration through negative attributions towards their staff, which is unlikely to be conducive in creating a trusting work environment.

In reality, distributing leadership was not always successful. One participant described a situation where the positional leaders had been content with superficial change in relation to the EYLF (ADEEWR 2009), which compromised the learning of educators: 'they became very, very skilled at being able to talk about how the EYLF supports the practice they currently use and they have no intention of changing!' While this insight could be interpreted as resistance to change, an alternative explanation may indicate limitations with the PL conditions within the centre. Learning occurs through ongoing, challenging reflection where existing beliefs are disrupted, allowing educators to reconsider the explanations that underpin their practice (Wong *et al.* 2012).

A key orienting concept in this research was the existence of a relationship between leadership and PL (Muijs *et al.* 2004, Oberhuemer 2005, Siraj-Blatchford and Manni 2007), with distributed leadership specifically found to promote PL and curriculum change in early childhood (Clarkin-Phillips 2007, Thortnon 2009, Heikka and Waniganyake 2011). All participants in this study recognised the link between leadership and PD&L. Although concepts of distributed leadership were not well understood, several directors were nevertheless attempting to distribute leadership to positional leaders. As such, an emergent theme from this study was that all positional leaders understood they had a role in supporting educators' PD&L within their centres.

Collaborative versus individualised approaches

Although there were accounts of successful collaborative PD&L, the majority of participants used external, one-off PD for their staff. Analysis revealed tensions in the participants' rationale regarding the purpose of PD: for three participants a primary focus was developing the competence of individual staff, while the majority recognised that collaborative work helped in translating new knowledge into practice.

One-off events

Of the 12 participants, 11 reported the use of one-off PD events referred to variously as 'training', 'PD' or 'a course' and indicating the prevalence of one-off events as a preferred PD response (Brown and Inglis 2013, Nabhani *et al.* 2014). Two participants aligned external PD to educators' existing knowledge and skills: 'make sure we are targeting them to a workshop that is appropriate for their level' – rationalising a need for differentiated levels of PD to motivate advanced educators or to provide technical information for educators with lower-level qualifications. In particular, conference attendance was valued by participants as suitable for motivating experienced educators to access new knowledge. An emerging theme was how subsequent follow-up work was viewed and organised within centres. Although individualised PD potentially supports personal understanding, impacts are enhanced when shared (Cherrington and Thornton 2013).

Educators' expectations also emerged as being likely to influence the use of individualised PD. Analysis of the data revealed participants' awareness that educators struggled to recognise in-centre collaborative work as constituting PD. One participant explained educators' perceptions as, 'devaluing of something that happens in-house …' Furthermore, this participant explained that despite participation in a PD&L project within the centre, educators claimed they were not receiving PD. Narrow conceptualisations of PD by directors and educators reflect historical understandings of PD where 'training' is understood as an external activity delivered by experts (Productivity Commission 2011). Yet four participants reported poor outcomes from external, one-off PD. One participant noted that, '… one-off training was not effective and it [PD] had to become embedded and we had to do it continually,' while another observed that, 'you can … send them on all of the professional development they like and not come back and not discuss it, so it doesn't go anywhere.' Such experiences reflect findings from other research that one-off events have limited impact in transforming practice (Winter 2003, MacNaughton and Hughes 2007, Nuttall 2013).

For many participants, one-off PD events were used as a response to individual educators' goals identified in annual performance reviews. From analysis, a common practice was for individual staff to select PD from training catalogues. Risks inherent in such approaches are that PD choices are *ad hoc*, may not align with centre needs and fail to support common goals and understanding. Only four participants had developed centre-wide PD plans for integrating PD choices into a coherent centre strategy.

Collaborative approaches

One participant reported only using whole-centre approaches for PD&L where collaborative processes were supported by an external expert or were facilitated within the centre to encourage team exploration. Eight participants had used project approaches where specific educators worked together towards a common goal. A participant explained such a project: 'so it was then very collaborative … building on each other's skills but sharing their knowledge as well.' Another participant had developed a 'curriculum renewal project' where educators acted as critical friends in reviewing each other's documentation of children's learning.

The benefits of collaborative PD&L were seen to assist educators to participate in professional dialogue about their pedagogy. This was articulated by a participant as:

> … a really useful tool of bringing them together, having questions, investigating … and so, for the whole process, basically they, just were forced to discuss and come and have some clarity about what it was going to look like.

Another participant commented that shared professional dialogue enabled educators to engage in change within their centre: 'through that dialogue and that empowering, to feel that [they] do have the opportunity to facilitate some change or try something new.'

Overall, the data collected in this research reveal that nine participants used some form of collaborative PD&L with processes consistent with PL communities (Stoll *et al.* 2006). The majority of participants reported using regular staff meetings to provide opportunities for professional dialogue and learning (Shields 2010). Collaborative PL processes enabled professional dialogue (Maloney and Konza 2011, Marbina *et al.* 2012). At least one-half of the participants reported that groups of educators were involved in learning collaboratively over extended periods of time (Clarkin-Phillips 2011). Participants' accounts suggested that project work involving a shared focus, cooperation and collaboration supported the development of shared meaning and contributed to building a centre culture (Hord 2009) conducive to professional learning and development.

For a small number of participants, PD&L was organised deliberately to ensure the promotion of collaborative processes. For instance, two participants had sent several educators to the same one-off event to enable projects to be undertaken. Subsequent follow-up project work involved examining the practice implications of the new information: '... what does that mean for us ... how can we use that to inform our practice?' Through developing their own practitioner research projects, centres created opportunities for authentic PL (Stoll *et al.* 2006, Groundwater-Smith and Campbell 2010), which encouraged shared professional conversations to process new information. There was evidence that professional dialogue included debate (Sumsion *et al.* 2009) enabling educators to examine differences in theoretical perspectives, as outlined by a participant: '... they had really massive differences in their thinking and it really helped bring it together and move the team forward in lots of positive ways.'

Whether transformative learning was taking place cannot be determined from the data collected in this research. Collaborative PD&L, however, was viewed as contributing to curriculum innovation and included critical reflection, professional dialogue and debate, and exploration of links between theory and practice (Timperley *et al.* 2007, Fleet *et al.* 2009, Urban *et al.* 2011). An ability for educators to participate in genuine debate is essential if existing practice is to be critically examined (Stoll *et al.* 2006) to promote understanding and make space for examining beliefs and the co-construction of new knowledge. The data suggested that in at least one-half of the centres collaborative PL had encouraged informal professional conversations that have the potential to strengthen educators' commitment to collaboration (Cardno 2008). These findings reveal the presence of PL communities within several centres.

Conceptualisation of professional development and learning as a continuum

The analysis of data from this study indicates that the majority of participants used a mix of individualised and collective PD&L approaches, attempting to juggle the need to develop skills, access new curriculum content knowledge and provide opportunities for educators to work collaboratively to explore new knowledge. Furthermore, analysis revealed that four participants were deliberately supplementing individualised, one-off events with follow-up work within the centre, revealing an active role in leading PD&L.

An emergent finding is that choices for PD&L may reflect a director's knowledge and beliefs about the purpose of PD. If a director believes that PL occurs through shared processes and is socially constructed, then PD&L is likely to be viewed as a predominantly collaborative and centre-wide phenomenon. In contrast, if a director prioritises improving an individual educator's knowledge, skills and capabilities, then their choices are likely to be predominantly individualised approaches. Not surprisingly, there appeared to be a correlation between a participant's account of previous positive experience of collaborative approaches and their preference to pursue follow-up collaborative activities in the centre. Those directors who were organising practitioner research within their centres had in excess of five years of experience as a director but significantly indicated past experience of an externally supported inquiry or action research project. In contrast, two directors who had less than two years' experience in their leadership role and one director who was not a qualified ECE educator appeared to favour skill development through individualised and external PD for their staff. Despite the obvious limitations of the small sample size, the directors in this study shed light on possible influences on directors' capacity to lead collaborative PD&L and more specifically practitioner research.

Planning follow-up activities for collaborative work to explore new knowledge suggests deeper-level understanding that professional knowledge is co-constructed within a group context (Campbell and McNamara 2010). The extent to which a director organises follow-up work after external PD distinguishes those directors who understand the nature of praxis and the need for time for professional dialogue and critical thinking in developing informed action and transformative possibilities (Petrarca and Bullock 2014). As an educational leader, the director's knowledge and understanding of PL approaches and how learning occurs cannot be easily ignored (Keay and Lloyd 2011a, Urban et al. 2011).

Directors' decisions about PD&L could be seen as falling along a continuum with one-off PD at one end and in-centre self-directed processes at the opposite end (Winter 2003). In this research, categories of 'collaborative' (focus on processing acquired knowledge and developing new contextual knowledge) and 'individualised' (focus on skills) emerged as distinct conceptual orientations that assist in describing and explaining how PD&L contributes to curriculum innovation. Figure 1 illustrates a continuum of PD&L from individualised to collaborative approaches.

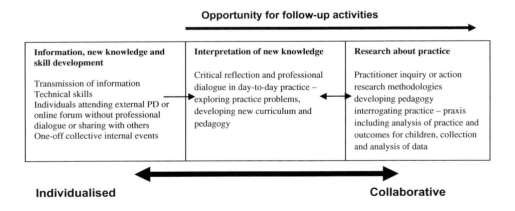

Figure 1. Continuum of professional development and learning.

Access to new information and knowledge via transmission approaches can lead to interpretation as depicted by the one-way arrow in Figure 1. Where there are opportunities for follow-up work with other educators, the two-way arrow between interpretation and research about practice depicts a reciprocal relationship between these forms of PL. When educators participate in research about their practice, processes can cycle back to enhancing interpretation of knowledge accessed. In turn, interpretation through critical reflection and professional dialogue can generate deeper-level contextual PL through practitioner research within centres.

Organisational structures

In practice, organising collaborative PD&L may be difficult to achieve in ECE centres (Brown and Inglis 2013). Furthermore, the work of developing organisational structures and work environments to sustain PL is a challenge for directors (Stamopoulos 2012). Data collected in this study reveal there was little understanding of the director's role in developing the centre infrastructure to support PL (Stamopoulos 2012). While knowledge and facilitation skills are required to support reflective practice (ADEEWR 2010, Marbina *et al.* 2012), organisational structures are also critical. As noted by Cardno (2008), participants in this research also reported several challenges including lack of time and opportunity, staff turnover and limited leadership capabilities of positional leaders. This has led to views that early childhood environments are not conducive of practitioner research and arguments that external facilitation is therefore required for deep-level PL in early childhood centres (Cardno 2008, Pirard 2011).

Although many participants made links between centre culture, common goals and educators' attitudes towards PL (Aubrey *et al.* 2013), there was limited understanding that collaborative PD&L actually contributes to shaping a positive culture (Fleet *et al.* 2009). Rather, directors in this study saw centre culture as achieved through overt processes where their own influence and expectations can shape educators' behaviours.

A widespread reliance on individualised PD plans at the expense of centre-wide plans (Nuttall 2013) is likely to reduce the effectiveness of PD&L efforts. Where centre-wide plans existed, directors appeared to plan for collaborative work following one-off PD. A director's ability to see PD&L opportunities as falling along a continuum (Winter 2003) may enhance their understanding of the limitations of one-off PD and emphasise the need for follow-up collaborative work. Deeper understanding about how PL occurs may encourage directors to create work environments with more opportunities for educators to process new knowledge, investigate their practice and learn from each other (Urban *et al.* 2011).

Figure 2 depicts PD&L processes, illustrating the interface between individualised and collaborative PD&L and the processes undertaken by educators to change their practice. While an individual may access new theories via one-off PD, the processes involved in changing practice within a team teaching environment involve exploring linkages between theory and practice, which occurs as educators participate in critical reflection and professional dialogue about their practice (depicted by large arrows). Practitioner inquiry processes are particularly useful in providing collaborative, contextualised and situated PL (Nuttall 2013).

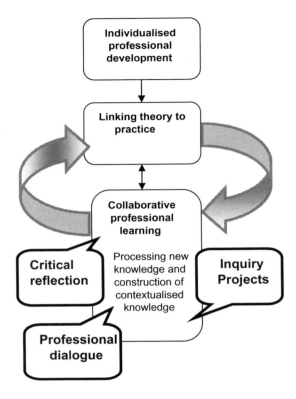

Figure 2. Professional development and learning components and interrelationships.

Directors may be encouraged to plan environments to ensure that individualised one-off PD events contribute to curriculum innovation through follow-up with learning undertaken collaboratively. Organisational structures such as child-free planning time, resources, staffing arrangements, the extent of collaborative opportunities and centre leadership arrangements interact to impact on educators' learning within the centre. Indeed, the manner in which the director shapes the work environment has a significant impact on the processes and interactions that sustain educators' learning.

Limitations

This research was small scale and exploratory. Participants in the focus groups were directors who were already engaging their staff in regular PD&L and the majority had achieved bachelor degrees as ECE teachers. These two factors are not present in all early childhood centres in Australia, and therefore these participants are not representative of the ECE workforce throughout the country.

A further limitation is that data were collected and analysed by one researcher. The focus group method has been commonly applied in exploratory stages of research, but a limitation is that individuals may not feel confident to express their own views in focus groups (Gibbs 1997). It is possible that the group dynamics may suggest stronger agreement than may be the case, however, because less confident group members may have been reluctant to speak out. In this research, focus groups were facilitated to support all participants to contribute and non-verbal responses were recorded in field notes.

Conclusion

This study explored directors' understanding about leadership and PD&L when undertaking curriculum reform in early childhood centres. As the site leader, the director fulfils a critical role, making both pedagogical and management decisions (Heikka and Waniganyake 2011) that influence the nature of PD&L for educators. The director was seen as the principal designer of the work environment, making decisions about organisational structures and therefore creating conditions conducive to PL.

The director's ability to support collaborative professional dialogue was a critical component of PD&L, revealing the specialist nature of the director's leadership role and the importance of pedagogical knowledge (Fasoli *et al.* 2007), fundamental in guiding educators in practitioner research linked to everyday practice (Fleet *et al.* 2009, Burgess *et al.* 2010). Findings from this study revealed the complexity of the director's PL support role and the subtleties required in leading professional dialogue and inquiry, knowing when to make decisions about how, when and where to intervene to guide staff learning or to step back to allow exploration. Directors require sophisticated interpersonal skills combined with professional knowledge to enable staff to explore different theoretical positions and provide subtle guidance as necessary. Through the exercise of such practice wisdom, directors build trust (Maloney and Konza 2011), which contributes to the growth of educator professional dialogue and collaboration, and also contributes to the development of a professional culture (Groundwater-Smith and Campbell 2010). The findings suggest that enabling factors within an organisation and the facilitation of PL are interdependent. Likewise, the relevance of 'strong' and visionary leadership in promoting PD&L is evident (Siraj-Blatchford and Manni 2007).

The findings further suggest that early childhood directors possess knowledge about the range of processes for leading PD&L. How such knowledge is acquired is not clear from this research but could constitute what Aubrey *et al.* (2013) describe as 'tacit' leadership knowledge. However, directors may lack understanding about how to assemble the possible components to develop supportive PL environments that embed change in everyday practice. Tensions were evident in directors' beliefs about the value of collaborative PD&L and their decisions to select one-off PD.

Collaborative approaches such as practitioner research seemed to be episodic rather than embedded in future planning and/or everyday practice. Nevertheless, elements of PL communities were evident in directors' accounts. Directors' years of experience may be a contributing factor in their preference for collaborative PD&L, but prior experience of practitioner research supported by an external provider seemed to be a factor in directors' decisions to attempt their own practitioner research within their centres.

This research is not suggesting there is no role for external PD. It does suggest that one-off external PD attended by individuals has limited impact in curriculum change unless there are follow-up opportunities to process new knowledge, enabling educators to collectively and collaboratively work together to examine new knowledge and the implications for their practice (Timperley *et al.* 2007). The importance of follow-up activities after PD events represents a critical step in PL that is essential for translating new curriculum knowledge into practice, which can then become embedded as everyday practice.

In sharing knowledge gained individually, educators can experience opportunities to build their own leadership capacity (Cherrington and Thornton 2013), which may be particularly useful in building motivation for PL and change. In representing PD&L as a continuum ranging from individualised to collaborative, directors and educators may be assisted to understand how PL and change occur, which could assist in the development of integrated and cohesive responses to PL within early childhood.

Finally, the research reveals that for curriculum reform, PD&L is situated and contextual, and intrinsically linked to everyday practice. PL results from a complex interplay of the director's pedagogical and organisational leadership, collaborative practice, organisational structures and leadership exercised throughout a group of educators. When the components come together, an environment conducive of PL is created, enabling educational change designed to improve children's learning and well-being.

Disclosure statement

No potential conflict of interest was reported by the authors.

References

Aubrey, C., Godfrey, R., and Harris, A., 2013. How do they manage? An investigation of early childhood leadership. *Educational management administration and leadership*, 41 (1), 5–29.

Australian Department of Education, Employment and Workplace Relations (ADEEWR), 2009. *Belonging, being and becoming: the early years learning framework for Australia* [online]. Available from: http://www.deewr.gov.au/Earlychildhood/Policy_Agenda/Qual ity/Pages/EarlyYearsLearningFramework.aspx [Accessed 2 April 2010].

Australian Department of Education, Employment and Workplace Relations (ADEEWR), 2010. *Educators belonging, being & becoming. Educators' guide to the early years learning framework for Australia*. Canberra: Commonwealth of Australia.

Beatty, B., 2007. Going through the emotions: leadership that gets to the heart of school renewal. *Australian journal of education*, 51 (3), 328–340.

Bennett, N., *et al.*, 2003. *Distributed leadership. Summary report*. Nottingham: National College for School Leadership.

Brown, A. and Inglis, S., 2013. So what happens after the event? Exploring the realisation of professional development with early childhood educators. *Australasian journal of early childhood*, 38 (1), 11–15.

Burgess, J., Robertson, G., and Patterson, C., 2010. Curriculum implementation: decisions of early childhood teachers. *Australasian journal of early childhood*, 35 (3), 51–59.

Buysse, V., Winton, P., and Rous, B., 2009. Reaching consensus on a definition of professional development for the early childhood field. *Topics in early childhood special education*, 28 (4), 235–243.

Campbell, A. and McNamara, O., 2010. Mapping the field of practitioner research, inquiry and professional learning in educational contexts. A review. *In*: A. Campbell and S. Groundwater-Smith, eds. *Connecting inquiry and professional learning in education. International perspectives and practical solutions*. New York, NY: Routledge, 10–25.

Cardno, C., 2008. Action research in early childhood centres: balancing research and professional development goals. *New Zealand research in early childhood education*, 11, 89–103.

Cherrington, S. and Thornton, K., 2013. Continuing professional development in early childhood education in New Zealand. *Early years: an international research journal*, 33 (2), 119–132.

Clarkin-Phillips, J., 2007. *Distributing the leadership: a case study of professional development*. Thesis (M Ed). University of Waikato, Hamilton, New Zealand.

Clarkin-Phillips, J., 2011. Distributed leadership: growing strong communities of practice in early childhood centres. *Journal of educational leadership, policy and practice*, 26 (2), 14–25.

Council of Australian Governments, 2008. *National partnership agreement on early childhood education*. Canberra: Author.

Dadds, M., 2014. Continuing professional development: nurturing the expert within. *Professional development in education*, 40 (1), 9–16.

Fasoli, L., Scrivens, C., and Woodrow, C., 2007. Challenges for leadership in Aotearoa/New Zealand and Australian early childhood contexts. *In*: L. Keesing-Styles and H. Hedges, eds. *Theorising early childhood practice: emerging dialogues*. Castle Hill: Pademelon Press, 231–253.

Fleet, A., *et al.*, 2009. School based practitioner enquiry as stepping stones to change. *Paper presented at the Australian Association for Research in Education annual conference*, 29 November–3 December, Canberra.

Fleet, A., *et al.*, 2011. *What's pedagogy anyway? Using pedagogical documentation to engage with the early years learning framework*. Sydney: Children's Services Central.

Fleming, J. and Kleinhenz, E., 2007. *Towards a moving school: developing a professional learning and performance culture*. Camberwell: Australian Council for Educational Research.

Gibbs, A., 1997. Focus groups [online]. *Social research update*, 19. Available from: http://sru.soc.surrey.ac.uk/SRU19.html [Accessed 12 May 2013].

Groundwater-Smith, S. and Campbell, A., 2010. Joining the dots: connecting inquiry and professional learning. *In*: A. Campbell and S. Groundwater-Smith, eds. *Connecting inquiry and professional learning in education. International perspectives and practical solutions*. New York: Routledge, 200–207.

Harris, A., 2004. Distributed leadership and school improvement: leading or misleading? *Educational management administration and leadership*, 32 (1), 11–24.

Heikka, J. and Waniganyake, M., 2011. Pedagogical leadership from a distributed perspective within the context of early childhood education. *International journal of leadership in education: theory and practice*, 14 (4), 499–512.

Heikka, J., Waniganayake, M., and Hujala, E., 2013. Contextualizing distributed leadership within early childhood education: understandings, research evidence and future challenges. *Educational management administration and leadership*, 41 (1), 30–44.

Hord, S., 2009. Professional learning communities. Educators work together toward a shared purpose – improved student learning. *Journal of staff development*, 30 (1), 40–43.

Hujala, E., 2004. Dimensions of leadership in the childcare context. *Scandinavian journal of educational research*, 48 (1), 53–71.

Johnson, B. and Christensen, L., 2004. *Educational research. Quantitative, qualitative and mixed approaches*. 2nd ed. Boston, MA: Pearson.

Keay, J. and Lloyd, C.M., 2011a. High quality professional development. *In*: J. Keay and C.M. Lloyd, eds. *Linking children's learning with professional learning*. Rotterdam: Sense, 47–59. doi: 10.1007/978-94-6091-645-8_2

Keay, J. and Lloyd, C.M., 2011b. Professional development, professionalism and professional knowledge. *In*: J. Keay and C.M. Lloyd, eds. *Linking children's learning with professional learning*. Rotterdam: Sense, 15–29. doi: 10.1007/978-94-6091-645-8_2

Lauer, P., *et al.*, 2014. The impact of short-term professional development on participant outcomes: a review of the literature. *Professional development in education*, 40 (2), 207–227.

Layder, D., 1998. *Sociological practice. Linking theory and social research*. London: Sage.

Layder, D., 2013. *Doing excellent small-scale research*. London: Sage.

Leithwood, K., *et al.*, 2006. *Successful school leadership. What it is and how it influences pupil learning*. Nottingham: National College for School Leadership.

Lewis, P. and Murphy, R., 2008. *Review of the landscape: leadership and leadership development*. Nottingham: National College for School Leadership.

MacNaughton, G. and Hughes, P., 2007. Teaching respect for cultural diversity in Australian early childhood programs: a challenge for professional learning. *Journal of early childhood research*, 5 (2), 189–204.

Maloney, C. and Konza, D., 2011. A case study of teachers' professional learning: becoming a community of professional learning or not? *Issues in educational research*, 21 (1), 75–87.

Marbina, L., Church, A., and Tayler, C., 2012. *Victorian early years learning and development framework. Evidence paper – practice principle 8: reflective practice*. Melbourne: Department of Education and Early Childhood Development.

Miller, L., 2011. Critical reflection. *Gowrie Australia reflections*, 45, 4–6.

Muijs, D., *et al.*, 2004. How do they manage? A review of the research on leadership in early childhood. *Journal of early childhood research*, 2 (2), 157–169.

Nabhani, M., O'Day Nicholas, M., and Bahous, R., 2014. Principals' views on teachers' professional development. *Professional development in education*, 40 (2), 228–242.

Nuttall, J., 2013. The potential of developmental work research as a professional learning methodology in early childhood education. *Contemporary issues in early childhood*, 14 (3), 201–211.

Nvivo qualitative data analysis software, QSR International Pty Ltd, Version 9, 2010.

Oberhuemer, P., 2005. Conceptualising the early childhood pedagogue: policy approaches and issues of professionalism. *European early childhood education research journal*, 13 (1), 5–16.

Ortlipp, M., Arthur, L., and Woodrow, C., 2011. Discourses of the early years learning framework: constructing the early childhood professional. *Contemporary issues in early childhood*, 12 (1), 56–70.

Petrarca, D. and Bullock, S., 2014. Tensions between theory and practice: interrogating our pedagogy through collaborative self-study. *Professional development in education*, 40 (2), 265–281.

Pirard, F., 2011. From the curriculum framework to its dissemination: the accompaniment of educational practices in care facilities for children under three years. *European early childhood education research journal*, 19 (2), 255–268.

Productivity Commission, 2011. *Early childhood development workforce, research*. Melbourne: Australian Government.

Rinaldi, C., 2006. *In dialogue with Reggio Emilia. Listening, researching and learning*. London: Routledge.

Rinaldi, C., 2012. *Principles of the Reggio Emilia educational project. Re-imagining childhood*. Adelaide Thinkers in Residence. Adelaide: Government of South Australia.

Robinson, V., Hohepa, M., and Lloyd, C.M., 2009. *School leadership and student outcomes: identifying what works and why. Best evidence synthesis [BES]*. Wellington: Ministry of Education.

Robinson, V. and Timperley, H., 2007. The leadership of the improvement of teaching and learning: lessons from initiatives with positive outcomes for students. *Australian journal of education*, 51 (3), 247–262.

Shields, C., 2010. Transformative leadership: working for equity in diverse contexts. *Educational administration quarterly*, 46 (4), 558–589.

Siraj-Blatchford, I. and Manni, L., 2007. *Effective leadership in the early years sector. The ELEYS study*. London: Institute of Education, University of London.

Stamopoulos, E., 2012. Reframing early childhood leadership. *Australasian journal of early childhood*, 37 (2), 42–48.

Stoll, L., *et al.*, 2006. Professional learning communities: a review of the literature. *Journal of educational change*, 7 (4), 221–258.

Sumsion, J., *et al.*, 2009. Insider perspectives on developing belonging, being & becoming: the early years learning framework for Australia. *Australasian journal of early childhood*, 34 (4), 4–13.

Thornton, K., 2009. *Blended action learning: supporting leadership learning in the New Zealand ECE sector*. Thesis (PhD). Victoria University of Wellington, New Zealand.

Thornton, K., 2010. 'School leadership and student outcomes': the best evidence synthesis iteration: relevance for early childhood education and implications for leadership practice. *Journal of educational leadership, policy and practice*, 25 (1), 31–41.

Timperley, H., *et al.*, 2007. *Teacher professional learning and development. Best evidence synthesis iteration (BES)*. Auckland: Ministry of Education.

Urban, M., *et al.*, 2011. *Competence requirements in early childhood education and care*. London and Ghent: University of East London and University of Ghent.

Waniganayake, M., *et al.*, 2008. *Practice potentials: impact of participation in professional development and support on quality outcomes for children in childcare centres*. Canberra: Professional Support Coordinators Alliance.

Winter, P., 2003. *Curriculum for babies and toddlers. An evaluation of the first phase (birth to age three) of the South Australian curriculum, standards and accountability framework in selected childcare centres in South Australia*. Thesis (PhD). University of South Australia.

Wong, S., Sumsion, J., and Press, F., 2012. Early childhood professionals and inter-professional work in integrated early childhood services in Australia. *Australasian journal of early childhood*, 37 (1), 81–88.

The role of motive objects in early childhood teacher development concerning children's digital play and play-based learning in early childhood curricula

Joce Nuttall, Susan Edwards, Ana Mantilla, Sue Grieshaber and Elizabeth Wood

Digital technologies are increasingly accepted as a viable aspect of early childhood curriculum. However, teacher uptake of digital technologies in early childhood education and their use with young children in play-based approaches to learning have not been strong. Traditional approaches to the problem of teacher uptake of digital technologies in early childhood curricula argue that more professional development is needed to help teachers learn to use the technologies with children. However, by focusing on children's play instead of teacher knowledge about using technologies with young children, the 'problem' of teacher uptake of technologies in the early years may be re-phrased as a field-specific problem concerned with defining and understanding young children's digital play. This argument is illustrated here through a recent study of teacher perspectives on digital play in the early years. Our aim is to offer an alternative response to the problem of uptake of digital technologies, whereby teachers' motives for engaging in professional development are understood in relation to children's play-based learning.

Introduction

This paper is drawn from a larger study (Nuttall *et al.* 2013) that is attempting to think differently about why digital technologies have had such limited impact on early childhood curriculum internationally (Grieshaber 2010, Yelland 2011). Solutions to this conundrum have so far mainly focused on the role of professional development in introducing early childhood teachers to using digital technologies with children (Barron *et al.* 2011) in an attempt to bridge the gap between children's contemporary life-worlds and the provision of play-based curriculum in early childhood education. In our attempt to question assumptions about teachers' uptake of digital technologies in early childhood settings, we have turned to the possibilities of cultural–historical activity theory (CHAT) and its claims about development. In particular, we have raised questions about the objects of early childhood teachers' professional development activities. In CHAT terms: what motivates teachers to participate in professional development about using digital technologies in the early childhood curriculum? Although we draw on empirical evidence from a recent study of young children's engagement with digital media, our purpose in this paper is to build theory in response to why professional development in this aspect of early childhood education has been largely unsuccessful to date.

The provision of better professional development opportunities seems a common-sense response to the problem of teacher uptake of digital technologies in education (Clarke and Zagarell 2012). If teachers struggle to incorporate digital technologies, then professional development opportunities should reasonably be designed to address these difficulties. Drawing on a survey of almost 300 early childhood teachers regarding their computer competence, Chen and Chang exemplify this assumption:

> To use technology effectively with young children, early childhood teachers require professional training that is current, comprehensive, and effective (Haugland 1999; Haugland and Wright 1997; NAEYC 1996). Effective training programs rely on updated, specific information regarding what early childhood teachers know about computers and how they use them in classrooms with young children. Training based on insufficient information cannot meet teachers' specific needs or build on skills and practices they have acquired. (2006, p. 170)

Why, then, have professional development efforts been largely ineffective? A clue perhaps lies in Chen and Chang's conclusions:

> The study contributes updated, specific information about the computer competence of early childhood teachers, including teacher attitudes, skills, classroom practices, and the interrelationship among them. The results raise research questions that call for more targeted studies of teacher technology competence. (2006, p. 183)

The claim that early childhood teachers' limited uptake of digital technologies can be traced back to teachers' attitudes and skills, or their confidence in using technologies to realise pedagogical goals (see, for example, McManis and Gunnewig 2012, Aubrey and Dahl 2014), is highly problematic because it implies that classroom practices arise primarily from the internal mental structures of individual teachers, such as beliefs. If this is so, then the role of professional development is to reshape these internal structures so that new knowledge, attitudes and skills are developed in ways that are subsequently evident in classroom practice. This view of professional development is at odds with recent understandings that view professional practice as routinised, recurrent, embodied and situated within specific historical and material conditions (Nicolini 2012, pp. 3–6) as well as within individual teachers' minds (Fisher and Wood 2012). This contemporary view of professional practice is not only found in CHAT but more broadly in practice theory (Schatzki *et al.* 2001), and suggests that a push for professional development focused on skills and attitudes in using digital technologies in early childhood curricula is potentially at odds with contemporary perspectives on teacher professional development.

We begin by clarifying what we mean by 'professional development' in the context of our research, since the meaning of this term is often taken for granted. We then outline some of the key assumptions and concepts, drawn from CHAT, that underpin the present study, particularly the specific meaning of 'motivation' within a CHAT-informed world-view. After a brief description of the study, we focus on how we interpreted the teachers' motivations to participate in the study, from a CHAT perspective. We conclude by reflecting on what their perspectives might mean for future efforts to foster the use of digital technologies in early childhood curricula.

Our critique of the literature about professional development in early childhood education

An everyday understanding of professional development proposes that it is any learning on the part of practitioners which results in persistent change in practice within that profession, either individually or collectively. However, as Buysse *et al.* (2009) argue, authoritative definitions of what constitutes professional development remain poorly developed in early childhood education, and this 'likely contributes to the lack of a common vision for the most effective ways of organizing and implementing professional development to improve the quality of the early childhood workforce' (2009, pp. 235–236).

However, in their attempts to define professional development, Buysse *et al.* make the common mistake of equating professional development opportunities with the notion of development itself:

> The term *professional development* encompasses all types of facilitated learning opportunities, for example, those that result in college credit or degrees as well as those that generally are less intensive and do not yield credits or degrees, those that occur largely through formal coursework, and those that are more informal and situated in practice. (2009, p. 238; original emphasis)

Such a definition not only skates over what we mean by 'development' in professional practice, but plays into the recent history of what governments and policymakers in Anglophone countries mean by professional development. In this context, professional development has taken on a strong instrumental cast, with changes in teachers' practice only considered worthwhile if they result in improved learning outcomes for children (Wood 2010). Since governments still largely fund professional development programmes, professional developers have become highly sensitised to government imperatives such as the implementation of new curriculum frameworks. At the same time, the policy formation process is increasingly located outside institutions of further and higher education that routinely critique policy directions (Ball 2012) and which have a long history of offering professional development programmes for teachers.

In accusing governments of instrumentalism, we do not mean to imply that better outcomes for children are not desirable; rather, we are wary of the way in which instrumental approaches to professional development position teachers not as subjects of professional development, but simply as some kind of conduit for curriculum implementation (Carson 2005). Nor do we mean to suggest that governments should not have a say in what these programmes should comprise. But even this brief contextualisation of professional development policy underlines the ways in which teacher development cannot be thought of as an individual phenomenon, since it is always connected to broader trends in governance, economics and culture. Perhaps professional development should be defined not as a constellation of events or opportunities, but as change that is evident within and across the profession. For this reason, we have turned to CHAT in our attempt to understand teachers' uptake (or not) of digital technologies within early childhood curricula, because it allows us to conceptualise human development as simultaneously individual, distributed and directed toward outcomes (i.e. children's learning). In this paper, our specific focus is on teachers' motives for their professional development. By understanding what motivates teachers, our ultimate intentions are to make professional development both meaningful for teachers *per se* and lead to better outcomes for children, since these should not be mutually exclusive aims.

Sensitising concepts drawn from cultural–historical activity theory

Amidst debates about the nature of professional development in early childhood education, the most neglected aspect seems to be what is meant by 'development'. The OECD, for example, offers the following tautological definition: 'Professional development is defined as activities that develop an individual's skills, knowledge, expertise and other characteristics as a teacher' (2009, p. 49). The analysis of teachers' motivations presented in the present paper, drawing on CHAT, suggests a series of possibilities for developing such a definition. First, CHAT views human development from a Vygotskian perspective (following Marx) as a response to systemic tensions that arise within cultural practices (Engeström 1999). A defining aspect of the notion of 'a profession' is that members of the profession collectively engage in shared cultural practices, which newcomers to the profession must also learn to navigate (Holland *et al.* 1998) in order to be recognisable members of that profession. Over time, contradictions or tensions within cultural practices arise when changes occur that are in dynamic relationship with those practices (Engeström 1993). In the present study, teachers' difficulty in adapting early childhood pedagogy in response to the rapid evolution of children's engagement with digital technologies is a classic example of such a contradiction (Edwards 2013a). Such contradictions are not necessarily unwelcome, since they hold within them the impetus for development (Roth 2005). As Engeström has argued, all practices both have a cultural history and offer the promise of the development of new forms of practice:

> An activity system always contains sediments of earlier historical layers, as well as buds or shoots of its possible future. These sediments and buds – historically meaningful differences – are found in the different components of the activity system including the physical tools and mental models of the subjects. They are also found in the actions and object units of the activity. (1993, p. 68)

Second, CHAT understands development both as an individual phenomenon and as collective, historically accumulating and multi-vocal (Nuttall 2013), with the development of self and society in a process of constant co-evolution (Beach 1999). For example, some teachers may have successfully integrated digital technologies into their early childhood practice. In order for the profession to develop as a whole, however, the resolution of contradictions between past and present practice needs to be evident at the level of the dominant cultural practices of early childhood education, not just in individual classrooms. Indeed, this is one of the most significant problems facing educational technology research more generally: how to move beyond localised technology innovations to more widespread adaptation and use. CHAT understands teaching, like any profession, as a specific form of labour. Engagement in professional development is a key part of the labour contributed by teachers to the continuation and renewal of contemporary culture that characterises all teaching. While this may seem self-evident, the rapid professionalisation of the early childhood field has served to partially obscure the realities of the physical and intellectual labour processes in which early childhood teachers engage. For CHAT theorists, these labour processes are necessarily collective and distributed, even if only between two teachers or between a teacher and a child. Furthermore, labour activities are always directed at a specific 'motive object' (Leont'ev 1978) that leads to a desired outcome:

> The main thing which distinguishes one activity from another, however, is the difference of their objects. It is exactly the object of an activity that gives it a determined direction. According to the terminology I have proposed, the object of an activity is its true motive. (Leont'ev 1978, p. 62)

These motive objects can be conceptualised as specific tasks or undertakings; 'facilitating play-based learning' is an example from early childhood teachers' work because it provides force and direction for teachers' activity whilst contributing to the larger outcome of fostering children's learning and development. Motivation is not understood by CHAT theorists in its everyday, common-sense definition as something essentially internal to individuals and bound up with willpower or 'goal orientation'. Rather, human activity is understood as directed toward outcomes that are desired and valued by a culture (in this case, the culture of early childhood education). Through the realisation of these outcomes, the culture is sustained and developed (Engeström and Kerosuo 2007).

Such objects are not neutral. They not only provide the motive force for development but are interpenetrated by affective forces, which can be experienced in both positive and negative ways. The object of fostering young children's learning through digital technologies is a specific case of a tension that is keenly felt by early childhood educators, compounded by its intersection with other controversial areas of children's contemporary lives including exposure to popular culture and consumerism (Edwards 2011) and fears about reduced outdoor play (Louv 2005), culminating in a socially constructed moral panic about young children's 'toxic childhoods' (Palmer 2007). In contrast, we believe it is essential to pay attention to the motive objects, including their affective dimensions, which teachers bring to professional development opportunities, if we are to design opportunities that are genuinely meaningful and can benefit teachers and children alike.

Finally, a third concept we have foregrounded from CHAT is the role of cultural tools in mediating between subjects (in this case, the teachers) and the motive objects of their activity (the learning and development of the children in their classrooms). A considerable amount of professional development activity during the last 30 years has been directed at getting digital technologies into the classroom (Phelps *et al.* 2004). Artefacts such as personal computers, digital video cameras and smartphones are now readily understood as cultural tools that can be used and adapted to foster learning (Plowman *et al.* 2012). In order for this to occur, teachers must master a hierarchy of actions and operations (Leont'ev 1978) (switching the device on, loading software, connecting to the Internet, creating and saving files) before the tool can be employed at the level of object-oriented activity. Early professional development efforts treated tools as the object of teachers' activity (Keengwe and Oncharwai 2009) – a necessary developmental stage if teachers have not previously been enculturated to routine computer use. A problem arises, however, if these technical aspects remain the object of teachers' activity. When teachers subsequently fail to effectively integrate digital technologies in the classroom, they are understood as not being 'digital natives' (Zevenbergen 2007) or as lacking in 'confidence' (Aubrey and Dahl 2014) about how to most effectively use technologies with young children. We have come to suspect that these interpretations misrecognise teachers' motive objects (see, for example, Guskey 2002) in using technologies with children and their desire to learn more about how to use technologies in early childhood curricula (Nuttall *et al.* 2013). Teachers do wish to engage with digital technologies but the professional development they have received has not yet enabled them to mobilise digital technologies to focus on the object of their labour process that gives developmental force to their professional activity: supporting children's learning through the provision of play-based curricula.

The broader study's aims and procedures

The project began with the following question: what do early childhood teachers recognise as digital play? In order to explore this question, we generated a series of video records of children engaging in traditional, consumerist and digital play that could then be shared with the participating teachers in individual interviews.[1] Seven children (six boys and one girl) and three teachers from suburban kindergartens in south-east Melbourne, Australia participated in the study. The teachers were invited to participate in the project through their local city council and each teacher invited families from their centre to participate. Data collection was conducted with teacher and parent consent and included the consent of each of the children (Harcourt and Conroy 2011). Each child was video-recorded engaging with either a traditional farm set or a generic wooden train set. The children were invited to show a researcher how they used the set while a second researcher filmed the child, and a series of pre-scripted questions were asked during the children's engagement with the artefacts. When the children indicated they had tired of using the generic artefact they were provided with a thematically related consumer artefact. For the child using the farm set, this was a Peppa Pig™ figure and some of her fellow characters from the Peppa Pig™ television programme; children who had selected the train set were given a set of Thomas the Tank Engine™ trains and railway track. Again, the children were invited to show the researchers how they used the artefacts and their engagement was video-recorded as both researchers interacted with the children. When the children indicated they had finished using these artefacts, they were provided with a final artefact in the form of thematically related application software ('apps') pre-loaded onto an iPad™. These included the Peppa Pig™ Happy Mrs Chicken™ app and the Thomas and Friends: Engine Activities™ app. If the children lost interest in the app after a few minutes, they were invited to explore other apps on the iPad™ to sustain their engagement with digital artefacts for at least 15 minutes, in order to ensure sufficient data for video analysis.

These video records were then collated for each child and presented to the children's respective teachers as stimulus material during individual semi-structured interviews, which were audio-taped and transcribed. In keeping with the emphasis on children's digital play, the interview questions included: 'When you watch this footage of the children, what do you recognize as play?', 'Which parts would you say are not play?' and 'When you think about what you recognize as play or not play, how do you see this as being related to early childhood curricula?' The resulting data-set was then reduced, principally by deductively focusing onto the teachers' responses to the *a priori* concepts embedded in the interview questions, including 'play' and 'not play'. This reduced data-set was then presented as stimulus material at a focus group interview with all three teachers, which was also video-recorded and transcribed.

The focus group interview, from which the present paper is drawn, was designed to shift the emphasis from what individual teachers recognised as digital play to the teachers' individual and collective commentary on wider issues of teacher knowledge about digital play. As the (de-identified) responses of each teacher from their individual interviews were shared with the other teachers, the focus group was asked the following questions:

- When you hear what teachers say about what they recognise as play from watching the footage of the children, what do you think teachers need to know about young children's play today?
- When you hear what teachers say about what characterises what they recognise as play from watching the footage of the children, what do you think teachers need to know about young children's play today?
- When you hear what teachers say about what they recognise and characterise as play, what do you think teachers need to know about contemporary play and curriculum?
- What do you consider to be the strengths and/or gaps in your knowledge, as early childhood teachers, about young children's play today?

The video record of the focus group was then inductively coded to identify concepts that appeared as patterns or important motifs in the teachers' talk, as well as the data being deductively coded against the *a priori* concepts in the focus group interview schedule, including 'curriculum', 'teacher knowledge' and 'contemporary play'.

To make thematic sense of the resulting data-set, we approached it from two angles. First, we employed three broad questions: 'What are these teachers talking about?', 'What else are they talking about?' and 'What are they not talking about?' Second, we turned to the conceptual tools offered by CHAT, particularly the notion of motive object. Our hunch was that understanding what had motivated these teachers to take part in this research project – specifically in CHAT terms, whereby objects provide the motive force for development – might point us to some of the underlying contradictions and affective forces surrounding the uptake of digital technologies in early childhood education. In the next section of this paper we describe how this was indeed the case.

Contradictions and affect in the teachers' discussion of children's digital play

Each of the teachers had responded to our call for participants with a combination of enthusiasm and anxiety. There were three entwined aspects to these early responses: they each recognised the ubiquity of digital technologies in the lives of the children they teach; they were committed to basing the provision of early childhood curricula on children's experiences of family, home and community; and they felt themselves adrift when trying to understand and mobilise children's home digital participation through play-based learning. As Anne (all names are pseudonyms) told us: 'I'm keen to take part because I want to learn more about what to do. I had some of this at uni[versity] but it wasn't enough'. For the teachers, their hope was that participation in the research would offer a form of professional development in response to the contradictions arising within their experience.

At the same time, one of the risks of professionalisation is that professionals become alienated from the feelings which contradictions provoke, particularly when knowledge about practice is conceptualised as being held in teachers' heads and professionals resort to notions such as 'optimal distance' (Foley 1994) to manage their emotions. For the teachers participating in the present study, their dominant emotion was a feeling of frustration, arising from a fundamental contradiction affecting their work as teachers. On the one hand, they had been thoroughly enculturated to the norms of the early childhood profession, including the primacy of children's home experiences as a source of curriculum:

Lynne: … I agree with Anne when she said that it depends on their prior experiences or their interests. I have a little boy who has got a very strong interest in dinosaurs so he's always playing dinosaur play and things in relation to dinosaurs. It depends on their knowledge, how much they know about things, which again comes back to their family background, how much exposure their family gives them to different experiences and new knowledge and different places and people and things like that.

Anne: That's true. We have a thing called 'Notes from Home' where the children bring stories in of what's important to them outside of kinder[garten] and often the majority of the stories are where they've been on holidays. And I've got a little boy who has never ever been on a holiday with his family and he loves it when other children stand up the front of the group and talk about 'I went to Fiji' or 'I went on an aeroplane' and he's frozen in time just listening. And he will often be quite sad afterward and he always says, 'I've never been on a holiday' and it just makes you want to cry.

On the other hand, the teachers in the study were well aware that the children with whom they work are growing up immersed in digital technologies and the consumption of popular culture artefacts at home and in the wider community (Ironico 2012), and that this was having consequences for their learning:

Tara: I feel it's all because of some of the technology that's come in; television, technology that's been introduced over the years. Children, their dramatic play is they're not using their own imagination; it's more about what they see on television. Superhero-type play has come in. Whereas back before then we were outside, we did a lot more imaginative play; there was a lot of using natural materials in their play, not so much the plastics and consumables. And I think the children were more focused and had a lot more opportunities to build on that and we'd come inside and make fairy wings out of paper, children were happy with that. Whereas now I find if someone brings up, say, the fairies, that topic, [the children say] 'They're not real', 'Oh they don't look good enough' or 'You need this'. They fall apart, they're not happy with the simple things and then the play just stops because they want the best and they don't take it further.

For teachers who have been enculturated into a historical view of children as emergent citizens, rather than active participants in digitally mediated consumer societies, such contradictions can bring up strong feelings about the romanticised role of early childhood education as a domain where children should be protected

THE PROFESSIONAL DEVELOPMENT OF EARLY YEARS EDUCATORS

from the 'evils' of consumer society. The teachers participating in the research felt that children's life-worlds in their home settings were becoming increasingly remote from their understandings of play-based curriculum and that this was having a profound influence on children's play behaviours – and, consequentially, on the teachers' capacity to successfully implement play-based learning. As Tara said:

Tara: My families don't go camping, they just sit inside, they don't even go outside. The children that I work with just adore to get outside and I give them the choice, 'Would you like to be inside today or outside?' and they will stay outside for six hours because they don't get it [outdoor experiences]. And I speak to the parents and I say, 'Oh what does your child do, do they get much outdoor time?' [and parents reply], 'Oh no we just stay inside all the time'. And so I think that will influence too is where their play is coming from. So if you've got kids that are just staying inside watching television all day ...

Anne: ... maybe they don't know how to play? ...

Tara: ... they don't know how to play and that's what I'm discovering over the years, and I've moved around from different areas [of the city] and I just find it fascinating that certain areas are very hard for their imaginative skills.

One interpretation of the teachers' statements presented so far is that they have reactionary, rather than responsive, views of children's changing experiences of technology (see, for example, Vangsnes *et al.* 2012, Flannery and Bers 2013). Our interpretation, however, is that the teachers, in the absence of a workable theory of digital play, are attempting to resolve the contradictions they are experiencing by positioning digital technologies as yet another tool to support their existing theories of play. This 'sedimented' orientation (Engeström 1993) to the possibilities of digital technologies is evident in the following sections of the focus group discussion:

Lynne: Yeah, I think an iPad, particularly if you had it connected to the internet, would be a very useful resource. One day – I don't know what was happening – but we were talking about turtles and a little boy said, 'Has a turtle got a nose?' And unless you've got a particular picture or a book in your library, if you can immediately get to a resource ...

Researcher: ... to pick up an iPad and Google 'turtle' ...

Tara: And that's where I see it as being really beneficial, more as a resource.

Lynne: You could immediately bring up a picture and then further discuss it [by asking the child], 'Well does it? Have a look. Does it have a nose? What do you think?'

Earlier in the discussion, Tara had also described how she saw 'the digital stuff' as an adjunct to her existing approach to play-based learning, which includes modelling of imaginative play:

Tara: I find that I do a lot of modelling of play. I actually sit down and show the children how to play. Once I used to sit down and be in the play but now I'm actually modelling the play. So, what I was thinking, with the dinosaurs you had with that little fellow, what I could see with the digital – that would be an extension of 'Let's go and find out the names of these dinosaurs' and we could use that as an extension of his interest and play. I don't actually see it as play itself but I see it as a resource.

Lynne: The digital?

> Tara: Yes the digital stuff. But I'm finding now I actually have to model play – children need to know how to speak to each other – and what is imaginative play. Because often they tell me, they say, 'Oh Tara, that's not real' and I said, 'Yeah, I've just seen a fairy over there, she just left the fairy dust there'. And they'll say, 'Oh, where?' and I have a whole pocket full of that sparkly stuff and I just put it there and they're [saying], 'No, we've got that in the pasting over there'. And I said, 'No'. And then the next day I left a whole lot of it out [because] I'm trying to encourage them to actually be more imaginative and get into it. They think I'm cuckoo.

Nevertheless, in the midst of their recourse to traditional theories of learning through play, the teachers were aware that digital technologies were inevitably traversing the threshold between home and centre:

> Tara: I've got a little fellow who actually brings his own [iPod™] in. He's one of my special needs children and it's the first time he ever was able to interact with other children; he's autistic. And when he brought that in he showed me first and he had monsters, his pet monsters, and he showed me those. And then there was a new boy who'd just started who's also autistic and I said [to the first child], 'Do you want to go and show him?' and he came over and it was the first time he allowed someone close next to him. And then he would start bringing it in because he's a little guy that needs to start [the centre session] outside, but in winter you couldn't do that so we used the [iPod™] – only for about the first 15 minutes and his mum would take it home. But he then started getting about five or six kids around him. So it was actually used in a social way, I must admit, for that little boy, particularly to show his friends because that was the way he interacted with his friends … And so that was a positive, I saw some positives within that happening there. But then they all wanted to have a go and the mum was a little bit nervous about that because it was her own personal one. But for him [she] brought it in and so we did that for the first 15 minutes; he could show a few of his friends and then she'd take it home.

Anne had also made a laptop computer and an iPad™ available to the children in the centre in limited ways:

> Researcher: And they're okay … with it?
> Anne: They're fine. I mean it's always a novelty when it's first introduced but there's just two chairs there, so two chairs, two children. And they use the laptop – we've got a game called Monster House or Spooky House or something, and they have to go into each room and it tells them what they have to find and what letter it starts with and they've got to find it. It's a whole convoluted kind of game but they love it. And they also use the laptop, we've got a digital microscope that we plug into it and they can put the microscope on their arm and the vision comes up on the laptop of the individual hairs on their arms, and they can keep the pictures and we can print them out later if they want to. Not that we do.
> Researcher: And you take photos with your iPad?
> Anne: Yeah.
> Researcher: So they know how to take photos or make movies?
> Anne: They haven't made movies but they use a digital camera to take photos as well, if they want to, and they know how to use the iPad to take photos. And then there's applications on the iPad that they can turn their own photos into funny stretched faces. They love that.

These types of experiences had provided the 'buds' (Engeström 1993) – small but sufficient possibilities for changes in practice – that prompted Tara and Anne to volunteer to participate in the project. As they participated, we came to understand that the teachers' descriptions of how they thought they might capitalise upon digital technologies remained at the level of tools through which they might enact their existing concepts of play-based learning. Our understanding of the situation in which teachers find themselves, by contrast, is that children's play is now characterised by a combination of traditional and digital activity (Marsh 2010, Goldstein 2011), and so now demands a qualitatively different form of pedagogy, drawing on the convergence of traditional and new forms of play (Edwards 2013b), if play-based learning is to continue to be a viable concept within early childhood curricula.

The importance of understanding of motive objects in teacher professional development

By focusing on the affect-laden motive objects reported by the teachers participating in the research, our aim is to develop a more sophisticated conceptualisation of teacher development, particularly with respect to children's digital play and its potential to inform curriculum provision in early childhood education. Although this paper reports the experiences of just three teachers, we are encouraged by the way in which a CHAT analysis alerted us to aspects of teachers' development that researchers (including ourselves) have hitherto neglected. Tara, Anne and Lynne's contributions to the focus group discussion give a clear sense of the motive objects at which their practice is directed: the development of imagination (Tara and the 'fairy dust'); the inclusion of children facing particular developmental challenges (Tara and the child with additional needs using his iPod™); the development of content knowledge (Lynne and the turtle); the development of process skills (Anne and the digital microscope); and learning to embrace fun (Anne and the stretched faces).

These objects are typical in early childhood education, but close attention to how the teachers described their objects draws our attention to two important features underpinning each of these objects. First is the teachers' deep commitment to children's home and community experiences as a source of meaningful curriculum (Anne and the 'Notes from Home'; Tara's questioning parents about children's outdoor play experiences; allowing a mother to bring her iPod™ to the centre for her son; Lynne's support for a child with a passionate interest in dinosaurs). Second is the powerful affective forces that imbue these objects (Anne wants to cry about the child who has never had a holiday; Tara is intrigued by the differences in children's experience of the outdoors; Tara's awareness that the children think her fairy play is 'cuckoo'; Tara's evident satisfaction about the impact of a child being allowed to show his mother's iPod™; and Anne's comments about the way the children 'love' their play with digital technology).

Taken as a whole, these motive objects are powerfully directed at the outcome of progressing children's learning and development through play-based learning connected with children's interests and home-based experiences. The findings suggest that these teachers do not need to be convinced that digital technologies are useful tools to add to their existing pedagogical 'tool kit', which is already extensive (modelling, discovery, seeking information, scaffolding, providing natural materials and asking questions are each invoked in the short sections of data reported here). Rather, these teachers need to find a way to understand children's engagement with digital technology as an object in its own right as a critical aspect of what it means to be a young child in the early twenty-first century. The field of multi-literacies (Kalantzis and Cope 2012) offers some clues about how such play-based curricula might be conceptualised in early childhood education (Edwards 2013a), but much work remains to be done. Our present focus is on the role professional development can play in promoting teacher development in response to children's contemporary circumstances, particularly children's experience of digital technologies. Three final points draw together the theoretical implications of this study.

Conclusion

First, our work with these teachers has reminded us of the need to be aware of and respect the history of the field when proposing professional development initiatives. The cultural tools employed by these teachers, particularly concepts related to play-based learning, have been appropriated by them through their active participation in the early childhood field. We argue that these theories, developed in 'pre-digital' times, have become a sedimentary feature of early childhood education, with thin but impermeable layers of knowledge laid down year after year as teachers participate in pre-service and in-service teacher education and re-inscribe these theories in the field through curricular practices such as observing and assessing play-based learning. This suggests that an important direction for professional development of early childhood teachers with respect to using digital technologies in early childhood curricula is to work with teachers to develop new concepts of digital play that will allow them to capitalise on children's play with digital technologies at home and in early childhood settings. This is our continuing work in this project.

Second, we are reminded of the need to extend our understandings of what motivates teachers to undertake professional development. It is common practice in professional development to invite participants to express 'what they want to get out of this experience' or 'what they want to learn' at the outset. In our experience, participants are often seeking new tools to assist in achieving their objects. In the case of digital play, we believe these objects have become obscured by a preoccupation with the technologies themselves. Furthermore, research has largely failed to help teachers to navigate through the feelings that arise when they want to embrace children's home experiences with digital technologies but also want to reject the consumption-oriented nature of many of those experiences.

Finally, we want to argue for the role of professional development as a form of consciousness-raising. Here we are using the phrase in a traditionally Marxian sense; that is, moving forward developmentally by bringing systemic contradictions into active awareness and working on them to find appropriate resolutions. Our experience in this and other projects is that these contradictions are often felt before they are understood in ways that teachers can readily express through the tool of language. Because motive objects are laden with affect, listening to how teachers express their embodied experiences of frustration, sadness and joy offers important clues about how to make professional development truly meaningful for teachers. The problem of teacher uptake of digital technologies in early childhood education may not be one of teacher failure or the need for more professional development, as much as it is a problem of how to harness teacher motives to use digital technologies with young children through the development of a new conceptualisation of digital play.

Disclosure statement

No potential conflict of interest was reported by the authors.

Note

1. Readers who are interested in the responses of the children within the study can find a detailed description of the project methodology and analysis of the children's participation in Nuttall *et al.* (2013).

References

Aubrey, C. and Dahl, S., 2014. The confidence and competence in information and communication technologies of practitioners, parents and young children in the early years foundation stage. *Early years*, 34 (1), 94–108.

Ball, S., 2012. *Global education inc. New policy networks and the neo-liberal imaginary.* London: Routledge.

Barron, B., *et al.*, 2011. *Take a giant step: a blueprint for teaching children in a digital age.* Stanford, CA: The Joan Ganz Cooney Center at Sesame Workshop and Stanford University.

Beach, K., 1999. Consequential transitions: a sociocultural expedition beyond transfer in education. *Review of research in education*, 24, 101–139.

Buysse, V., Winton, P.J., and Rous, B., 2009. Reaching consensus on a definition of professional development for the early childhood field. *Topics in early childhood special education*, 28 (4), 235–243.

Carson, T., 2005. Beyond instrumentalism: the significance of teacher identity in educational change. *Journal of the Canadian association for curriculum studies*, 3 (2), 1–8.

Chen, J. and Chang, C., 2006. Using computers in early childhood classrooms. Teachers' attitudes, skills and practices. *Journal of early childhood research*, 9 (3), 169–188.

Clarke, G. and Zagarell, J., 2012. Technology in the classroom. Teachers and technology: a technological divide. *Childhood education*, 88 (2), 136–139.

Edwards, S., 2011. Lessons from 'a really useful engine'™: using Thomas the Tank Engine™ to examine the relationship between play as a leading activity, imagination and reality in children's contemporary play worlds. *Cambridge journal of education*, 41 (2), 195–210.

Edwards, S., 2013a. Digital play in the early years: a contextual response to the problem of integrating digital technologies and play-based learning in the early childhood curriculum. *European early childhood education research journal*, 21 (2), 199–212. (Special issue: Promoting play for a better future).

Edwards, S., 2013b. Post-industrial play: understanding the relationship between traditional and converged forms of play in the early years. *In*: J. Marsh and A. Burke, eds. *Children's virtual play worlds: culture, learning, and participation.* New York, NY: Peter Lang, 10–26.

Engeström, Y., 1993. Developmental work research as a test bench of activity theory: the case of the primary medical care practice. *In*: S. Chaiklin and J. Lave, eds. *Understanding practice: perspectives on activity and context.* Cambridge: Cambridge University Press, 65–103.

Engeström, Y., 1999. Activity theory and individual and social transformation. *In*: Y. Engeström, R. Miettinen, and R–L. Punamäki, eds. *Perspectives on activity theory.* Cambridge: Cambridge University Press, 19–38.

Engeström, Y. and Kerosuo, H., 2007. From workplace learning to inter-organizational learning and back: the contribution of activity theory. *Journal of workplace learning*, 19 (6), 336–342.

Fisher, J. and Wood, E., 2012. Changing educational practice in the early years through practitioner-led action research: an adult-child interaction project. *International journal of early years education*, 20 (2), 114–129.

Flannery, L.P. and Bers, M.U., 2013. Let's dance the "robot hokey-pokey!": children's programming approaches and achievement throughout early cognitive development. *Journal of research on technology in education*, 46 (1), 81–101.

Foley, G., 1994. Parent-professional relationships: finding an optimal distance. *Zero to three*, 14 (4), 19–22.

Goldstein, J., 2011. Technology and play. *In*: A. Pellegrini, ed. *The Oxford handbook of the development of play*. New York, NY: Oxford University Press, 322–341.

Grieshaber, S., 2010. Beyond discovery: a case study of teacher interaction, young children and computer tasks. *Cambridge journal of education*, 40 (1), 69–85.

Guskey, T., 2002. Professional development and teacher change. *Teachers and teaching: theory and practice*, 8 (3), 381–391.

Harcourt, D. and Conroy, H., 2011. Informed consent: processes and procedures: seeking research partnerships with young children. *In*: D. Harcourt, B. Perry, and T. Waller, eds. *Researching young children's perspectives. Debating the ethics and dilemmas of educational research with children*. New York, NY: Routledge, 38–52.

Holland, D., *et al.*, 1998. *Identity and agency in cultural worlds*. Cambridge, MA: Harvard University Press.

Ironico, S., 2012. The active role of children as consumers. *Young consumers: insight and ideas for responsible marketers*, 13 (1), 30–44.

Kalantzis, M. and Cope, B., 2012. *New learning. Elements of a science of education*. New York, NY: Cambridge University Press.

Keengwe, J. and Oncharwai, G., 2009. Technology and early childhood education: a technology integration professional development model for practicing teachers. *Early childhood education journal*, 37 (3), 209–218.

Leontev, A.N., 1978. *Activity, consciousness and personality*. Englewood Cliffs, NJ: Prentice-Hall.

Louv, R., 2005. *Last child in the woods: saving our children from nature-deficit disorder*. Chapel Hill, NC: Algonquin Books.

Marsh, J., 2010. Young children's play in online virtual worlds. *Journal of early childhood research*, 8 (1), 23–39.

McManis, L. and Gunnewig, S., 2012. Finding the education in educational technology with early learners. *Young children*, 67 (3), 14–24.

Nicolini, D., 2012. *Practice theory, work & organization: an introduction*. Oxford: Oxford University Press.

Nuttall, J., 2013. The potential of developmental work research as a professional learning methodology in early childhood education. *Contemporary issues in early childhood*, 14 (3), 201–211.

Nuttall, J., *et al.*, 2013. The implications of young children's digital-consumerist play for changing the kindergarten curriculum. *Cultural-historical psychology*, 2013 (2), 54–62.

Organisation for Economic Co-operation and Development (OECD), 2009. *Creating effective teaching and learning environments: first results from TALIS*. Paris, France: Author.

Palmer, S., 2007. *Toxic childhood. How the modern world is damaging our children and what we can do about it*. London: Orion Books.

Phelps, R., Graham, A., and Kerr, B., 2004. Teachers and ICT: exploring a metacognitive approach to professional development. *Australasian journal of educational technology*, 20 (1), 49–68.

Plowman, L., McPake, J., and Stephen, C., 2012. Extending opportunities for learning: the role of digital media in early childhood education. *In:* S. Suggate and E. Reese, eds. *Contemporary debates in childhood education and development*. New York, NY: Routledge, 95–105.

Roth, W.-M., 2005. *Doing qualitative research: praxis of method*. Vol. 3. Rotterdam: Sense.

Schatzki, T.R., Knorr-Cetina, K., and von Savigny, E., 2001. *The practice turn in contemporary theory*. London: Routledge.

Vangsnes, V., Økland, N., and Krumsvik, R., 2012. Computer games in pre-school settings: didactical challenges when commercial computer games are implemented in kindergartens. *Computers & education*, 58 (4), 1138–1148.

Wood, E., 2010. Reconceptualising the play and pedagogy relationship: from control to complexity. *In*: L. Brooker and S. Edwards, eds. *Engaging play*. Maidenhead: Open University Press, 11–24.

Yelland, N., 2011. Reconceptualising play and learning in the lives of young children. *Australasian journal of early childhood*, 36 (2), 4–12.

Zevenbergen, R., 2007. Digital natives come to preschool: implications for early childhood practice. *Contemporary issues in early childhood*, 8 (1), 19–29.

Preschool teachers' informal online professional development in relation to educational use of tablets in Swedish preschools

Leif Marklund ⓘ

This paper focuses on preschool teachers' use of online social networks for discussions about tablets in preschools. Posts initiating discussions ($n = 465$) were analysed to increase understanding of what questions tablets raise among preschool teachers and to understand online communication from a professional development perspective. Posts were analysed using thematic analysis in combination with the Technological Pedagogical Content Knowledge framework, which illustrates what kind of knowledge teachers need in order to teach efficiently with technology. The results indicate that traditional means of professional development are frequently discussed but that the newness of tablets in preschools makes it difficult for preschool teachers to find support in research, training and literature. Thus, communication can partly be described as collegial support. Questions often aim at urgent and specific forms of desired knowledge, possibly challenging to address by acts of reading literature, attending courses or lectures. Furthermore, market interests become visible, as providers of services and products promote lectures, books, websites and applications. As rapidly changing technologies enter the preschool practice, it seems that preschool teachers will increasingly be dependent on more direct and flexible forms of professional development.

Introduction

A contemporary development in Swedish preschools is that tablets are increasingly being introduced as an educational technology within preschools. This educational phenomenon is also visible in preschool teachers' discussions in online social networks dealing with the pedagogical use of tablets in preschools. Towards the end of her working day, a preschool teacher writes the following message to such a discussion group:

> *I* will soon begin my work at a preschool where they use tablets a lot. We don't use tablets where I'm working now. I don't have any tablet at home so I don't know anything about them. At my new job I have a colleague who knows more about tablets than I do, so I guess I will be able to learn from her in the beginning. I hope to learn things here as well.

This paper focuses on preschool teachers' use of online social networks for discussions about the educational use of tablets in preschool.

Background

The citizens' use of information technology in Sweden

In international comparisons, Sweden stands out as one of the most prominent countries regarding information technology (IT) infrastructure and Internet penetration among its citizens (OECD 2014). Bergström and Sveningsson (2014) highlight how important it has become for Swedish citizens to be able to access the Internet for services and information. They argue that those who do not participate online are excluded from parts of society. Statistics Sweden (2013) reports that 94% of the citizens in the age span of 16–74 have access to both computers and the Internet in their homes. An annual study on Internet habits reveals that this penetration also concerns young children, as 45% of two year olds have used the Internet (Findahl 2013). The annual study also brings attention to how the attitudes towards young children's use of the Internet have changed since the millennium shift, at which point in time adults did not consider it to be a natural part of children's lives to the extent they do now. The more positive attitudes could be related to the fact that children's early reading experiences today are increasingly coming from using computers and new media (Riddersporre and Persson 2010). Findahl (2013) considers tablets to be one factor that increases young children's use of the Internet and he also stresses the fact that the opportunities which Swedish children have to acquire digital experiences vary, as some are found to be daily users and some do not use it at all.

The use of information technology in the Swedish educational system

The need to master IT early in life can be viewed as a matter that concerns democracy, rights and equality and thus, irrespective of background and gender, children must all be given equal access to IT (Sheridan and Samuelsson 2003). Unfortunately the Swedish educational system currently fails in addressing the IT-related inequalities arising from different socio-economic conditions in upbringing (Samuelsson 2014). Two main reasons for this failure are presented. First, the current inequalities related to the access to and use of IT within the Swedish educational system. Second, that the instructions to the educational system on how to work with IT are vague (Samuelsson 2014). This creates a situation where local conditions and teachers' varying degrees of competence in the educational use of IT currently greatly influence the IT-related education being offered. A government commission, working towards a digital agenda for Sweden, recently shared one part of their conclusion (SOU 2014:13), stating that digital competence should be acknowledged as a key competence within the curriculum, and that there is a need to revise the contemporary curriculum by adding a digital perspective to its content. The need to develop teachers' digital competence by professional development is also highlighted in the conclusion.

The Swedish preschool

In Sweden the preschool represents a first step in the educational system and has had a curriculum of its own since 1998, later revised in 2010 (Lpfö 98 Revised 2010). A new school jurisdiction in 2011 reinforced this position within the educational system and also increased the emphasis on the educational, school preparing, aspect of the preschool practice (SFS 2010:800). The Ministry of Education and Research (2014) states that the purpose of the preschool is to stimulate children's development and learning in a secure and caring environment. However, Jönsson *et al.* (2012) argue that it is important to study and analyse how recent changes in policy documents and how goals are affecting the balance between education and care in preschools. Sheridan *et al.* (2011) argue that these changes put preschool teachers in a position where they need to develop a shared understanding of what teacher competence means, in their contemporary and future professional lives, and that this understanding will ultimately affect the conditions of children's learning in preschools. The Swedish preschool is a non-mandatory part of the educational system for one-year-old to six-year-old children, a system in which 96% of all six-year-old children attended a more school-oriented practice, labelled preschool class, in 2011/12 (Skolverket 2013b). The attendance rates are also high among younger children (Skolverket 2013a). For one-year-old to four-year-old children, these attendance rates are significantly higher than the OECD average (OECD 2013). Statistics Sweden (2014) reports that the reforms which aimed to overcome the influence of children's socio-economic backgrounds on attendance in preschool have been successful; that is, children with unemployed parents or with parents on parental leave with other children are still able to attend preschool. Economic regulations on fees and a general, increased interest in pedagogical aspects of preschools are also believed to have contributed to this development.

The educational use of tablets in preschools

According to Riddersporre and Persson (2010), one important task for preschools is to compensate for socio-economic effects on children's development and learning. The curriculum states that the preschool should support families in the care and development of their children, and that multimedia and IT can be used to develop children's creativity and communicative skills (Lpfö 98 Revised 2010). These factors could possibly explain the interest in using tablets within the preschool practice, along with the previously mentioned statistics on how IT and the Internet have become an integral part of the lives of most Swedish citizens. According to Granberg (2011) the introduction of educational use of IT has been a slow process within Swedish teacher education, thus it is not likely that preschool teachers have had any training in how to use tablets in preschools included in their university studies. A study by Hylén (2013) also indicates that investments in educational technology must be accompanied by teacher professional development in order for them to become successful in an educational perspective. Hylén (2013) also brings attention to discussion groups in online social networks and considers them as an opportunity for teachers to extend their collegial discussions in relation to the tablets. He also states that these discussion groups have often been created by dedicated teachers who also maintain them. He thus indicates that through the way the Internet has developed, new opportunities have emerged for teachers to create their own online environments for collegial communication.

Avalos (2011) argues that teachers' professional learning is a complex process that requires cognitive and emotional involvement, both as individuals and as a collective, and that both formal and informal forms of professional development can be purposeful depending on the teachers' and their students' objectives and needs. Avalos (2011) further states that professional development initiatives are unlikely to be experienced as relevant by all teachers. Dede *et al.* (2009) bring attention to how formal professional development initiatives can be experienced as time consuming and ineffectual in the already busy work schedules of teachers, and that the failure to provide day-to-day professional support and mentoring for teachers has a negative effect on new teachers' willingness to remain teachers. This is supported by Turner (2006), who states that the learning of inexperienced teachers ideally should be self-directed and oriented towards educational issues that are close to their needs and that mentors would enhance the learning.

Barab *et al.* (2003) highlight the fine balance between designing online communities for professional development and letting them develop from the needs and agendas of the members. It has been found that professional development initiatives with a top-down approach have difficulties in becoming successful, effective and sustainable over time, partly because of teachers' lack of ownership of the professional development process (Olofsson 2010). This is also supported by Schlager and Fusco (2003), who question the value of creating larger online communities for professional development because these often exclude existing local professional communities of teachers in the design process. Instead they direct attention to the greater potential of the Internet in supporting local communities of teachers. Dede *et al.* provide further insight into the needs of these local communities of teachers:

> The need for professional development that can fit with teachers' busy schedules, that draws on powerful resources often not available locally, and that can create an evolutionary path toward providing real-time, ongoing, work-embedded support has stimulated the creation of online teacher professional development (oTPD) programs. (2009, p. 9)

One example of such a formal initiative had the purpose of enabling information and communication technology-related discussions among teachers in online forums (Prestridge 2010). The findings distinguish between collegial discussions and critical discussions, suggesting that collegial discussions are important for developing and maintaining the online community and that critical discussions are important for changing teachers' beliefs. Scott (2010) argues that technology-facilitated professional development generates two positive outcomes: the profession-related learning of teachers and that those teachers also get a chance to improve their knowledge about technologies with which their students are already familiar. Lloyd and Duncan-Howell (2010) argue that professional development should be perceived as a circular process during which teachers are allowed to change in subtle, iterative and self-determined ways. If perceived and supported in this way, they argue that online communities can support ongoing and effective professional development. However, Zygouris-Coe and Swan (2010) bring attention to how creating online communities for teacher professional development is much easier than the task of sustaining them over time. This, they argue, requires awareness of what purpose the online community serves, knowledge of how to sustain it, awareness of participants' needs and what activities will help facilitate learning.

Teachers are using the opportunities of the Internet for collegial communication on work-related issues in different ways. Johannessen (2011) found that secondary teachers shared ideas and practical ways of using digital resources in their communication within an online community. This study also indicates that teachers do not seem to critique each other's practices and that they do not touch upon digital didactic issues to any substantial extent in their online discussions. In a questionnaire

THE PROFESSIONAL DEVELOPMENT OF EARLY YEARS EDUCATORS

study, directed to an online community where teachers share and discuss lessons and lesson plans, Olofsson (2010) found that one-half of the participating teachers thought that the online discussions had contributed to their professional development over time. It had influenced both their understandings of the teacher profession and how they work.

Purpose

The purpose of this study was to examine what questions and information preschool teachers ask and share regarding educational use of tablets in preschools within online social network discussions. This in turn will increase the understanding of how online communication relates to the professional development of preschool teachers.

Method

This study used an online ethnographical method which, according to Parker Webster and Marques Da Silva (2013), has become relevant through the way offline and online activities are mixed and blurred in our daily lives. Different concepts have been used to describe online ethnographical methods and this study can be described as inspired by netnography, a method that Kozinets (2010) describes as participant-observational research based in online fieldwork that can generate an ethnographic understanding of a cultural or communal phenomenon.

Procedure

A commonly used online social network in Sweden was chosen for this study. A search inquiry, using the internal search engine of the social network and the Swedish equivalent of the word 'preschool' (*förskola*) as a keyword, resulted in the finding of numerous groups discussing different issues related to preschools. This list of discussion groups was then narrowed down to two of the groups, those that strictly focused on discussing the Swedish preschool and the educational use of tablets in that particular context. The names and the descriptions provided by the moderators of these groups indicated that they clearly targeted preschool teachers as contributors. Similarities between the two groups led to the decision to treat them as one set of data for analysis in this study. They were found similar in the following respects: topic of discussion, participant target group, time of creation, duration and frequency of discussion activity, the moderators' educational background and work profession. Furthermore, the discussions were composed of posts with similar characteristics; that is, about one-half of the posts in each of the groups were posed as questions and the remaining posts were sharing information. To access the ongoing group discussions a request was sent to each of the moderators, and the requests were approved, one on the same day and one on the following day, without any further need to provide information. Posts that had initiated discussions in the two discussion groups from the day when each group was created to the date of data collection, a period of little less than two years, were collected for further analysis.

Analysis

As this study was concerned with preschool teachers' questions and the information that they share in online discussion groups, it was not relevant to include all aspects of the online discussions in the analysis. Posts that initiated discussions in the two discussion groups were targeted in the analysis and the responses to these posts were excluded from the data material. The posts were initially placed in two separate text documents for analysis, one document for each of the two discussion groups. A first analysis revealed that the posts in the discussions had different characteristics; some were posed as questions and other posts shared information. The data from the two discussion groups were therefore organized into one document with informative posts and one document with posed questions.

The Technological Pedagogical Content Knowledge (TPACK) framework was used in the analysis of the posed questions (Figure 1). TPACK describes three kinds of teacher knowledge and how these knowledge types intersect to enable effective implementation of educational technology in a certain educational context (Koehler and Mishra 2009, Koehler 2014). The framework is sensitive to the fact that every educational situation is unique and that factors like differences in educational contexts, culture and teachers' preferences and knowledge will influence the way that educational technology is being introduced and effectively used for pedagogical purposes. The framework provided a possibility to classify the preschool teachers' questions on the basis of their different orientation; that is, if they regarded technological issues, teaching content in relation to technology use or pedagogical issues when using technology. By applying TPACK to the questions posed, it was possible to examine what kind of questions preschool teachers ask when they introduce tablets in their educational practice.

Using its constituting parts, the TPACK framework generated seven categories for the analysis: TPACK; Technological Knowledge (TK); Technological Content Knowledge (TCK); Content Knowledge; Pedagogical Content Knowledge;

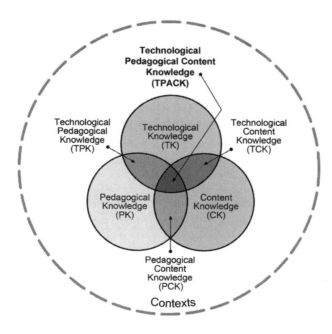

Figure 1. TPACK framework.
Note: Reproduced by permission of the publisher, © 2012 tpack.org.

Pedagogical Knowledge; and Technological Pedagogical Knowledge (TPK). The categorization of the questions resulted in three categories: TK, TCK and TPK. In order to further explore the content and nature of the discussions, thematic analysis was used to search for patterns in the issues that the preschool teachers had raised in each of the three categories (Clarke and Braun 2013).

The TPACK framework was not relevant to use on the informative posts. Instead the informative posts were analysed using a single step of thematic analysis in order to establish their purpose in the discussions; that is, to increase the understanding of how the information in these posts was associated with the professional development of preschool teachers.

Ethical considerations

The study adheres to the ethical guidelines of the Swedish Scientific Council (Hermerén 2011), and the Association of Internet Researchers' guidelines on ethical issues were used to orientate the decision-making in the research process (Markham and Buchanan 2012). Their advice to consult other research and research review boards regarding ethical considerations was applied. Accessing the online discussion groups required a request to the moderators. This level of openness is described by Sveningsson (2009) as a semi-public environment, and she recommends that the information should be treated as being somewhere between public and private. Zimmer (2010) argues that researchers must be sensitive to the contextual nature of privacy when studying social networks. Sveningsson (2009) argues that the aspect of privacy protects research subjects' integrity and freedom to decide what information to share. The moderators were therefore seen as gatekeepers (see, for example, Cohen *et al.* 2011) in the sense that they were informed and gave their consent before the participants were approached with information. Although the information shared in the discussions was found to be non-sensitive and not considered potentially harmful to the participants, they were informed about the study and the opportunity to have their posts excluded from the data material, just by requesting this from the researcher. They were also informed that the name of the online social network, the discussion groups and their identities would be confidentially treated in the analysis and reporting of the findings. This information was delivered to the participants as a message within each of the discussion groups, and none of them decided to withdraw from the study.

Participants

The two discussion groups will be introduced separately, but in the analysis they were treated as one set of data.

Group A

At the time of the data collection Group A had been an active online discussion group for a little less than two years. In total, 1320 participants were part of the group. A majority of the participants were silent followers of the discussions and their level of engagement regarding the shared information is unknown. Thirteen posts were excluded, as they did not concern preschools. The active participants had written 240 posts, 118 questions and 122 informative posts, which initiated discussions related to the pedagogical practice of preschools. The moderators describe the purpose of the group in the following way:

> A group for enthusiastic teachers where we can discuss news, pedagogical issues, come up with suggestions, ideas, thoughts and questions. Furthermore the group addresses how teachers and children can develop media awareness and digital competence from working with tablets.

Group B

At the time of the data collection Group B had been an active online discussion group for a little less than two years. In total, 2066 participants were part of the group. A majority of the participants were silent followers of the discussions and their level of engagement regarding the shared information is unknown. Eight posts were excluded, as they did not concern preschools. The active participants had written 225 posts, 121 questions and 104 informative posts, which initiated discussions related to the pedagogical practice of preschools. In a welcoming message the moderators of Group B expressed their ambition that participants would be able to share experiences and ideas and be inspired in their work with tablets.

Results

When the TPACK framework was applied to the question posts (*n* = 239/465) they could be ordered into three of the framework's seven categories: TK, TCK and TPK. The following sections will report on the thematic analysis of questions within these categories and the thematic analysis of the informative posts (*n* = 226/465), illustrated in Figure 2.

Thematic analysis of question posts

Technological Knowledge

The knowledge represented by the TK category is described as:

> Knowledge about certain ways of thinking about, and working with technology, tools and resources. (Koehler 2014)

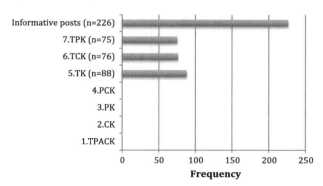

Figure 2. All posts in the discussions.
Note: TPACK, Technological Pedagogical Content Knowledge; TK, Technological Knowledge; TCK, Technological Content Knowledge; CK, Content Knowledge; PCK, Pedagogical Content Knowledge; PK, Pedagogical Knowledge; TPK, Technological Pedagogical Knowledge.

The questions in this category often relate to the challenge of handling technology and software. The first theme, 'Direct and specific' ($n = 88/88$), regards the nature of these questions; that they aim to solve issues of technical nature which interfere with the pedagogical intentions. For example:

> I heard that it is possible to lock the software the children work with, so that they cannot switch between applications. Can anyone explain how?

A general reflection is that different levels of technical complexity can be found among the TK questions, and that the discussions in this respect appear to be inviting and open-minded.

The second theme, 'Purchasing technology' ($n = 22/88$), includes posts indicating difficulties in deciding what technology, hardware and software, to purchase for educational use. For example:

> What are the pros and cons with tablet version 4, I mean in relation to the previous versions 2 and 3?

Technological Content Knowledge

The TCK category's sense is described in the following way:

> Teachers need to understand which specific technologies are best suited for addressing subject-matter learning in their domains and how the content dictates or perhaps even changes the technology – or vice versa. (Koehler and Mishra 2009, p. 65)

The third theme, 'Intentions and applications' ($n = 60/76$), illustrates how questions about applications are being phrased: how the pedagogical intention is initially described and how the question that follows indicates an unawareness of what applications might be educationally useful. For example:

> We will work thematically during the spring semester and the topic is water. Can anyone suggest applications, suitable for children aged 1–5 years old?

The fourth theme, 'New pedagogical aid' ($n = 11/76$), includes questions in which preschool teachers ask for applications that can support their pedagogical work with children with special educational needs. For example:

> In February we will get a child who only speaks Tigrinya as a native language. I cannot find any application for translation that includes Tigrinya as an option. Can anyone help us?

The fifth theme, 'Digital representation' ($n = 9/76$), includes questions indicating that traditional pedagogical activities are getting a digital representation. For example:

> Does anyone have suggestions for good applications to help us in our work with values and emotions?

The sixth theme, 'School subject orientation' ($n = 15/76$), includes questions regarding school-oriented skills that the preschool teachers want their children to practice with the tablets. For example:

> Does anyone know any good applications for developing Swedish skills? Spelling, sounding, writing … anything is of interest to me.

THE PROFESSIONAL DEVELOPMENT OF EARLY YEARS EDUCATORS

Technological Pedagogical Knowledge

The knowledge represented by the TPK category is described as:

> ... knowing the pedagogical affordances and constraints of a range of technological tools as they relate to disciplinarily and developmentally appropriate pedagogical designs and strategies. (Koehler and Mishra 2009, p. 65)

The seventh theme, 'New educational technology' ($n = 21/75$), includes questions revealing the newness of tablets in Swedish preschools. For example:

> I have just begun working at a preschool for younger children and I would like to work with tablets. What have you done? What kind of applications is good? I appreciate any suggestions or ideas.

The eighth theme, 'Professional development, literature and research' ($n = 10/75$), includes questions aiming to locate courses, research and literature about tablets in preschools. For example:

> Does anyone know of any good research on digital tools in the preschool environment?

The ninth theme, 'Changes in practice' ($n = 13/75$), includes questions where preschool teachers raise critical reflections regarding the use of tablets in their practice. For example:

> I think a lot about if it is right or wrong when children are leaving traditional play for the tablets ... how should we relate to that? What are your thoughts?

The 10th theme, 'Sharing applications' affordances and constraints' ($n = 23/75$), includes questions that indicate the need of confirmation from colleagues regarding applications' affordances and constraints. For example:

> Does anyone have experience of application X? Is it suitable to use for pedagogical documentation in preschool?

Thematic analysis of informative posts

About one-half of the posts in the discussion were informative in nature; that is, not phrased as questions ($n = 226$). Thematic analysis was used to establish their purpose in the discussions as well as their relation to professional development of preschool teachers. Ten themes emerged and the distribution of posts among these themes is illustrated in Figure 3. The main purpose of the informative posts was to promote services, products and online resources that had relation to the educational use of tablets in preschools. Some of the informative posts also revealed how the discussion groups were used for communication between participants and other actors, such as authors, lecturers and developers.

Purpose of promoting web resources, services and products

A majority of the posts ($n = 82/226$) promote web resources, such as websites, blogs or online social network groups, that relate to the topic of tablets in preschools. Internet and media resources experienced to be of value are shared among the participants. One example of such resources is the blogs that some preschools maintain about their work with the tablets, information that other preschool teachers can relate to when making their educational choices about tablets. However, some posts have

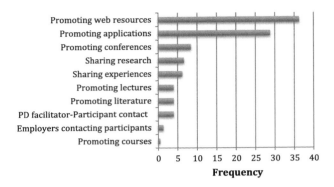

Figure 3. Distribution of informative posts into themes.
Note: PD, professional development.

more of an agenda to them, in the way they promote websites and blogs. These promoted websites mainly offer the service of making applications more accessible to the teachers by categorizing them and making them searchable using different criteria of relevance to educators. The maintainers of these websites appear to be actively promoting their websites in the discussions, illustrated by:

> Many of you have probably read my earlier messages ... but take a look at this website where you will find some of my best advice regarding preschool applications.

Authors of blogs share their experiences and reflections regarding tablets in preschools in the discussions, and some take on the role of experts. These enthusiastic participants are often also involved in lecturing and some are authors of books or maintainers of websites on the topic of tablets in preschools. Thereby their presence in the discussion groups could possibly be understood both as an act of contributing to the sharing of knowledge and as a presence serving market interests.

Many posts often promote applications ($n = 65/226$), by announcing that they are available free of charge. Application developers are also actively promoting their own applications in the discussions, and some posts indicate interdependency between these developers and preschool teachers, illustrated by:

> Hi all! We have developed a first version of an application to help develop children's vocabulary when expressing emotions, for ages 3–4 and upward. It is free and all feedback is most welcome ... enjoy.

The frequency of posts like this one in the discussions indicates that the Swedish preschool is recognized as a market by developers of applications. Applications are also being promoted among colleagues, possibly indicating a need to confirm the choices of educational applications with other preschool teachers.

Posts promoting conferences ($n = 21/226$) also include promotion of smaller educational events like workshops, or educational days. These posts are almost exclusively written by lecturers at these events.

Posts promoting lecturers are closely connected to the posts that promote conferences, but sometimes a lecturer's attendance at an event is central to the information being shared in the post ($n = 9/226$).

In some posts ($n = 9/226$) authors promote their books, and one single post ($n = 1/226$) was found that promotes courses about tablets in preschool.

THE PROFESSIONAL DEVELOPMENT OF EARLY YEARS EDUCATORS

Purpose of sharing information and experiences

Only a few posts share information about research (n = 15/226), possibly indicating that limited research is available or known to these preschool teachers. This could, on the other hand, indicate that they have found other preferred channels of information.

In some posts (n = 13/226) preschool teachers announce their feelings or experiences, without necessarily looking for a response on their post. Most frequently these are announcements that they are happy to get tablets to their preschool, or messages that someone from the media has shown an interest in the way they work with tablets.

Purpose of establishing contact between actors

Some posts (n = 9/226) reveal dialogues between preschool teachers and the authors and lecturers that arrange professional development events. These dialogues included messages expressing gratitude for the event or messages with follow-up questions in relation to the event.

In a few posts (n = 3/226) employers announce job offers where preschool teachers with a special devotion to the educational use of tablets are targeted. For example:

> Do you feel like working with storytelling as a foundation for learning where digital tools are a daily part of the pedagogical practice? Now you have the chance at preschool X in municipality Y.

Discussion

The first aim of this study was to examine the professional development needs of Swedish preschool teachers using tablets in their pedagogical practice.

The analysis of the posed questions indicates that the introduction of tablets in preschools generates a professional development need among these preschool teachers with three different orientations. They need to overcome knowledge gaps in relation to: technological knowledge (TK); the interplay between technological knowledge and content knowledge (TCK); and the interplay between technological knowledge and pedagogical knowledge (TPK).

The TK questions were direct and specific in nature and the climate of discussion was found to be generous and open-minded. The technologically related knowledge gaps seem to interfere with both the process of purchasing the technology, hardware and software, and the process of implementing tablets in the teachers' educational practice. The questions also reveal an enthusiasm about overcoming technological barriers, and technological issues are collaboratively addressed in the discussions.

The TCK questions indicate a lack of awareness about what applications could be useful to the pedagogical intentions of the teachers. It seems as if pedagogical intentions are at the forefront when these preschool teachers approach the tablets for educational use, rather than their technological awareness. It seems as though the preschool teachers are trying out new approaches to reach pedagogical goals by using tablets. Moreover, some questions indicate that applications can provide a new kind of pedagogical support when working with children who have special needs or with children who speak another mother tongue. This kind of novelty, brought to

THE PROFESSIONAL DEVELOPMENT OF EARLY YEARS EDUCATORS

the preschool practice by the tablets, also seems to generate uncertainties regarding how to make proper use of them for educational purposes. Questions about applications that can support school-oriented skill development are quite frequent among the TCK questions, and questions about how to play with tablets or questions about game applications are almost absent in these discussions. These questions possibly indicate that tablets are primarily used in order to support learning activities for which preschool teachers have developed a clear pedagogical intention for their educational use. Another possibility is that this kind of tablet functionality is looked upon as self-evident or perhaps gaming applications are not considered valid from a pedagogical perspective among these preschool teachers.

The TPK questions also indicate knowledge gaps regarding how to introduce tablets in pedagogical practice. Questions concerning available courses, lectures, research and literature on the topic of tablets in preschools could indicate that these supportive functions are difficult to attain due to the newness of the educational phenomenon of tablets in preschools, or that these preschool teachers are unaware of available research on this topic. It could also indicate that they use other channels of information to learn more about tablets. Most participants who posed questions seem convinced of the educational affordances of tablets in preschools, but some also raise critical questions in relation to the changes they have experienced in their pedagogical practice from having introduced tablets to the children. Some questions also indicate a need among preschool teachers to obtain feedback from other colleagues regarding pedagogical affordances and constraints of applications.

These results indicate that there is a need for providing Swedish preschool teachers with the opportunity to improve their digital competence in a time when tablets are increasingly being introduced in their practice. Professional development initiatives of this kind have also been suggested in other recent studies (Hylén 2013, SOU 2014:13). The contemporary changes in the Swedish preschool, with increased emphasis on the educational and school-related aspects of the practice, are to some extent visible in these discussions. Jönsson *et al.* (2012) expressed concerns regarding how these changes will affect the balance between education and care in the preschool. Among the questions posed, only a few mention games or play in relation to the use of tablets in preschool and quite many concern ways of using tablets to improve the children's more school-oriented skills. Perhaps this is an indication that educational aspects are emphasized when preschool teachers use tablets. This issue of how preschool teachers should perceive and use tablets in their practice could perhaps represent another example of when changes in practice create a need for them to develop a shared understanding of their teacher competence (Sheridan *et al.* 2011). The questions reveal that tablets have been introduced at different points in time and that preschool teachers have reached different levels of knowledge about tablets and their educational affordances. Thereby it seems as though the claim of Samuelsson (2014) – that local conditions and teachers' proficiency in the educational use of IT currently have a great influence on the IT-related education that is offered to children – can also be applied to the Swedish preschool context. These preschool teachers' enthusiasm about and positive attitude towards using tablets could be perceived as one expression of the change in attitudes towards children's use of technology that has been observed in Swedish society (Findahl 2013). Riddersporre and Persson (2010) claim that children's early reading and writing experiences increasingly come from using computers and new media. This seems to be recognized among the participants, as they appear to be largely convinced that tablets have educational affordances for their work supporting the learning of young children. The importance of a mentor for the learning process in professional development has been emphasized by Turner (2006). Some participants are more active than others in the discussions, and they have taken on the role of experts, which could possibly be seen as a mentoring role. Whether these participants are conscious of this role is unknown, but they do have a central role in the communication. It might therefore be fruitful to raise their knowledge about mentoring, and its relation to learning, as a way to enhance the professional development effect of these informal initiatives for professional development.

The second aim of this study was to examine the communication in the online social network groups used by preschool teachers for discussions about educational use of tablets.

The informative posts had different purposes in the discussions. Some shared information about tablets and experiences from using them in practice. A few posts indicated that these online social networks are places where different actors can contact each other. Employers can reach potential employees with job advertisements, for example. The social networks also provide an opportunity for enablers of professional development events, authors of literature and blogs, to correspond with their audience; that is, preschool teachers who want to improve their knowledge about the educational use of tablets.

A majority of the informative posts had the purpose of promoting web resources, services and products related to the educational use of tablets in preschools. Although shared among the participating preschool teachers, this information was mainly contributed by maintainers of websites, lecturers, authors and application developers to the discussions. This indicates that preschools are increasingly being recognized as a market by these actors as a result of the introduction of tablets in Swedish preschools. This is a consequence of the tablet introduction in preschools that could possibly be explained using the perspective of Peres *et al.* (2010), who bring attention to the fact that marketization forces always accompany the introduction of innovations (for example new technologies). Both the staff at preschools and actors that could be interpreted as having more of a market interest make use of the social web's opportunities to create and share information about tablets in preschools (O'Reilly 2005).

The discussions in the online social network exemplify this use of the social web, and altogether more than 3000 persons had joined the discussion groups. Some participants were actively participating by posting in the discussions and some were passive followers, and as Friesen (2010) suggests there are difficulties in knowing to what extent the discussions are contributing to the professional learning of all participants in online social networks. Those who actively post questions and information seem to do this in order to provide and receive the day-to-day professional support and mentoring that professional development initiatives often fail to provide teachers with in their work (Dede *et al.* 2009). The topics in the discussions are to a large extent about issues that are close to the participants' needs. The slow introduction of technology within Swedish teacher education makes it plausible to suggest that most preschool teachers who introduce tablets are unskilled when it comes to using technology in their teaching (Granberg 2011). Turner (2006) argues that professional development of inexperienced teachers ideally should be self-directed and directed towards educational issues close to their needs. If the preschool teachers can be regarded as unskilled in using tablets for educational purposes, the online social network discussions seem to support them in developing their skills in a self-directed way. In this online setting they also appear to have ownership of their professional development, one important factor for successful, effective and sustainable professional development (Olofsson 2010). As these discussion groups have often been created and are being maintained by dedicated teachers, they can perhaps avoid discarding the needs and agendas of the participants, which constitute possible drawbacks of top-down initiatives for professional development (Barab *et al.* 2003, Hylén 2013). Even though the participants work in different parts of the country, they have still gathered within the discussion groups to discuss the educational issue of tablets in preschool. In this respect they could perhaps be looked upon more in terms of a local community of teachers, which Schlager and Fusco (2003) suggest is suitable to be supported over the Internet. Moreover, the discussions seem to provide real-time, ongoing, work-embedded support that may help teachers even though they have busy schedules. Also, information that is not always available locally is shared in these networks (Dede *et al.* 2009).

Only posts that initiated discussions were examined in this study, so it is difficult to know whether the preschool teachers critique each other's work in these discussions, an aspect of online discussions that according to Prestridge (2010) is an important factor for changing teachers' beliefs. It is also difficult to determine whether these social network discussion groups are allowing preschool teachers to change in the subtle, iterative and self-determined ways that Lloyd and Duncan-Howell (2010) argue are important aspects of how online professional development should be perceived and supported. However, the current lack of other channels of information about tablets in preschools (i.e. from research, literature and courses) makes it likely that this kind of online communication in social networks has an impact on how tablets are used in Swedish preschools, a conclusion which tallies with Olofsson's (2010) study on teachers' experiences of using an online community for discussions about lesson plans.

Conclusions

From this study it is possible to conclude that many preschool teachers are involved in a learning process about the educational use of tablets, and that the studied online discussions are one aspect of that learning process. Question posts in the discussions reveal that preschool teachers are in need of professional development as a consequence of the increased use of tablets in their practice. Their professional development needs have three different orientations. They need to improve their technological knowledge (TK), their knowledge about the interplay between teaching content and technology (TCK) and their knowledge about the interplay between pedagogy and technology (TPK). The posts of an informative nature in the discussions are, topic wise, highly connected to traditional means of professional development as they share information about conferences, lectures, literature and research. The informative posts also reveal that a market interest in preschools and in the professional development of preschool teachers is accompanying the introduction of tablets in Swedish preschools.

The analysed posts only reveal the preschool teachers' questions and shared information; they do not reveal their underlying thoughts or justifications for their educational choices. They furthermore do not reveal how tablets are being used in the practice and how preschool teachers experience the educational effects of tablets on the preschool children and on themselves in their preschool teacher profession.

However, in the planning for continuous professional learning and development of preschool teachers it is important to know that informal initiatives for professional development, like the ones described in this study, exist. The online discussion groups described in this study have both affordances and constraints, and can therefore be seen as a source of inspiration and information for future professional development initiatives that focus on the educational use of technology. The affordance of the communication in these online discussions seems to be that it covers educational issues that are closely connected to the participants' needs of knowledge. Moreover, many are also willing to share their experiences, and together they seem to be able to offer direct support that can help participants achieve their pedagogical intentions in relation to the tablets. A key message from this study is therefore that preschool teachers seem to become increasingly dependent on more flexible forms of professional development as educational technology is being introduced in their pedagogical practice.

The moderators and participants in these online discussion groups could possibly find ways forward that could strengthen the professional development effect of this kind of online communication by considering the outcome of this study. One way forward would be gradually to shift the focus from the direct and specific questions of technical nature towards more challenging didactic questions in order to enhance the professional development effects of the discussions. Currently it seems as though it is mostly preschool teachers with a positive attitude towards tablets who have found their way to these discussion groups. Inviting preschool teachers to the discussion groups who are more reserved towards using tablets might be one way to deepen the didactic discussions and a way to collaboratively build strong arguments for the educational use of tablets in preschools, arguments that hopefully a majority of preschool teachers can support.

Participants and mentors of these discussion groups should also reflect on how the choice of language affects our possibilities to perceive our social reality. This mainly concerns the fact that the phrase 'application for learning' is used in these discussions for a wide range of applications with very different characteristics. Words like play or games rarely appear in the discussions about tablets, even though at least game applications are an intrinsic functionality of the tablets. Therefore I would like to forward the following question to the participants in these online discussion groups. Could this use of language, when applications with different characteristics are grouped under one and the same concept, potentially limit the way it is possible for preschool teachers to talk about, and develop, the way in which tablets are used for different pedagogical purposes in preschools?

Disclosure statement

No potential conflict of interest was reported by the author.

ORCID

Leif Marklund http://orcid.org/0000-0003-3856-1519

References

Avalos, B., 2011. Teacher professional development in *Teaching and teacher education* over ten years. *Teaching and teacher education: an international journal of research and studies*, 27 (1), 10–20.

Barab, S.A., MaKinster, J.G., and Scheckler, R., 2003. Designing system dualities: characterizing a web-supported professional development community. *The information society*, 19 (3), 237–256.

Bergström, A. and Sveningsson, M., 2014. *Deltagande och delaktighet i digitala miljöer* [Participation and inclusion in digital environments]. Medie-Sverige 2014. Statistik och analys.

Clarke, V. and Braun, V., 2013. Teaching thematic analysis. *Psychologist*, 26 (2), 120–123.

Cohen, L., Manion, L., and Morrison, K., 2011. *Research methods in education*. 7th ed. London: Routledge.

Dede, C., *et al.*, 2009. A research agenda for online teacher professional development. *Journal of teacher education*, 60 (1), 8–19.

Findahl, O., 2013. *The Swedes and the internet* [online]. Available from: http://www.soi2013.se/en/children-and-young-people/ [Accessed 17 February 2015].

Friesen, N., 2010. Education and the social web: connective learning and the commercial imperative [online]. *First Monday*, 15 (12). Available from: http://firstmonday.org/ojs/index.php/fm/article/view/3149/2718 [Accessed 25 January 2015].

Granberg, C., 2011. *ICT and learning in teacher education*. (Doctoral thesis). Umeå University, Umeå.

Hermerén, G., 2011. *God forskningssed* [Research guidelines from the Swedish Research Council]. Stockholm: Vetenskapsrådet.

Hylén, J., 2013. *Utvärdering av Ipad-satsning i Stockholms stad Juni 2013: Stockholms stad* [Evaluation of the investment in tablets in the city of Stockholm June 2013]. Stockholm: Utbildningsförvaltningen.

Johannessen, R.E., 2011. *Lærere sin bruk av sosial web. "Del&bruk" - en møteplass for professjonell utvikling?* [Teachers' use of the social web – a meeting-place for professional development?]. Master thesis in Pedagogics. University of Bergen.

Jönsson, I., Sandell, A., and Tallberg Broman, I., 2012. Change or paradigm shift in the Swedish preschool? *Sociologica problemas e' practicas*, 69, 41–61.

Koehler, M.J., 2014. *TPACK explained* [online]. Available from: http://www.matt-koehler.com/tpack/tpack-explained/ [Accessed 28 March 2014].

Koehler, M.J. and Mishra, P., 2009. What is technological pedagogical content knowledge? *Contemporary issues in technology and teacher education*, 9 (1), 60–70.

Kozinets, R.V., 2010. *Netnography*. Los Angeles, CA: Sage.

Lloyd, M. and Duncan-Howell, J., 2010. Changing the metaphor: the potential of online communities in teacher professional development. *In:* J. Ola Lindberg and A.D. Olofsson, eds. *Online learning communities and teacher professional development: methods for improved education delivery*. Hershey, PA: Information Science Reference, 60–76.

Lpfö 98 Revised, 2010. *Curriculum for the preschool Lpfö 98*. Stockholm: Skolverket.

Markham, A. and Buchanan, E., 2012. *Ethical decision-making and internet research – recommendations from the AoIR ethics working committee* (Version 2.0). Available from: http://aoir.org/reports/ethics2.pdf [Accessed 17 February 2015].

Ministry of Education and Research, 2014. *The pre-school system* [online]. Available from: http://www.government.se/sb/d/7172 [Accessed 2 June 2014].

O'Reilly, T., 2005. *Web 2.0: compact definition?* [online]. Available from: http://radar.oreilly.com/2005/10/web-20-compact-definition.html [Accessed 17 February 2015].

OECD (Organisation for Economic Co-operation and Development), 2013. *Sweden: education at a glance 2013: country note* [online]. Available from: http://www.oecd.org/edu/Sweden_EAG2013%20Country%20Note.pdf [Accessed 17 February 2015].

OECD (Organisation for Economic Co-operation and Development), 2014. *Broadband and telecom, OECD broadband statistics update* [online]. Available from: http://www.oecd.org/internet/broadband/broadband-statistics-update.htm [Accessed 23 June 2014].

Olofsson, A.D., 2010. Discussions in online learning community forums – do they facilitate teachers professional development? *The University of the Fraser Valley research review*, 3 (2), 54–68.

THE PROFESSIONAL DEVELOPMENT OF EARLY YEARS EDUCATORS

Parker Webster, J. and Marques da Silva, S., 2013. Doing educational ethnography in an online world: methodological challenges, choices and innovations. *Ethnography and education*, 8 (2), 123–130.

Peres, R., Muller, E., and Mahajan, V., 2010. Innovation diffusion and new product growth models: a critical review and research directions. *International journal of research in marketing*, 27 (2), 91–106.

Prestridge, S., 2010. ICT professional development for teachers in online forums: analysing the role of discussion. *Teaching and teacher education*, 26 (2), 252–258.

Riddersporre, B. and Persson, S., 2010. *Utbildningsvetenskap för förskolan* [Educational science in preschool]. Stockholm: Natur & Kultur.

Samuelsson, U., 2014. *Digital (o)jämlikhet? IKT-användning i skolan och elevers tekniska kapital* [Digital inequity? ICT usage in school and pupils' technological capital]. Dissertation in Education (No. 23). School of Education and Communication, Jönköping University.

Schlager, M.S. and Fusco, J., 2003. Teacher professional development, technology, and communities of practice: are we putting the cart before the horse? *The information society*, 19 (3), 203–220.

Scott, S., 2010. The theory and practice divide in relation to teacher professional development. *In*: J. Ola Lindberg and A.D. Olofsson, eds. *Online learning communities and teacher professional development: methods for improved education delivery*. Hershey, PA: Information Science Reference, 20–40.

SFS, 2010:800. *Skollag* [Swedish Code of Statutes Education Act]. Stockholm: Utbildningsdepartementet.

Sheridan, S. and Samuelsson, I.P., 2003. Learning through ICT in Swedish early childhood education from a pedagogical perspective of quality. *Childhood education*, 79 (5), 276–282.

Sheridan, S., *et al.*, 2011. Preschool teaching in Sweden – a profession in change. *Educational research*, 53 (4), 415–437.

Skolverket, 2013a. *Barn och grupper i förskolan 15 oktober 2013* [Children and groups of children in preschool October 15th 2013] [online]. Available from: http://www.skolverket.se/statistik-och-utvardering/statistik-i-tabeller/forskolan/barn-och-grupper/barn-och-grupper-i-forskolan-15-oktober-2013-1.215853 [Accessed 2 June 2014].

Skolverket, 2013b. *Beskrivande data 2012. Förskola, skola och vuxenutbildning* [Descriptive data 2012. Preschool, school and adult education]. Rapport nr. 383. Stockholm: Skolverket.

SOU, 2014:13. *Delbetänkande av Digitaliseringskommissionen: En digital agenda i människans tjänst – en ljusnande framtid kan bli vår* [Report from the Digitalization committee: a digital agenda in the service of humanity – a brightening future can become a reality]. Stockholm: Regeringskansliet.

Statistics Sweden, 2013. *Privatpersoners användning av datorer och Internet 2013* [Private citizens' use of computers and the internet 2013: Statistics Sweden]. Stockholm: Statistiska centralbyrån.

Statistics Sweden, 2014. *De flesta barn i förskola – oavsett bakgrund* [Most children attend preschool – regardless of their background] [online]. Available from: http://www.scb.se/sv_/Hitta-statistik/Artiklar/De-flesta-barn-i-forskola–oavsett-bakgrund/ [Accessed 2 June 2014].

Sveningsson, M., 2009. How do various notions of privacy influence decisions in qualitative internet research? *In*: A. Markham and N. Baym, eds. *Internet inquiry: dialogue among researchers*. Thousand Oaks, CA: Sage, 69–87.

Turner, C., 2006. Informal learning and its relevance to the early professional development of teachers in secondary schools in England and Wales. *Journal of in-service education*, 32 (3), 301–319.

Zimmer, M., 2010. "But the data is already public": on the ethics of research in Facebook. *Ethics and information technology*, 12 (4), 313–325.

Zygouris-Coe, V.I and Swan, B., 2010. Challenges of online teacher professional development communities – a Statewide case study in the United States. *In*: J. Ola Lindberg and A.D. Olofsson, eds. *Online learning communities and teacher professional development: methods for improved education delivery*. Hershey, PA: Information Science Reference, 114–133.

Reflecting on reflection: improving teachers' readiness to facilitate participatory learning with young children

Naomi McLeod

This paper explores whether teachers' habits and assumptions about their practice can be enhanced by continued professional development through nurturing self-awareness of lived experiences. Within the paper a practical understanding of critical reflection as a process is explored and particular attention is given to Moon's assertion that one person cannot make another person reflect. Reflection as a process is re-evaluated through the application of Theory U and the axiom that reflection needs to start with the self. The paper's central argument is that at the heart of critical reflection is the need for embodied readiness. Without such openness as the first step, critical reflection is misinterpreted. The main outcome of the study was the development of '9 R's of Reflection', a practical framework that enabled critical reflection to become part of teachers' day-to-day practice, enabling them to focus positively on the challenges they faced within the applied educational setting. The findings of the study demonstrate that the '9 R's' broke down sites of conflict between the desire to follow children's interests and the pressure to conform to the technical demands that dominate modern education so that the teachers changed their habits and became better at participatory teaching.

Introduction

The article details the findings from a research study that explored whether it was possible to influence teachers' views, assumptions, understanding and practice of participatory teaching with young children through the facilitation of continuing professional development (CPD) that developed deep self-awareness and critical reflection. Using such processes the study developed, with participant teachers, a shared understanding of participatory teaching, and explored whether it could be sustained through a process of critical reflection ('9 R's of Reflection', which developed as an integral part of the research process).

This research then started with the needs and interests of teachers and responded to their personal interests, motivations and practices of working with young children. The study's contextual axiom is that our lived traditions produce values, biases and beliefs that influence the manner in which we consciously or unconsciously form our professional identity, our priorities and understandings of working with young children (Beijaard *et al.* 2004, Hassan 2005). It is these embodied experiences, especially those unconscious ones that we need to understand if we want to understand the 'richness and subtlety of human experience' (Leitch 2006, p. 551). Within the context of education, teachers tend to feel restricted by an outcome-driven curriculum and targets imposed by government as part of a top-down approach. As a result there is the tendency to sometimes 'play it safe' and follow rules without questioning (Wilkins 2011). Being aware of these power relations promotes a consciousness of reality so that teachers are more able to make informed decisions and take ownership of their practice (Freire 1994, Mac Naughton 2005).

The paper's central argument is that critical reflection requires and begins with self-awareness, which can be developed through CPD activities that nurture embodied openness and readiness. In the development of such attitudinal dispositions the paper applies Theory U to demonstrate the need for openness. The main focus is to show how the process of becoming open was supported by a practical framework for reflection, named here as the '9 R's of Reflection'. This framework emerged as a result of the study and proved to be an essential foundation to teachers' development of critical reflection, which in turn was a catalyst to them focusing positively on the processes that promote participatory teaching and learning.

Developing critical reflection through self-awareness of embodied lived experiences

In relation to education, critical reflection is regarded as a meta-cognitive (reflexive) process (Bolton 2005) that assumes and requires awareness and self-examination of what people do and think. It is an internal process that consists of exploring personal beliefs, emotions, assumptions, thoughts and actions (King and Kitchener 2004, McLellan 2004). van Manen (1995) refers to critical reflection as 'finding oneself', an experience that can be both difficult and uncomfortable. Becoming a reflective professional as an agent of change (Price and Valli 2005) is gained by reflection upon the difficulties of classroom practice and the ability to 'stand back' and see different perspectives (Etherington 2004). Critical reflection in relation to teachers (and the participation of young children), then, means that teaching as a whole becomes an examination through different 'lenses'. In a sense, it becomes an ongoing 'learning journey' as part of professional development. Awareness by the teacher of the issues of power and control leads to more deliberate thinking about creating democratic classrooms. In this formulation, critical reflection becomes crucial for twenty-first-century teachers as a means of enhancing practice in the development of meaningful CPD (Edwards *et al.* 2002, Reed and Canning 2010, McLeod 2011). My argument is the need to nurture and develop open-mindedness and a readiness to see as the necessary starting point for critical reflection: 'Failure to see is the biggest barrier towards tackling our challenges' (Hassan 2005, p. 6). As Dimova and Loughran (2009) clarify, open-mindedness requires being ready to listen to more sides than one as an active listener. This means being prepared to hear views and ideas that may be contrary to our own and being able to admit that a prior belief may be incorrect, particularly in relation to pedagogy (Rinaldi 2006). To start this 'opening process' there is the need to be ready and demonstrate an openness of mind, heart and will (Scharmer 2009, p. 37).

An emancipatory theoretical framework

The study takes critical social theory as its underpinning, based on the principles of empowerment, social justice, emancipation and freedom. It is predominantly informed by Freire's (1994) theory of 'conscientization', which involves questioning assumptions that have been taken for granted and raises awareness of new perspectives and personal actions that can lead to the transformation of oppressing professional customs (Mezirow 1997, Jacobs and Murray 2010). Within this paper, a practical understanding of critical reflection in relation to participation, relevant for the present day, is explored (Dewey 1933, Schön 1987, Brookfield 1995) through the '9 R's of Reflection' (McLeod 2012). Particular attention is given to Moon's (2008) assertion that one person cannot make another person reflect; they can only facilitate or foster a critically reflective approach through appropriate conditions. In doing so, Theory U (Scharmer 2009) is presented as a means of exploring in detail the complex and challenging internal processes involved as part of being ready to be open and develop self-awareness (Hassan 2005).

First, however, it is necessary to define participation, participatory teaching and participation of young children in the pedagogical space and context of this study.

'Participation' in the context of this study and the need for developing personal/embodied awareness of underpinning beliefs, values and habits

In the context of this study, participation is understood as a child's right to be involved in their learning and sharing responsibility and power for decision-making about matters that affect their lives (United Nations 1989, Article 12, Hill *et al.* 2004, Davies and Artaraz 2009). Participation is underpinned by progressive steps involving listening to and consultation with children (Shier 2001, Lancaster 2003), which are crucial in building a pedagogical space that contributes to children's learning and well-being where they can make independent choices, share responsibility and make sense of their learning (Nutbrown 1996, Clark 2004, 2005).

Within the framework of this study, listening, consultation and participation are contextualised and understood as integrated parts of Shier's (2001) Pathways to Participation model. His five levels of participation are defined as follows:

Listening:

(1) Children are listened to.
(2) Children are supported in expressing their views.

Consultation:

(3) Children's views are taken into account.
(4) Children are involved in decision-making processes.

Full participation:

(5) Children share (some) power and responsibility for decision-making.

At the heart of participatory learning spaces, children are respected as individuals, and learning is supported through constructive thought and communication rather than on the transmission of knowledge and skills (Malaguzzi 1992, Villen 1993). This can be a challenging process for adults because the value attributed to a child's participation is subject to adult self-awareness and issues of power imbalance that adults have over the child. These power relationships must be unpicked if participatory teaching is to be effective (Feldman and Weiss 2010). Unless teachers are able to identify such embedded and unconscious influences on their epistemological beliefs and pedagogical approach, then any changes in critical reflection will remain ornamental and tokenistic rather than genuine and meaningful. This paper, then, takes a fresh look at critical reflection and the need to start with a personal readiness through the application of nurturing an open mind, heart and will (Theory U; Scharmer 2009).

Theory U: becoming open and ready

Here I use Theory U to reinforce the prominence that needs to be attributed to the initial and vital stage of nurturing an open, receptive authentic approach as well as demonstrating the complex and challenging internal processes involved in becoming critically reflective (Hassan 2005). As Moon (2008) notes, one person cannot make another person reflect, they can only facilitate or foster such an approach through appropriate conditions in relation to the habits already formed by teachers. Such conditions were nurtured through the '9 R's of Reflection', as explained later.

As Figure 1 indicates, an open mind, heart and will is the nucleus for embodied readiness, essential for critical reflection. Next I provide a summary of the different 'spaces' involved that in reality are not straightforward or easy (Hassan 2005). This can involve a journey of fluid movements forwards and backwards with different spaces blending into each other. It is also a journey that involves feeling uncomfortable. For this reason, it is helpful to see the spaces as areas for personal self-awareness rather than a precise and prescriptive order of actions. Rather than a

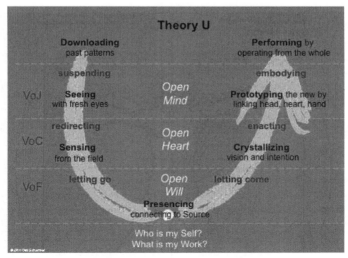

Source: www.presencing.com.

Figure 1. Theory U (Scharmer 2010, p. 6).

fixed self as part of research, the self is fluid and is created in the process of the professional development as part of a reflexive process of coming to know oneself (Lincoln and Guba 2000).

An open mind

Opening the mind is based on accessing the cognitive or intellectual, so that a person sees differently (Scharmer 2009, Titchen and McCormack 2010). To be open and to move from a conception of knowledge (formation or interpretation) towards a contextual understanding (reformation), Moon (2008) emphasises an understanding of the context in which critical reflection is required. Hassan (2005) clarifies the complexity of this process and the difficulties because of the lifetime biases and beliefs attached. Here 'the voice of judgement' (VOJ in Figure 1) may cause a person to play safe, follow the imposed rules (Scharmer 2009, p. 42, Wilkins 2011) and not take risks (which as a result can prevent a participatory teaching approach). Scharmer (2009) and Titchen and McCormack (2010) argue that for a person to see and act differently, a deeper level of *feeling* beyond the mind is needed. An open heart is required.

An open heart

Having an 'open heart' entails accessing personal emotions that relate to empathising with others and a person's ability to see from another perspective or 'through the eyes' of someone else (Scharmer 2009, Titchen and McCormack 2010). This is central to critical reflection and is also important in terms of helping teachers to explore and understand their identities (Nias 1996, Noddings 1996, Hargreaves 2001). While emotion can distort critical reflection and the need that teachers can feel to be right (De Bono 1983), cultivating an open heart by being vulnerable and honest can promote trust and enable emotions to be put to one side. Here Scharmer (2009) warns of the 'voice of cynicism' (VOC in Figure 1) or scepticism, which can prevent a person putting themselves in vulnerable positions such as being open and honest. Recognising the value of emotions strengthens the significance of an open heart through self-awareness and the sometimes unquestioning acceptance of life experience and assumptions. Active engagement or questioning of how we know what we know is crucial (Mezirow 1997), particularly in teaching. Thus an open will is required.

An open will

Opening the will refers to 'letting go' and being true and honest. This is crucial but ultimately depends on being able to drop the 'habitual self' (Scharmer 2009, p. 41). Often 'the voice of fear' (VOF in Figure 1) can block an open will; for example, the fear of being in the minority. As Scharmer (2009, p. 42) outlines, the journey to openness is 'always the road less travelled' because of the complex and difficult inner work it involves in relation to self. This embodied openness is situated at the heart of a series of fluid spaces that facilitate the uncomfortable process of coming to know oneself.

The spaces of Theory U

Downloading represents the beginning, through open conversations about past experiences, practice or habits in relation to the challenges as part of teaching, which in reality, as Dewey (1933) highlights, is not straightforward and can involve confusion and doubt.

Seeing involves becoming aware of personal habits or practice that previously a person may not have been conscious of (Scharmer 2009).

Sensing requires being able to view the context from another perspective (such as the child's perspective). Here there is a grasping of the context as a whole that comprises a consideration of our own relationship to the wider work environment and a questioning. This is essential as part of developing an awareness of imposed conventions on teachers (Gilroy 1993).

Presencing entails connecting to the deepest source in order to 'let go' so that 'letting come' is possible. Letting go is 'about putting ourselves into a state of profound openness' and involves courage, 'leaving the shores of our certainty ... [and] overcoming our fear of the unknown' (Hassan 2005, p. 8). 'Letting come' is about being open to change, which can be a time of anxiety, emotional difficulty and the most vulnerable stage of the process, but likewise it can also be one of new creation (Hassan 2005). This stage represents a realisation and a shift in action. It is referred to as 'passing through the eye of the needle' (Scharmer 2009, p. 42) because it requires 'dropping everything that isn't essential' (2009, p. 191). In an active classroom situation, van Manen (1995) questions the reality of this happening because of the necessity to act on the spot, without having time to step back and consider alternatives.

Crystallizing is concerned with the new vision or possibilities that can emerge as a result of embracing new awareness. Again, van Manen (1995) draws attention to the complexity of this happening as part of the active practice of teaching.

Prototyping requires exploring the future through dialogue with the head, heart and will; the will being the action or commitment that Shier (2001) refers to so that new understanding impacts directly on teaching. Prototyping is driven by vision and trust, and is different from a set plan. It is about 'letting come' in a similar way to *phronesis praxis* as described by Aristotle (Barnes 1976, Grundy 1987). Instead of an unreflective technical product approach, the teacher focuses on the process and what makes for human flourishing (Kemmis 2010).

Performing is exemplified in a new commitment, comparable with the deliberate and committed open 'plan of action' to which Dewey referred (McDermot 1973, p. 505).

The study and appropriate methods used to support openness and insight

The study was conducted in two phases over a period of seven months. The focus of Phase One (January–June) was on developing a shared understanding of participation (based on Shier's [2001] Pathways to Participation) through critical reflection. Phase Two (over the period of one month – July) explored whether participation could be sustained through a process of critical reflection – the '9 R's of Reflection' that emerged as an ongoing part of the analysis (McLeod 2012). The study departure point was that of the needs and interest of two teachers in relation to participatory teaching (Loucks-Horsley *et al.* 2003, p. 47). Two teachers who were part of the Foundation Stage were involved: one was a reception teacher (RT) and the other a nursery teacher (NT). The overriding aim was to develop a deep insight into the teachers' experience of developing a reflexive approach as I worked 'with' them (Clough and Nutbrown 2007). Through previous projects we had developed a positive, open working relationship built on a mutual respect of the value and commitment to listening to young children. Involving other participants may have changed the dynamics of the group and the trusting, secure environment required for embodied readiness and openness.

Because the focus of this study was to understand and explore the teachers' perspectives and experiences of participation with young children, the research was designed to be participatory and emancipatory by nature (Goldstein 2000, McCormack and Boomer 2007), using methods that reflected this by choosing open and engaging approaches. The study employed a multi-method creative and exploratory approach that provided the flexibility to respond to the emerging nature of the data (Corbin and Holt 2005). It began with an open questionnaire followed by conversations about the teachers' views and understanding in respects of consultation and participation with young children. The findings were used to inform the framework for Phase One; the collaborative (CPD) workshops over a six-month period. A qualitative thematic analysis approach drawing on a conceptual framework of creative hermeneutics (McCormack and Boomer 2007) was utilised as a way of embracing the theoretical and methodological underpinning consistent with the approach of openness and engagement. In doing so, the analysis of data did not wait until the end of the study. Instead, all elements were considered to be data (workshop transcripts, reflective tasks, teachers' journals as well as my own ongoing journal) and were continuously compared with each other in order to obtain themes for understanding and interpreting the nature of the relationship between consultation and participation and critical reflection. Throughout the study, the two teachers actively participated in both the generation of data, through their engagement in the study, and the analysis of data (through the identification of themes and categories) by commenting on significant elements and aspects as a result of reading each workshop transcript, as part of Phase One and Phase Two. The involvement of the teachers in the analysis process was crucial as part of the inductive, reflective nature of the combined thematic and creative hermeneutic approach. The collaborations offered a means of 'capturing the essence' of their stories (Corbin and Holt 2005, p. 52).

The mentor workshops in Phase One were the hub of the research and learning process, supported by the relaxed atmosphere, openness and desire of both teachers to engage. The focus was on the following:

- Knowing yourself – personal values and beliefs.
- Perceptions of children.
- Consultation and participation with young children.
- The benefits of consultation.
- Understanding Shier's (2001) Pathways to Participation.
- Becoming critically reflective.
- Supporting participation through keeping a reflective journal.
- Creative evaluation for Phase One.

As a result, they were able to tap into seemingly forgotten memories and emotions. This in turn unearthed a consciousness of themselves that enabled fresh perspectives of how personal experiences influenced their very being (Leitch 2006). We explored new, individually tailored concepts that in turn presented fresh challenges. All of the workshops followed this format:

(1) Reflections on transcript (10 minutes).
(2) Sharing follow-up task (10 minutes).
(3) Aligning practice with Shier's model (5 minutes).
(4) New theme explored (25 minutes).
(5) Supportive reading (5 minutes).
(6) New agreed task (5 minutes).

Each workshop began by spending time reflecting on the transcript of the previous session to identify anything the teachers found interesting, valuable or challenging, or were particularly proud of, and points of agreement or dissent. Time was also dedicated to discussing the follow-up agreed tasks that the teachers had reflected on in their journals. These tasks were individually tailored and agreed between us in relation to the personal and professional needs and challenges of each of the teachers. Examples included teacher planned sessions (with individual children, pairs, small or larger groups), or 'continuous provision' (activities chosen by the children). Each reflected the teachers' personal readiness and openness to engage in the study. This meant each task was aptly pitched in terms of motivation and challenge (Platteel *et al.* 2010), but perhaps most importantly the task focus was decided by the individual teachers.

Almost one-half of the workshop time was spent exploring a new participatory concept through exchange of knowledge involving collaboration and open discussion. This enabled the teachers to identify a deeper self-awareness, and unearth a consciousness of personal strengths and weaknesses pertinent to participatory learning and teaching, which consequently presented fresh challenges and areas for development that ultimately required openness. I provided supportive reading for each workshop in the form of accessible hand-outs as a way of enhancing the teachers' developing understanding of participation, which as Moon (2006) identifies can be a way of supporting professional understanding and development. Through the teachers' engagement in the reflective and collaborative nature of the workshops, '9 steps of reflection' emerged. These '9 R's of Reflection' are distinctly relevant to this study and are presented in Figure 2.

Phase Two of the study involved exploring whether participation through a process of critical reflection was sustainable over a period of one month with the participant teachers. Two workshops were provided over the period of a month, after which a final collective creative evaluative session took place.

At the end of both phases, creative evaluation sessions were planned to capture the essence of the teachers' personal learning as a result of engaging in the study. These included collages (Simons and McCormack 2007), the use of creative hermeneutic cards (Bijkerk and Loonen 2009) and metaphors crafted into poetic haiku (McIntosh 2010a). Together these highlighted visual journeys of transformation experienced by the teachers (Titchen and McCormack 2010). In doing so, a deeper kind of knowledge was available (Jupp 2006, p. 133). The use of creative hermeneutic arts-based approaches facilitated a reflexive approach and enabled the teach-

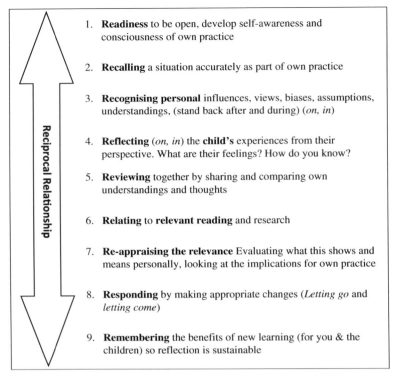

Figure 2. '9 Steps of Reflection' as a tool for sustaining critical reflection (McLeod 2012).

ers to articulate and summarise the essence of their experience of the project and their transformational learning. Further insight in relation to the creative methodologies as part of the project is available in McLeod (2014).

It was the gradual development of these '9 R's of Reflection' as a practical framework that reinforced the essential nature of embodied readiness (Scharmer 2009) at the heart of critical reflection. The '9 R's' enabled the teachers to focus positively on the challenges and difficulties they faced within the applied educational setting on a day-to-day basis and provided insight into what participation felt like from a child's perspective. As a way of demonstrating how the '9 R's of Reflection' evolved and empowered the teachers to become critically reflective, and follow children's interests as is necessary for participatory teaching rather than conforming to the pressures that dominate modern education (Corbin and Holt 2005, Scharmer 2009), the findings and the discussion from the research are analysed through referring back to the themes espoused by Theory U (Scharmer 2009) – namely downloading, seeing, sensing, presencing, crystallising, prototyping and performing, facilitated through the '9 R's'. This approach is adopted as a way of demonstrating the embodied readiness displayed by the participant teachers as well as indicating how appropriate conditions were created (McCormack and Boomer 2007) as an integral part of the '9 R's of Reflection'. The following account therefore unravels the reciprocal relationship between the '9 R's of Reflection' and readiness (embedded throughout Theory U) as an integrated experience.

The unravelling and analysis of readiness (Theory U) through the '9 R's of Reflection'

Right from the start of the project, the space created was valued as a chance to collaborate, share and develop together. The teachers saw it as a protected, safe space where risks could be taken, and time was set aside for exploring past experiences and influences on their personal views. It was the beginning of 'downloading' and 'seeing' afresh (Scharmer 2009) so that challenges and uncertainties were openly discussed without fears of being judged. Downloading was evidenced as part of the open discussions by the teachers about their childhood experiences and memories and their views of children as part of society. For one of the teachers, this involved memories of parents who were 'over protective and safety conscious'. She became aware of the influence of her background and upbringing on her behaviour 'to always please and do what I was told to', which often resulted in thoughtful but passive actions. She lacked confidence in her pedagogical reasoning and recognised the impact of this on her teaching and her discomfort in sharing power with children as part of their learning. For the other teacher, connections were made between emotional experiences linked to family relationships. This was particularly challenging and uncomfortable as it evoked many emotions and forgotten feelings (Dewey 1933). She recalled not liking how it made her feel and noted the emotions provoked (Scharmer 2009). The impact for each of the teachers was a realisation of how they viewed children as part of society. Seeing and Sensing (as processes of Theory U) (Scharmer 2009) were evident here. The Reception teacher explained how she felt about 'sharing power with children':

> It's definitely not right. I think there should be more of a balance. Children's experiences are limited and in terms of safety and everything else that goes along with it … but I don't see children as having any power in society, not enough anyway. Children's views aren't very appreciated in society at the moment … Power should be shared … but more weighted with the adults in terms of responsibility. Having conversations isn't adult talk and children listening. I think there should be a balance. One without the other is not right and one is wrong. It's a balance between the two … it's consultation. If you don't listen to children they don't feel valued, they're not going to share their ideas or flourish into the people that they can be. It's about respect. Until you question where that's come from you don't question and think.

In terms of what influenced her views and understandings, she noted, 'I think with me, it's innate, it's something that I automatically do'. She was uncertain of where her personal views came from, but she demonstrated a connection and developing awareness of 'seeing' and her personal understanding of valuing the children's perspective (Brookfield 1995, Lancaster 2003) as underpinning her pedagogical approach (McAlpine and Weston 2000):

> From my own practice, I can see the benefits but I feel I would like additional knowledge on the pedagogy behind children's learning … I've got confidence but I also want to know research that backs up the fundamental values of children's views and opinions.

In a sense, she saw the barrier as herself in terms of requiring further knowledge about the reasons why consultation underpinning participation is important. She demonstrated evidence of valuing children as part of society and the 'need to question' her underpinning values. The NT was very clear that different views and approaches taken 'depend on your background and understanding and how you were brought up'. In terms of her understanding of children in society, she was clear that, 'children make their own choices but the power lies with the adult so it's up to the adult whether they agree with the child's choice' (Moss *et al.* 1999, Lancaster 2003). One of our early CPD sessions revealed her uncertainty. She used 'safety' as a means of demonstrating the need for children to listen to adults as part of adult-led teaching and considered how 'a child may struggle' in terms of giving their views. But ultimately she viewed this as the child's problem rather than seeing the role of a teacher as enabling talk. Following a moment of thought, she added, 'but if we don't listen to children ... they're not really going to want to listen to you'. She was clear that consultation was 'about both sides being involved', but she was not comfortable in letting go or taking the risk of giving children the choice of consultation and participation. She appeared to want to believe in participation but had doubts (Hassan 2005). As part of this stage in the process of developing readiness, she was 'sensing' (Scharmer 2009) by developing an awareness of imposed conventions (Gilroy 1993).

During one conversation, the RT noted:

> We all make assumptions about how we think we know best and how we see other adults doing the same and we make those assumptions on children's behalf. We assume they can't do this or won't be happy about that, instead of just giving them the opportunity to show us.

She had developed an appreciation of the value of stepping back and sensing the importance of not making assumptions about what children can or cannot do, as well as a realisation of how personal misunderstandings impact on practice. What was also significant through our open collaborations was the growing awareness of critical reflection as a means for appreciating and seeing practice more holistically (Mezirow 1997, Pollard *et al.* 2008). During one of the CPD sessions, the NT grew in confidence as she shared her new learning:

> The first thing I noticed was everything we're doing now is much more natural so I notice the whole process of participation much more as I'm doing it and as I follow it through more than ever than I did before.

They were engaging in meaningful reflection as part of everyday practice (Schön 1983, Kemmis 2010).

The teachers noted the opportunity to 'review together' as essential in becoming more open. This was supported by the additional reading I provided, which enabled a sense of relevance, purpose and authority for the teachers. During one of the 'participation' workshops, the RT demonstrated further personal links between relevant reading (United Nations 1989, Lancaster 2003, Shier 2001) and her developing ability to provide openings and opportunities for young children as part of her teaching. She noted how 'the reading really encourages me and backs up my practice'. Her engagement in this process enabled a sense of permission, empowerment and justification of participatory teaching in terms of her own professional development as well as her teaching (Eun 2011). It was their desire for relevant reading that essentially provided the courage that allowed/enabled them to leave the shores of certainty and overcome their fears (presencing) (Hassan 2005). It provided the authority they felt they needed to focus positively on challenges associated with participatory teaching. The implementation of the '9 R's' supported the breaking down of the conflict between the teacher's desire to follow children's interests and ideas and the pressure to conform to the technical demands that dominate modern education, which can result in following rules and targets without sometimes questioning (Claxton 2003, Wilkins 2011). The reading promoted a consciousness that enabled the teachers to question, make informed decisions and take ownership of their practice (Freire 1994, Mac Naughton 2005). Together we decided that 'Relating to Relevant Reading' should be added as an essential 'R for Reflection'.

New participatory possibilities emerged (crystallized) (Scharmer 2009) as a result of embracing new awareness through engaging in the collaborative CPD sessions (the 'R's of Reflection').

The teachers noted the following:

> RT: I find as well that this [the process of the 9 R's] has helped, when you talk about your practice to other people or when other people say 'how do you do that?' and I've found that it pulls everything together really and gives you the justification for what you're doing, so it's not just 'we've got to play outside because that's what the Early Years Foundation Stage says'.

> NT: It also highlights what you do without realising that you do it naturally, but when you have to tell someone about it, it makes you consider more.

This indicated the valuable nature of the collaborative process in contrast with van Manen's (1995) concern that reflecting together interferes with the natural process of teaching. In the case of this study, the collaborative nature of the CPD workshops provided a sense of ownership of knowledge, empowerment and understanding of why alongside the open, reflective approach of the teachers, as they questioned their practice rather than simply accepting a strategy or framework (Freire 1994, Hassan 2005, Moon 2008, Scharmer 2009). As they shared their reflective accounts, their thoughts often included connected emotions (King and Kitchener 2004, McLellan 2004, Leitch 2006) and a sense of personal efficacy.

They realised the value of their evolving transformative participatory practice for both the children as well as their own practice. In turn, the open collaborative nature of the CPD workshop conversations promoted a sense of active involvement in, and ownership of learning; and meta-cognition (Moon 1999). Essentially they were able to explore the future through dialogue with the head, heart and will; the will being the action or commitment that Shier (2001) and Scharmer (2009) refer to in the form of 'prototyping'. Together we agreed on the following as valued future actions:

- Seeing and appreciating other perspectives.
- Valuing a reflective approach.
- The adult as the one required to offer an opening in order to make changes.
- The need to be more flexible in following the children's interests and ideas as part of teaching.
- The dilemma of the pressure of targets and external barriers.
- The importance of being able to justify participatory teaching.

The RT said: 'I can see the benefits for the children and for us and I can justify why'. She had questioned the unequal power balances and control as part of her practice and was able to think more deliberately about the creation of democratic practice (Brookfield 1995, Carr 1998, Scharmer 2009). However, there was still the dilemma of the pressure of targets when teaching activities that had been planned (Dimova and Loughran 2009, Tickell 2011, Wilkins 2011).

The collaborative nature of sharing through the evolving '9 R's of Reflection' played a central role in the teachers becoming critically reflective and valuing participation (McCormack and Boomer 2007). Both teachers became more confident in exploring aspects of their planned teaching. A new deliberate commitment, comparable with 'performing' or transformational learning (Shier 2001, Scharmer 2009), is provided below as a way of demonstrating the final 'space' of Theory U necessary for embodied readiness and commitment.

The RT referred to the Steps of Reflection as a way of embedding a meaningful reflective approach as part of her everyday practice (Schön 1983):

> I was outside with the boys who wanted to play football but the ball kept rolling under the ramp so by the afternoon there were no balls left. I encouraged them to think of how they could retrieve the balls. I wanted them to work it out for themselves. They tried a bat and realised it wasn't long enough, so they decided to get the brush poles and things with long handles. Instead of saying, 'No, do it this way', I offered it as a real problem so we were sharing responsibility. They couldn't play football if they didn't have the football.

> There was so much open discussion. I listened and watched. Every now and then I said, 'Did that work?' or 'Why do you think that was?' It took them a long time to get the brush poles themselves. They weren't worried about getting dirty, probably because I wasn't. They were openly discussing and thinking together. I could see their delight and empowerment. I asked how they felt. One child said 'Me mum wouldn't let me do it 'cos I'd get me jumper dirty', and another said 'When we get the ball we can play football again'. We've got to encourage them to think for themselves and be empowered, not dominated.

> In terms of implications and responding, I can see I need to stand back and let them work it out for themselves. So by letting go, there was more participation and involvement for the children. I could really see how much they understood and I also realised, I needed to talk to the classroom assistant about needing to let the children do more of this, because we can set problems up but if it doesn't come from them, it's not as meaningful, like when we're on the carpet and I say 'I need to find out which one is taller' and they think that's a boring problem.

> I encouraged them to think. I wanted them to work it out for themselves and see the operationalization of Theory U.

The RT responded directly to the children's suggestions and made appropriate changes as part of her practice as it happened. She understood the relevance of children needing to be empowered and not dominated and she recognised their valuable understanding as part of problem-solving learning experiences. She also valued the importance of asking the children how they felt about their experience, rather than relying on her assumptions. She clearly valued and appreciated the experience from their perspective. What was also significant was her realisation of the consequences of her reflective practice and her new-found confidence and decision to challenge

THE PROFESSIONAL DEVELOPMENT OF EARLY YEARS EDUCATORS

wider issues (Taylor 1993, Freire 1970, 1994, Brookfield 1995, Mac Naughton 2005, Athey 2007, Scharmer 2009).

In reality, the first step of 'Readiness' was only added towards the end of the project when we reflected together about the importance of being open and aware of the influence of past experiences on practice (Scharmer 2009). The realisation of being ready dawned on the RT: 'It suddenly hit me that this wouldn't have been possible unless we were ready and open to question ourselves'. As the workshops progressed, the teachers became more expert at evaluating and *Reappraising the Relevance* of their teaching in relation to participation (Shier 2001). This included a heightened awareness of the need to question and challenge personal ideas and habits. They became more proficient at evaluating their participatory teaching and the implications (Moon 2006, 2008). As part of the re-appraising process, both teachers became more critical of their own practice and began to re-appraise the relevance by identifying and appreciating the benefits for the children as well as for themselves. Responding was added as an R.

Finally, at the end Phase One of the study, 'Remember' was a collective suggestion as our ninth step of reflection. The teachers recognised that remembering the '9 R's of Reflection' as a process of value, empowerment and encouragement would be important in sustaining participation as part of their teaching in the future (Kemmis 2010, McIntosh 2010b).

The structure of the '9 Steps of Reflection' provided practical steps that enabled the teachers to focus on obstacles and problems associated with consultation and participation which they encountered as part of their teaching (Marcos *et al.* 2009). The evolving steps also acted as a framework around which the teachers were able to construct written reflections about their practice. The significance and potential value of this tool as a means of supporting critical reflection as part of daily teaching became clearer, more significant and more detailed as we analysed the data as an ongoing part of the study (Corbin and Holt 2005, McCormack and Boomer 2007). The Reciprocal Relationship arrow represents the 'golden thread' connecting each aspect of the cyclical process. This indicates the fluid and live relationship between the conceptual steps (R's) as part of the purposeful process of critical reflection. The term 'step' was used simply to indicate the depth of the processes involved in becoming reflective and is used to indicate the supportive and flexible process. It should not be seen as a restrictive set of rules to be followed rigorously. Equally, the term sequence represents the connectedness as a whole rather than a particular pattern that should be followed.

Findings from Phase Two of the study: sustaining openness through the '9 R's of Reflection'

Phase Two of the study reported in this paper was concerned with whether participation could be sustained by embedding the '9 R's of Reflection' as part of ongoing teaching. The text is a transcription of the narrative spoken by the RT as she reflected on her participatory teaching and her experience of reflection before the project, during the project and thoughts on her future practice.

THE PROFESSIONAL DEVELOPMENT OF EARLY YEARS EDUCATORS

The reception teacher: before

I felt like I had a massive mountain going on and really I just needed to understand that there are such huge benefits that come out of reflection. It's just letting go and not letting it get to you. It was scary because you leave a lot behind but the R's make sure the scary doesn't take over.

During

I think this project has been about getting stuck in … just going for it and just totally immersing yourself. It never ends or finishes. It's a continuum. It's on-going, never ending and something you will always do using the R's. Because of the process we've been through together it's just something I need to carry out now. Now that we've realised and experienced the importance of participation and listening to children through reflection, it's something that I'll do forever. It's become a part of life.

It's the experiencing for ourselves and valuing it. I've specified specific reflection time … it's just an additional thing that I do now so I'm reflecting as I'm doing. Using our developing Steps [of Reflection] has definitely enabled a deeper level of reflection than just thinking. Yes, because when you write it down you're more engaged in it and you question it and think it through more than just thinking 'Oh that was good'. It sort of goes from thinking it to talking it to writing it down in three stages but more clearly.

Forwards into the future

The way I see it, the journey's not finished yet, we've got further to go and I don't think we'll ever be finished. I also liked the way that she's trying to pass something to her friend and we need to do the same thing now. We need to share with other people and to help them realise the importance of participation with children. The benefits are huge. it's just a case of opening the door.

I love where the project has brought us. I love that you know that we dedicate time to reflecting, I love the freedom we've found.

The RT reflections indicate a genuine passion, readiness, enthusiasm and commitment as part of engaging in the reflective process (the 9 R's), particularly in light of initial uncertainties (Scharmer 2009). The importance of collaboration is emphasised as well as the need to remember and share her new-found confidence (Kemmis 2010). The RT recognised the benefits both for herself and for the children. Having experienced the process of reflection, she is committed to making time to reflect as both part of daily teaching and keeping a journal (Bolton 2005, Moon 2008).

Concluding thoughts

This study demonstrates the essential need for an embodied 'opening process' of mind, heart and will as the starting point for critical reflection (Scharmer 2009, p. 37) (Theory U) in the context of appropriate conditions (McCormack and Boomer 2007), which was developed, supported and sustained by the 'R's of Reflection' (Kemmis 2010, McLeod 2012). By facilitating openness, self-awareness and personal questioning over a period of time as part of professional development, the teachers' experience was one of a personal sense of purpose, meaning and relevance that promoted empowerment, ownership of knowledge, permission to question and confidence in taking necessary risks (Freire 1994, Brookfield 1995). As part of their day-to-day teaching they were able to focus positively on processes that promote participatory teaching, and became better at listening to, consulting and participating with young children. The NT's concluding comments were as follows:

I think that until you go through this process you don't realise how important it is.

The following points were recommended by the teachers for teachers as a means of sustaining critical reflection as part of professional learning and development:

- Be ready, open and willing to develop self-awareness.
- Be prepared to explore emotions as part of understanding one's own identity.
- Commit time and enthusiasm.
- Be prepared to let go, take risks and make changes.
- Commit to sharing the value of participation with other colleagues.
- Remember the benefits for the children and teachers.
- Be prepared to respect and value children's ideas and interests.
- Identify listening, consulting and participating with children as a personal area of interest and priority for professional development.

Each of the above suggestions pertinent to reflection is situated within the '9 R's of Reflection' (Figure 2), signifying perhaps the relevance and purpose of the '9 R's' for other teachers. Ultimately, of course, further research involving the sustainability of the '9 R's of Reflection' with the teachers involved in this study is needed (despite the fact that they are no longer teaching in the same school). As Hughes (2008), Givvin and Santagata (2011) and Tickell (2011) reinforce, change takes time if it is to be embedded and sustainable as a valuable part of teaching. Therefore, further research could focus on how to nurture action research to support embodied readiness through creating appropriate collaborative conditions (McCormack and Boomer 2007), involving teachers and university tutors working and researching together (Stenhouse 1971, 1976). The practical focus would be on enhancing both individual and collective transformations. Likewise, the '9 Steps / R's of Reflection' need further evaluation against other models that have been found to support the key features of critical reflection and participation as part of a meaningful process.

In terms of considerations for the wider teaching population, there is the need to recognise the importance of starting with and working with teachers' personal priorities and interests as a means for purposeful collaborative inquiry. In addition, creating the right conditions is essential, such as an open and trusting safe environment so that uncertainty and willingness to take personal risks are embraced. To a certain extent these recommendations are dependent on policy-makers valuing the contribution that critical reflection can make alongside the constraints and tensions caused by Local Authority targets and Standard Assessment Tests.

References

Athey, C., 2007. *Extending thought in young children: a parent – teacher partnership*. 2nd ed. London: Paul Chapman.

Barnes, J., 1976. Introduction to Aristotle: *The Nicomachean ethics ('Ethics')*. Harmondsworth: Penguin.

Beijaard, D., Meijer, P., and Verloop, N., 2004. Reconsidering research on teachers' professional identity. *Teaching and teacher education*, 20 (2), 107–128.

Bijkerk, I. and Loonen, I., 2009. *Water naar de zee dragen* [Carry water to the sea]. Houten, The Netherlands: Springer Uitgeverij / Media.

Bolton, G., 2005. *Reflective practice: writing and professional development*. 2nd ed. London: Sage.

Brookfield, S.D., 1995. *Becoming a critically reflective teacher*. San Francisco, CA: Jossey-Bass.

Carr, W., 1998. The curriculum in and for a democratic society. *Curriculum studies*, 6 (3), 323–340.

Clark, A., 2004. *Listening as a way of life: why and how we listen to young children*. London: National Children's Bureau for Department for Education & Science.

Clark, A., 2005. Listening to and involving young children: a review of research and practice. *Early child development & care*, 175 (6), 489–505.

Claxton, G., 2003. *The intuitive practitioner: on the value of not always knowing what one is doing*. Maidenhead: Open University Press.

Clough, P. and Nutbrown, C., 2007. *A student's guide to methodology*. London: Sage.

Corbin, J. and Holt, N.L., 2005. Grounded theory. *In*: B. Somekh and C. Lewin, eds. *Research methods in the social sciences*. London: Sage, 49–55.

Davies, S. and Artaraz, K., 2009. Towards an understanding of factors influencing early years professionals' practice of consultation with young children. *Children and society*, 23 (1), 57–69.

De Bono, E., 1983. *Practical thinking*. Harmondsworth, Middlesex: Penguin.

Dewey, J., 1933. *How we think: a restatement of the relation of reflective thinking to the educative process*. New York: Heath and Company.

Dimova, Y. and Loughran, J., 2009. Developing a big picture understanding of reflection in pedagogical practice. *Reflective practice*, 10 (2), 205–217.

Edwards, A., Gilroy, P., and Hartley, D., 2002. *Rethinking teacher education: collaborative responses to uncertainty*. London: Routledge Falmer.

Etherington, K., 2004. *Becoming a reflexive researcher: using our selves in research*. London: Jessica Kingsley.

Eun, B., 2011. A Vygotskian theory-based professional development: implications for culturally diverse classrooms. *Professional development in education*, 37 (3), 319–333.

Feldman, A. and Weiss, T., 2010. Understanding change in teachers' ways of being through collaborative action research: a cultural-historical activity theory analysis. *Educational action research*, 18 (1), 29–55.

Freire, P., 1970. *Cultural action for freedom*. M. Bergman, trans. Harmondsworth: Penguin.

Freire, P., 1994. *Pedagogy of hope*. New York: Continuum.

Gilroy, P., 1993. Reflections on Schön: an epistemological critique and a practical alternative. *In*: P. Gilroy and M. Smith, eds. *International analyses of teacher education*. Abingdon: Carfax, 125–142.

Givvin, K.B. and Santagata, R., 2011. Toward a common language for discussing the features of effective professional development: the case of a US mathematics program. *Professional development in education*, 37 (3), 439–451.

Goldstein, L., 2000. Ethical dilemmas in designing collaborative research: lessons learned the hard way. *International journal of qualitative studies in education*, 13 (5), 315–330.

Grundy, S., 1987. *Curriculum: product or praxis?* Oxford: Routledge Falmer.

Hargreaves, A., 2001. Emotional geographies of teaching. *Teachers' college record*, 103 (6), 1056–1080.

Hassan, Z., 2005. *Connecting to source* [online]. Available from: www.worldchanging.com/ [Accessed 24 July 2010].

Hill, M., *et al.*, 2004. Moving the participation agenda forward. *Children and society*, 18 (2), 77–96.

Hughes, J., 2008. Change takes time. *Early education*, 56, 10.

THE PROFESSIONAL DEVELOPMENT OF EARLY YEARS EDUCATORS

Jacobs, G. and Murray, M., 2010. Developing critical understanding by teaching action research to undergraduate psychology students. *Educational action research*, 18 (3), 319–335.

Jupp, V., ed., 2006. *The Sage dictionary of social research methods*. London: Sage.

Kemmis, S., 2010. What is to be done? The place of action research. *Educational action research*, 18 (4), 417–427.

King, P.M. and Kitchener, K.S., 2004. Reflective judgment: theory and research on the development of epistemic assumptions through adulthood. *Educational psychologist*, 39 (1), 5–18.

Lancaster, P., 2003. *Listening to young children*. Maidenhead: Open University Press.

Leitch, R., 2006. Limitations of language: developing arts-based creative narrative in stories of teachers' identities. *Teachers and teaching: theory and practice*, 12 (5), 549–569.

Lincoln, Y.S. and Guba, E.G., 2000. Paradigmatic controversies, contradictions and emerging confluences. *In*: N.K. Denzin and Y.S. Lincoln, eds. *Handbook of qualitative research*. 2nd ed. London: Sage, 191–216.

Loucks-Horsley, S., *et al.*, 2003. *Designing professional development for teachers of science and mathematics*. 2nd ed. Thousand Oaks, CA: Corwin Press.

Mac Naughton, G., 2005. *Doing Foucault in early childhood studies*. London: Routledge.

Malaguzzi, L., 1992. *A charter of rights*. Reggio Emilia, Italy: Municipality of Reggio Emilia.

Marcos, J.J.M., Miguel, E.S., and Tillema, H., 2009. Teacher reflection on action: what is said (in research) and what is done (in teaching). *Reflective practice*, 10 (2), 191–204.

McAlpine, L. and Weston, C., 2000. Reflection: issues related to improving professors' teaching and students' learning. *Instructional science*, 28 (5), 363–385.

McCormack, B. and Boomer, C., 2007. *Creating the conditions for growth. Report on the Belfast City Hospital and The Royal Hospitals Collaborative Practice Development Programme*. Belfast, NI: Belfast Health and Social Care Trust.

McDermot, J., ed. 1973. *The philosophy of John Dewey*, Volumes 1 & 2. New York: Springer.

McIntosh, P., 2010a. The puzzle of metaphor and voice in arts-based social research. *International journal of social research methodology*, 13 (2), 1–13.

McIntosh, P., 2010b. *Action research and reflective practice. Creative and visual methods to facilitate reflection and learning*. London: Routledge.

McLellan, E., 2004. How reflective is the academic essay? *Studies in higher education*, 29 (1), 76–89.

McLeod, N., 2011. Exploring early years educators' ownership of language and communication knowledge and skills: a review of key policy and initial reflections on *Every Child a Talker* and its implementation. *Education 3–13: international journal of primary, elementary and early years education*, 39 (4), 429–445.

McLeod, N., 2012. *Critical reflection as a tool for developing pedagogical participation with young children in their learning*. Thesis (EdD). University of Sheffield library.

McLeod, N., 2014 forthcoming. Evoking new ways of seeing through creative hermeneutic methods: working with teachers to improve participatory teaching with young children.

Mezirow, J., 1997. Transformative learning: theory to practice. *In*: P. Cranton, ed. *Transformative learning in action: insights from practice: new directions for adult and continuing education* (No. 74). San Francisco, CA: Jossey-Bass, 5–12.

Moon, J., 1999. *Reflection in learning and professional development*. London: Routledge Falmer.

Moon, J., 2006. *Learning journals: a handbook for reflective practice and professional development*. London: Routledge.

Moon, J., 2008. *Critical thinking: an exploration of theory and practice*. Oxford: Routledge.

Moss, P., Petrie, P., and Poland, G., 1999. *Rethinking school: some international perspectives*. York: Joseph Rowntree Foundation.

Nias, J., 1996. Thinking about feelings: the emotions in teaching. *Cambridge journal of education*, 26 (3), 293–306.

Noddings, N., 1996. Stories and affect in teacher education. *Cambridge journal of education*, 26 (3), 435–447.

Nutbrown, C., ed., 1996. *Respectful educators – capable learners: children's rights and early education*. London: Paul Chapman.

Platteel, T., *et al.*, 2010. Forming a collaborative action research partnership. *Educational action research*, 18 (4), 429–451.

Pollard, A., *et al.*, 2008. *Reflective teaching*. 3rd ed. London: Continuum.

Price, J.N. and Valli, L., 2005. Pre-service teachers becoming agents of change. Pedagogical implications for action research. *Journal of teacher education*, 56 (1), 57–72.

Reed, M. and Canning, N., 2010. *Reflective practice in the early years*. London: Sage.

Rinaldi, C., 2006. *In dialogue with Reggio Emilia: listening, researching and learning*. London: Routledge.

Scharmer, C.O., 2009. *Theory U: leading from the future as it emerges*. San Francisco, CA: Berrett-Koehler.

Scharmer, C.O., 2010. The blind spot of institutional leadership: how to create deep innovation through moving from egosystem to ecosystem awareness [online]. Paper prepared for the *World Economic Forum Annual Meeting of the New Champions 2010*, Tianjin, People's Republic of China, 13–15 September. 1–13. Available from: www.presencing.com/docs/publications/execsums/Theory_U_Exec_Summary.pdf.

Schön, D.A., 1983. *The reflective practitioner: how professionals think in action*. New York: Basic Books.

Schön, D.A., 1987. *Educating the reflective practitioner: toward a new design for teaching*. San Francisco, CA: Jossey-Bass.

Shier, H., 2001. Pathways to participation: openings, opportunities and obligations. *Children and society*, 15 (2), 107–117.

Simons, H. and McCormack, B., 2007. Integrating arts-based inquiry in evaluation methodology: challenges and opportunities. *Qualitative inquiry*, 13 (2), 292–311.

Stenhouse, L., 1971. The humanities curriculum project: the rationale. *Theory into practice*, 10 (3), 154–162.

Stenhouse, L., 1976. *An introduction to curriculum research and development*. London: Heinemann.

Taylor, P., 1993. *The texts of Paulo Freire*. Buckingham: Open University Press.

Tickell, C., 2011. *The early years: foundations for life, health and learning. An independent report on the early years foundation stage to Her Majesty's government*. London: Department for Education.

Titchen, A. and McCormack, B., 2010. Dancing with stones: critical creativity as methodology for human flourishing. *Educational action research*, 18 (4), 531–554.

United Nations, 1989. *Convention on the rights of the child*. New York: United Nations.

van Manen, M., 1995. Epistemology of reflective practice. *Teachers and teaching: theory and practice*, 1 (1), 33–50.

Villen, K., 1993. Pre-school education in Denmark. *In*: T. David, ed. *Educational provision for our youngest children: European perspectives*. London: Paul Chapman, 18–34.

Wilkins, C., 2011. Professionalism and the post-performative teacher: new teachers reflect on autonomy and accountability in the English school system. *Professional development in education*, 37 (3), 389–409.

Do reflections on personal autobiography as captured in narrated life-stories illuminate leadership development in the field of early childhood?

Sara Layen

Research demonstrating the importance and impact of the earliest years on long-term outcomes is now well established, and the link between effective leadership and quality provision has been clearly made. However, the nature of the best preparation for such leadership remains contested. The qualitative research reported here is related to the early childhood sector in England and is based on a series of in-depth interviews conducted over a four-month period with three early childhood leaders selected through purposeful sampling. The research study focuses on the key area for exploration – whether reflecting on and analysing autobiographical stories, both personal and linked to leadership experiences, has the potential to support leadership development by increasing self-awareness and self-concept. Links are made between 'lived experience' and leadership practice and effectiveness. The study highlights the importance of such reflections and indicates that this approach to leadership development has a positive and constructive impact on the participants' views of themselves as people and leaders, and as such might be an additional approach to developing new leaders and supporting the continuing development of existing leaders.

Introduction

The concept of leadership within the early years sector has not traditionally enjoyed the same attention as in other fields and as a result there has been a lack of research available to inform and guide thinking and practice relating to leadership development in the field (Rodd 2005). Research demonstrating the importance and impact of the earliest years on long-term outcomes is now well established (Field 2010, Allen 2011, Tickell 2011) and has significantly influenced the development of national and international policy in terms of emphasis on and funding for early childhood education and care across the globe. Key to delivering policy into practice and supporting better educational outcomes for children is the quality of leadership for provision and practice (Siraj-Blatchford and Manni 2007, Centre for Excellence and Outcomes in Children's and Young People's Services 2010). According to Nutbrown (2012), highly qualified and passionate leaders play the biggest part in raising standards and improving the quality of provision in the sector. The case for the nurturing of effective leadership is strong.

Effective leaders are 'reflective practitioners who influence and develop people by setting an example and providing a model, both morally and purposefully' (Siraj-Blatchford and Manni 2007, p. 22). However, influencing colleagues has been identified as one of the key barriers affecting the ability of early childhood leaders to effect change (Hadfield *et al.* 2010).

The question necessarily arises of 'what is the most effective preparation for leadership in the sector?' Definitions of leadership do not usually refer to training of leaders and there is an underlying assumption that leadership skills are acquired in other ways (Waniganayake 2002). If leadership is a skill learnt through interactions and reflecting on those interactions (Siraj-Blatchford and Manni 2007), then this needs to figure highly and integrally in early childhood leadership preparation. The question as to what are the significant interactions and experiences that develop leadership also needs to be addressed. Fitchman and Yendel-Hoppey (2005) assert that childhood experiences may be directly linked to the way in which leadership is understood, perceived and played out by early years leaders and that these experiences contribute to the development of a vision for early years which includes a wider vision for society.

The qualitative research reported here relates to the early childhood sector in England and is based on the analysis of in-depth interviews conducted over a four-month period with three participants selected through purposeful sampling. The research focuses on the leaders' perceptions of what has supported their leadership and goes on to look at the key area for deeper exploration: whether reflecting on personal and professional (leadership-linked) autobiographical stories has the potential to support leadership development by increasing self-awareness and sharpening self-concept. The study highlights the importance of such reflections and shows why this approach to leadership development has a positive consequence. It demonstrates the constructive impact of reflections on the participants' views of themselves as people and leaders. It is suggested that this might be used as an additional approach to developing new leadership and enhancing the development of existing early years leaders. The study therefore has implications for policy and practice beyond England.

For the purposes of this paper, it is assumed essential that effective leaders have an advanced understanding of early childhood pedagogy (Nutbrown 2012), a factor that was fully reflected in participants' evaluation of the impact of their higher-level qualifications on their leadership development (data not included in this report).

Early childhood leadership development: current situation in England

The route into early years leadership has historically been more fluid than in other educational fields, and there has been a belief that success as an early years practitioner will necessarily translate into the ability to be an effective leader (Siraj-Blatchford and Manni 2007). Training and support for developing leaders had been piecemeal over the years until the advent in 2004 of the National Professional Qualification in Integrated Centre Leadership (NPQICL), a master's-level qualification predominantly for children's centre leaders and deputies, and the Early Years Professional Status (EYPS) in 2007, a leader/practitioner status for graduates aimed to underpin leadership development in the field. Leadership training before the introduction of these qualifications consisted mainly of in-service or short courses (Rodd 1998, Siraj-Blatchford and Manni 2007), with only a minority of practitioners engaging in long-term study of leadership (Siraj-Blatchford and Manni 2007).

Dedicated leadership courses in England (NPQICL, EYPS, New Leaders in Early Years) under the current Coalition government (2010–present) are now being replaced by a wider range of longer-term leadership development opportunities such as work-based action research projects, specialist higher degree qualifications, mentoring and coaching opportunities and leadership development programmes that are longer term and practice based (Rodd 2013).

The EYPS with its underpinning leadership strand has been superseded by the Early Years Teacher (EYT) status, which builds on and replaces the EYPS. EYT is designed to provide 'overall pedagogical leadership for a setting, working directly with children and families, and supporting staff with lower levels of qualifications' (Nutbrown 2012, p. 46) although there is no dedicated leadership element reflected in the EYT standards. There remains a significant further group of lower qualified early childhood leaders (NVQ Level 3), who as yet have no access to 'whole setting' leadership development. These leaders may hold the overall lead for private, voluntary and independent settings (which make up a significant proportion of early childhood provision in England), a role that bears some resemblance to the role of leaders of children's centres but on a smaller scale. Support for their development remains piecemeal, with EYT the only formal professional development available once practitioners have achieved a degree.

It could be argued that this return to a more piecemeal approach is not sufficient preparation for the demanding, complex and diverse role that has the potential to encompass administration and management of diverse services and leadership of a multi-disciplinary team in addition to pedagogical leadership (Muijs *et al.* 2004, Krieg *et al.* 2014). Current training for early years practitioners (Early Years Educator and EYT) does not prepare them to appreciate and take on leadership roles, but instead focuses on child-centred education and care. Leaders require mature and sophisticated understanding of the complex dynamics of children, families and communities, knowledge and skills in addition to those required for provision of education and care (Cecchin 2009, Rodd 2013). Consequently there is a gap developing between the aspirations and vision for continuous quality improvement that supports outcomes for all children, and particularly for disadvantaged groups, and the support for the development of practitioners to take on the complex and challenging role of leader.

The content and delivery of training and future professional development that best support leadership development have yet to be closely researched, together with an understanding of how leadership develops (Fitchman and Yendol-Hoppey 2005). Alongside this, the relationship between training and specific practitioner behaviours and skills that are most likely to raise the quality of provision and outcomes for children still needs to be determined (Mathers *et al.* 2011, p. 107).

Experiential and reflective experiences and leadership theory

In order for early childhood leaders to be able to influence others on the basis of trusted, positive and constructive relationships at both individual and team levels, leaders need a range of skills including 'emotional intelligence and the ability to draw on a repertoire of strategies for inspiring, influencing and negotiating with others' (Children's Workforce Development Council 2010, p. 7).

Emotional intelligence encompasses self-awareness (understanding of one's own goals and values), self-management (control of emotions that enhances an environment of trust and fairness), social awareness (high motivation characteristics such as optimism, commitment and achievement) and empathy, which includes consideration and awareness of the perspective of others in any situation (Goleman 1998). These are personal characteristics that the effective leader will manifest, and which can be developed through self-reflection.

The value of self-reflection is a well-developed theme in leadership literature, being linked to the potential to 'reveal the underlying aspect of self' (Chak 2006, p. 32), to support the leader in being available to others and 'externally open', to enhance the leader's ability to transform self, groups and organisations (Rosenberg 2010, p. 12) and to nurture the ability to decrease negative emotions and increase positive ones (Seligman cited Rosenberg 2010). Further beneficial outcomes of self-reflection include coherence of thoughts, feelings, motivation and behaviour (Rosenberg 2010), all themes that strongly resonate with Goleman's dimensions of emotional intelligence.

Self-reflection may also encompass development of an understanding of one's own experiences, particularly through critical reflection on childhood memories, in order for leaders to understand how social and political forces have shaped identities as early childhood educators and leaders (Fitchman and Yendol-Hoppey 2005, p. 200). The construction and sharing of autobiographies may support insight into leadership styles and abilities, and could potentially be a first step to 'the ongoing self-enquiry and reflection inherent in leadership', thus resonating with Lee's assertion that 'our pasts have enormous influence on our futures' (2008, p. 97). Understanding past experiences may also have the potential to lead to understanding of how to energise early childhood leaders in their role (Fitchman and Yendol-Hoppey 2005, p. 204).

The leader who has developed a critical understanding of their own personal experiences in the context of the broader world of political, social and economic reality may well be better placed to develop a philosophy that relates to community. Lee (2008, p. 9) suggests that groups can be influenced by those who have a philosophy relating to community.

The development of a personal approach to leadership theory and development through the exploration of emotional intelligence and self-reflection links to the relatively new theory of authentic leadership. There are many definitions of authentic leadership (Chan 2005), but they all refer to leadership that is genuine, trustworthy and honest (Northouse 2013), qualities that are paramount in a sector whose focus is children, families and community (Alasuutari 2010). For the purposes of this article, a closer analysis of the literature relating to a developmental definition, which regards authentic leadership as something that can be developed and nurtured, is most relevant when considering the question of how to best support the professional development of early childhood leadership.

Authentic leadership according to the developmental definition develops from and is grounded in a leader's positive psychological qualities (which include confidence, hope, optimism and resilience) and strong ethics (Walumbwa *et al.* 2010). Both dimensions are in harmony with the ethos and culture of early childhood leadership and acclaimed early years pedagogy in the twenty-first century (Dahlberg and Moss 2005, Rodd 2013). Furthermore, authentic leadership is recognised as being made up of four related components – self-awareness, an internalised moral perspective, balanced weighing of options and relational transparency (Walumbwa *et al.* 2010). Authentic leaders have the capacity to make ethical decisions, which enable them to make decisions that serve the greater good, promote justice and achieve what is right for the community (Northouse 2013). These characteristics resonate strongly with the type of leadership that is needed in the early childhood sector – ethical, transparent, positive, hopeful, resilient, motivating and trustworthy in respect of children and families (Dahlberg and Moss 2005). They also correspond closely with the aspirational nature of early years provision to mitigate the effects of inequality and poverty.

The extent to which the authentic leader is effective is in direct relation to the consistency between a leader's true self, as expressed in their values, purpose and voice, and their behaviours (Sparrowe 2005). This alignment makes the leader transparent to their 'followers' and increases credibility and capacity to influence.

If this is the case, the literature pertaining to the support and development of authentic leadership may be relevant to the question of how to support the development of leadership in the early childhood sector, whilst simultaneously bearing in mind the styles and skills of effective early childhood leadership highlighted in the Effective Leadership in the Early Years Sector study (Siraj-Blatchford and Manni 2007) – reflective practice, a focus on collaboration and positive constructive relationships that will enable a secure and shared contextual vision to be developed at setting and community levels.

A common element for all of the definitions of authentic leadership is the depth of self-knowledge and self-concept that supports the two dimensions (ethical position and psychological) referred to above. The telling of life-stories helps to develop greater self-knowledge and clarity, and through understanding life experiences leaders become more authentic and more effective (Luthans and Avolio 2003). The telling of life-stories also increases the potential for leaders to identify values and convictions and develop a personal meaning system (Northouse 2013) organising experiences and establishing connections (Shamir and Eilam 2005, p. 436). As Pearce (2003, p. 21) asserts, every idea that is held passionately has a background in personal experience.

One of the major ways to develop potential through exploring personal stories is through a guided reflection process (Shamir and Eilam 2005). This involves engaging leaders in the narration of 'trigger events' to increase self-awareness (Luthans and Avolio 2003) and pursuing a narrative journey in autobiographical memory that supports the self-awareness which leads towards authenticity (Sparrowe 2005, p. 431). This approach to leadership development would involve a shift of styles, away from an emphasis on development of skills and behavioural styles towards an emphasis on leaders' self-development and especially to the development of their self-concepts through construction of life-stories (Shamir and Eilam 2005, p. 436) – from the public to the personal.

Research on leadership from a life-story perspective is very limited but may be another thread to add to the existing approaches to early childhood leadership development, proving fruitful in developing the self-awareness and self-knowledge that support emotional intelligence, clarity about values, clearer moral perspective and transparent relationships. The resulting increase in authenticity has the potential to increase the influence such a leader may have on individuals and communities.

Methodology

This interpretive study sought to describe and understand the phenomenon of leadership development through individuals' exploration of significant personal stories, integrating autobiographical narratives with reflection and analysis supported by the researcher.

The research was phenomenological in its design, believing behaviour to be determined by the phenomena of experience (Cohen *et al.* 2007) and the active consciousness of such experience to have the potential to bestow meaning upon it (Curtis 1978). The stories told by the participants recreated fragments of the unbroken stream of their lived experiences, which are given meaning and understood retrospectively through reflexivity (Burrell and Morgan 1979).

Integral to the study was the acknowledgement that the story told by the individual is relevant, is meaningful and has the potential to reveal truths and insights, resonating with Seidman's (2006, p. 7) assertion that the stories of individuals are 'of worth', and have the potential to be educative. An implicit assumption of the research design was that meanings may be constructed from experiences, stories, dialogue and reflections (Seidman 2006, p. 7, Squire 2013, p. 43), and that construction of meaning can be supported in partnership with a sensitive other through further discussion, reflection and analysis.

The views of the individual participant about any episode were regarded to be as valid as that of the researcher, acknowledging the possibility of multiple interpretations of and perspectives on single events and situations, reality being multilayered and complex (Cohen *et al.* 2007, p. 21).

The participant data consisted of personal stories, relating to significant events in both their personal lives and leadership lives. The stories are viewed as having the potential to be rich in authentic and live data (Thody 1997), data that are regarded authoritatively as respectable (Bauman 1986).

Sampling

Participants were selected through purposeful sampling, a non-random method, whereby participants are identified who are likely to be 'information-rich' in order to support the research focus (Patton 2001, Creswell 2007). The participants were selected according to criteria identified by the researcher, which included the following: current experience in early years leadership; deemed to be effective through Ofsted evaluation or authoritative opinion in the field; willing and prepared to devote time to the project; and able to build on and maintain a previously established professional and mutually respectful relationship with the researcher (Plummer 1983). Settings from which the participants were selected included an Early Years Foundation Stage state school with a children's centre on site, and two independent settings both of which were registered as charitable organisations (non-profit making). It is acknowledged that this limited number of participants does not reflect the entire spectrum of diverse settings that exist in the early childhood sector in England, but for the purposes of this study their selection was deemed pertinent.

Ethical issues

Participants were fully briefed about the aims of the study, the extent and nature of their involvement and the researcher's credentials, prior to their agreement to take part (Adelman 1976). Research processes were transparent and issues relating to anonymity and the identification of participant data were addressed. Participant ownership of their data was underlined, together with their right to withdraw data at

THE PROFESSIONAL DEVELOPMENT OF EARLY YEARS EDUCATORS

any time during the study. The content and structure of each interview were discussed and agreed beforehand (Bell 2010).

A systematic approach of sharing interview transcriptions with the participants and inviting review and reflection upon them, together with sharing analysis and emerging themes, was an integral part of the research design. The mode of data analysis was also shared with participants, who were additionally assured that their perspective was an integral facet of the study and was valued and respected.

Data collection

Interviews

A series of three individual 40-minute unstructured and semi-structured in-depth interviews took place with each participant, in which a number of autobiographical narratives were collected, analysed and reflected upon. Researcher reflections and responses to the interviews were captured as an integral part of the data together with participant responses to transcripts, retrospective reflections on the interviews and responses to analyses.

To surface the data of most relevance to the research focus, consideration of the general areas for exploration was pre-planned and shared with participants prior to the interviews (Hitchcock and Hughes 1995, p. 162).

The first two interviews in the interview sequence were unstructured and focused on the telling of one or two autobiographical stories that captured significant events; Interview 1 was focused on stories that related to the participants' childhood and Interview 2 on those that related to their professional 'leadership' lives. Guiding themes were introduced in the form of open-ended questions that provided a sense of direction but allowed the respondent to tell their stories in their own way (Sargent 2004, p. 176), allowing them greater and freer flow and the space 'to travel' wherever they liked (Bell 2010) within the context of the theme of the interview. This facilitated the potential for interviewees to delve more deeply into their stories without the pressure on the researcher to cover a pre-set agenda, which is a particularly appropriate approach to gathering what are potentially highly personal materials (Bell 1999). Participants were therefore able to draw on details that they felt were relevant, and the potential for the researcher and participant to co-construct new insights was created (Bold 2012, p. 100).

Data analysis

Analysis of the autobiographical narrative data followed a phenomenological analytical process (Polkinghorne 1989, Moustakas 1994), where the researcher goes through a process known as 'horizonalization' in order to analyse and distil experience to its essences (Moustakas 1994). Moustakas uses the analogy of the 'horizon' to indicate the endless possibilities and potential for discovery and understanding that reflecting on and becoming aware of experience offers, and the potential to discover our own nature from the vantage point of self-awareness. The process involves highlighting significant statements, sentences or quotes from the transcript from which clusters of meaning are identified, which are then used to develop themes (Creswell 2007). These are considered in relation to the research focus and those that relate directly are extracted and are condensed into assertions which represent the data. The assertions are thus grounded in the lived experiences of current early childhood leaders.

The validity of the analysis was triangulated by the participants who had opportunities to comment on and add to the transcripts after each interview, and to review and comment on the clusters of meaning and identification of themes. The researcher aimed to retain the authentic meaning of the subject's words and phrases at all times, in order to minimise researcher intrusion on the data (Plummer 1983). Over-interpretation was mitigated against, by the researcher listening carefully to participants and defending interpretations to them whilst at the same time acknowledging that there is room for divergence and possibility of misinterpretation (Squire 2013).

Verbatim interview transcripts for each of the participants' three interviews were initially read in their entirety. From these readings, clusters of meaning began to emerge. These were noted and a second reading of the transcripts took place looking for confirming or disconfirming evidence. Further readings enabled the data to be organised into emerging themes. In order to validate the analysis, the themes emerging from each interview were presented, discussed and verified with each participant in order to ensure trustworthiness of interpretation. The themes were finally condensed into assertions linking themes emerging from the participants' personal stories and their leadership stories. These were discussed and rated in relation to the extent to which the participant felt they resonated as meaningful within their leadership, on a scale of one to five (low to high).

Findings

An analysis follows of the findings in relation to the question of whether a focus on supporting leaders to reflect on their own narratives, both personal and linked to leadership, has the potential to develop the self-awareness and self-concept that will strengthen their leadership. The discussion will be grouped into three related sections that link to the research question: firstly, that reflection on personal narratives results in increased self-awareness; secondly, that reflecting on personal narratives supports leadership development; and finally, that reflecting on personal narratives is of value to leaders.

Reflecting on personal narratives results in increased self-awareness

Seidman (2006, p. 7) reflects that the telling of stories is essentially a meaning-making process, pointing out that the narrator will select what they see as relevant details from their 'stream of consciousness'. Bruner (1986) likewise suggests that the storytellers' identities may be revealed in their life-stories, identities that are the products of the experiences themselves and the organised stories of these experiences, thus pointing to the necessity of reflecting upon and extracting the meaning from them. The process of clarifying the meaning of such experiences in terms of self is a means to developing the self-concept that supports authentic leadership (Boyd and Fales 1983), an approach that organises life events into a structure that establishes connections hitherto unperceived (Shamir and Eilam 2005, p. 402).

One of the surprises to all three participants was the relationship between their childhood experiences and the impact of these on the values that influenced the way in which they manifested their leadership, unconscious links that had been running strongly throughout but were unperceived (Tables 1–3). The importance of hearing

THE PROFESSIONAL DEVELOPMENT OF EARLY YEARS EDUCATORS

Table 1. Two assertions that relate the way in which Jo manifests her leadership to her lived experiences.

Jo's emerging themes	Assertions
• Engaging in life-long learning is the means to improve outcomes and support self-actualisation, through the development of skills, knowledge, understanding, concepts of identity, self-belief and self-esteem • A learning disposition supports the potential for a leader to influence others and to develop pedagogy • Believing in and supporting the innate potential of others, generously (looking to support their development), is integral to effective early childhood leadership • Caring for and gathering people into a positive community is integral to the early childhood leadership vision • Early childhood leaders need an awareness of the complexity of people's lived experiences, enabling them to understand perspectives, empathise and support constructive interactions and relationships • Women need to be liberated from restrictive attitudes and actions that men sometimes impose on them in order to control them[a] • The early years sector, being predominantly female, is a context in which women can flourish, express and develop their potential while simultaneously putting children at the centre of the vision • Early childhood leadership is underpinned by relationships, mutual respect and working together towards desired goals and outcomes • A vision for childhood that is ethical, respectful and joyful is a pre-requisite to visionary provision • The early years leader needs to be an advocate: understanding that children develop in the context of their family and community; that the early childhood leader has a responsibility to work in partnership with families in order to support outcomes for their children	Childhood experiences are directly linked to the manner in which early childhood leadership is manifested, perceived and understood A vision and desire to encourage and draw children, practitioners and communities together through relationship and learning and to promote their aspirations underpins early childhood leadership

Notes: Jo rated all emerging themes as highly relevant to the way in which she felt she manifested her leadership. All scored four or five on a scale of one to five (low–high), [a]except one that was scored three.

and responding to the voice of the child, as manifested in their own leadership practices, sprang from the participants' own experiences of their own childhood, and underpinned this dedication. Commitment to supporting children's well-being, happiness and autonomy was likewise linked to childhood experiences, forming themes in the initial interviews. An example of this is found as Jo comments on a childhood story:

> I always remember thinking I wasn't listened to as a child. [...] We didn't have any emotional support as children. (Jo, Interview 1)

These experiences are linked to Jo's vision for childhood of being listened to, celebrated and emotionally secure, which are depicted in her leadership stories (Interview 2).

THE PROFESSIONAL DEVELOPMENT OF EARLY YEARS EDUCATORS

Table 2. Two assertions that relate the way in which Lorraine manifests her leadership to her lived experiences.

Lorraine's emerging themes	Assertions
• Early years leaders need to operate in and create a culture of openness and honesty within which confident children are nurtured • Early years leaders make decisions and develop ethical policies that are child-centred, and which support children's well-being • Early years leaders value and develop partnerships and cultures that are child-focused, whilst taking into account the varying perspectives of stakeholders • Early years leadership must focus on children's learning and development in order to support long-term outcomes and social mobility[a] • It is the role of the early childhood leader to be an advocate for children, within the setting and wider community, standing up for beliefs and values that support positive outcomes for children • Early years leaders need to create a team culture in which practitioners approach their role professionally, setting high standards and expectations, in order to raise the status and quality of the sector	Experiences in childhood directly affect the way in which the role of the early childhood leader is played out, understood and perceived. Such experiences have the capacity to underpin a commitment to supporting children's learning and development and their long-term outcomes The role of an effective early childhood leader encompasses values of honesty, trust, openness and commitment to high standards of professionalism in order to support a healthy team culture, partnerships with families and advocacy in the wider community

Notes: Lorraine rated all emerging themes as highly relevant to the way in which she felt she manifested her leadership. All scored five on a scale of one to five (low–high), [a]except one that was scored four.

Childhood experiences were also perceived to underpin values relating to social justice, valuing all people regardless of ethnicity, gender or social grouping, manifesting themselves in a leadership that is committed to supporting outcomes and aspirations of all children and their families. Lorraine's childhood stories reflect the emphasis on the equal value of every individual and the strengthening value of family and community in supporting a child's self-concept and identity:

> My dad would never judge who we brought home … it didn't matter what they'd got or what they hadn't … it enabled me to mix with all sorts of people and value them. (Lorraine, Interview 1)

> My grandma used to get out all the [family] pictures … we knew all the family history … we've always been a family who have 'aired and shared'. (Lorraine, Interview 2)

Pearce (2003, p. 21) recognises the importance of life experience, stating that 'Your passion about what you want to change grows from the foundation of values that have been formed by your life experiences', pointing out that every idea which is passionately held has a foundation in personal experience. This was found to be the case in the narratives of all study participants, and as such supports the case for leaders in a sector that is dedicated to social justice to explore and make meaning from and links between their own life experience and their leadership.

The increase in self-awareness and self-concept resulting from telling and reflecting on their personal narratives reflected in the participants' comments indicated that reflecting on childhood experience and linking it to their leadership role did support the participants' self-awareness and self-concept:

THE PROFESSIONAL DEVELOPMENT OF EARLY YEARS EDUCATORS

Table 3. Two assertions that relate the way in which Sarah manifests her leadership to her lived experiences.

Sarah's emerging themes	Assertions
• Early childhood leadership is complex and challenging and leaders need adequate professional development in order to be able to meet the demands of the role, together with a vocational commitment to the sector • The early childhood leadership role requires a high level of personal resilience and the ability to engage positively with the challenges inherent in the role • The early childhood leader needs to have an underpinning vocation and a vision for provision that supports children's well-being, learning dispositions and educational outcomes. This vision includes a commitment to the development of a workforce who are specialists in early childhood • For new leaders, the gap between expectation and reality can helpfully be mediated by professional support and encouragement[a] • Effective early childhood leadership develops successful provision that is underpinned by a shared ethos that is child-centred. A clear and shared vision may support the development of such a culture • Effective early childhood leadership leads by example and facilitates the development of professional learning communities • Effective leadership recognises the value of processes and protocols that support and monitor provision • Emotional intelligence and constructive, respectful relationships are integral to effective (early childhood) leadership • Early childhood leadership is committed to the support and development of others as a means of improving provision	Childhood experiences shape the manner in which leadership is understood and manifested, and contribute to a vision for childhood that the early years leader seeks to support through the development of a highly skilled and committed team Early childhood leadership is complex and demanding as it seeks to support and meet the needs of a variety of participants while at the same time seeking to maintain a focus on quality child-centred provision that supports well-being, creativity and positive outcomes

Notes: Sarah rated all emerging themes as highly relevant to the way in which she felt she manifested her leadership. All scored five on a scale of one to five (low–high), [a]except one that was scored three.

I've never given it any deep thought, why I've done the job, where I am, and whether it has got any connections with me as a person. It's not until you unpick it that those things come through. (Jo, Interview 1)

Very interesting ... To see it in black and white ... how it relates to the job I've chosen, the career and how I do it, and how I want to make a difference to other people. (Lorraine, Interview 1)

The analysis ... it was interesting to see what it says about me as a person and a leader. (Sarah, Interview 1)

However, it is relevant to note that alternatively it has been suggested that the events and experiences which authentic leaders choose to share are chosen in order to reflect their self-concept and their beliefs relating to leadership (Shamir and Eilam 2005). Both perspectives, however, do highlight self-concept and increase self-awareness as the events are reflected upon and analysed.

THE PROFESSIONAL DEVELOPMENT OF EARLY YEARS EDUCATORS

Reflecting on personal narratives supports leadership development

Shamir and Eilam (2005) highlight the individuals in their research whose life-stories were less coherent in terms of links to their leadership, describing them as leaders who tended to 'perform' leadership functions but whose role remained external to their self-concept. Many of these individuals appeared to have entered the leadership role by default, echoing the situation of many early childhood setting leaders who have come into the role as a result of circumstance rather than choice (Caldwell 2003, Ebbeck and Waniganayake 2003, Siraj-Blatchford and Manni 2007). It could be claimed that the leader who 'performs' lacks the credibility and authenticity needed in order to influence others and that this in turn could be related to the difficulty some early childhood leaders experience in influencing colleagues to change and develop practices (Hadfield *et al.* 2010). It would follow therefore that if a leader's authenticity, which is supported by an understanding of their 'true self' (Sparrowe 2005), can be enhanced by nurturing the links between life's experiences and leadership experiences, then reflecting on and analysis of lived experiences could be considered as a further approach to supporting development of and commitment to leadership.

Participants in the study selected several stories in Interview 2 which they had chosen to reflect their leadership 'best self' and also to show how they had successfully overcome difficulty. The style of their leadership resonated closely to the self-concept, values and aspirations identified in their personal narratives – thus Lorraine's story linked values of openness, trust and commitment to supporting children's well-being and outcomes; Jo's stories foregrounded belief in the capacity of individuals to develop and achieve their aspirations in the face of difficulty, and her commitment to children's well-being and voice; and Sarah's stories foregrounded how she had overcome her own inexperience through establishing constructive relationships and giving generously of her time to colleagues. The linking of the way in which their leadership was manifested to their personal selves was deemed to be extremely positive:

> It's been quite liberating. It's been a confidence builder. (Jo, Interview 2)

> It's given me more determination to achieve and support others to fulfil their dreams and wishes. That's come out of telling the stories. (Jo, Interview 2)

> It's enabled me to further understand the reasons why I enjoy my role as a leader and put me in touch with my own feelings and beliefs about the importance of the work of an EY leader. (Jo, Interview 2)

> It confirms me. This strengthens the leader I feel I am … It strengthens why I do what I do. (Lorraine, Interview 2)

> Since this, I have had more self-belief. (Sarah, Interview 3)

> It is very motivating for me. (Sarah, Interview 3)

Shamir and Eilam (2005) point out that this approach helps leaders to discover their strengths and contributions and broaden their self-concepts. Additionally, in this study it enabled the participants to celebrate their leadership.

Reflecting on personal narratives is of value to leaders

Luthans and Avolio (2003) point to the value of understanding life's experiences in supporting growth in individuals, and in supporting them to become stronger leaders.

The resulting increase in clarity about who they are, together with increase in self-knowledge, helps individuals to develop a deeper understanding of their leadership role. The participants in this study similarly were able to identify the value of sharing, reflecting and analysing their narratives, describing it as a learning process (Jo, Interview 3) rather than a content-based process that focuses on concepts, skills or behaviours as part of courses or on-the-job training (Conger 1992):

> You're unpicking where things came from and you can see why it is so important to me to be the authentic leader and not just someone who does the job 9–3 pm for them. (Jo, Interview 3)

> It's really interesting that the stories have told this. I can't believe that all this rambling has come to this [analysis]. (Lorraine, Interview 2)

> It's been a very therapeutic experience … the process was really positive. (Sarah, Interview 3)

Participants also described how the process had helped them sharpen their vision and highlight the relationship between their vision, their leadership actions and relationships with the children, their families and the wider community. The emerging themes and assertions (Tables 1–3) were rated as highly relevant. Only one theme was rated slightly lower (score of three) and this may reflect the participants' continued working out of current circumstances. This suggests that the telling of stories can surface important and meaningful threads which shape the way in which the leadership role is manifested, highlight areas for further reflection and development, and help to explicitly reveal the values, the moral framework and the vision that underpin leadership.

The impact of the process on the participant who had less experience and a less developed knowledge and understanding of leadership theory was in contrast to the impact on the others. Additionally, she found the process to be very therapeutic and helpful as she reflected on challenging situations in her leadership.

It is acknowledged that a greater number of interviews with participants would have allowed more detailed exploration and would have strengthened the data analysis further. However, initial agreements between the researcher and participants relating to time commitment were adhered to.

To sum up, the discussion of the analysis of data in this study suggests that the following assertions may be relevant when considering the relationship of personal lived experience to leadership development:

- Reflecting on personal autobiography in the form of narrated life-stories supports and increases self-concept, self-awareness and self-belief.
- Making links between personal and leadership narratives may have the potential to increase clarity of vision, motivation and clarity of moral perspective.
- Making visible the links between personal narratives and leadership helps leaders to understand the way in which they manifest their leadership.
- Professional leadership development is supported by reflection on and analysis of experiences.
- Leaders might benefit from reflecting on their stories in different ways, depending on their experience and understanding of leadership and where they are in their leadership journey.

THE PROFESSIONAL DEVELOPMENT OF EARLY YEARS EDUCATORS

The data are not able to reveal a longer-term impact on the participants' leadership and whether the process does result in an increase of influence. In order to corroborate or refute this, further data will need to be collected at a later date. However, the increase in self-awareness and self-knowledge the process has brought about might suggest that the resulting augmentation of emotional intelligence (Goleman *et al.* 2002) might lead to this.

Conclusion and recommendations

This research study set out to explore whether there was value in adding a further thread to current early childhood leadership development approaches through analysis and reflection on personal narratives and consideration of their relationship to the way in which three early childhood leaders manifested their leadership. The rich data obtained through narratives of lived experience provided an accessible and 'human' means to locating and exploring meaning in partnership with a sensitive and empathic 'other'. The emerging relationship between the participants' personal and leadership narratives (Tables 1–3) enabled participants in this study to reflect in depth on their leadership and to understand how it was inextricably linked to them personally.

The response of the study participants to this approach was very encouraging, with all three leaders engaging enthusiastically and valuing the opportunity to explore a focus on themselves, an opportunity that none of them had hitherto experienced. The process of making meaning from their personal narratives and relating it to the way in which they perceived, understood and manifested their leadership provided valuable insights into the underpinning philosophy of their leadership and its origins, although it is acknowledged that due to time constraints further relevant data remained unrevealed. However, the understanding that was developed may in turn better place them to develop a philosophy relating to community (Lee 2008), a current and topical element which is integral to successful early intervention (Field 2010). Furthermore, the insights gained may have potential to increase resilience, motivation and commitment and develop leadership maturity (Luthans and Avolio 2003).

The impact of this approach to early childhood leadership development was seen to differ somewhat between the three participants. Jo found the process to be very revealing in relation to herself; Lorraine found it to be confirming of the person and leader she understood herself to be; and Sarah, a newer and younger leader, found the process to be therapeutic, supporting and repairing her self-belief. The contrasting outcomes may be related to a number of factors, including age and experience (both in terms of life and professional), and the participants' confidence and disposition to reflect deeply on issues personal to them. The context in which the three participants played out their leadership may also be a relevant factor, with Sarah actualising her leadership within a hierarchical school structure whereas Jo and Lorraine held leadership positions in independent settings. The effect of the work context on leaders' positive psychological characteristics and capacity for authentic leadership is a further variable that may need to be taken into account. However, taking these issues into consideration, the positive outcomes for all three participants in this study suggest that this approach may prove fruitful for other early years leaders in a diverse and varied sector. Furthermore, in view of the significant proportion of for-profit early childhood settings in England, it would be of relevance to explore the impact of neoliberal agendas on a leader's ability to align authentic, ethical leadership relating to agendas of social justice with private-sector for-profit goals that have the potential to impact values, behaviours and pedagogy (Woodrow and Press 2008), although this was not a theme that emerged within this small-scale research study with leaders from non-profit-making organisations.

Triangulation of the data by the participants in this study securely underpinned their ownership of the data. However, the researcher acknowledges that a third-party analysis of the data would have further strengthened the research.

The outcome of the study for the three participants supported the alignment of the leaders' selves with their leadership behaviours, an alignment that has the potential to strengthen credibility and increase capacity to influence (Luthans and Avolio 2003, Sparrowe 2005); as such, the approach could be considered as a further constructive strand to current professional development of early childhood leaders.

The following issues would need to be considered prior to integrating this approach into professional early childhood leadership development:

- The interpersonal skills of any interviewer (Lofland 1971), which play a key role in supporting the telling of autobiographical stories.
- Issues of power and influence related to the interviewer/participant relationship, which may affect the data and their interpretation (Bell 1999).
- Researcher influence and effect emanating from the personal and biographical characteristics of the researcher (Hitchcock and Hughes 1995).
- Issues relating to time.
- Consideration of where this approach might be most constructively situated in the professional development of leaders.

The complexity of leadership of pedagogical institutions requires secure, confident, authentic and knowledgeable leaders (Siraj-Blatchford and Manni 2007, Cecchin 2009). The findings of this study suggest that reflecting on and analysing personal narratives and linking them to the leadership role is a process that could benefit a range of other early childhood leaders.

Disclosure statement

No potential conflict of interest was reported by the author.

References

Adelman, C., Jenkins, D., and Kemmis, S., 1976. Re-thinking case study: notes from the second Cambridge Conference. *Cambridge journal of education*, 6 (3), 139–150.

Alasuutari, M., 2010. Striving at partnership: parent-practitioner relationships in Finnish early educators' talk. *European early childhood education research journal*, 18 (2), 149–161.

Allen, G., 2011. *Early intervention: the next steps. An independent report to Her Majesty's government*. London: Cabinet Office. Available from: http://www.dwp.gov.uk/docs/early-intervention-next-steps.pdf [Accessed 14 February 2015].

Bauman, R., 1986. *Story, performance and event*. Cambridge: Cambridge University Press.

Bell, J., 1999. *Doing your research project*. 3rd ed. Milton Keynes: Open University Press.

Bell, J., 2010. *Doing your research project: a guide for first-time researchers in education, health and social science*. 5th ed. Maidenhead: Open University Press.

Bold, C., 2012. *Using narrative research*. London: Sage.

Boyd, E.M. and Fales, A.W., 1983. Reflective learning: key to learning from experience. *Journal of humanistic psychology*, 23 (2), 99–117.

Bruner, J.S., 1986. *Actual minds, possible selves*. Cambridge, MA: Harvard University Press.

Burrell, G. and Morgan, G., 1979. *Sociological paradigms and organizational analysis*. London: Heinemann Educational.

Caldwell, R., 2003. Models of change agency: a fourfold classification. *British journal of management*, 14 (2), 131–142.

Cecchin, D., 2009. Pedagogical institutions as objects for leadership. *In: Integrating leadership and pedagogy in early childhood institutions: professional pedagogical leadership* [online]. BUPL, The Danish Federation of Early Childhood Teacher and Youth Educators. Available from: http://www.bupl.dk/iwfile/BALG-88FH3D/$file/Professional%20Pedagogical%20leadership%20Engelsk%20udgave%20brugt%20til%20EECERA%202009.pdf [Accessed 14 February 2015].

Centre for Excellence and Outcomes in Children's and Young People's Services (C4EO), 2010. *Grasping the nettle: early intervention for children, families and communities*. London: C4EO.

Chak, A., 2006. Reflecting on the self: an experience in a preschool. *Reflective practice*, 7 (1), 31–41.

Chan, A., 2005. Authentic leadership measurement and development: challenges and suggestions. *In*: W.L. Gardner, B.J. Avolio, and F.O. Walumbwa, eds. *Authentic leadership theory and practice: origins, effects and development*. Oxford: Elsevier Science, 227–251.

Children's Workforce Development Council (CWDC), 2008. *Guidance to the standards for the award of early years professional status*. Leeds: Children's Workforce Development Council.

Children's Workforce Development Council (CWDC), 2010. *The common core of skills and knowledge*. Leeds: Children's Workforce Development Council.

Cohen, L., Manion, L., and Morrison, K., 2007. *Research methods in education*. 6th ed. Abingdon: Routledge.

Conger, J., 1992. *Learning to lead: the art of transforming managers into leaders*. San Francisco, CA: Jossey-Bass.

Creswell, J.W., 2007. *Qualitative inquiry and research design: choosing among five approaches*. London: Sage.

Curtis, B., 1978. Introduction to B. Curtis and W. Mays, eds. *Phenomenology and education*. London: Methuen, ix–xxvi.

Dahlberg, G. and Moss, P., 2005. *Ethics and politics in early childhood education*. Abingdon: RoutledgeFalmer.

Ebbeck, M. and Waniganayake, M., 2003. *Early childhood professionals. Leading today and tomorrow*. Sydney: MacLennan and Petty.

Field, F., 2010. *The Foundation Years: preventing poor children becoming poor adults. The report of the Independent Review on Poverty and Life Chances*. London: Cabinet Office.

Fitchman Dana, N. and Yendol-Hoppey, D., 2005. Becoming an early childhood teacher leader and an advocate for social justice: a phenomenological interview study. *Journal of early childhood teacher education*, 26 (3), 191–206.

Goleman, D., 1998. *What makes a leader? Harvard business review*. Boston, MA: Harvard Business Press.

Goleman, D., Boyatzis, R., and McKee, A., 2002. *Primal leadership: learning to lead with emotional intelligence*. Boston, MA: Harvard Business School Press.

Hadfield, M., *et al.*, 2010. *First national survey of practitioners with early years' professional status*. Leeds: Children's Workforce Development Council.

Hitchcock, G. and Hughes, D., 1995. *Research and the teacher: a qualitative introduction to school-based research*. 2nd ed. Abingdon: RoutledgeFalmer.

Krieg, S., Davis, K., and Smith, K.A., 2014. Exploring the dance of early childhood educational leadership. *Australasian journal of early childhood*, 39 (1), 73–80.

Lee, W., 2008. ELP: empowering the leadership in professional development communities. *European early childhood education research journal*, 16 (1), 95–106.

Lofland, J., 1971. *Analyzing social settings*. New York, NY: Wadsworth.

THE PROFESSIONAL DEVELOPMENT OF EARLY YEARS EDUCATORS

Luthans, F. and Avolio, B.J., 2003. Authentic leadership development. *In*: K.S. Cameron, J.E. Dutton, and R.E. Quinn, eds. *Positive organizational scholarship*. San Francisco, CA: Berrett-Koehler, 241–258.

Mathers, S., *et al.*, 2011. *Evaluation of the Graduate Leader Fund: final report* [online]. London: Department for Education. Available from: https://www.gov.uk/government/uploads/system/uploads/attachment_data/file/181480/DFE-RR144.pdf [Accessed 14 February 2015].

Moustakas, C., 1994. *Phenomenological research methods*. Thousand Oaks, CA: Sage.

Muijs, D., *et al.*, 2004. How do they manage?: a review of the research on leadership in early childhood. *Journal of early childhood research*, 2 (2), 157–169.

Northouse, P.G., 2013. *Leadership: theory and practice*. 6th ed. London: Sage.

Nutbrown, C., 2012. *Foundations for quality: the independent review of early education and childcare qualifications* [online]. Available from: https://www.gov.uk/government/uploads/system/uploads/attachment_data/file/175463/Nutbrown-Review.pdf [Accessed 10 February 2015].

Patton, M., 2001. *Qualitative research & evaluation methods*. Thousand Oaks, CA: Sage.

Pearce, T., 2003. *Leading out loud*. San Francisco, CA: Jossey-Bass.

Plummer, K., 1983. *Documents of life: an introduction to the problems of a humanistic method*. London: Allen & Unwin.

Polkinghorne, D.E., 1989. Phenomenological research methods. *In*: R.S. Valle and S. Halling, eds. *Existential-phenomenological perspectives in psychology*. New York, NY: Plenum, 41–60.

Rodd, J., 1998. *Leadership in early childhood*. 2nd ed. Buckingham: Open University Press.

Rodd, J., 2005. *A discussion paper. Leadership: an essential ingredient or an optional extra for quality early childhood provision?* [online]. Available from: http://tactyc.org.uk/pdfs/Reflection-rodd.pdf [Accessed 14 February 2015].

Rodd, J., 2013. *Leadership in early childhood*. 4th ed. Maidenhead: McGraw Hill.

Rosenberg, L.R., 2010. Transforming leadership: reflective practice and the enhancement of happiness. *Reflective practice*, 11 (1), 9–18.

Sargent, P., 2004. Between a rock and a hard place: men caught in the gender bind of early childhood education. *The journal of men's studies*, 12 (3), 173–192.

Seidman, I.E., 2006. *Interviewing as qualitative research*. New York, NY: Teachers College Press.

Shamir, G. and Eilam, G., 2005. "What's your story?": a life-stories approach to authentic leadership development. *The leadership quarterly*, 16 (3), 395–417.

Siraj-Blatchford, I. and Manni, L., 2007. *Effective Leadership in the Early Years Sector (ELEYS) study*. London: The Institute of Education, University of London.

Sparrowe, R.T., 2005. Authentic leadership and the narrative self. *The leadership quarterly*, 16 (3), 419–439.

Squire, C., 2013. Experience-centred and socioculturally-orientated approaches to narrative. *In*: A. Andrews, C. Squire, and M. Tamboukou, eds. *Doing narrative research*. London: Sage, 47–71.

Thody, A., 1997. Lies, damned lies – and storytelling. *Educational management and administration*, 25 (3), 325–338.

Tickell, C., 2011. *The early years: foundations for life, health and learning. An independent report on the Early Years Foundation Stage to Her Majesty's government*. London: Department for Education (DfE).

Walumbwa, F.O., *et al.*, 2010. Psychological processes linking authentic leadership to follower behaviours. *The leadership quarterly*, 21 (9), 901–914.

Waniganayake, M., 2002. Growth of leadership: with training, can anyone become a leader? *In*: V. Nivala and E. Hujala, eds. *Cross-cultural perspectives on leadership*. Oulu: Oulu University Press, 115–126.

Woodrow, C. and Press, F., 2008. (Re)positioning the child in the policy/politics of early childhood. *In*: S. Farquhar and P. Fitzsimons, eds. *Philosophy of early childhood education: transforming narratives*. Oxford: Blackwell, 88–101.

Preschool teachers' insights about web-based self-coaching versus on-site expert coaching

Darbianne Shannon, Patricia Snyder and Tara McLaughlin

Implementation science defines training and coaching as two important competency components to support fidelity of implementation of evidence-based practices. The present study explores the perspectives of 21 preschool teachers, located in the United States, about the professional development (PD) they received, which included training and coaching. The PD was designed to support their planning, implementation and evaluation of embedded instruction practices for young children with disabilities. The PD involved: 16.5 hours of workshops distributed across four to six weeks; the provision of job-aids; and 16 weeks of on-site coaching or 16 weeks of prompts to engage in self-coaching using a project-developed website. An interpretivist theoretical perspective of symbolic interactionism using grounded theory methods was adopted to guide the analysis of focus group data obtained from teachers following their participation in the PD. We describe the components of the PD that teachers characterized as effectively transcending the web-based and on-site coaching, the challenges they experienced with embedded instruction implementation and their recommendations for enhancing coaching. Implications are offered for considering individual and environmental factors that influence knowledge acquisition and practice implementation in the classroom and sustaining teacher learning through follow-up implementation support.

Introduction

Providing professional development (PD) that prepares and supports a knowledgeable and skilled early childhood workforce is receiving significant attention in the United States in both research and policy contexts (Zaslow *et al.* 2010, Rhodes and Huston 2012, Winton *et al.* in press). Informed by principles from implementation science, PD that includes training and coaching has been identified as important for enhancing practitioners' competence and confidence to implement evidence-based practices with fidelity (Snyder *et al.* 2011, Metz and Bartley 2012). In early childhood PD there has been a renewed emphasis on ensuring practitioners have the knowledge, skills and dispositions to design high-quality learning environments,

THE PROFESSIONAL DEVELOPMENT OF EARLY YEARS EDUCATORS

implement evidence-based interactional and instructional practices, and use child progress and outcomes information to inform and refine their practices (Winton *et al.* in press).

A significant corpus of recent research has focused on characterizing the features of PD necessary to achieve measureable change in teacher practice and related child outcomes (Pianta *et al.* 2005, Desimone 2009, Snyder *et al.* 2011, Diamond *et al.* 2013). Among the PD features identified to date are: PD is sustained over time rather than episodic, one-shot experiences; PD is focused on a specific curriculum or set of explicit practices rather than general teaching methods; and PD includes the provision of job-embedded supports, using systematic approaches that involve teachers' implementation of practices in the classroom and reflection, as well as pro-viding specific feedback about practice implementation from a coach, mentor or peers. A meta-analysis conducted by Joyce and Showers (2002) suggested that features of PD associated with what they termed 'executive implementation' of prac-tices in classrooms included a combination of pedagogical strategies such as theory and discussion, plus explicit demonstrations of practices in training, plus practice with feedback in training, plus coaching in the classroom. Based on estimates from their meta-analysis, these authors noted that PD including all of these features would achieve fidelity of implementation as high as 95%.

Several recent studies have contributed quantitative evidence about noteworthy impacts of PD on practitioners' implementation of evidence-based practices, particu-larly when the PD included coaching (Snyder *et al.* 2012). Coaching in these studies focused on supporting implementation of an explicit and coherent set of environ-mental, interactional or instructional practices associated with positive developmen-tal and learning outcomes for young children, including children at risk for learning challenges or those with identified disabilities. Coaching included systematic and cyclical processes of collaborative goal-setting related to practice implementation, providing repeated practice implementation opportunities in job-embedded contexts and engaging in guided reflection with explicit feedback about implementation. This form of practice-focused coaching was demonstrated to be effective for enhancing teachers' implementation of social–emotional practices (Fox *et al.* 2011, Hemmeter *et al.* 2011), positive behavior support strategies (Artman-Meeker and Hemmeter 2012, Vo *et al.* 2012), interactional practices (Pianta *et al.* 2005), literacy practices (Diamond and Powell 2011, McCollum *et al.* 2013) and mathematics practices (Rudd *et al.* 2009).

Despite promising evidence, policy-makers, training and technical assistance pro-viders, and practitioners identify coaching as a time-intensive and cost-intensive form of PD. Much remains to be learned about what forms (e.g. expert coaching, peer coaching), delivery formats (e.g. face to face, web-based) and doses of coach-ing are reliably associated with desired levels of practice implementation for which practitioners and under what circumstances. Unpacking these and other features of coaching is needed to support increased access and flexibility of use (Snyder *et al.* 2012). Moreover, as practice-focused coaching gains increased momentum in imple-mentation science, it is important to examine practitioner perspectives about features of PD that are viewed as acceptable and feasible to support professional learning and implementation of evidence-based practices.

The present study is a qualitative analysis of focus group data obtained from pre-school teachers who participated in PD designed to support their implementation of embedded instruction practices for young children with disabilities. Embedded instruction is a multicomponent approach for providing learning opportunities for young children with disabilities in the context of naturally occurring classroom activities, routines and transitions (Snyder *et al.* 2013). The PD for teachers in the present study included: 16.5 hours of small-group workshops distributed across four to six weeks; the provision of job-aids for planning, implementing and evaluating embedded instruction; and 16 weeks of coaching provided either on-site by a project-trained coach or through prompts and access to a self-coaching website. The focus in the present study was on teachers' perspectives about the PD and coaching they experienced as well as the extent to which the PD supported their implementation of embedded instruction practices when coaching form and format were varied, but dose frequency was balanced. Using a grounded theory approach, the following research questions guided the analyses:

(1) Which features of PD effectively transcended the coaching delivery forms (self versus expert) and formats (web-based versus on-site)?
(2) Which features of the web-based self-coaching or on-site expert coaching facilitated teachers' perceived competence about implementing embedded instruction practices?
(3) What were teachers' implementation challenges under the web-based self-coaching condition or the on-site expert coaching condition?

Study context

The data were obtained as part of a larger potential efficacy study that involved 36 preschool teachers of young children with disabilities which focused on the impact of a multicomponent PD intervention on preschool teachers' use of embedded instruction practices (Snyder *et al.* 2013). Teachers were enrolled from three school districts located in three states and were randomly assigned at each site to one of three experimental conditions: face-to-face workshops plus on-site coaching ($n = 12$); face-to-face workshops plus self-coaching via a project-developed website ($n = 12$); and business-as-usual PD offered by the school districts ($n = 12$). Coaching implementation data showed that all teachers in the on-site coaching condition received 16 weeks of coaching, but only 2 of the 12 teachers assigned to the self-coaching condition used all available features on the self-coaching website. Eight teachers assigned to the self-coaching condition used one to three of the available features on the self-coaching website while two teachers did not access the self-coaching website during the study. Teachers assigned to the self-coaching condition displayed lower levels of implementation of embedded instruction learning trials in their classroom, when compared with teachers who received on-site coaching. Teachers in both coaching conditions, however, wrote higher-quality embedded instruction learning targets when compared with teachers in the business-as-usual condition.

Participants

Certified teachers working in preschool classrooms of three school districts located in Florida, Wisconsin and Washington participated in the study. The focus of the present study was on teachers enrolled in the two coaching conditions who participated in focus groups at the end of the study and not teachers receiving business-as-usual PD. Ten of 12 participants in the self-coaching condition and 11 of 12 participants in the on-site coaching condition consented to participate. Years of early childhood teaching experience for self-coaching teachers averaged six years (standard deviation = 4) while the on-site coaching teachers averaged 9.3 years of experience (standard deviation = 6).

Coaches

A project-employed coach trained in both the practice-focused coaching protocol and embedded instruction worked with teachers in the on-site coaching condition at each site. All coaches had experience as early childhood teachers and experience with research. One coach had a doctoral degree and the other two coaches had master's degrees.

Professional development intervention

The 16.5 hours of interactive workshops were distributed across four to six weeks at each site. Teachers received job-aids (including implementation guides, activity matrixes and video cameras) for use during and after workshops. Active learning strategies were used throughout the workshops and included video exemplars, case studies and application exercises to implement in the classroom between workshop sessions. Across both coaching delivery formats, a practice-focused coaching approach was used. This approach involves specification of a targeted set of practices, needs assessments completed by teachers related to implementation of practices, goal-setting and action planning, observation/self-observation, reflection and performance feedback (Snyder *et al.* 2009). In the present study, 14 embedded instruction practices were specified and focused on what to teach, when to teach, how to teach and how to evaluate embedded instruction implementation and child learning outcomes (Snyder *et al.* 2013).

On-site expert coaching

Each teacher in the on-site condition participated in a face-to-face coaching orientation followed by coaching in her classroom. The coach followed a systematic coaching protocol to enact the practice-focused approach. On-site sessions typically consisted of live classroom observation by the coach, followed by a meeting between the coach and teacher that included reflective conversation and provision of performance feedback. On-site coaching occurred every other week for 16 weeks. On alternate weeks, the coach contacted the teacher by email, telephone or video-conference to review the action plan and embedded instruction implementation activities carried out by the teacher following the reflection and feedback conducted during the previous week. The coach therefore had weekly contact with the teacher for 16 consecutive weeks.

Web-based self-coaching

Each teacher in this condition was given a face-to-face orientation to the self-coaching website. The orientation provided information about navigating the self-coaching website, self-coaching processes supported by the website and forms/materials located on the website. Instructions and forms available on the website for teachers to self-coach aligned with the on-site coaching protocol (i.e. self-assessment of needs, goal-setting and action planning, self-monitoring and self-evaluation of embedded instruction and child learning outcomes). After the orientation, teachers had access to the self-coaching website for 16 weeks. When teachers accessed the website, they would see a tip of the week related to embedded instruction and articulated website navigation videos highlighting key website features. Teachers in this condition were sent a weekly email from research project staff that encouraged them to visit the website, engage in self-coaching, complete self-coaching forms and view new resources or exemplar videos for embedded instruction and the tip of the week.

Method

An epistemological stance of constructionism and an interpretivist theoretical perspective of symbolic interactionism guided the inductive analysis (Crotty 2011). According to Blumer (1969), symbolic interactionism abides by three fundamental assumptions: 'human beings act toward things on the basis of the meaning these things have for them'; 'that the meaning of such things is derived from, and arises out of, the social interaction that one has with one's fellows'; and 'that these meanings are handled in and modified through, an interpretive process used by the person in dealing with the things he/she encounters.' Research within this perspective seeks to develop theory about the relationship between participants' perspectives of their context and the meaning they assign to both objects and experiences within that context (Crotty 2011).

Data generation and collection

Focus group data were collected at the conclusion of the potential efficacy trial as a component of gathering social validity data from teachers about the feasibility, acceptability and utility of both coaching and embedded instruction. A total of six focus group interviews, lasting one to two hours, were conducted across the three sites (one for each condition at each site) using a semi-structured interview protocol. Members of the research team who were not directly involved in coaching facilitated the focus groups. All sessions were audio and video recorded and transcribed for analysis. Completed transcripts were read concurrently with the audio for accuracy and tone. Quotes presented have been altered for readability in two ways: grammatically, including syntax and punctuation; and speech disfluencies (e.g. like, um, er) have been removed. In the quotes presented below sites are labeled A, B, and C. Within each site there were participants who received expert coaching (EC) and self-coaching (SC). The numbers represent the lines from the original transcription document.

Data analysis

Transcripts were analyzed using the constructivist grounded theory method, which emphasizes learning about the dimensions of experience or action embedded within relationships, situations and systems over time (Charmaz 2006). Additionally, constructivist grounded theory seeks to describe action in relation to meaning, including the participants' assumptions, their intentions and the consequence of their actions on the world (Charmaz 1996). Although the method emphasizes grounding findings in the data, it must be acknowledged that the researchers' background, interests and familiarity with the field lend foundational concepts to the process, serving as 'points of departure' for further theoretical development (Charmaz 1996, p. 32).

Two focus group transcripts, one from each coaching condition, were coded line by line using gerund-based phrases (e.g. using new materials, assuming, feeling frustration), which supported an understanding of the phenomenon grounded in the data. The data and codes were reviewed and words/phrases were collapsed into more theoretical focused codes (e.g. awareness of students), which were applied to four additional transcripts, two from each condition/location (Glaser 1978, Charmaz 1996). When new concepts arose, previous transcripts were recoded. This interactive process led to categories that subsumed multiple concepts and focused codes (e.g. 'intensive coaching supports' combined collaborative partnership, accountability for implementation and access to feedback), which, in turn, explicate the properties and relationships among the focused codes (cf. Glaser 1978, Charmaz 1996, 2006).

The movement from code to category was facilitated throughout the analysis by the process of memo-writing – a method for recording emergent understanding of the data, which grows increasingly theoretical over time (Glasser and Strauss 2009). Finally, a theoretical model was designed to illustrate the categories and their relationship to one another (see Figure 1). Notably, the credibility or trustworthiness of this work lies in the reader's ability to find meaning within the categories and model described (Creswell 2013). In addition, the analytic process was systematic and included measures of quality such as use of an audit trail, the constant-comparative method, peer debriefing and disconfirmatory cases (Branlinger *et al.* 2005, Creswell 2013).

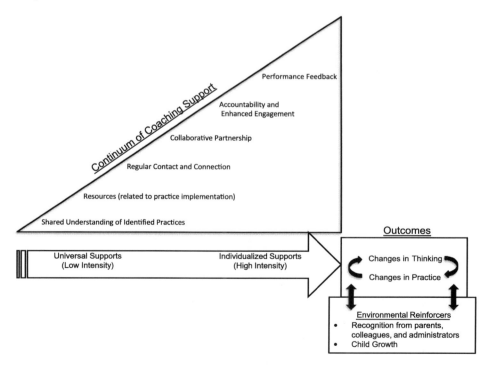

Figure 1. Change mechanisms model.

Findings

The practice of educators is embedded within a multi-layered system, which has the potential to support or challenge the quality of the classroom environment, including the interactions taking place between teachers, assistants and young children (see Figure 2). Acknowledging the complex nature of the classroom environment where the teachers' learning – changed and unchanged thinking and practices – took place is essential in understanding the variability of experience. The major constructs of this phenomenon are presented concentrically, moving from distal factors influencing the context in which the PD and teacher learning took place, to proximal mechanisms associated with changes in thinking and practices. Given the path from distal to proximal influences, the findings are organized to describe: contextual influences surrounding the learning environment; teachers' perceived and lived experiences with the PD and varied coaching formats; and participants' insights into their changed thinking and practices. The findings conclude with a description of the participant-reported challenges related to embedded instruction implementation, and concurrent recommendations for enhancement of both coaching and the embedded instruction practice content provided as part of the PD.

The learning context

Within the United States, society's understanding of early learning and development is constantly evolving. Guided by both socio-political and economic factors, the interpretation of desired outcomes for young children and proficiency benchmarks for their teachers are often unclear and evolving (Zigler *et al.* 2011). This ongoing repositioning of early childhood teachers within what has traditionally been a kindergarten–12th grade system has raised questions about the potentially

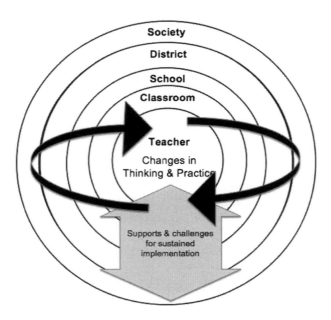

Figure 2. Learning and implementation context.

deleterious impacts of perpetuating the divide between birth to five teaching and learning experiences and the primary grades (Takanishi 2011). Several teachers described being disconnected, misunderstood or 'isolated' from their school and district colleagues (SiteC_EC_894–895). A teacher from Site B contrasted her on-site coaching experience with the support traditionally provided through administrative supervision, stating:

> We take data on the kids all the time. It was really nice having someone take data on me. To see am I doing it? Am I not? Is there growth? ... Yet no one [from an administrative or supervisory position] comes in [to observe]. I think it was that accountability piece [in the coaching]. So many times we get in our classroom and the principal may come in twice a year and do this 30-minute observation, but then he's gone ... (SiteB_EC_766–770)

Although teachers commented that support and knowledge of early childhood special education (ECSE) by district and school administrative leadership fell along a continuum, teachers across all sites described that essential elements of their professional role(s) were misunderstood by colleagues and supervisors outside the ECSE community, often resulting in feelings of professional isolation.

District-level administrators specializing in ECSE, however, played a significant role in communicating with university personnel and teachers affiliated with the study. For example, they conveyed to school administrators the relevance of having teachers participate in the study, and validated the additional hours worked by the teachers through the provision of district in-service recertification points. The teachers' ability to access meaningful PD within their schools and districts was a persistent challenge, leading teachers to speak abrasively, as they expressed their frustration: 'I'm not just going out and taking useless crap just so we can get points and get recertified' (SiteA_EC_1904–1905). Teachers were eager to learn new strategies and to improve their practice, but sought meaningful PD. Due to the professional learning context, teachers described feeling eager, yet hesitant, when they volunteered for the study. This was most apparent in the reflections of teachers who engaged in on-site coaching as they contrasted their lived experience with their underlying fears. For example, one teacher stated: '[My coach] is not intrusive or intimidating. I think having the right person there is important, because you don't want to feel like somebody's judging you or criticizing you' (SiteA_EC_463–465). Participating in the study opened new doors to a professional network, but sharing their practice beyond the secure walls of their classroom was uncharted territory for most participants.

Professional development and coaching

All participants who received coaching came to the partnership with a unique set of knowledge, skills and dispositions – a learning history, which interacted with the resources and coaching format they received in particular ways. Yet consistent themes emerged across participants' experiences. The theoretical model (Figure 1) illustrates the continuum of PD and coaching support, which served as a mechanism of change for participants. PD and coaching supports ranged from universal (e.g. establishing a shared understanding of identified embedded instruction teaching practices, providing resources and establishing connections) to more individualized (collaborative partnership, including affective support; enhanced accountability and engagement; and feedback on practice implementation). Teachers in the self-coaching condition experienced less intensive support when compared with the on-site condition despite the focus on a balanced weekly dose. Moreover, the self-coaching supports were experienced on a continuum because teachers demonstrated agency in their access to and implementation of self-coaching. For example, 6 of 12 teachers in the self-coaching condition uploaded a video of their process to receive feedback on how to engage in the practice-focused coaching cycle. In contrast, all 11 teachers in the on-site condition were guided through the coaching cycle each week. The findings related to PD and coaching describe: universal supports provided to all teachers; and more intensive supports that resulted from on-site coaching.

Universal professional development supports

Universal PD supports were provided to teachers who received coaching. These included the 16.5 hours of workshops distributed across four to six weeks and 'job-aids', which were considered foundational for teachers to write learning targets, implement practices and monitor progress. The material resources or job-aids included digital video cameras, access to model implementation videos and practice guides including forms such as an embedded instruction action plan and activity matrix with exemplars. Weekly check-in emails were provided to teachers in self-coaching, and weekly contact through alternating on-site and distance sessions (email, telephone, videoconferencing) was provided for teachers in the on-site coaching condition.

Shared understanding of identified practices. Workshops were intended to introduce a set of identified practices and ensure some level of shared understanding prior to coaching. During the workshops, teachers in both coaching conditions were introduced to embedded instruction practices, materials and resources. Teachers noted features of the workshops that helped to increase their knowledge and sense of self-efficacy related to the practices. First, teachers valued the systematic review of how to do concrete tasks related to the identified practices in combination with opportunities for supported practice. For example, this teacher highlights why guided practice opportunities were critical as she adopted new practices:

> If we had been thrown all of [the resources] all at once, you look at that and go, 'Oh it's way too much'. So, [the workshops] kind of took it in these little pieces and we did this little assignment and we saw, okay, now we're going to develop a plan … we're going to develop the matrix and we're going to use that. So, I think the pacing was pretty good to get us from point A to point B. (SiteC_EC_436–440)

Another example of a step-by-step guided practice during the workshop was the use of self-assessments to develop action plans and the use of action plans to link children's individualized education program goals to the embedded instruction learning targets or planned interactions taking place in the classroom between the teacher and child. Pulling all these documents together can be challenging for classroom teachers. As one participant shared:

> [The workshop] gives you that automatic step-by-step processing … I really like the workshop to bring out that action plan and the self-assessment … saying: Are you doing this [embedded instruction]? Do you know what a real good goal is? Do you have this in your goals? Do you have this in your targets and to … really stop and think am I really doing this in my classroom? (SiteA_SC_1929–1942)

Time for reflection and self-assessment about their embedded instruction practice supported the teachers by identifying potential growth areas and motivating engagement through the explicit alignment between the implementation supports they were receiving and the teachers' work contexts. Having time was noted as a strength in some contexts. For example, a teacher said: 'we actually practiced how to write learning targets … you actually had time to stop everything and think about it' (SiteB_EC_493–495). Yet, time was also a challenge, which will be discussed in a later section. Overall, teachers identified the systematic nature of the workshop process, including new content paired with guided practice and the tools to implement the practices in the classroom, as critical for supporting their confidence and competence to implement embedded instruction practices with children in their classrooms.

Resources

Digital video cameras, video exemplars, workshop materials and practice guides make up the resources to support practice implementation. Each of these resources and their perceived utility are explained below.

Digital video cameras. A video camera was provided to all teachers across both conditions and was introduced during the workshops. Video cameras were used for recording and reflecting on classroom practices, for reviewing and recording child data related to learning trials or for showing growth over time either in teachers' implementation of embedded instruction learning trials or in child learning or both. Although some teachers reported that more training on how to use the camera would have been helpful or indicated they and their assistants did not feel comfortable in front of the camera, other teachers embraced this resource to aid their implementation of embedded instruction. For example, teachers across coaching conditions shared the videos with parents to celebrate the success of children in their class and to illustrate growth in children's skills targeted for embedded instruction. Teachers who had not yet attempted to use the video camera expressed the desire to continue experimenting with this tool.

Exemplar videos. Exemplar videos illustrating non-study teachers implementing embedded instruction in preschool classrooms were available to all participants in the workshops, through the coaches for the on-site coaching condition and through the self-coaching website. Across both conditions, the videos were perceived as valuable. The videos showed teachers what was possible within an evidence-based embedded instruction framework, which participants overwhelmingly reported to fit with their idea of good and intentional instruction. One teacher spoke of the videos affirming and extending her instructional approach, stating: 'There was always room for improvement in different areas and when I saw the videos during the training, I was like there's something else I can do … it was a validation and an extension of what to do' (SiteA_SC_107–114). After the workshops, there were two primary ways in which teachers reported using the videos: to review practices and to communicate and model for their classroom support staff, who had not attended the workshops, how to carry out embedded instruction practices.

Workshop materials and practice guides. Teachers in both coaching conditions were provided with several embedded instruction documents for reference, planning, implementation and record-keeping; however, these tools were not perceived to be as independently useful as the exemplar videos. Participants said using these documents in the classroom required more intensive support. As previously noted, teachers in both coaching conditions improved in their ability to write higher-quality learning targets; yet their self-confidence and perceptions of the documents' utility did not match teachers' demonstrated skill capacity outside the workshop context. Teachers who were participating in self-coaching noted the difficulty they experienced in using these documents without follow-up support from an on-site coach, stating:

> When you go to the workshop and you take [the documents], you're like yes, I knew exactly what you were talking about and then you go into the classroom and you start looking at the individual children and you're like I don't understand it. There's a difference, you're in the workshop and you're in and you think you've got it and then when you sit down with the children and your [learning] targets ... there's all these little intricate things that you have to remember. (SiteA_SC_615–622)

Although participants received guidance in how to use these resources in workshops and were provided with models for reference, additional support and feedback were desired. A teacher who received on-site coaching confirmed the statement above. As she explained it:

> The individualization to be able to go, 'I don't get this. This is my question.' You can't do that with a book ... we go to all these workshops ... and it's really exciting and you learn this and you have these materials, but I just – I think any professional development model, if you don't have some kind of follow through, it's not going to get used ... There needs to be some kind of follow through to really help teach – force teachers to implement – because you want to. Our intentions are always good. But man, oh man, it just gets hard to do. So I think that coaching there was just paramount. (SiteC_EC_362–370)

Across conditions, teachers communicated the need for more intensive support when implementing new practices in the classroom. The workshop materials and initial support to demonstrate the embedded instruction practices were universally accessible; however, the utility of the materials did not transcend to the web-based self-coaching format. The teachers who received on-site coaching concurred with existing PD research about the need for follow-up and accountability to buttress the 'good intentions' of teachers who attend workshops.

Weekly check-ins

Both coaching conditions were designed to have weekly contact with teachers. Weekly contact was important to establish and maintain a connection with participating teachers and to support teachers' use of the embedded instruction practices. For teachers in the self-coaching condition, contact occurred as a weekly email that was sent from research project staff. The structured email format encouraged active participation on the self-coaching website, informed participants about new website resources and requested procedural documents from self-coaching teachers. Teachers in the on-site condition experienced weekly contact alternating between face-to-face and email coaching sessions. The bi-weekly, on-site coaching emails provided individualized notes and feedback based on the coach's on-site classroom observations and teacher–coach reflection and feedback following the observation. The emails referred teachers to specific videos, documents or other materials to implement embedded instruction practices with particular children in their classroom. The individualized nature of the on-site coaching contacts, including the personalized emails, was significant to the participants, as evidenced by their comments, demonstrating the perceived value of universally available support manifested differently in each coaching format.

Several participants in the self-coaching group stated they did not know they had received a weekly email or did not find it useful. One teacher responded, 'I was reading through a 100 e-mails at a time' (SiteA_SC_1385–1387); others noted that required administrative tasks interfered with their ability or time to view new resources posted on the website. Given the structured format of the email, one teacher commented: 'They kind of always seem to say the same thing. Towards the end I kind of just skimmed over them to make sure nothing was due' (SiteC_SC_572–574). Two teachers who reported exploring the recommended web-based resources mentioned in the emails noted that they took personal time at home, including nights and weekends, to review suggested links. Self-allocated planning time within the busy school day was difficult to prioritize for teachers engaged in self-coaching. Furthermore, some teachers in self-coaching expressed guilt over not accessing the resources shared in the email, while others appeared to develop a fear of this non-personalized email, stating: 'I didn't miss them [the emails], every time I got one I'd go oh, what did I do wrong? Or what did I forget?' (SiteA_SC_1259– 1260).

In contrast, teachers who received on-site coaching valued the personalized, on-site verbal feedback most, but also noted that customized emails served as a valuable reminder of their reflection and feedback debriefing and next steps. One teacher said:

> [the email] just reminded me again [of my responsibilities] because it is at the end of the day, you're just – [tired sigh] – It's what kept me on track, more on things that I was going to look up or work on. (SiteA_EC_1426–1427)

Although both coaching conditions had a mechanism for weekly contact and establishing a connection with teachers, the individualized contact of on-site coaching including personalized emails appeared to be more effective for reducing teachers' feelings of being overwhelmed and repositioning them as knowledgeable and capable of implementing embedded instruction.

Intensive support

Across the universal supports described above, the way in which participants accessed and used the implementation supports and resources was influenced by the coaching delivery format. Coaches were in the classroom to observe embedded instruction implementation, to model how to use the resources and to facilitate the process of applying job-aids in the classroom. The on-site coaching condition contained three critical constructs associated with participants' self-efficacy and implementation of embedded instruction that were not apparent in self-coaching participants' data: participation in a collaborative partnership; accountability for implementation; and consistent supportive and constructive feedback.

Participation in a collaborative partnership. The presence of a coach made the embedded instruction knowledge, performance feedback and support readily available, in the form of a partnership. As demonstrated previously within the learning context, teachers often felt isolated and received little external support and feedback on their teaching practices. The role of coaches fulfilled both needs. Teachers' comments regarding their coaches were overwhelmingly positive, stating they were like friends, mentors and 'one of us.' Coaching was individualized and communicated to teachers that they were doing their job well, even when they could not see it for themselves:

> We didn't get a lot of praise for what went on in the classroom. So for [my coach] to come in and say, 'Wow, what a difference, what a change.' [Was important for me] just because she saw it and now I'm seeing it. Even with kids who weren't the target. Just to get feedback that you are doing something right … I don't know about other buildings or things like that, but we don't have people walking in our room and saying those kinds of things to us. (SiteB_EC_571–576)

All coaches had expertise working with young children and were trained to implement embedded instruction; feedback was therefore perceived as both credible and non-punitive. Furthermore, coaches participated in the workshops and could facilitate teachers' application of the teaching practices by drawing on their shared learning experiences and providing specific praise. One teacher described on-site coaching as:

> a collaborative effort as opposed to, 'This is what you need to work on'; it's more like 'What do you want to work on? What do you feel?' I like that aspect. It made me think and reflect and see what I needed to do. (SiteA_EC_1263–1265)

Although support was provided around an identified set of embedded instruction practices, coaches honored teachers' self-awareness and knowledge of their classroom. Opportunities for choice further developed teachers' trust and rapport with coaches.

Accountability for implementation. Coaches sustained the teachers' learning momentum after the workshop. They played a critical role in ensuring that teachers: acknowledged their successes; accessed and implemented embedded instruction with the job-aids provided; and problem-solved when challenges arose rather than abandoning their 'good intentions.' Teachers commented that coaching sessions motivated their implementation: 'And it's easy to say, oh, let's just put it off for a couple of weeks. It'll be shoved under the table, but when you know your coach is coming, you work on it' (SiteA_EC_308–309). A few teachers questioned whether they would continue completing the tasks when they no longer received coaching, because the level of accountability would decrease.

Feedback was accessible. Coaches provided both supportive and constructive feedback, which scaffolded teachers to align their practice with the evidence-based processes of embedded instruction and increase their fidelity of implementation. Teachers admitted they were unsure about receiving constructive feedback, fearing it might be punitive, but were surprised by the partnership they formed with the coach and how they came to value their presence and the supportive and constructive feedback provided:

> I [liked] having someone observe … to see what we live and then also be able to say, 'Hey, this was okay' or good or whatever, but 'This is a little way you could tweak this or you could have someone help in this situation' … that immediate feedback was nice. (SiteB_EC_740–746)

THE PROFESSIONAL DEVELOPMENT OF EARLY YEARS EDUCATORS

Teachers particularly commented on the importance of feedback from the coach that included implementation data and the summary email. Teachers indicated that feedback provided them with the motivation to continue implementing embedded instruction and specific suggestions on areas to improve.

In contrast to the experiences of teachers in the on-site coaching condition, teachers in the self-coaching condition did not experience a sense of partnership. They wanted more accountability for their implementation and external feedback from a coach. One teacher noted: 'Help would have been nice. To have somebody go through your learning targets and say hmm, "Let's look at these again." and "How can we maybe improve the learning targets and make them more specific to what we're seeing?"' (SiteA_SC_628–631). Another indicated:

> it wasn't feasible for me because I had to rely on myself to do it. If someone else was to come in and I had to have time, then I would have consciously taken that time. Otherwise I don't do it. (SiteC_SC_576–578)

Experiences of the self-coaching teachers highlight their longing for comparable types of intensive supports provided by on-site coaching – partnership, accountability, external feedback – within the online environment.

Environmental reinforcers

Participation led to perceived symbiotic changes in teachers' thinking and practice across the on-site coaching and self-coaching conditions (see Figure 1). When the teachers changed their practices in response to their new learning, they received natural reinforcement through interactions with people in their work environment. Positive environmental feedback reinforced the teachers' implementation, making the new practices a valued part of classroom routines; whereas negative responses or an absence of a positive response (i.e. recognition for effort) led teachers to abandon practices and materials, concluding they were ineffective. This section describes the significance of the transactional relationship between teachers' changed or unchanged practices and their contextual work environment.

One of the most significant changes reported was how teachers perceived the children in their classroom. They moved beyond conventional labels (e.g. voluntary pre-kindergarten, exceptional student education, dual language learners) to seeing children's unique abilities as assets and their needs as opportunities for development of teachers' skills in embedded instruction and, in turn, child-learning outcomes. Teachers who participated in both coaching conditions described: being more aware of their children's individual preferences and abilities; being more intentional in their lesson planning; and communicating lesson plans and embedded instruction learning targets with assistants and other members of children's support team(s). The ability to improve child outcomes through embedded instruction learning trials reinforced teachers' use of the practices in powerful ways. One teacher described her multifaceted growth process:

> I think that it's made me a better special education teacher in a full inclusion environment. I think that piece is easily lost and I should say I kind of move my kids through their days and saw them being successful, but now I *know* they're successful. Now I'm probably deeper into my IEPs (individualized education programs) than I have been able to be [in the past], which is good. It almost made me feel bad at the beginning, because I don't [*sic*] know these kids as well as I thought I did. So, it went from feeling kind of guilty to realizing that there is a way for me to do both things [teach

children with disabilities and their typically developing peers] and do both things well. I think it brought me balance. (SiteC_EC_180–186)

Parents and colleagues also reinforced teachers' perceived value of the changes taking place in the classroom. Some teachers described how celebrating successes with enthusiastic parents and being approached by colleagues for tips played critical roles in building self-efficacy and the motivation to continue implementing embedded instruction. For example, after reflecting on the excitement of a student's increasing language, one teacher shared: 'he's talking two or three words ... I feel confident ... and today my colleagues ask ... can you help me with this child' (SiteA_EC_154–160). The combined positive feedback and emergent professional network for the continued pursuit of enhanced fidelity of implementation of practices by colleagues was important for teachers as they spent a reported 10+ additional hours a week planning, implementing and evaluating their embedded instruction practices.

Simultaneously, some teachers' responses revealed how classroom and school environments have the potential to challenge teachers' implementation. Across conditions, teachers noted time as one of the most difficult aspects of implementation to navigate. This challenge arose in relation to: familiarity with resources and how to access them; working with paraprofessionals; and balancing the provision of individualized instruction and the ability to meet all students' needs. Teachers in the self-coaching condition expressed feeling challenged more often than teachers who received on-site coaching. For example, one teacher explained how the absence of administrative and collegial support was a significant deterrent to her continued efforts to implement embedded instruction practices as intended:

I was sat down by [my administrator] and told that maybe I was focusing too much on the ESE (exceptional student education) children and I needed to focus more on the other students in the classroom, that the parents had concerns that I was spending more time on the focus children than I was on the other students. (SiteA_SC_367–396)

In the absence of a professional network or coach, teachers reported they did not possess the needed support for trouble-shooting how to respond to the difficulties of integrating new practices into their daily routine. Furthermore, they lacked the confidence and the experience to defend their use of embedded instruction practices as they worked out the kinks.

Challenges and implications for practice

The social validity data gathered in the focus groups afforded insight into opportunities for improving future PD including workshops and coaching delivery formats. Two major themes emerged: the use of the self-coaching website and associated materials was dependent on the quality of available equipment and participants' comfort with technology; and participants sought professional networks to augment their self-coaching.

Technology

Although technology has the potential to increase access to resources offered through web-based platforms (Dede *et al.* 2009), it also requires initial investments in the form of equipment and training. This study provided digital video recorders for teachers to upload videos and a face-to-face orientation to the web-based delivery format. Despite the technical support provided, however, computer software and bandwidth were reported to be somewhat persistent challenges. The frustration of not being able to efficiently access the site was a challenge for some participants. One participant noted:

> I didn't have a computer that was functioning well … I was behind and I never seemed to get caught up … I didn't discuss it with anyone, because I felt like I was a naughty child not doing my work … I'm already behind so let me just continue with what I know how to do. (SiteA_SC_ 264–271)

In this reflection we hear 'good intentions' mixed with fear of punishment and a desire to feel competent. Difficulty with technology demonstrates the importance of knowing participants' learning histories and work context to ensure support is readily available, especially when introducing new knowledge (i.e. embedded instruction practices) in combination with a new learning format (i.e. a web-based self-coaching delivery). Even those who expressed comfort and a commitment to using the website noted technological difficulties. For example, one teacher said:

> I had trouble at my school watching the videos and stuff. My computer would just freeze … I could do it at home, but I couldn't do it at school. I tried to share it with [my teaching assistants], and it was just so [motioning slow] – you'd get half way and then it would just freeze. … So that was frustrating when I wanted to share [the videos]. (SiteC_SC_63–68)

Based on this feedback, it became apparent that prior to engaging teachers in web-based PD, providers should: assess teachers' technological self-efficacy and baseline knowledge of the delivery format; make on-site assistance available; and work with district personnel to ensure access to current technology, required software and adequate bandwidth.

Professional networks

Across conditions, collaboration with colleagues who had a shared vision for high-quality instruction around embedded instruction practices surfaced as participants discussed potential supports for continued implementation. As one teacher shared: 'I think it would be nice for us to get to talk and then we could build up a community ourselves … then maybe if we had questions, we could e-mail each other about it' (SiteA_EC_400–403). Another participant concurred, adding: 'we could be each other's support system' (SiteA_EC_405). Echoing the need to circumvent feelings of isolation associated with often being the only ECSE teacher at their school, one teacher suggested a discussion board might allow teachers to flexibly share ideas and resources. Teachers felt a professional network could provide additional accountability too:

> It would be nice to have all the embedded instruction people … to discuss what we're going to do for the upcoming year, how we're going to implement. Maybe even make ourselves partner up with somebody and make ourselves check-in, 'Are you doing it?' Just saying, 'What are you doing, how is it coming?' (SiteA_SC_1754–1760)

The potential face-to-face, online and blended formats for implementation support described by participants across conditions demonstrate that teachers want a professional network for support, sustained momentum, continued learning and accountability. Future PD involving coaching, especially when adopting a web-based delivery format, could structure a supportive partnership or professional network where participants can engage with colleagues about their experiences as they implement new practices.

Discussion

Teachers are situated within complex environmental systems, which facilitate or constrain access to both human and material resources (Bronfenbrenner 1979). The experiences of focus group participants offered important insights into: the intersection of evidence-based practices and the organizational and ecological realities of classrooms; the acceptability, feasibility and utility of two variant forms of practice-focused coaching; and the required level of support to implement a multicomponent intervention such as embedded instruction. Currently, the gap between research and effective implementation of evidence-based practices within the classroom context has been documented to be in excess of 20 years (Metz *et al.* 2013). Odom (2009) contends the extent to which educators perceive new practices to be useful and accessible impacts their motivation to learn and their ability to implement the practices. Therefore, it is essential for PD providers to make explicit and intentional connections between evidence-based practices and the classroom context to increase effective implementation. To accomplish this, PD providers require knowledge about: for whom practices are likely to 'fit,' including teachers' beliefs and values and their classroom and organizational context; what teachers need to know and be able to do to implement; and how to facilitate the learning process (National Professional Development Center on Inclusion 2008). For example, within this study it became apparent that self-coaching in a web-based delivery format required individual participants to have a strong grasp of the content, self-motivation and technological self-efficacy to successfully access the available supports. However, even teachers who possessed all of these characteristics still described implementation to be challenging in the absence of a network of support or accountability. Despite the potential for broader access with web-based delivery formats (Dede *et al.* 2009), the present study highlights the importance of examining the mechanisms that result in effective PD across delivery formats (Snyder *et al.* 2011).

Moreover, McCollum and Catlett (1997) suggest a relationship exists between what teachers need to know and be able to do (i.e. implementation of evidence-based practices) and how the learning process is facilitated. That is, the degree of teacher change:

> is assumed to be related to the degree of active involvement that the participant has in the training process, with active involvement defined as the extent to which the learning activity allows the participant to experience knowledge, skills, and attitudes in the same way they will be required in the work setting. (McCollum and Catlett 1997, p. 115)

Teachers who received on-site coaching had sustained opportunities to experience the use of embedded instruction practices in the context of a supportive coaching partnership with regular supportive and constructive feedback, which facilitated their increased level of implementation.

Recognizing that more intensive forms of PD are likely to require additional human and material resources, sustainable and scalable implementation of these delivery formats might impede their adoption. Implementation science has emerged in response to the research-to-practice gap and seeks to inform organizations and providers of early childhood education about a framework designed to install and improve infrastructures required to effectively adopt evidence-based practices. This framework includes five stages: exploration; installation; initial implementation; full implementation; and sustainability (Metz *et al.* 2013). Through these stages, organizations can ensure individual PD initiatives are responsive to who, what and how learning takes place; but can also establish the ecological system for supporting PD providers and teachers.

Children and teachers will always be situated within complex systems; however, it is the pathways forged through shared understanding toward common goals, acknowledgement of teachers' lived experiences and the establishment of intentional infrastructures to support those goals and experiences that will close the research-to-practice gap with the aid of well-aligned PD models. The present study has provided teachers' insights into their lived experiences of practice-focused PD and coaching while contrasting these experiences across delivery formats to contribute to the theoretical and empirical PD evidence base.

Disclosure statement

No potential conflict of interest was reported by the authors.

Funding

Work reported in this paper was supported, in part, by a grant from the National Center for Special Education Research, Institute of Education Sciences, US Department of Education to the University of Florida [R324A070008 Patricia Snyder, Principal Investigator]. The opinions expressed are those of the authors, not the funding agency.

References

Artman-Meeker, K.M. and Hemmeter, M.L., 2012. Effects of training and feedback on teachers' use of classroom preventive practices. *Topics in early childhood special education*, 33 (2), 112–123.

Blumer, H., 1969. The methodological position of symbolic interactionism. *In: Symbolic interactionism: perspective and method*. Oakland, CA: University of California Press, 1–60.

Brantlinger, E., *et al.*, 2005. Qualitative studies in special education. *Exceptional children*, 71 (2), 195–207.

Bronfenbrenner, U., 1979. *The ecology of human development: experiments by nature and design*. Cambridge, MA: Harvard University Press.

Charmaz, K., 1996. The search for meanings – grounded theory. *In:* J.A. Smith, R. Harre, and L. Van Langenhove, eds. *Rethinking methods in psychology*. London: Sage, 27–49.

Charmaz, K., 2006. *Constructing grounded theory: a practical guide through qualitative analysis*. Newbury Park, CA: Pine Forge Press.

Creswell, J.W., 2013. *Research design: qualitative, quantitative, and mixed methods approaches*. Thousand Oaks, CA: Sage.

Crotty, M., 2011. *The foundations of social research: meaning and perspective in the research process*. Thousand Oaks, CA: Sage.

Dede, C., *et al.*, 2009. A research agenda for online teacher professional development. *Journal of teacher education*, 60 (1), 8–19.

Desimone, L.M., 2009. Improving impact studies of teachers' professional development: toward better conceptualizations and measures. *Educational researcher*, 38 (3), 181–199.

Diamond, K.E. and Powell, D.R., 2011. An iterative approach to the development of a professional development intervention for Head Start teachers. *Journal of early intervention*, 33 (1), 75–93.

Diamond, K.E., *et al.*, 2013. *Synthesis of IES research on early intervention and early childhood education*. Washington, DC: National Center for Special Education Research, Institute of Education Sciences, US Department of Education.

Fox, L., *et al.*, 2011. Coaching early childhood special educators to implement a comprehensive model for promoting young children's social competence. *Topics in early childhood special education*, 31 (3), 178–192.

Glaser, B.G., 1978. *Theoretical sensitivity: advances in the methodology of grounded theory*. Vol. 2. Mill Valley, CA: Sociology Press.

Glaser, B.G. and Strauss, A.L., 2009. *The discovery of grounded theory: strategies for qualitative research*. Piscataway, NJ: Transaction.

Hemmeter, M.L., *et al.*, 2011. Impact of performance feedback delivered via electronic mail on preschool teachers' use of descriptive praise. *Early childhood research quarterly*, 26 (1), 96–109.

Joyce, B.R. and Showers, B., 2002. *Student achievement through staff development*. Alexandria, VA: Association for Supervision and Curriculum Development.

McCollum, J.A. and Catlett, C., 1997. Designing effective personnel preparation for early intervention: theoretical frameworks. *In*: P. Winton, *et al.*, eds. *Reforming personnel preparation in early intervention: issues, models, and practical strategies*. Baltimore, MD: Brookes, 105–126.

McCollum, J.A., Hemmeter, M.L., and Hsieh, W.Y., 2013. Coaching teachers for emergent literacy instruction using performance-based feedback. *Topics in early childhood special education*, 33 (1), 28–37.

Metz, A. and Bartley, L., 2012. Active implementation frameworks for program success. *Zero to three*, 32 (4), 11–18.

Metz, A., *et al.*, 2013. The key components of successful implementation. *In*: T. Halle, A. Metz, and I. Martinez-Beck, eds. *Applying implementation science in early childhood programs and systems*. Baltimore, MD: Brookes, 21–42.

National Professional Development Center on Inclusion, 2008. *What do we mean by professional development in the early childhood field?* Chapel Hill: The University of North Carolina, FPG Child Development Institute.

Odom, S.L., 2009. The tie that binds: evidence-based practice, implementation science, and outcomes for children. *Topics in early childhood special education*, 29 (1), 53–61.

Pianta, R.C., *et al.*, 2005. Features of pre-kindergarten programs, classrooms, and teachers: do they predict observed classroom quality and child-teacher interactions? *Applied developmental science*, 9 (3), 144–159.

Rhodes, H. and Huston, A., 2012. Building the workforce our youngest children deserve. *Social policy report*, 26 (1), 3–32.

Rudd, L.C., *et al.*, 2009. Professional development + coaching = enhanced teaching: increasing usage of math mediated language in preschool classrooms. *Early childhood education journal*, 37 (1), 63–69.

Snyder, P., *et al.*, 2009. *Coaching preschool teachers to use embedded instruction practices* [Manual and coaching protocols]. College of Education, University of Florida, Gainesville, FL.

Snyder, P., Hemmeter, M.L., and McLaughlin, T., 2011. Professional development in early childhood intervention: where we stand on the silver anniversary of PL 99-457. *Journal of early intervention*, 33 (4), 357–370.

Snyder, P., *et al.*, 2012. Characterizing key features of the early childhood professional development literature. *Infants and young children*, 25 (3), 188–212.

Snyder, P., *et al.*, 2013. Embedded instruction to support early learning in response to intervention frameworks. *In:* V. Buysse and E. Peisner-Feinberg, eds. *Handbook of response-to-intervention in early childhood*. Baltimore, MD: Brookes, 283–298.

Takanishi, R., 2011. Transforming America's primary education system for the 21st century: integrating K-12 education with pre-kindergarten. *In*: E. Zigler, W.S. Gilliam, and W.S. Barnett, eds. *The pre-K debates: current controversies and issues*. Baltimore, MD: Brookes, 181–184.

Vo, A.K., Sutherland, K.S., and Conroy, M.A., 2012. Best in class: a classroom-based model for ameliorating problem behavior in early childhood settings. *Psychology in the schools*, 49 (5), 402–415.

Winton, P.J., Snyder, P., and Goffin, S., in press. Beyond the status quo: rethinking professional development for early childhood teachers. *In:* L. Couse and S. Recchia, eds. *Handbook of early childhood teacher education*. New York, NY: Routledge.

Zaslow, M., *et al.*, 2010. *Toward the identification of features of effective professional development for early childhood educators: literature review* [online]. Washington, DC: Office of Planning, Evaluation and Policy Development, US Department of Education. Available from: http://www.ed.gov/about/offices/list/opepd/ppss/reports.html [Accessed 16 February 2015].

Zigler, E., Gilliam, W.S., and Barnett, W.S., eds., 2011. *The pre-K debates: current controversies and issues*. Baltimore, MD: Brookes.

The nature of professional learning communities in New Zealand early childhood education: an exploratory study

Sue Cherrington and Kate Thornton

Professional learning communities are receiving increasing attention within the schooling sector but empirical research into their development and use within early childhood education contexts is rare. This paper reports initial findings of an exploratory study into the development of professional learning communities in New Zealand's early childhood sector. The study found that the characteristics of effective school-based professional learning communities are also applicable to early childhood settings, and that development of supportive structural and relational conditions is required if the promise of professional learning communities evident in the schooling sector is to be achieved in early childhood education.

Introduction

Internationally, professional learning (PL) in both the schooling and early childhood education (ECE) sectors has received widespread attention from policy-makers and researchers over recent years (for example, Mitchell and Cubey 2003, Desimone 2009, Sheridan *et al.* 2009, Thornton 2009, Cherrington and Thornton 2013, Earley and Porritt 2014). Internationally, PL activities are also described as professional development and continuing professional development, depending on the context. In this article, we use the term PL except where the literature cited uses an alternate term. Opfer and Pedder's review of research into effective PL found that:

> teachers learn most effectively when activities require them to engage with material of practice ..., when activity is school-based and integrated into the daily work of teachers ..., and when the pedagogy of PD [professional development] is active and requires teachers to learn in ways that reflect how they should teach pupils. (2011, p. 385)

Analysis of successful continuing professional development projects in British schools identified several key features, including ensuring collaborative approaches to continuing professional development, having a focus on pupil outcomes and understanding how to evaluate impact (Earley and Porritt 2009, p. 137).

In the early childhood (EC) context, Mitchell and Cubey's (2003) best evidence synthesis of effective professional development linked to enhanced pedagogy and children's learning emphasised the situated nature of effective professional development and the importance of participants actively investigating their own practices through analysing data collected from their settings, and through critical reflection on their practices. Factors influencing the extent to which New Zealand PL programmes have enhanced EC teachers' practices are evident from evaluations of such programmes (for example, Cherrington and Wansbrough 2007) and the Centre of Innovation programme (Gibbs and Poskitt 2009). These factors include the influence of positional and pedagogical leaders, the existence of strong internal features (such as a positive team culture, supportive management, strong team motivation, and ownership of the PL focus), supportive workplace conditions and advice and support from outside the EC setting.

Empirical studies of PL in EC are predominately small-scale, qualitative projects focused on particular approaches to PL rather than on enhancing children's learning and developmental outcomes. Such studies include Thornton's (2009) study of blended action learning to support leadership development and Mitchell's (2003) study of an EC teacher network using an action research (AR) methodology. Several studies have utilised a 'community of practice' (Lave and Wenger 1991) framework to explicate the situated nature of PL within the EC context (for example, Ryder 2007). Other scholars, such as Edwards and Nuttall (2009, p. 2), advocate a post-developmental approach to PL which recognises that 'the nature, processes, and purposes of professional learning are highly dependent upon specific social, cultural, economic, historical and interpersonal contexts'.

The study reported here focused on a particular approach to PL that has received considerable attention in the literature on PL in schooling contexts but which has been largely absent from the ECE literature: professional learning communities (PLCs). Our interest in PLCs emerged from our extensive professional backgrounds in EC teacher preparation and PL. Further, we surmised that PLCs could make a useful contribution to a sector achieving variable success in prioritising and ensuring that learning occurs for all children (Education Review Office 2013), and where gathering and critically analysing robust data about children's learning is not the norm. In exploring the nature of EC PLCs in New Zealand, we hoped to examine how contextual factors unique to EC settings (such as variable levels of teacher preparation, team teaching approaches and limited opportunities for team discussions and continuing professional learning) influenced the development and activities of four PLCs and enhanced children's learning. Four specific research questions were asked:

- What factors contribute to effective PLCs in ECE?
- How does involvement in an ECE PLC support changes in teacher practices that lead to improved teaching and enhanced learning?
- What organisational and structural factors influence the effectiveness of PLCs in ECE?
- What relational and interpersonal factors influence the effectiveness of PLCs in ECE?

This article introduces this exploratory study and discusses what characterised these PLCs, together with conditions that hindered or enabled their development.

Professional learning communities

Grossman *et al.* asked, 'what distinguishes a community of teachers from a group of teachers sitting in a room?' (2001, p. 987). In their work on teacher community, they

THE PROFESSIONAL DEVELOPMENT OF EARLY YEARS EDUCATORS

suggested 'such communities must be equally concerned with student learning and with teacher learning' (2001, p. 952). Hipp and Huffman's recent definition of PLCs as 'professional educators working collectively and purposefully to create and sustain a culture of learning for students and adults' (2010, p. 12) highlights the intentional and continuous focus on learning success for all students. Two models of PLCs exist: school-wide (or sub-sets thereof) PLCs that have emerged primarily from the school reform literature (for example, DuFour and Eaker 1998); and subject-discipline PLCs such as those evident in video clubs (for example, Borko *et al.* 2008).

Characteristics of professional learning communities

Consensus is building about what characterises PLCs, particularly for school-based PLCs – they possess: a shared vision and values; shared and supportive leadership; the application of collective learning; shared personal practices; and supportive structural and relational conditions (DuFour and Eaker 1998, Hord and Sommers 2008, Hipp and Huffman 2010). In addition, DuFour and Eaker (1998) suggest that PLCs are focused on continuous improvement and are both action and results orientated, whilst Stoll *et al.* (2006) also highlight mutual trust, respect and support amongst members, inclusive membership and openness, networks and partnerships.

For school-based PLCs, creating a shared vision and values builds shared ownership and commitment amongst community members. Hipp and Huffman suggest that developing this vision is the first task for a PLC as it leads 'to binding norms of behaviour that the staff support' (2010, p. 5). PLC leaders play a key role (DuFour and Eaker 1998, Hipp and Huffman 2010) in engaging members in creating a shared vision and values and then using these as the ongoing focus for change. The importance of shared and supportive leadership is noted within the PLC literature. Leadership is not located solely with the positional leader; rather, the adoption of a distributive model in which 'power, authority, and decision-making are shared and encouraged' (Hord and Sommers 2008, p. 10) builds capacity and commitment to the PLC's work (Stoll *et al.* 2006, Hipp and Huffman 2010). Dufour and Eaker (1998, p. 196) suggest that positional leaders use a 'loose/tight' leadership style, 'encouraging autonomy while at the same time demanding adherence to shared vision and values' in order to empower PLC members.

The characteristic of collective learning combines a focus on continuous learning (Hord and Sommers 2008) and the collaborative nature of that learning in order to improve practice and student outcomes (DuFour and Eaker 1998). Hipp and Huffman (2010) suggest teachers learning together create a powerful sense of community. Closely aligned with the characteristic of collective learning is that of shared personal practices. McLaughlin and Talbert (2006) describe this as de-privatising practice where teachers observe, whether directly or via video-recordings, each other's teaching, share new practices, give feedback (Hipp and Huffman 2010) and reflect collectively on their practice (Hord and Sommers 2008).

Effective, sustainable PLCs require supportive structural and relational conditions: Hipp and Huffman suggest these conditions are 'the glue that holds all other dimensions together' (2010, p. 19). Structural conditions include providing regular time and space for members to easily meet and talk together, and offering support through external facilitators, district offices and networks (Stoll *et al.* 2006, Hord and Sommers 2008). Further, school-based PLCs benefit when the school is smaller and members teach in close proximity, have collaborative teaching roles and responsibilities, autonomous school units and effective communication systems (Hipp and Huffman 2010). Central to supportive relational conditions is trust and respect between group members; building and maintaining trust is a key obligation for positional leaders (Hord and Sommers 2008, Hipp and Huffman 2010) so that members feel safe participating in activities where their practice is de-privatised. Similarly, managing group dynamics and power relationships amongst members is important (Dana and Yendol-Hoppey 2008).

When investigating the relevance of these characteristics to the New Zealand EC context, Thornton and Wansbrough (2012) found that although respondents to their national survey felt their centres reflected many PLC characteristics, five aspects required strengthening: effective professional leadership; opportunities for feedback, coaching and mentoring; strengthening relationships with family/*whānau*[1] to keep children's learning to the fore; embedding change into the service's culture; and prioritising time for shared reflection and meaningful conversations around learning and teaching (Thornton and Wansbrough 2012).

Models of professional learning community development

Several models have been developed to explain how PLCs develop and evolve over time. Grossman *et al.* (2001) theorised that teacher professional communities move from a beginning stage through an evolving to a mature stage across four key dimensions: group identity formation and norms of interaction; addressing different subject matter emphases across disciplines; negotiating tensions between student-focused and teacher-focused learning; and communal responsibilities for individual growth. Across these dimensions, teachers move from an individual to a collective orientation, become more willing and able to acknowledge and address conflict, and accept and appreciate divergent ideas. In their three-stage model, McLaughlin and Talbert (2006) suggest that teacher learning communities at a novice stage struggle to use inquiry processes, such as collecting and analysing data. Intermediate-stage communities use inquiry cycle processes more effectively and become less reliant on external facilitators but lack 'a strong norm of collective responsibility and service ethic to drive and sustain their progress' (McLaughlin and Talbert 2006, p. 33). In contrast, in the advanced stage the whole school has an evidence-based approach with teachers 'collecting and analysing data, and taking action based on that analysis' (2006, p. 34). Martin-Kniep (2008) suggests a continuum of four levels – beginning, developing, established and systemic – that PLCs go through as they develop and mature. As PLCs evolve through these stages, members move from focusing on their own individual self-development to being fully committed to the achievement of the wider organisation's goals, and to working collaboratively and reflectively with others. Finally, Hipp *et al.*'s (2008) investigation of how two schools recultured themselves as PLCs used data collected in an initial two-year project together with follow-up data three years later. Drawing on Fullan's change model, whereby innovations move through three distinct levels – initiation, implementation and institutionalisation – Hipp *et al.* found that:

> The process of reculturing schools as professional learning communities is a journey as evidenced by the time and energy exerted to move schools from one level to the next – from initiation to implementation to institutionalization or sustainability. Some schools take two small steps forward – one step back; some move along in the efforts at a steady pace; others seem to stall never really reculturing; and others beat the odds

and persist (Fullan 2000). Each school is unique and cultures develop organically, thus affecting the entire school community. (2008, p. 192)

Methodology

Research design

An interpretive paradigm underpinned this study because our intention was to understand the complex nature of PLCs and how they develop within the EC sector. Interpretive research endeavours to 'understand and interpret the world in terms of its actors' (Cohen *et al.* 2000, p. 28), hence the choice of mainly qualitative data collection methods. Four PLCs were established and studied over a period of 10 months using a case-study approach. Merriam (1998) notes that case studies are appropriate when processes rather than outcomes are the focus of investigation and that their heuristic quality enhances understanding of the phenomena being studied.

In addition to the case-study methodology used by the researchers, PLC members were simultaneously investigating aspects of their teaching practice using AR. This approach was chosen as it was perceived most likely to meet the aims of a PLC; that is, an intentional focus on teacher and student learning. AR has been described as a systematic process involving action that is informed, purposeful, committed and intentional (McNiff and Whitehead 2010) and is particularly suitable for teachers investigating their own practice.

The two researchers in this study facilitated the PLCs in addition to researching the case studies. This joint role was similar to that taken by the first researcher in her doctoral research (Thornton 2009) and has been termed that of engaged researcher (Nandhakumar and Jones 1997). Our activities as facilitators and as researchers overlapped in many of our interactions with participants. This overlap and the need to frequently move between such activities are recognised by Nandhakumar and Jones (1997), who suggest these roles cannot be viewed as discrete. An example of this overlap was the use of knowledge gained about team dynamics from participants' reflective journals when facilitating the PLC meetings. Factors that helped us balance these roles included our previous PL facilitation experience, our professional credibility within the local ECE sector and the use of an online site for gathering and storing data.

Research participants

Two PLCs established for this project were whole-centre PLCs where the entire teaching team within a single EC centre focused on investigating an area of interest determined by that centre. Two other PLCs were clusters of pairs of teachers from several centres, one focused on strengthening leadership and one on enhancing reflective practices, reflecting the researchers' expertise. Within these cluster PLC foci, each participating centre identified a specific question for investigation. The two structures reflected typical current practices for PL delivery within the New Zealand EC sector and were familiar to potential participants. We were interested in exploring how these organisational structures – whole-centre versus cluster PLCs – influenced their development and effectiveness. An invitation to register interest in participating in this project was emailed to EC centres in the wider provincial region in which our university is located. Services were able to indicate interest in participating in either

PLC model. Two centres indicated interest in participating as whole-centre PLCs and were both selected. Ten centres initially indicated interest in participating in the cluster PLCs; of these, one was declined approval to participate by their umbrella organisation and another elected not to proceed due to other workplace priorities. The remaining eight centres were able to join the cluster of their choice.

The four PLCs established and their focus questions are outlined in Table 1. Pseudonyms have been used for each centre and teacher throughout.

Data collection tools and procedures

Data collection occurred in three phases over a 10-month period in 2012, as outlined in Table 2.

The meetings with each PLC followed a timeline developed to give structure to the PLC process (see Table 3) drawing on Easton's (2011) processes for designing and developing PLCs. Each researcher facilitated meetings for two PLC groups, supported by a research assistant. Between meetings, PLC groups worked on an individual AR investigation, collecting data and trying out changes in their practices agreed to at the PLC meetings. Support for their data collection activities was available from the research assistant who was able to video-record practice and collect observational data, at the participants' request.

Alongside this process, each PLC had its own Moodle[2] site where resources relating to PLCs and to their AR investigations were uploaded, and members documented their AR journeys. Each member kept an individual reflective journal, visible only to them and the researchers. Reflective questions were posted each month to support participants in this process. This data source was particularly valuable in gaining honest responses about the nature of the relational and interpersonal factors influencing the effectiveness of PLCs.

Data analysis

This article draws on the qualitative data only. Minutes of PLC meetings and the group interview were kept by our research assistant; audio-recordings of these sessions were also transcribed. These data, together with participants' reflective journals and online discussions of their AR projects, were coded against characteristics of effective PLCs identified in the literature: collective learning and application; shared personal practice; shared and supportive leadership; shared vision and values; supportive conditions – relationships; and supportive conditions – structural. In addition, in a process referred to as thematic analysis (Braun and Clarke 2006), data were carefully read and re-read to identify factors that supported or hindered development of the PLCs, together with changes in practices or development of new practices.

Results

The four PLC groups in this study developed and worked in quite unique ways. The pre-existing characteristics of individual members (and, with regards to the two whole-centre PLCs, their characteristics as a team) were influential in how teachers engaged in their PLC and in how we planned and facilitated meetings. The analysis of each PLC presented below highlights how each demonstrated some but not all of the characteristics of PLCs outlined earlier, in quite distinctive ways.

Table 1. Participating PLCs.

PLC	Characteristics	PLC focus
Pīwakawaka Early Learning Centre (PLC)	• Whole-centre PLC • Full-day programme for children aged six months to five years • Teachers worked in two teams: one with children younger than two years and one with older children	• How can we develop our practices in *tikanga me te reo Māori*[a]?
Riroriro PLC	• Whole-centre PLC • Full-day programme for children aged six months to five years • Teachers worked in two teams: one with children younger than two years and one with older children	• How can we make the most of rituals and routines to include all children and create a peaceful environment within the centre?
Leadership cluster	• 11 teachers from 5 centres • Mix of full-day and part-day programmes	• Hioho ELC: what leadership strategies do teachers need to use to empower children to practice *ako*[b]? • Miromiro ELC: how can the Miromiro ELC teachers help lead the development of a collaborative community planning process, around working together to ensure 'School readiness for our children'? • Korimako ELC: how can we encourage leadership amongst our teaching team? • Mohua ELC: how can we develop leadership in the teaching team? • Whio ELC: how does our practice recognise and foster children's leadership?
Reflective practice cluster	• Eight teachers from three centres • Mix of full-day and part-day programmes	• Ocean ELC: how effective is our culture within our team meeting to enable us to critically look at our own and each other's practice to enhance learning and teaching? • Ngā Putiputi ELC: how can we enhance our team's critical reflections on our investigative project approach to strengthen intentional teaching? • Totara ELC: how can we enhance our teaching practice to support children's social competence?

Notes: [a]Māori language and culture.
[b]*Ako* is a Māori word meaning teaching and learning.

THE PROFESSIONAL DEVELOPMENT OF EARLY YEARS EDUCATORS

Table 2. Data collection phases.

Project activities	Time period	Data collected
Initial online survey (adapted from Hipp and Huffman 2010)	February (prior to seminar)	• Quantitative and qualitative responses
Seminar introducing project (addressing AR for teacher projects; PLCs; ethical aspects; using Moodle; research expectations)	February	• None
Five meetings for each PLC	March–July	• Meeting notes • Transcripts of meetings from audio and video recordings
Online activities using Moodle	March–July	• Forums, blogs and reflections
Follow-up online survey	August	• Quantitative and qualitative responses
Group interview	November	• Meeting notes • Transcripts of audio and video recordings

Table 3. Timeline for the PLC process.

Stage of PLC		PLC meetings
Defining	• Creating shared meaning around the topic	Meeting One
	• Formulating overall AR question	
	• Identifying next steps	
	• Gathering evidence: identifying current practices and underlying assumptions	Own centre work
Exploring	• Sharing reflections on current practices and assumptions	Meeting Two
	• Refining research questions	
	• Identifying resources and next steps	
Experimenting	• Deciding on actions	Own centre work
	• Exploring new practices	
	• Sharing new practices	Meeting Three
	• Identifying next steps	Meeting Four
Reflecting	• Documenting new practices	Own centre work
	• What is working?	
	• Where to next?	
Sharing	• How has working in a PLC enhanced our teaching and learning practices?	Meeting Five

Note: Model adapted from Easton's (2011) processes for designing and developing PLCs.

Pīwakawaka whole-centre PLC

Pīwakawaka PLC's development was dominated by pre-existing relational and leadership issues. The head teacher volunteered the centre for the research but did not take an active role in the PLC process, allowing leadership from other team members to emerge. Early reflections by team members and discussions during PLC meetings indicated both a level of excitement at the possibilities for PL and recognition of trust and relational issues within the team, as illustrated by the following reflective journal entry:

> Trust is an important issue, and one I thought we all shared in equal amounts, however the deeper into the project we go I have found this is not so. However I do believe this action research will provide a good opportunity to build and work on trust within staff. (Frances)

Several suggestions for their AR focus were offered by team members and the decision to work on developing their use of *tikanga me te reo* (language and culture) Māori practices appeared to be a deliberate choice to focus on a 'neutral' topic. All New Zealand ECE services are required to focus on bicultural practice as part of their commitment to the Treaty of Waitangi and their implementation of the EC curriculum document *Te Whāriki* (New Zealand Ministry of Education 1996). Their choice enabled a relatively new team member to adopt a strong leadership role, based on her expertise in bicultural practices.

Developing a shared vision of how *tikanga me te reo Māori* would be evident within the centre emerged as a key task for this team, and was a central focus in early meetings alongside recording and analysing their current practices. By the end of their third meeting, the following vision statement had been drafted:

> Children, whānau, staff and visitors will know/understand the unique place of te reo me nga tikanga Maori through experiencing daily life at Pīwakawaka ELC.

Some progress was made in working towards this vision and in how they worked together as a PLC; however, contributions and progress were uneven. Thus, the characteristics of collective learning and shared personal practice were only evident amongst some participants. Successes were had in trialling approaches reflective of *tikanga* when welcoming new children and their families and farewelling those off to school, but other shifts in practice were primarily individual rather than collective changes. For example, individual teachers increased their use of *te reo Māori*, actively seeking guidance on pronunciation and sentence structure from the teacher leading the project. Other planned actions, such as visiting the local *marae*[3], did not occur.

Similarly, variable progress was made in addressing relational issues within the team and in developing trust and collegial practices. Members became more willing to disagree and offer alternative viewpoints, and some felt that discussions were more collaborative and that trust was building. A reflection written six months after the beginning of the project explained this progress:

> I feel that establishing ourselves as a PLC has been the key to enabling teachers to voice their opinions about best practice and hopefully there will be other areas we can open up to discourse and examination, so that our practice becomes a constantly evolving enterprise. (Chloe)

Others experienced greater tension and found themselves feeling increasingly isolated within their sub-team, but did not voice these feelings outside their reflective journals. The effectiveness of this PLC was also impacted on by external issues including the absence of the head teacher due to commitments in the wider organisation and the temporary relocation of the service for unexpected renovations.

By the end of the project, the Pīwakawaka PLC had made some gains but was not in a position to be described as a true PLC. Rather, elements of what Grossman *et al.* (2001) describe as a pseudo-community were apparent in how these teachers worked together because they were still unwilling and unable to tackle the underlying conflict within the team. Their ability to sustain changes made through their AR project was also questionable; the one teacher from this team who attended the final group interview reported that no further progress had been made towards achieving their vision statement.

Riroriro whole-centre PLC

The Riroriro PLC team was highly diverse: across the nine teaching staff, five different cultural groups were represented; individuals had varying degrees of teaching experience; and there was a mix of in-training and qualified teachers. These factors influenced how this PLC developed and how individuals participated: senior staff took a more proactive role during scheduled PLC meetings, in online discussion forums and in their PLC work between meetings. These teachers recognised their role in supporting other staff to become more involved:

> This PLC as a group and particularly our topic has aroused some strong feelings, lots of talk in the centre and a bit of finger pointing. As leaders we cannot stop one teacher feeling that they do more work than the other one, but I can try harder to ensure each teacher feels valued, and has the ability and opportunity to make a contribution to our centre. (Valerie, reflective journal)

Within their broader focus on rituals and routines, these teachers chose to focus on developing peaceful lunchtime routines where children and adults had time for conversation and where eating together was a pleasurable activity. They identified that the period leading up to children's lunchtime and through until children were settled for an afternoon sleep was hectic, and that organising these routines often took priority over engaging in positive learning interactions with children. A key task for us, as researchers, was supporting the team to gather and analyse data about their current practices and to discuss proposed changes as a collective, rather than rushing into implementing new strategies. The use of the online site as a forum for asynchronous discussions between meetings helped this team delay making decisions about changed practices until everyone had been consulted and consensus gained on their next steps:

> I have found the Moodle very helpful as it is a way for everyone to write down their thoughts and everyone else gets to see and have a say, I think it is an extremely useful tool as we get to do it in our own time and not necessarily be put on the spot at a staff meeting in front of everyone. (Lorraine, reflective journal)

These teachers actively engaged in gathering data about their practices, including video-recording the current lunchtime routines and asking the older children what they liked and disliked about lunchtimes, and agreed on changes to the physical environment, the timing of lunch for younger and older children, and on their interactions with the children at lunchtime. Their focus expanded beyond the routine itself as they provided parents with information about healthy food and easy packaging to help children be more independent with their lunchboxes.

Several PLC characteristics were evident with this group. Firstly, although individual teachers' contributions varied, the team was committed to a collective approach and to following the process of data collection, analysis and consensus decision-making presented in the project – a process described by one teacher as 'a "gift" to educators because it slows the pace enough for them to reflect' (Sharon, reflective journal). In-depth discussions were held via the online site as well as during staff meetings and scheduled PLC meetings. Secondly, teachers consistently paid attention to relational aspects in order to progress their work, resulting in increased levels of trust and a greater sense of teamwork:

> Nurturing respectful trusting relationships is vital and I think we strengthen these through times of resolving conflict and supporting each member of the team. Understanding by listening, reflecting, empowering and encouraging teachers is so important. (Alison, reflective journal)

Finally, supportive structural conditions were also evident as the centre management provided financial support, along with the active commitment of the team leaders.

Whilst many of the practical changes this team made to their lunchtime routine were subtle, evidence gathered at the end of phase two indicated that the routine was more peaceful, children were more independent, and teachers and children engaged in more sustained conversations. Riroriro PLC's greatest changes, however, were in their shift from an individual to a collective approach for working together: three months after the conclusion of phase two, team members felt 'the model of that review process is something that will stay with each of us' (Sharon, group interview).

Leadership cluster PLC

The leadership cluster PLC comprised teachers from five centres, each with a different AR question related to leadership. Initial discussions revealed that individuals had markedly different perceptions and experiences of leadership. This diversity of views, experiences and AR foci was both useful and challenging. Whilst most participants reported that they found hearing others' perspectives on leadership helpful, a process described by Olivia in the final interview as 'the cross-pollination of ideas', some found these differences frustrating. Similarly, the different research questions posed by each centre contributed to some teachers feeling confused about the parallel AR and PLC research processes whilst others found that the different projects helped broaden their thinking about leadership.

Centres varied in the achievement of their individual AR goals, with several factors influencing progress. Some teachers took several meetings to refine their AR questions and begin examining current practices. Teachers from two centres – Korimako ELC and Mohua ELC – experienced wider changes within their centres, making it challenging to concentrate on a narrower leadership-focused AR question, whilst a third centre, Miromiro ELC, needed support to link leadership to their intention to work with their local community to re-develop their transition to school policies. The head teacher from this centre developed a greater understanding of the power of distributive leadership as a result of involving the centre's parent committee in the re-development of their transition to school procedures:

> My increased confidence has made me a more effective leader because I know to trust the consultation process and I no longer feel threatened by parents' suggestions that we do not prepare our children well enough. (Tina, reflective journal)

Two centres, whose research questions focused on leadership involving aspects of children's learning, experienced shifts in teachers' thinking and practices: the teachers at Whio ELC became more attuned to differences in how leadership was enacted by individuals and groups of children. Teachers at Hioho ELC reported

THE PROFESSIONAL DEVELOPMENT OF EARLY YEARS EDUCATORS

shifts in practice for themselves, children and parents as they explored and emphasised the construct that everyone in the centre was both a learner and a teacher, and planned to continue their focus on *ako* (teaching and learning) beyond the research project. Although they appeared to be already operating as a PLC in their own context they valued their participation in the cluster, suggesting that:

> Getting those perspectives on what you're doing, gives you [the] ability to think deeper about what you're doing. (Olivia, group interview)

The characteristics of supportive structural and relational conditions (Hipp and Huffman 2010) presented differently with a cluster PLC, as participants were both part of the PLC and members of their centre team. Whilst we, as researchers, could address some structural and relational conditions affecting how the PLC worked, we had no influence over the barriers and enablers within participants' own settings, which were challenging for some participants. For example, the teachers from Korimako ELC experienced significant staffing and structural changes within their centre, resulting in increased responsibilities for them. These teachers reported that the PLC enabled them to share issues and seek feedback, and that they learnt a great deal from working alongside other teachers in leadership positions:

> I feel a lot more confident being a leader ... You feel more empowered that you know what you are doing is right and those sorts of things. (Helen, group interview)

Early in the project, participants identified that, as a newly formed group with diverse AR questions, it would take time to develop trust in each other. By the end of the study, however, participants reported that the collaborative and open nature of the group supported them to engage in robust and meaningful discussion and that they were comfortable sharing their ideas. Engaging in collective learning with colleagues from different centres prompted reflection and was valued by many participants. Less effective was the online platform for discussion and reflection between PLC meetings, with several teachers noting it may have been more helpful if they were all working on the same AR focus.

In summary, then, this PLC made progress in developing several characteristics of an effective PLC: its members were engaged in collective learning and were increasingly de-privatising and sharing their practices. As a group they had developed supportive relational structures including trust and were giving feedback and engaging in robust discussion. Developing a shared vision as a PLC took time to achieve, partly due to the differences in each centre's AR question, although shared understandings about constructs of leadership did emerge.

Reflective practice cluster PLC

The reflective practice cluster PLC involved eight teachers from across three EC centres. The smaller numbers of centres participating in this cluster meant that centres were invited to involve three, rather than two, teachers; two centres took up this option. The cluster's overarching focus on reflective practice was instrumental in shaping how participants worked together from the outset. It enabled us, as researchers, to explicitly position critical reflection as a key activity within each PLC meeting, encouraging members to engage through questioning, clarifying, challenging and supporting each other to be critically reflective. Participants found the process challenging and rewarding:

Sometimes some of the questions you guys posed I just went, 'ohh this is taking me a bit out of my comfort zone and I don't want to do this' but you did it because it is almost like an assignment you have to do it. Because of that you just gained immensely, you gained so much out of it. (Marion, group interview)

Despite their different AR questions, this group quickly established trust and effective norms for working together: they readily asked questions and clarified what others were saying, offered suggestions and feedback, openly shared progress with their projects, and empathised with challenges that some experienced in encouraging their centre colleagues to participate in collective reflection on their practices. Not all members, however, were able to respond publicly when they disagreed with others' views, sharing their views instead in their reflective journals:

I felt a wee bit offended by one person's comments … about how young new teachers only bring in theory. (Ann, reflective journal)

Each centre team reported shifts in practice as a result of their AR project and from their engagement in the PLC. Teachers at Totara ELC, who focused on how their teaching supported children's developing social competency, used video-recorded episodes to analyse children's turn-taking approaches and teachers' strategies to support these behaviours. Teachers developed a wider repertoire of strategies, and used these more deliberately to support children's turn-taking; children also used a greater range of strategies to negotiate turn-taking and were more responsive to other children's requests. As one teacher wrote in her journal:

I feel I am more conscious of my turn taking strategies and techniques and reflect more on how I could do things differently. I find myself having more informal discussions with my colleagues on ways that they have used to tackle similar or different scenarios and in doing this I [have a] new understanding of particular children's behaviours or other teachers' own prior experiences, philosophy and teaching practices. Together we seem to be sharing our knowledge and understanding or experiences more often and openly. (Helga)

The Ngā Putiputi ELC team reported shifts in their individual and collective reflections on their teaching, and felt that their team was working together more cohesively and openly. They consciously engaged in intentional teaching during their interactions with children, and actively shared their teaching and reflections with parents through pedagogical documentation displayed in the centre.

In contrast, Ocean ELC experienced both success and disappointment in their project to develop a critical team culture. Teachers experienced significant shifts in their team interactions as they practised reflecting critically on their own teaching and giving feedback to each other, reporting that 'we were just flying. We were having robust debates' (Marion, group meeting). However, staff changes during the project impacted negatively on their new critical team culture. A new teacher was reluctant to engage in critical reflection on her own practice and this, together with another teacher taking long-term leave, resulted in critical conversations occurring between individuals rather than across the team. Reflecting back on their experiences at the final group meeting, the centre's head teacher shared her sorrow at the loss of open debate and reflection but expressed a determination to try again in the New Year.

This cluster PLC was developing many characteristics of an effective PLC. They shared a common understanding of critically reflective practice and practised this during PLC meetings and with their centre colleagues. Trusting relationships developed to the point where members were willing to de-privatise their practices

THE PROFESSIONAL DEVELOPMENT OF EARLY YEARS EDUCATORS

and express vulnerability with each other. This group developed shared personal practice and engaged in collective learning, despite their different research questions.

Discussion

Over the timeframe in which we worked with teachers in this exploratory study, each of the four PLCs made progress with their AR investigations and in developing into PLCs as identified in the literature (for example, DuFour and Eaker 1998, Hipp and Huffman 2010). Our data reveal that the project's timeframe was insufficient, however, for each group to demonstrate the characteristics of, or develop into, a self-sustaining PLC. Given the empirical evidence about the development of self-sustaining PLCs in the schooling literature, this finding is unsurprising. For example, the two schools in Hipp *et al.*'s (2008) study had begun development as PLCs prior to their participation in the initial project, suggesting an internal commitment to school improvement. Hipp *et al.* suggest that these schools 'mirror the literature regarding the multiple (3–10) years needed to bring about organizational change in schools' (2008, p. 191).

When considered alongside the models of PLC development presented earlier, the PLCs in this study were located predominately at the novice (McLaughlin and Talbert 2006) or beginning (Grossman *et al.* 2001, Martin-Kniep 2008) stages, although there were individual variations. Pīwakawaka PLC was clearly still in Grossman *et al.*'s (2001) beginning stage, where several teachers remained firmly located in furthering their own goals and agendas and the team had not collectively reached a point where they were willing to acknowledge and address underlying conflicts. Whilst leadership for the AR project had been devolved to a recently employed teacher, this may have been more a response to the absence of strong positional leadership. Although attempts were made to engage in collaborative learning activities, when initial plans for these were unsuccessful team members either focused on developing their own practices or offered minimal contributions to the project. In contrast, the Riroriro PLC was making progress towards McLaughlin and Talbert's (2006) intermediate stage: they had become committed to gathering and bringing data to their team meetings for discussion, and were using these processes more effectively and with less support from the researchers. Although individual differences were still evident amongst teachers' commitment to the team's collective goals, the positional leaders had proactively sought to engage and support teachers who were more reticent about sharing their views or who remained more focused on their own individual perspectives.

Members of the two cluster PLCs faced a double challenge in that they were, firstly, working in a newly established PLC group and, secondly, leading their AR projects in their centres with colleagues less involved in the project. Whilst participating in a new group required the establishment of group norms and trust, the very newness of these two groups created space for paying deliberate, careful attention to these issues without having to attend to 'baggage' that an existing team may carry. For the reflective practice PLC, having an explicit expectation that we would collectively practise being critically reflective and establishing ground rules for such practice were instrumental in building a collaborative approach to discussing each centre's individual project: these teachers made considerable progress towards being an evolving (Grossman *et al.* 2001) and developing (Martin-Kniep 2008) PLC.

Leading AR projects back in their centres created challenges for several members of the cluster PLCs, predominately around their colleagues' willingness (or otherwise) to commit to the projects and the PLCs participants' ability to influence or control external influences. Thus, both the owner from Mohua ELC and the teachers from Korimako ELC found it challenging to encourage distributed leadership within their centres, with teachers not always willing to make decisions and take on new responsibilities. Similarly, teachers from Ocean ELC found it frustrating when a new team member was unwilling to engage in critical reflection with her colleagues.

Supportive structural and relational conditions

The PLC literature (for example, Hord and Sommers 2008, Hipp and Huffman 2010) is rich with discussion about the importance of supportive conditions, both structural and relational. Likewise, there is empirical evidence of the impact of structural and relational aspects on the development of effective teams and of effective ECE PL relevant to this study (Mitchell 2003, Ryder 2007, Thornton 2009, Cherrington 2011). Structural aspects were particularly influential on these PLCs: Pīwakawaka ELC moved location during the project; and Mohua ELC changed their licensing conditions, bringing two previously separate centres together under one license, creating, in effect, a single teaching team. Significant team changes occurred for both Ocean ELC and Korimako ELC whilst one of the participating teachers at Totara ELC resigned. Frequent staffing changes are endemic in New Zealand EC services: annual turnover of between one-fifth and one-quarter of teaching staff in ECE centres has been recorded by the New Zealand Ministry of Education (2014b), whilst a recent evaluation of an EC ICT PL programme found that 48% of teachers involved at the beginning of the programme had left their centre 18 months later (Cherrington *et al.* 2009). Hipp *et al.* (2008) note that changes to key personnel or school organisational structures have the potential to disrupt progress in the development and sustainability of PLCs; an issue pertinent to this project and to the establishment of PLCs more widely within the New Zealand EC sector.

A further structural condition – that of time for PLC team members to meet together – is particularly problematic within the EC sector (Cherrington and Wansbrough 2007). In this study, each PLC meeting, other than the initial Saturday seminar, was scheduled for the early evening (usually 5.30–7.30 pm) to enable members to participate after centre programmes had finished for the day. Although Hord and Sommers (2008) suggest that providing time within the school day for members to meet together sends a clear message that the PLC is valued, this is not easily achieved in ECE services which offer full-day programmes. No recompense for attending night meetings was available to these teachers from the research funding; rather, in an environment where access to ongoing PL is extremely limited, they elected to participate for the PL opportunities the project provided. Mitchell (2003) has argued that the provision of supportive structural conditions, including time and space for teachers' discussion and reflection and management commitment to PL for staff, is essential within the EC sector. Given the importance of supportive structural conditions, any effort to establish PLCs more broadly within the New Zealand EC sector will require recognition from service management that the work of a PLC is more intensive and long-lasting than traditional PL approaches and, thus, requires commitment for appropriate levels of resourcing.

Earlier discussion has noted how the development of trust amongst members was a key relational element influencing the extent to which each PLC was able to engage in open discussion and reflection on their practices, paralleling previous New Zealand research (for example, Thornton 2009, Cherrington 2011). Despite being used to working closely together in teams, usually in the same physical environment, there is empirical evidence that developing relationships of trust and criticality together can be problematic for EC teachers (Nuttall 2004). Addressing issues of power and group dynamics is another component of enabling supportive relational conditions within a PLC. Dana and Yendol-Hoppey's (2008) discussion of how five types of power – positional, assigned, knowledge, personal and factional – positively or negatively influence group dynamics within a PLC is useful for considering the power influences at play within this project. For example, positional power was used positively by the leaders within Riroriro ELC to surface and address one team member's unwillingness to critique her own practice that contributed to her standing apart from the growing collective culture within the centre. In contrast, the positional leader at Pīwakawaka ELC was mostly absent from the work of this PLC, creating space for factional power influences to emerge.

Developing a model for supporting PLC development in ECE

The model developed for this project provided a helpful structure given that the notion of a PLC was new for the participating teachers, and given the project's limited lifespan. Furthermore, although all of the research team had previous experience and expertise in delivering PL, this was our first experience of combining facilitating and researching PLCs. Creating a timeline outlining each stage of the project helped slow teachers' inclination to make assumptions about current practices and to forge ahead with changes before they had gathered, analysed and discussed data on current practices. Shifting teachers into an evidence-based approach is a necessary development within the New Zealand EC sector. A recent New Zealand Education Review Office[4] (2009) report identified that considerable work is required to build self-review capacity in ECE services, as only 14% of almost 400 services had a strong understanding of, and well-implemented, self-review processes. The ECE self-review processes (New Zealand Ministry of Education 2006), which include a four-stage cycle of preparing for review, gathering data, making sense of that data and deciding on changes to be made, are appropriate for use within PLCs and align well with the model developed for this project.

Limitations

Our finding that the timeframe of the project was insufficient highlights the main limitation of this exploratory study; the short-term nature of the project necessitated by the scope of the funding grant. Although the 10-month timeframe is relatively long for a New Zealand ECE PL programme, Hipp *et al.* (2008) have emphasised the time and energy necessary for effective PLCs to develop. The centres involved volunteered to participate in this study and, without funding for release time or expenses such as travel, their involvement over a calendar year was considered a sufficient time commitment. Future projects, building on this pilot, will utilise a longer timeframe.

The characteristics of the participating centres signal a further limitation of this study. Their decision to volunteer for the project indicated a commitment to engaging with in-depth PL and to examining their practice unlikely to be universal across the sector. Offsetting this, however, the reduction of PL programmes funded by the New Zealand Ministry of Education has left many services unable to access in-depth PL, and may have encouraged participation. We note, too, that the challenges faced by many of the participating teachers, particularly in relation to supportive structural and relational conditions, are, in our experience, relatively typical in New Zealand EC centres.

Implications

The research reported here offers initial empirical evidence, in a field dominated by research in the schooling sector, that the model of PLCs has potential within the EC sector for improving teachers' professional practices, which may lead to enhanced learning for children. Our data also reveal that a complex set of factors, particularly concerning structural and relational conditions, influence the development of PLCs within EC, some of which are unique to this sector. Further analyses of the data gathered in this project are intended to report in more detail shifts in teachers' practices, leadership facets and building professional communities within cluster groups. In addition, further research is required into the longer-term development and sustainability of EC PLCs, and to this end a three-year project is planned. Beyond this, research into the effectiveness of PLCs in different EC service types within New Zealand and internationally is required to build more complete understandings of PLCs within EC contexts.

Developing PLCs in EC will require shifts in teachers' thinking and ability to engage in robust data collection and critical reflection as they engage in deeper, more intensive PL over a longer timeframe than that which has traditionally been available to the sector. Such shifts will prove challenging to those practitioners who have not been prepared for such an approach to PL through their initial teacher education programme and to the 23.8% of staff who are currently unqualified (New Zealand Ministry of Education 2014a). In addition, paying 'unrelenting attention to student learning success' (Hord and Sommers 2008, p. 10) has not been a strong feature of ECE PL programmes in New Zealand, and thus requires a shift in emphasis to improving and enhancing learning for *all* children.

Acknowledgements

The authors express their appreciation to Marg Bleasdale, their research assistant, for her exemplary work on this project and to the participating teachers for their willingness to stretch their own professional learning and de-privatise their practices.

Disclosure statement

There are no conflicts of interest arising from the funding source for the project that this manuscript draws from, for either author.

Funding

The project was funded by a Victoria University of Wellington Internal Research Fund Grant in 2012 [grant number 108768].

THE PROFESSIONAL DEVELOPMENT OF EARLY YEARS EDUCATORS

Notes

1. *Whānau* is the Māori word for extended family.
2. Moodle (Modular Object-oriented Dynamic Learning Environment) is a web-based learning management system that allows a range of online tools to be used for collaborative synchronous or asynchronous interaction.
3. *Marae* are the social and cultural hub within Māori communities.
4. The Education Review Office undertakes regular reviews of all schools and licensed ECE services.

References

Borko, H., *et al.,* 2008. Video as a tool for fostering productive discussions in mathematics professional development. *Teaching and teacher education*, 24 (2), 417–436.

Braun, V. and Clarke, V., 2006. Using thematic analysis in psychology. *Qualitative research in psychology*, 3 (2), 77–101.

Cherrington, S., 2011. Early childhood teachers' thinking and reflection within their communities of practice. Unpublished PhD thesis, Victoria University of Wellington, Wellington, NZ.

Cherrington, S. and Thornton, K., 2013. Continuing professional development in early childhood education in New Zealand. *Early years: an international research journal*, 33 (2), 119–132. doi:10.1080/09575146.2013.763770.

Cherrington, S. and Wansbrough, D., 2007. *Final report to the ministry of education on the national evaluation of ECE professional development programmes*. Wellington: NZ Ministry of Education.

Cherrington, S., *et al.,* 2009. *Evaluation of the early childhood education information and communication technology professional learning programme final report*. Wellington: NZ Ministry of Education.

Cohen, L., Manion, L., and Morrison, K., 2000. *Research methods in education*. London: Routledge Falmer.

Dana, N.F. and Yendol-Hoppey, D., 2008. *The reflective educator's guide to professional development: coaching inquiry-oriented learning communities*. Thousand Oaks, CA: Corwin Press.

Desimone, L.M., 2009. Improving impact studies of teachers' professional development: towards better conceptualisations and measures. *Educational researcher*, 38 (3), 181–199.

DuFour, R. and Eaker, R., 1998. *Professional learning communities at work: best practices for enhancing student achievement*. Bloomington, IN: National Educational Service.

Earley, P. and Porritt, V., eds., 2009. *Effective practices in continuing professional development: lessons from schools*. London: Institute of Education and TDA, Bedford Way series.

Earley, P. and Porritt, V., 2014. Evaluating the impact of professional development: the need for a student-focused approach. *Professional development in education*, 40 (1), 112–129.

Easton, L.B., 2011. *Professional learning communities by design: putting the learning back into PLCs*. Thousand Oaks, CA: Corwin Press.

Education Review Office, 2009. *Implementing self-review in early childhood services*. Wellington: NZ Education Review Office.

Education Review Office, 2013. *Priorities for children's learning in early childhood services*. Wellington: NZ Education Review Office.

Edwards, S. and Nuttall, J., 2009. Introduction. *In*: S. Edwards and J. Nuttall, eds. *Professional learning in early childhood settings*. Rotterdam: Sense, 1–8.

Fullan, M., 2000. The three stories of education reform. *Phi delta kappan*, 81 (8), 581–584.

Gibbs, R. and Poskitt, J., 2009. *Report on the evaluation of the early childhood centres of innovation programme*. Wellington: NZ Ministry of Education.

Grossman, P., Wineburg, S., and Woolworth, S., 2001. Toward a theory of teacher community. *Teachers college record*, 103 (6), 942–1012.

Hipp, K.K. and Huffman, J.B., eds., 2010. *Demystifying professional learning communities: school leadership at its best*. Lanham, MD: Rowman & Littlefield Education.

Hipp, K.K., *et al.,* 2008. Sustaining professional learning communities: case studies. *Journal of educational change,* 9 (2), 173–195.

Hord, S.M. and Sommers, W.A., 2008. *Leading professional learning communities: voices from research and practice.* Thousand Oaks, CA: Corwin Press.

Lave, J. and Wenger, E., 1991. *Situated learning: legitimate peripheral participation.* Cambridge: Cambridge University Press.

Martin-Kniep, G.O., 2008. *Communities that learn, lead, and last: building and sustaining educational expertise.* San Francisco, CA: Jossey-Bass.

McLaughlin, M. and Talbert, J., 2006. *Building school-based teacher learning communities: professional strategies to improve student achievement.* New York, NY: Teachers College Press.

McNiff, J. and Whitehead, J., 2010. *You and your action research project.* London: Routledge.

Merriam, S., 1998. *Qualitative research and case study applications in education.* San Francisco, CA: Jossey-Bass.

Mitchell, L., 2003. Shifts in thinking through a teachers' network. *Early childhood folio,* 7, 22–27.

Mitchell, L. and Cubey, P., 2003. *Characteristics of professional development linked to enhanced pedagogy and children's learning in early childhood settings: best evidence synthesis.* Wellington: NZ Ministry of Education.

Nandhakumar, J. and Jones, M., 1997. Too close for comfort? Distance and engagement in interpretive information systems research. *Information systems journal,* 7 (2), 109–131.

New Zealand Ministry of Education, 1996. *Te Whāriki: early childhood curriculum.* Wellington: Learning Media.

New Zealand Ministry of Education, 2006. *Ngā arohaehae whai hua: self-review guidelines for early childhood education.* Wellington: Learning Media.

New Zealand Ministry of Education, 2014a. *Early childhood education statistics: ECE teachers* [online]. Available from: http://www.educationcounts.govt.nz/statistics/ece2/staffing [Accessed 26 August 2014].

New Zealand Ministry of Education, 2014b. *Early childhood education statistics: teacher turnover in ECE* [online]. Available from: http://www.educationcounts.govt.nz/statistics/ece2/staffing [Accessed 26 August 2014].

Nuttall, J., 2004. Why don't you ask someone who cares? Teacher identity, intersubjectivity, and curriculum negotiation in a New Zealand childcare centre. Unpublished PhD thesis, Victoria University of Wellington, Wellington, New Zealand.

Opfer, V. and Pedder, D., 2011. Conceptualizing teacher professional learning. *Review of educational research,* 81 (3), 376–407.

Ryder, D., 2007. Making meaning: a team of early childhood education teachers working towards registration from a group perspective. Unpublished Masters thesis, Canterbury University, Christchurch, New Zealand.

Sheridan, S.M., *et al.,* 2009. Professional development in early childhood programs: process issues and research needs. *Early education & development,* 20 (3), 377–401.

Stoll, L., *et al.,* 2006. Professional learning communities: a review of the literature. *Journal of educational change,* 7 (4), 221–258.

Thornton, K., 2009. Blended action learning: supporting leadership learning in the New Zealand ECE sector. Unpublished PhD thesis, Victoria University of Wellington, Wellington, New Zealand.

Thornton, K. and Wansbrough, D., 2012. Professional learning communities in early childhood education. *Journal of educational leadership, policy and practice,* 27 (2), 51–64.

'Accept the change and enjoy the range': applications of the Circles of Change methodology with professionals who support early childhood educators

Kym Macfarlane, Ali Lakhani, Jennifer Cartmel, Marilyn Casley and Kerry Smith

Inclusion Support Facilitators support Early Childhood Education and Care centres in Australia to provide an inclusive environment for the children they serve. To date no research has examined the causes of job stress faced by these professionals. Similarly, no research has explored how interventions aimed at supporting Inclusion Support Facilitators' practice may impact their work. This research explored how the first of a set of critical reflection workshops instructing on the use of the Circles of Change methodology impacted the practice of Inclusion Support Facilitators. The research was undertaken in two stages. The first stage involved collecting baseline data to investigate current levels of job stress amongst Inclusion Support Facilitators. The second stage involved gathering qualitative data to explore the opinions of professionals about how such stresses might be changed following an initial critical reflection workshop. Findings from this research suggest that job demands may be a potential cause of stress for Inclusion Support Facilitators. Findings also suggest that the Circles of Change methodology may be helpful in encouraging personal reflection, communication and transformational change amongst professionals who support those working in childcare. Such notions are critical to how professionals manage both job stress and workplace change.

Introduction/background

Inclusion Support Agencies (ISAs) are publically funded agencies supporting Early Childhood Education and Care (ECEC) centres within 67 regions across Australia (Department of Education, Employment and Workplace Relations [DEEWR] 2012). The purpose of ISAs is to, '… assist eligible ECEC services to build the knowledge and confidence – they need to be able to offer quality inclusive ECEC environments to children with additional needs' (DEEWR 2012, p. 22). ISAs provide support services to ECEC providers working with priority children, including those who are differently abled and also including children from Aboriginal and Torres Strait Islander, refugee or culturally and linguistically diverse backgrounds (DEEWR 2012). ISA support is dynamic and encourages inclusiveness in ECEC centres while 'promot[ing] and support[ing] access to quality ECEC services …' (DEEWR 2012, p. 22).

ISAs employ Inclusion Support Facilitators (ISFs) to support ECEC centres working with priority children. Specifically, ISFs '... work directly with eligible ECEC services, to provide support, information and guidance that assists [ECEC centres] to provide inclusive quality ECEC environments' (DEEWR 2012, p. 23). The focus and work roles of ISFs are multifaceted and require that they both support ECEC centres in providing care to priority groups they serve, while also aiding centres to attain resources required to support those priority groups. Particular to supporting ECEC centres' ability to service priority children, ISFs have a variety of responsibilities – including promoting ECEC centres' awareness of the priority groups they serve, providing professional suggestions that are targeted to the needs of ECEC centres and providing ongoing on-site support to centres to ensure that they are practicing as inclusive environments (DEEWR 2012). In relation to resources, ISFs aid ECEC centres by assisting centres in completing applications for funding and recommending additional support services for ECEC centres when required (DEEWR 2012).

To date no research exists investigating the causes of job stress faced by ISFs whose primary role is to work with educators in this sector. Similarly, no research has explored how interventions aimed at supporting ISF practice may impact their work. Considering the close relationship that ISFs have with ECEC settings and ECEC service provision, it is possible that they are facing stress similarly to childcare workers in Australia. This means that the stresses of the ECEC sector impact the work of the ISFs who are trying to support childcare centres.

Over the last three decades a body of research has investigated the causes, consequences and levels of job stress in childcare workers throughout the West (see, for example, Maslach and Pines 1977, Townley *et al.* 1991, Grantz and Claffy 1996, Goelman and Guo 1998, Curbow *et al.* 2000, Hale-Jinks *et al.* 2006, Brennan *et al.* 2008, Li Grining *et al.* 2010). Specific to Australia, research investigating the experiences of early years educators is limited (Yost 2012) and a segment of research in this area has focused on employee retention (for example, see Sumsion 2007, Jovanovic 2013). Research that has investigated early years educators' experiences in Australia has characterised employment in the childcare sector as stressful, and has highlighted some causes (see Fenech 2006). Yost (2012) investigated the work experiences of early childhood educators from 28 schools in Tasmania. Results from Yost's research include the notion that '... stress was the most cited concern reported by [those interviewed]' (2012, p. 104) and a large workload was a factor contributing to this stress. Similarly, research by Kelly and Berthelsen (1995, 1997) characterises the Australian early childcare profession as stressful and identified sources of stressors for Queensland early years educators. Some of the factors contributing to stress include issues of time, managing the needs of children and parents, and keeping up with advances in early years education practice and philosophy (Kelly and Berthelsen 1995, 1997). Therefore, it is clear that ISFs are working in a sector with individuals who are also subject to significant job stress and that these factors may influence the way in which ISFs are able to work with these educators.

Critical reflection and reflective practice are methods useful for evaluating practice and problem-solving within the early childhood education and care profession (Moss and Pence 1994, Perry 1997, Moss 2000, National Childcare Accreditation Council 2002, Noble 2003, Macfarlane and Cartmel 2012). It is also a means of coping with situations that involve stress and tension. Furthermore, problem-solving as a part of critical reflection enables the construction (Macfarlane *et al.* 2004) and reconstruction (Yost *et al.* 2000) of new knowledge. Results from research investigating the use of critically reflective programmes within teacher development and education have identified such programmes as factors contributing to empowerment of beginning teachers (Wideen *et al.* 1998, Yost *et al.* 2000) while also supporting their identification of problems and development of collaborative solutions (Gün 2011). Such information can also be applied to this case, where critical reflection was viewed as a means of enabling ISFs to cope with issues of job stress in their environment. The model of critical reflection chosen here was implemented because of its usefulness in producing transformational change and its relevance to the early years sector as a whole.

Consequently, this research aimed to examine the job stressors that ISFs face while exploring how the first of a set of critical reflection workshops impacted their practice. The research was undertaken using a mixed-method approach (Creswell 2003) that utilised survey data and Most Significant Change questions (Davies and Dart 2005). The baseline survey data were intended to measure current levels of stress, and the Most Significant Change questions aimed to explore whether the critical reflection workshop assisted the ISFs in adapting to the stresses in their workplace.

Methodology

Initially, ISFs were administered an adapted version of the Child Care Worker Job Stress Inventory (CCW-JSI; Curbow *et al.* 2000) via a paper or online survey prior to an introductory workshop centring on critical reflection and transformational change. Eighteen of the 37 participants who completed the survey did so online at their workplace. The remaining 19 participants completed a physical copy of the survey at their workplace prior to the introductory workshop.

As part of the qualitative component, the initial workshop was conducted within a conference room at the workplace of ISFs practicing in Queensland. Forty-eight participants attended the introductory workshop and 44 agreed to have their reflection following the workshop included within the study. Qualitative data were gathered prior to a second critical reflection session, three months after the initial workshop. The qualitative data included participants' written responses to a question: 'What is the most significant change that has happened in your professional work since our previous workshop?' For clarity it is important to highlight that ISFs involved in this study remain anonymous in their qualitative responses, and have been randomly assigned identification numbers. These numbers have no relation to the number of participants within the study.

Sample

Thirty-six ISFs and one Team Leader working in Queensland completed an adapted version of the CCW-JSI. The ISFs included in this sample represented over one-half of the ISFs servicing Queensland. The entire sample was female and ranged in age from over 20 to older than 60. Approximately 41% of the sample fell within the age range of 50–60. Of the 44 participants who consented to the inclusion of their qualitative reflections, 5 were administrative staff, 38 were ISFs and 1 was the Team Leader.

Quantitative instrument

Curbow *et al.* (2000) outline their development of a childcare worker job stress inventory and provide results from their administration of the inventory instruments amongst two sample populations: family day-care providers and childcare centre workers. They suggest that their inventory is a tool to:

> ... compare child care environments, track stressor levels in new workers over time, assess the spillover effects of stressors from one group in the network to another, and to suggest possible interventions that might allay the effects of work place stressors. (Curbow *et al.* 2000, p. 520)

The inventory accounts for the domains of job control and job demands as included within the Hurrell (1987) NIOSH Job Stress Model and offers benefits over other generic job stress inventories as it is intended for a distinct population; that is, childcare workers (Curbow *et al.* 2000). The final version of the inventory included three scales – job controls, job resources and job demands – and each of these includes 17 items answerable on a five-point Likert scale ranging from one (rarely/never) to five (most of the time). Increased scores on these subscales imply that educators feel 'more control in their daily activities and routines, greater resources at their work, and more work-related demands' (Zhai 2011, p. 446). The CCW-JSI therefore becomes a tool to understand how those employed in childcare characterise their work.

The CCW-JSI was adapted to better suit the ISFs' work focus. Considering that ISFs work with childcare centres and in most instances not directly with children, the items within each scale were adjusted to reflect the job roles of someone working with centres and not providing a primary service for children. For example, the original job demands item 'I feel there are major sources of stress in the children's lives that I can't do anything about' was adjusted to read 'I feel that ECEC service centres face issues that I can't do anything about'. Similarly, the original job resources item 'I know the children are happy with me' was adjusted to read 'I know the ECEC service providers are happy with me'. The inventory resulted in a job demands scale with 19 items, a job resources scale of 11 items and a job control scale of 6 items.

Intervention

The intervention is the first of a set of four workshops focusing on critical reflection and transformational change. The workshop ran for seven hours over one day and involved practicing and training about the application of the Circles of Change (COC) methodology (see Macfarlane *et al.* 2004, 2008, Macfarlane and Cartmel 2012). The COC methodology includes a combination of the concept of Learning Circles (Lovett and Gilmore 2003) and a specially designed critical reflection model – Deconstruct, Confront, Theorise and Think Otherwise. The methodology aims to encourage dialogue and critical discussion amongst childcare professionals (Macfarlane and Cartmel 2012) in a safe space of interaction. Initially developed for university child and family students, the '... main aim of COC is to challenge thinking; that is, develop the ability to be a critical and insightful thinker' (Macfarlane and Cartmel 2012, p. 846). Previous evaluations of the model have identified it as one which provides a space for future practitioners to discuss and learn from their colleagues (Macfarlane *et al.* 2008). The model has enabled practitioners to confront their own biases (Macfarlane and Cartmel 2012) and those who have learnt the model have been able to successfully apply it in their work settings (Macfarlane *et al.* 2008).

THE PROFESSIONAL DEVELOPMENT OF EARLY YEARS EDUCATORS

During the first workshop participants learnt the COC process and practiced the stages involved; namely, deconstruct, confront, theorise and think otherwise. The stages addressed during this first session allowed participants to: describe a phenomenon of interest (deconstruct); clarify their perspective about the phenomenon of interest challenging their own values and beliefs (confront); examine the characteristics of the phenomenon from a variety of professional and theoretical perspectives (theorise); and encourage themselves to think outside the dominant perspective (think otherwise) (Macfarlane *et al.* 2004, 2008, Macfarlane and Cartmel 2012). The aim of the workshop was for participants to develop an understanding of the COC process, which could then be applied to their workplace.

Data analysis

As stated previously, the purpose of this research was to investigate the impact of an initial critical reflection workshop on ISF practice and to develop an understanding of the stresses relating to job demands, job resources and job control faced by ISFs prior to the critical reflection workshop. Quantitative data analysis of the CCW-JSI was conducted using SPSS software. Descriptive statistics allowed researchers to determine how inclusion support facilitators perceive their job demands, resources and control. Distributions were presented in frequency tables and included the mean and standard deviation of every item within each scale and each scale as a whole.

The qualitative data were analysed using a grounded theory approach (Strauss and Corbin 1997) and involved multiple in-depth readings of the data to generate themes and subthemes, and to investigate how they may be related to one another (Strauss and Corbin 1997). The themes generated are highlighted within this paper and include negotiating perspectives, thinking otherwise and interdisciplinary dialogue.

Results

Quantitative

Demographics

Questions within the demographics section focused on work experience. The sample of ISFs included within this research have extensive knowledge in children's services, with roughly 41% of the sample having between 15 and 25 years' experience in this area. Approximately 65% of the sample has worked as an ISF for over 5 years. Additionally, over three-quarters of the ISFs included within this study have attained tertiary education and in total four facilitators spoke a language in addition to English.

Job resources, job demands and job control

Descriptive statistics for the three scales – job demands, job resources and job control – are presented in Tables 1, 2 and 3 respectively. The job demands scale had a total mean of 69.79, an average skewness of –0.41 and kurtosis of –0.36. The job demands average, computed by dividing the total mean by the amount of items in the scale, provided a value of 3.67; positioned between the ratings for 'a fair amount' and 'frequently' on the grading scale. Participants rated 16 of the 19 items

THE PROFESSIONAL DEVELOPMENT OF EARLY YEARS EDUCATORS

Table 1. Job demands.

	Mean	Skewness	Kurtosis
Early childhood education & care (ECEC) services expect me to provide practical and professional advice.	4.22	−1.604	3.311
ECEC services expect me to provide on-site assistance to develop service support plans.	4.19	−1.181	1.075
ECEC services expect me to provide on-site assistance to review service support plans.	3.62	−0.181	−0.990
I need to know about adult learning principles.	3.47	0.000	−1.167
Child development knowledge is important to the role.	4.38	−0.647	−0.609
I need to know about guiding change in ECEC services.	4.19	−0.799	−0.680
I need to know about inclusive practice.	4.19	−0.964	−0.501
I need to know about reflective practice.	4.22	−1.104	0.009
I need to know approaches that help build capacity.	4.19	−1.009	−0.281
I need to know about family-centred practice.	3.35	−0.208	−0.899
I must have cross-cultural competencies.	3.92	−0.343	−1.138
I need to know about innovations and changes in child care practice.	4.32	−1.218	0.769
I feel that I am required to build interdisciplinary team work and interagency collaboration.	3.68	−0.240	−0.844
ECEC services have issues that are hard to deal with.	3.03	0.259	−1.087
ECEC services face issues that I can't do anything about.	2.73	0.558	−0.644
I feel I should be paid more for the work that I do.	3.67	−0.366	−1.403
I feel I need to be nice no matter how I really feel.	3.58	−0.156	−1.280
I feel like I need to be both a friend and colleague to the ECEC service provider.	2.81	0.298	−1.025
I have to work long hours.	2.03	1.200	0.585

Table 2. Job resources.

	Mean	Skewness	Kurtosis
I know the ECEC service providers are happy with me.	3.73	−0.110	−0.015
I know the ECEC service providers want me to work with them.	3.65	−0.578	0.470
I know that I am appreciated by the ECEC service providers.	3.51	−0.045	−0.441
I know that I am respected for the work that I do.	3.41	−0.704	−0.044
I feel the satisfaction of knowing that I am helping the ECEC service provider.	3.68	−0.926	0.389
I feel satisfaction of knowing that I am helping ECEC services to offer quality inclusive environments.	3.73	−0.621	−0.185
I feel that my work is making a difference with ECEC service providers.	3.54	−0.128	−0.644
I feel like I am doing a 'real' job.	3.86	−0.473	0.172
I know that the work that I am doing is important.	4.22	−0.283	−0.714
I feel like I am helping ECEC service providers grow and develop.	3.56	0.118	−0.507
I enjoy my work with ECEC service providers.	4.16	−0.719	0.854

as occurring greater than 'a fair amount', and 8 of these 16 items as occurring frequently. The highest rated item within the job demands scale was 'child development knowledge is important to the role', which was positioned between 'frequently and very frequently' on the grading scale, at a mean of 4.38. The lowest rated item

THE PROFESSIONAL DEVELOPMENT OF EARLY YEARS EDUCATORS

Table 3. Job control.

	Mean	Skewness	Kurtosis
How often do you work late?	2.00	1.119	0.639
How often do you get the ECEC service providers to put your suggestions into practice?	2.97	0.057	−1.568
The resources I need to complete my job are available.	3.41	−0.373	−0.757
ECEC service providers follow guidelines and policies.	3.44	0.221	0.003
How easy would it be for you to change jobs?	2.69	0.164	−0.704
How easy is it for you to take time by yourself during the work day?	2.16	0.321	0.398

was 'I have to work long hours', and was almost directly positioned on 'sometimes' at a mean of 2.03.

The job resources scale included 11 items and resulted in a total mean of 41.04, an average skewness of −0.41 and kurtosis of −0.06. The job resources scale average mean, computed by dividing the total mean by 11, resulted in a value of 3.73 and placed between the ratings 'a fair amount' and 'frequently' on the grading scale. Participants rated each of the 11 items as occurring greater than 'a fair amount', with 2 of the items occurring greater than 'frequently'. The highest rated item within the job resources scale was 'I know that the work I am doing is important', which was positioned between 'frequently' and 'very frequently' on the grading scale at a mean of 4.22. The lowest rated item was 'I know that I am respected for the work that I do', which was placed between 'a fair amount' and 'frequently' at a mean of 3.41 on the grading scale.

The job control scale resulted in a total mean of 16.67, an average skewness of 0.25 and kurtosis of 0.33 across the six items. The job control scale average mean, computed by dividing the total mean by six, was 2.78 and placed closest to the rating 'a fair amount' on the grading scale. Participants rated two of the six items as occurring between 'a fair amount' and 'frequently'. Four of the items were rated as occurring equal to or greater than 'a fair amount' and one of the items, 'How often do you get the ECEC service providers to put your suggestions into practice?', was placed almost directly on 'a fair amount' at a rating of 2.97. The highest rated item within the job control scale was 'ECEC service providers follow guidelines and policies', and was positioned between 'a fair amount' and 'frequently' on the grading scale at a mean of 3.44.

Qualitative

An analysis of responses from ISFs about the most significant change to their practice following the initial workshop resulted in three themes. Although the question posed to participants centred on the most significant change that has taken place in their practice, participant responses were not isolated to changes in their practice. Participants shared their opinions about transdisciplinary dialogue and their own perspectives about the process. For this reason the themes gathered from the data address the most significant changes faced by participants and their thoughts concerning the dialogue process. The three themes are unpacked below.

THE PROFESSIONAL DEVELOPMENT OF EARLY YEARS EDUCATORS

Negotiating perspectives

The second most populated theme emerging from the qualitative data was negotiating perspectives, and 18 of the 44 participants made reference to this theme. The theme breaks down into three subthemes, which include acknowledging multiple perspectives, facilitating multiple perspectives and reflecting about self-perspectives.

Acknowledging multiple perspectives. Participants highlighted a change in their practice in their acknowledgement and acceptance that multiple perspectives exist within their practice. For example, participants highlighted that following the initial workshop they were able to '… be open minded and to see others perspectives' (ISF No. 15), while also recognising 'the importance of marginalised perspectives' (ISF No. 6).

Participants clarified that recognising multiple perspectives may potentially contribute to a well-thought-out professional practice, where action is based on thorough inquiry. For example, concerning multiple perspectives ISF No. 8 clarified a significant change as:

> Acknowledging the process – honouring the opinions of all involved. Not jumping to a solution. Thinking about the questions that will support the inquiry further – digging deeper.

The idea of respecting all professional opinions when making decisions concerning professional practice was echoed by five others in the group (ISF Nos 1, 6, 15, 20 and 24). Similarly, ISF No. 144 identified the importance of basing decisions on multiple perspectives and realised the importance of '… taking into account personal theories and then "Thinking Otherwise"'.

The linking of multiple perspectives and thinking otherwise was echoed by other participants, and six (ISF Nos 3, 12, 15, 20, 25 and 38) considered thinking otherwise to be a useful practice.

Facilitating multiple perspectives. Participants described factors that contribute to and hinder the facilitation of multiple perspectives, critical inquiry and reflective practice. For example, particular to encouraging the inclusion of multiple perspectives, participants highlighted the importance of initiating a safe space and characterised the concept of safe space. For example, ISF No. 24 highlighted the importance of:

> …be[ing] very considerate [to] creat[e] a safe, trustworthy and comfortable space during reflective questioning.

This was done to encourage multiple perspectives and transdisciplinary dialogue. Building on this idea, participants also identified that it was important to acknowledge the perspectives and personal thoughts of others who share within reflection. For example, participants noted the importance of:

> [t]alking about feelings when we discuss issues [and] the importance of fully talking things through. (ISF No. 13)

Participants also highlighted some of the barriers to encouraging multiple perspectives and a transdisciplinary dialogue. Participants suggested aggression and lack of trust as factors that may prevent a dialogue from occurring. For example, ISF No. 26's response included:

THE PROFESSIONAL DEVELOPMENT OF EARLY YEARS EDUCATORS

[i]f the team members do not trust each other or feel like someone is aggressive in the group, the circle cannot work.

This perspective that a lack of trust or cohesion within the circle can prevent the facilitation of the dialogue was voiced by others (ISF Nos 21, 24 and 27) and is best exemplified by comments made about the dialogue process. For example, ISF No. 145 observed, '[h]ow easily the circle process closed down/changed when someone else entered the group'.

Results from the data suggest that participants were able to identify which environmental conditions support transdisciplinary dialogue and which become barriers.

Reflecting about self-perspectives. ISFs developed an understanding of their own perspective and how it may influence their practice and their contribution to professional dialogue. For example, ISF No. 23 suggested that the COC process allowed her to:

... become more aware of where I am coming from – my perspective, and why I have it.

Participants also identified ways to develop and present their perspective in the larger group. For example, ISF No. 28 analysed her own practice and highlighted:

... I listen + engage at the same time [and I] find it interesting to 'look' at self during the process. Need Practice!!!

Thus, ISF professionals generally developed an awareness of their own perspective and identified listening as a tool to encourage self-reflection.

ISFs were also able to identify issues concerning self-perspective that arise while in a larger group. Specifically, they clarified that the COC process may potentially limit their own perspective, and that developing a balance is important to maintaining their own perspective while encouraging perspectives from the entire group. For example, ISF No. 30 identified a challenge with transdisciplinary dialogue and decision-making and shared:

[h]ow to balance [my] personal/professional philosophy with processes that undermine (potentially) my philosophy, e.g.: inclusion.

This meant that some participants were still ambivalent about how the COC process might actually play out for them in practice.

Transdisciplinary dialogue

Twenty-three of the 44 participants reflected on using a transdisciplinary dialogue through COC. Two general categories emerged. One included reflections concerning the COC process, specifically highlighting outcomes from its use. The second highlighted reflections that focused on the feelings which participants had throughout transdisciplinary dialogue. For this reason, the two subthemes below are transdisciplinary dialogue outcomes and feelings towards the transdisciplinary dialogue process.

Outcomes. Participants described how transdisciplinary dialogue became possible through the COC method and potential outcomes from the process. For example, change in practice was identified as an outcome from the COC process and the COC process was described:

> ... as a tool to engage stakeholders in a critical reflection + reflective practices to bring about change. (ISF No. 39)

Additionally, participants described the COC process as a tool to support the investigation of a phenomenon from multiple perspectives. They also described the process as a method, which enables a professional's identification of factors that contribute to, or are impacted by, a phenomenon. For example, ISF No. 146 identified that interdisciplinary dialogue through COC enabled individuals to '... deconstruct a topic ... and really think about all the elements involved'. Therefore, participants saw the COC method as a useful way to engage in critical reflection.

Participants also characterised COC as a process which can be applied throughout their practice. For example, ISF No. 4 shared a significant change in becoming '[m]ore conscious to follow "Circles of Change Steps" in my role'.

Similarly, ISF No. 37 also suggested that a significant change in their practice involved '... the whole Circles of Change process, realising ... to use it continually'. It was therefore clear that participants identified a variety of outcomes from the COC method while recognising that it can become a framework to use within their daily practice.

Feelings throughout the process. Participants provided an account of their feelings while implementing, and following the implementation of, a transdisciplinary dialogue through COC. A segment of participants were enthused by the COC process and shared their feelings about being involved in the transdisciplinary dialogue circle. For example, participants found that it was, '... great to be a part of the practice circle [and that] taking part made it more real ...' (ISF No. 2).

Similarly, participants shared that being in the COC was pleasing and that it was important to:

> Understand that a change [had] already taken place and ... [to] accept the change and enjoy the range. (ISF No. 31)

Participants also felt that it was, '... great to have a roadmap to practice with [line break] finally' (ISF No. 41).

In addition, participants identified that the process was effective and easily implemented; for example, a participant suggested that it was '[s]urpris[ing] that the Circles of Change process flowed automatically' (ISF No. 15).

The data made clear that engaging in reflection brought about feelings of relief, excitement, surprise and happiness.

Thinking otherwise

Seven participants described how the COC methodology enabled them to consider thinking otherwise, or to begin to think otherwise. Participants characterised what thinking otherwise meant to them personally, and how thinking otherwise was an activity related to multiple perspectives. For this reason, thinking otherwise was broken down into two subthemes; the first focusing on the personal and the second on multiple perspectives.

Personally. Participants characterised what thinking otherwise meant to them and described thinking otherwise as a process that countered their own perspectives, and their developed understandings of truth. For example, ISF No. 11 suggested that thinking otherwise meant the opposing of their own practice and shared that for themselves it involved '... do[ing] something differently'.

For certain members of the group, thinking otherwise meant challenging well accepted standards in their practice. For example, ISF No. 25 aligned thinking otherwise with '... confront[ing] understandings of truth ...'. In this way, COC became a tool for individuals to challenge their traditional ways of practice.

Participants also characterised thinking otherwise as a place within their practice that is unheard or unexplored. They suggested that thinking otherwise requires that professionals move to a new space. For example, ISF No. 3 shared the importance of lifting personal restrictions, and identified thinking otherwise as a place where you must '... allow yourself to go'.

Similarly, ISF No. 38 characterised the unthinkable as a place that must be travelled to and, when reflecting on thinking otherwise, shared: '... go to the space of the unthinkable'. These comments suggest that thinking otherwise became a journey for participants and required that they shift their perspective and practice.

Multiple perspectives. Participants also characterised thinking otherwise as an activity that is supported by multiple perspectives. For certain members of the group, thinking otherwise encouraged an acknowledgement of multiple perspectives and acceptance that different views are inherent within groups. This is best summarised by the response of ISF No. 20, who shared:

> Different people do things differently – think otherwise – [w]e may have different styles but the process is the same.

Through COC, acknowledging multiple perspectives surrounding an issue became possible, and this encouraged individuals' abilities to think otherwise about what had previously been taken for granted.

Discussion

The mixed-methods design provided data that describe the work environment of professionals supporting ECEC centres in Australia while also suggesting some benefits that professional development interventions which focus on critical reflection may have for their practice. This section will first discuss the findings from the CCW-JSI instrument, highlighting how the data characterise the work role of ISFs in Queensland, Australia. The following section will illustrate the implications of the intervention and how the outcomes may support areas of ISF practice that they have identified as challenging.

Data from the CCW-JSI suggest that job demands are an area of the ISFs' role that provides challenge to their practice. Participants perceived that they have an average or above-average amount of job controls and job resources, implying that they have an adequate amount of both traits to complete their work effectively. At the same time, the sample of ISF professionals included within this research perceived that they have between a fair and a frequent amount of job demands at a mean of 3.67, suggesting that their work is demanding. The survey results position job demands as an area that may cause stress to ISFs in Queensland.

Three items from the job demands scale were identified as particularly important for the work of ISFs, and this also encouraged the intervention. These items include 'I need to know about guiding change in ECEC services' (mean 4.19), 'I need to know about reflective practice' (mean 4.22) and 'I must have cross-cultural competencies' (mean 3.92). The COC model is a tool that may address these items as it is currently being identified by participants as a method that can assist in encouraging reflective practice in dynamic education settings. For example, Macfarlane and Cartmel (2012) implemented the COC method in their research with professionals working in children's services. They found that the use of COC engendered change in people's minds because it encouraged them to consider multiple perspectives. These authors also found that COC changed the way participants approached particular issues and led to changes in the practice of those who used the model. In this study, users of COC also experienced increases in understanding of content and knowledge (Macfarlane and Cartmel 2012). These results suggest that the COC methodology is a useful framework for practitioners to negotiate multiple perspectives. Additionally, their results suggest that the COC methodology may work to limit professionals' job stress by supporting their ability to see their work situation from different points of view.

This usefulness was further evidenced following the first workshop where participants shared how their use of the COC methodology impacted their practice. Participants highlighted how the initial COC workshop allowed them to reflect on their own practice and perspective while taking into consideration the perspectives of their colleagues. This outcome is significant when the quantitative data are considered. Within the job demands scale, ISFs established the importance of reflective practice to their work. The initial workshop using the COC methodology allowed individuals to take on multiple points of view and this may also aid them in dealing with their job stress. Again, this means that conflict and related demands could be minimised or reduced. Additionally, participants highlighted that the COC process may become a useful roadmap for them to encourage changes within their work. This point is significant because quantitative data also suggested that practitioners were required to support change in ECEC settings. Given the COC methodology's ability to support change in ISFs' workplace, the model when used in practice during negotiations with ECEC settings may support ISFs' ability to encourage change in ECEC settings. Critical reflection tools such as COC then become important interventions, which provide professional training in areas where practitioners face job stress related to their job demands.

The initial findings from this research support the contention that reflective practice may be a tool to reduce the job stress faced by professionals working in ECEC. Recent research exploring this phenomenon has found positive results. Diaz (2012) utilised a quasi-experimental design to explore how a reflective practice intervention may reduce job stress amongst early childcare educators in the state of California. Within the reflective practice intervention, participants were invited to identify a challenge or issue within their workplace, outline the factors contributing to an issue and take into account the perspectives of others involved (Diaz 2012). Similar to our findings, Diaz (2012) found that the reflective practice workshops provided a venue for participants to converse about an issue and encourage changes to their practice. Furthermore, Diaz (2012) found that teachers involved in reflection workshops reported that their workplace stress decreased. Results from Diaz (2012) and this

THE PROFESSIONAL DEVELOPMENT OF EARLY YEARS EDUCATORS

study suggest that interventions focusing on reflective practice may reduce job stress and facilitate change.

Participants involved in the critical reflection exercise suggested that their participation encouraged their ability to account for multiple perspectives and think otherwise about stereotypes they held. Similar results were identified in Dvir and Avissar's (2014) case study of a learning programme meant to develop critical professionals in education. They found that participation in a critical reflection learning programme allowed candidates to learn about different cultures and perspectives within the communities they served. Specifically, participants' work within diverse communities allowed them to reconceptualise education and think outside their own perspective in terms of content delivery. Additionally it allowed participants to challenge the opinions that they may have held about individuals living within low socio-economic areas.

Finally, this research has limitations that may impact the strength of the findings, and are important to address. The study included a small sample of professionals that support ECEC centres in Queensland, Australia. Given the sample size, and their unique role, it is fair to say that results cannot be generalised to all professionals working in the ECEC field. Additionally, results from this research, which concern the effectiveness of the intervention, do not provide insight into how the COC method might impact practitioners in the long term. This research explored the perceptions of practitioners following the first of a series of eight workshops that will take place over a period of two years. Understanding the long-term outcomes of this intervention will require gathering practitioners' perspectives throughout and following the project.

Recommendations

This research provides evidence supporting reflective practice workshops as effective in encouraging transdisciplinary dialogue between professionals who support ECEC centres. It is expected that reflective practice can support the reduction of job stress amongst professionals working in childcare (Diaz 2012) and those who support childcare professionals. Considering the limited research that explores the perspectives of Australian early childhood professionals (Yost 2012), evaluations of similar programmes are needed in order to draw concrete conclusions about the effectiveness of reflective practice workshops. Additionally, research will benefit from exploring how such interventions impact professionals in the long term, and how long-term interventions may reduce job stress and encourage change in ECEC settings.

Conclusion

The present study suggests some of the short-term outcomes that professionals working with ECEC centres experienced as a result of their participation in an initial critical reflection workshop. Critical reflection encouraged individuals to account for multiple perspectives in decision-making and provided them with a safe space to have their opinions heard. Additionally, participants highlighted that the COC process encouraged them to think otherwise about their practice. The COC model was identified by participants as an effective methodology to encourage critical reflection amongst a group.

To date minimal research has explored the perspectives of early childhood educators and professionals who support their practice (Yost 2012). Results from this study suggest that supporting ECEC centres is challenging, and that professionals working within this capacity have high job demands partially resulting from the interdisciplinary nature of their work. The development and facilitation of programmes that encourage critical reflection is one approach which may reduce job demands faced by professionals working in ECEC. Furthermore, the implementation of programmes provides the opportunity for individuals working within the field to collaboratively identify areas for concern, and ways to make change happen.

Disclosure statement

No potential conflict of interest was reported by the authors.

Funding

Funding for this research was provided by Uniting Care Queensland.

References

Brennan, E.M., *et al.*, 2008. The evidence base for mental health consultation in early childhood settings: research synthesis addressing staff and program outcomes. *Early education & development*, 19 (6), 982–1022.

Creswell, J.W., 2003. *Research design: qualitative, quantitative, and mixed method approaches*. Thousand Oaks, CA: Sage.

Curbow, B., *et al.*, 2000. Development of the child care worker job stress inventory. *Early childhood research quarterly*, 15 (4), 515–536.

Davies, R. and Dart, J., 2005. *The 'Most Significant Change' (MSC) technique: a guide to its use* [online]. Available from: www.mande.co.uk/docs/MSCGuide.pdf [Accessed 5 March 2010].

Department of Education, Employment and Workplace Relations (DEEWR), 2012. *Inclusion and professional support program guidelines 2013–2016* [online]. Available from: http://deewr.gov.au/inclusion-andprofessional-support-program [Accessed 30 March 2013].

Diaz, E.K., 2012. *The effects of reflective practice on teacher perceptions of work related stressors for early childhood educators*. Master of Science. San Diego State University, San Diego, CA.

Dvir, N. and Avissar, I., 2014. Constructing a critical professional identity among teacher candidates during service-learning. *Professional development in education*, 40 (3), 398–415.

Fenech, M., 2006. The impact of regulatory environments on early childhood professional practice and job satisfaction: a review of conflicting discourses. *Australian journal of early childhood*, 31 (2), 49–57.

Goelman, H. and Guo, H., 1998. What we know and what we don't know about burnout among early childhood care providers. *Child & youth care forum*, 27 (3), 175–199.

Gratz, R.R. and Claffey, A., 1996. Adult health in child care: health status, behaviors, and concerns of teachers, directors, and family child care providers. *Early childhood research quarterly*, 11 (2), 243–267.

Gün, B., 2011. Quality self-reflection through reflection training. *ELT journal*, 65 (2), 126–135.

Hale-Jinks, C. and Knopf, H., 2006. Tackling teacher turnover in child care: understanding causes and consequences, identifying solutions. *Childhood education*, 82 (4), 219–226.

Hurrell, J.J., 1987. An overview of organizational stress. *In:* L.R. Murphy and T. Schoenborn, eds. *Stress management in work settings*. New York, NY: Praeger, 31–45.

Jovanovic, J., 2013. Retaining early childcare educators. *Gender, work and organization*, 20 (5), 528–544.

Kelly, A.L. and Berthelsen, D.C., 1995. Preschool teachers' experiences of stress. *Teaching and teacher education*, 11 (4), 345–357.

Kelly, A.L. and Berthelsen, D.C., 1997. Teachers coping with change: the stories of two preschool teachers. *Australian research in early childhood education*, 1, 62–70.

Li Grining, C., *et al.*, 2010. Understanding and improving classroom emotional climate and behavior management in the "real world": the role of Head Start teachers' psychosocial stressors. *Early education & development*, 21 (1), 65–94. doi:10.1080/10409280902783509.

Lovett, S. and Gilmore, A., 2003. Teachers' learning journeys: the quality learning circle as a model of professional development. *School effectiveness and school improvement*, 14 (2), 189–211.

Macfarlane, K. and Cartmel, J., 2012. Circles of change revisited: building leadership, scholarship and professional identity in the children's services sector. *Professional development in education*, 38 (5), 845–861.

Macfarlane, K., Cartmel, J., and Maher, C., 2008. Challenging traditional notions of practice through circles of change. *Educating young children*, 14 (1), 21–26.

Macfarlane, K., Noble, K., and Cartmel, J., 2004. Pedagogy in the nursery: establishing practitioner partnerships in high-quality long day care programs. *Australian journal of early childhood*, 29 (4), 38–44.

Maslach, C. and Pines, A., 1977. The burn-out syndrome in the day care setting. *Child care quarterly*, 6 (2), 100–113.

Moss, P., 2000. Training of early childhood education and care staff. *International journal of educational research*, 33 (1), 31–53.

Moss, P. and Pence, A., 1994. *Valuing quality in early childhood services*. London: Paul Chapman.

National Childcare Accreditation Council. 2002. *Putting children first: quality improvement and accreditation system handbook*. Canberra: NCAC.

Noble, K., 2003. Graduate programs for students working in the ECEC sector. Refereed paper submitted to the *New Zealand Association of Research in Education/Australian Association of Research in Education conference*, Auckland, New Zealand, 29 November–4 December.

Perry, R., 1997. *Teaching practice*. London: Routledge.

Strauss, A. and Corbin, J.M., eds., 1997. *Grounded theory in practice*. London: Sage.

Sumsion, J., 2007. Sustaining the employment of early childhood teachers in long day care: a case for robust hope, critical imagination and critical action. *Asia-Pacific journal of teacher education*, 35 (3), 311–327.

Townley, K.F., Thornburg, K.R., and Crompton, D., 1991. Burnout in teachers of young children. *Early education & development*, 2 (3), 197–204. doi:10.1207/s15566935eed0203_2.

Wideen, M., Mayer-Smith, J., and Moon, B., 1998. A critical analysis of the research on learning to teach: making the case for an ecological perspective on inquiry. *Review of educational research*, 68 (2), 130–178.

Yost, D.S., Sentner, S.M., and Forlenza-Bailey, A., 2000. An examination of the construct of critical reflection: implications for teacher education programming in the 21st century. *Journal of teacher education*, 51 (1), 39–49.

Yost, H.F., 2012. *"Things are always changing": investigating Tasmanian early childhood teachers' perceptions of teaching*. Doctor of Education. University of Tasmania.

Zhai, F., Raver, C.C., and Li-Grining, C., 2011. Classroom-based interventions and teachers' perceived job stressors and confidence: evidence from a randomized trial in Head Start settings. *Early childhood research quarterly*, 26 (4), 442–452.

Head Start classroom teachers' and assistant teachers' perceptions of professional development using a LEARN framework

Ilham Nasser, Julie K. Kidd, M. Susan Burns and Trina Campbell

This study investigates early childhood education teachers' and assistant teachers' views about a year-long professional development model that focuses on developing intentional teaching. The study shares the results of interviews conducted with the teachers at the end of the implementation of a one-year experimental professional model in Head Start settings in a large metropolitan area. The purpose was to gather feedback on the model, which included large-group, on-site and one-on-one interactions. Teachers and assistant teachers were asked about the various components of the model and the influence the professional development opportunities had on their practice and classroom interactions. The results of this study support the importance of providing networking opportunities across sites and sharing usable knowledge and strategies that can be applied directly to their work with young children.

Introduction

Teacher educators have concluded that teaching is an ongoing learning process that expands beyond the formal university training and continues in actual classrooms in the form of professional development (PD) and mentoring relationships (Blank 2010). Early childhood teachers need continuous and sustainable PD, and according to Cummins, 'what is needed are personal, ongoing relationships that can make a difference, and provide the understanding that mentoring is an important teacher PD strategy' (2004, p. 257). Despite this assertion, there is a lack of clarity in the United States about the most effective forms of PD in early childhood education and the impact on teachers' development and improving practice (Diamond *et al.* 2013). There is also a lack of consistency regarding agreed-upon professional standards that promote teachers' development and preparation (Zaslow *et al.* 2010). There is agreement, however, on the need for effective PD that leads to better instruction and improved student learning (Diamond *et al.* 2013), especially when it is specific to curriculum materials (Holland 2005).

Our goal in this study was to provide further insights and contribute new knowledge to the field on guiding the planning of PD by shedding light on teachers' and assistant teachers' perspectives and views about the relationships and interactions they encountered, the structure of the PD (i.e. individual, small-group and large-group learning opportunities) and the content that was addressed. We did not set out to answer the questions raised in Diamond *et al.*'s (2013) US Institute of Education Sciences report, *Synthesis of IES Research on Early Intervention and Early Childhood Education*, about the effectiveness of particular components of PD (i.e. coaching, communities of practice and use of technologies). Rather, we wanted to tap into the teachers' and assistant teachers' satisfaction with the particular components and what they believe did or did not support their growth as professionals. They often find themselves required to take part in workshops and listen to speakers without a voice in what aspects of PD promote change. These findings provide insights that will help researchers and others develop and refine PD models that can ultimately be implemented and compared to more fully answer questions about ways to help teachers and assistant teachers develop the knowledge and skills needed to be effective teachers who contribute to positive outcomes for all students.

It is also important to note that the uniqueness of this study stems from its focus on teachers' as well as assistant teachers' views to address PD needs of both groups in early childhood classrooms. In US prekindergarten classrooms, there are typically at least two adults working with each group or class of children. One often serves as the lead teacher, referred to in this study as the teacher. The other adult often serves in a supportive role that may range from teaching with the teacher, to assisting the teacher with some guidance, to assisting the teacher with high levels of guidance. In this study, we used assistant teacher to refer to any of these adults who are not in the lead teacher role.

Our study is also unique in its implementation of various PD structures and mentoring relationships that were developed and occurred over the span of the academic year. Teachers and assistant teachers had one-on-one in-classroom mentoring and small-group on-site community meetings as part of their PD program in addition to full days of large-group PD sessions, which are described in more detail below. The PD was delivered by a group of faculty and doctoral students in an early childhood education program in the same region.

Related literature

The question of how teachers learn and how they apply the knowledge, especially in early childhood settings, has been an ongoing interest in teachers' professional training (Blank 2010). Planning interventions that reflect the principles of adult learning and promote deep content knowledge and application of information in the classroom has also been highlighted in PD literature (Hofman and Dijkstra 2010). Research on PD that supports teacher effectiveness provides important convergent findings on such issues as the importance of a more specialized and experienced peer in guiding a continuous teacher development (Whitebook and Bellm 1996) and the ineffectiveness of one-time workshops and short-term mentoring (Birman *et al.* 2000, Diamond *et al.* 2013). Nevertheless, other research reports conflicting findings in areas such as the nature of embedded mentoring, duration and intensity, and impact on child's outcomes (Assel *et al.* 2007, Wong and Premkumar 2007). These findings are critical in cases where teachers' accountability is high stakes – as in Head Start, which is a federally funded program in the United States that was established in 1965 to provide services such as health, nutrition and education to children and families in poverty (Zigler and Styfco 2010). In these contexts, measures of teacher quality and child success outcomes drive whether a Head Start program will have ongoing funding (US Department of Health and Human Services 2009). This intensifies the need for effective PD that results in positive student outcomes for all children.

Most studies point to the importance of ongoing opportunities for PD, especially the need for learning formats that go beyond the one-shot workshops prevalent in many PD designs (Onchwari and Keengwe 2008, Simon *et al.* 2011, Diamond *et al.* 2013). Guidance on effective PD is multifaceted, and programs typically lack well-developed, focused plans that are research based (Loucks-Horsley *et al.* 2010). Recommendations from the field support the importance of considering the form, duration and prior knowledge of participants in designing successful PD (Puig and Recchia 2008), including integration of content knowledge and opportunities to enact newly learned information and reflect on that enactment individually and in groups (Van Driel and Berry 2012). In a meta-analysis of PD literature, Birman *et al.* (2000) suggested new insight into these factors. According to their study, more hands-on PD, more time combined with more contact, and collective participation are essential components and show greater potential for achieving results. Mentoring relationships potentially allow for more time spent in classrooms and direct contact with teachers in their own classrooms, and as a result lead to improved practice.

A high level of support, whether teachers are veteran or novice, is important in promoting teachers' professional knowledge on the job. Nevertheless, debates around the most effective PD activities continue. For example, Anders *et al.* (2000) concluded that quality PD is characterized by the following features: intensive/extensive commitments; monitoring/coaching/clinical support; reflection; deliberation, dialog and negotiation; voluntary participation/choice; and collaboration. A recent study by Wei *et al.* (2010) suggested that PD conceived along these lines is effective. In addition, PD that allows feedback and modeling had greater impact on teachers' practice and ensured change continues after the intervention (Joyce and Showers 2002). Diamond *et al.* (2013) also concluded that effective PD focuses on the learner, takes place in a collaborative environment, includes opportunities to enact the content addressed and is supported by constructive feedback.

Previous research suggests the importance of carefully planning the structure and nature of mentoring interactions. A few studies reported that some teachers considered mentoring/coaching as an added job and a time-consuming process (Puig and Recchia 2008). Others documented successes gained in mentoring relationships, especially when focused and individualized (Domitrovich *et al.* 2009). Furthermore, teachers expressed higher satisfaction with mentoring activities and found mentoring more attractive when conducted in a non-evaluative manner (Evans-Andris *et al.* 2006, Domitrovich *et al.* 2009). In the Evans-Andris *et al.* (2006) study, teachers described mentors as supportive, respectful and helpful. Close mentoring allows participants to build a relationship that is more personalized and encourages teachers to be more receptive to new ideas (Onchwari and Keengwi 2008).

Furthermore, a site-based PD forum, where teachers collaborate and learn together, is an effective way to improve practice without overwhelming the teacher (Kuh 2012). In Kuh's (2012) study, positive effects were found when teachers practiced working as a team with their peers at the same site. Evans-Andris *et al.* (2006) reported learning new information from formal and informal networking opportunities provided in the program. Teachers also recommended that mentoring

THE PROFESSIONAL DEVELOPMENT OF EARLY YEARS EDUCATORS

needs more structure, including guidelines for what to talk about, how long to meet for and when to meet (Evans-Andris *et al.* 2006).

Professional development framework

Previous learning frameworks such as Bybee (1997) and Donovan *et al.* (1999) put emphasis on problem-solving and scientific inquiries as a foundation for learning. In this study, we used a framework we refer to as the Learn, Enact, Assess, Reflect, and Network (LEARN) framework, which was developed by Snow *et al.* (2005) and promotes the importance of engaging in learning, enacting, assessing and reflecting to enhance adult learning. Preschool teachers and assistant teachers in this study were engaged in continuous PD opportunities that enabled them to learn new knowledge, enact it in their classrooms, assess the effectiveness, reflect on the results, and network with others in communities of practice and learning networks. This cyclical framework allows teachers to learn more about their practice and ways it affects students' learning. In addition, it provides the opportunity to try new knowledge in real classrooms. The structure of the developed PD allowed participating teachers and assistant teachers to gain knowledge that is applicable. The PD model responded to the need for enactment identified in the literature as one of the issues lacking in PD activities. According to Hammerness *et al.* (2005) and Van Driel and Berry (2012), teachers are given knowledge but not how to transfer it to the classroom.

Our work with the teachers and teacher assistants focused on promoting intentional teaching across content areas. Intentional teaching has been identified as a mechanism to promote teachers' effectiveness (Bredekamp and Copple 2009) and is defined in the following way in our study:

> Intentional teaching means that teachers provide learning opportunities designed to meet the individual needs, interests, and prior knowledge of all children in their instructional settings. This takes place through reciprocal, codirected conversation between teachers and children in learning centers/small groups. Conversation happens with all children, rather than a selected few, and takes place on a consistent basis (high quantity as well as high quality). Children's ideas are developed, and thinking is demanded using rich curriculum content (e.g., in science, creative arts, and social studies). Planned instructional strategies/ activities take place within a positive classroom climate. (Burns *et al.* 2012, p. 284)

Epstein (2007) identified several strategies to promote intentional teaching practices when working with young children, such as structuring the physical environment, planning curriculum, scheduling the program day, interacting with children, building relationships with families and authentic assessment. Epstein's strategies balance the adult-guided experiences with the child-initiated ones, keeping in mind methods in which the intentional teacher uses best practices identified by the National Association for Educators of Young Children (Bredekamp and Copple 2009).

In our work, we focused the PD model on six broad instructional strategies: culturally responsive practice; including all children; differentiated instruction; effective teaching strategies; bridging assessment, instruction and curriculum; and integrating intentional teaching with the current curriculum model. These strategies form a comprehensive system for enhancing teachers' effectiveness by building upon and making connections across components and modeling intentional teaching. The above strategies were chosen for their appeal across content areas and their interconnectedness in actual practice in early childhood settings. We believe that serving all children requires knowledge of culturally responsive practice, differentiation strategies and assessment; all are components of intentional teaching.

Professional development components

As mentioned above, the model included different delivery methods. Teachers and assistant teachers had monthly one-on-one, in-classroom mentoring sessions and small-group, on-site community meetings as part of their PD program in addition to five full days of large-group PD sessions. Each large-group session lasted for a whole day (seven to eight hours) and mainly focused on delivering the knowledge base for the strategies mentioned above that were implemented in PD.

One-on-one mentoring

In this study, we adopted the definition of mentoring that highlights the expertise of the mentor and his or her attempt to provide a focused intervention that is not evaluative and is constructed in partnership with the mentee. In a recent publication from the National Association for the Education of Young Children, mentoring is defined as:

> ... a relationship-based process between colleagues in similar professional roles, with a more-experienced individual with adult learning knowledge and skills, the mentor providing guidance and example to the less-experienced protégé or mentee. Mentoring is intended to increase an individual's personal or professional capacity, resulting in greater professional effectiveness. (2011, p. 11)

The in-classroom mentoring involved mentors going into the classroom and working with the teachers and assistant teachers on challenges they identified. To plan for the in-classroom mentoring, we asked teachers and assistant teachers to identify one child and one intentional teaching strategy to target during each visit. We also asked them to indicate whether they wanted the mentor to observe and provide feedback, demonstrate the enactment of a strategy or co-teach with the mentee. We asked the teachers and assistant teachers to each complete a form prior to the in-classroom mentoring session and fax or email it to the mentor to enable the mentor to prepare for the mentoring session.

On-site community of learning and practice groups

Teachers and teacher assistants also participated in an on-site community of learning and practice group that met on a monthly basis. Communities of practice were described by Wenger and Snyder as, 'groups of people informally bound together by shared expertise and passion for a joint enterprise' (2000, p. 139). The community is a place to share, 'experiences and knowledge in free-flowing creative ways that foster new approaches to problems' (2000, p. 140). Communities form based on a common interest with a commitment to developing the abilities of others in the group and sharing knowledge and expertise (Wenger and Snyder 2000). Communities are mutually engaged in sustained pursuit of 'what matters' by building on collective goals and knowledge (Brouwer et al. 2012, p. 403). As teachers build a community, they offer and consider more divergent perspectives from team members, collaborate on problem-solving and accept constructive input from coworkers.

The on-site community meetings were held in each school and included teachers and assistant teachers who worked at the site. They provided a less formal context for learning that included the learning of new information as well as time to assess and reflect on the enactment of knowledge in the classroom. These meetings included time for each mentor and teaching team to discuss what was enacted in the classroom and skills and strategies to address issues raised by teachers. The mentors introduced content through readings, videos, assignments and/or discussion prompts.

Online community of practice and learning groups

Continuous PD also included participation in online learning experiences using Blackboard software. Stella and Gnanam (2004, p. 144) suggested that with technological advances and their integration in different aspects of learning a convergence has been created and resulted in the use of a broad-based term 'distributed learning.' They add that distributed learning can happen either on campus or off, its intentions are to provide greater flexibility and more time spent on learning. An online component allows situated and spontaneous learning that can respond to specific group needs without time or location constraints (Ayling *et al.* 2012). Use of online mentoring and collaboration enabled members of the learning and practice communities to continue to share and support each other even when they were not at the same school. The mentors facilitate these online groups.

The three above components were combined to provide support in multiple forms and spaces and to meet individual needs of teachers. In order to add to the knowledge already existing in the field about ways in which successful PD works, the current study attempted to explore the following research questions:

(1) What was the teachers' and assistant teachers' overall satisfaction with a year-long PD model that included large-group institutes, small-group community meetings and individual in-classroom mentoring?
(2) What elements of the PD model did teachers and assistants perceive supported their PD?
(3) What improvements to the model did teachers and assistants perceive were needed to better support their PD?

Methods and procedures

Context

This study was part of a larger study funded through a grant by the Administration for Children and Families in the US Department of Health and Human Services that focused on the development of a PD model for Head Start teachers and assistant teachers. Two staff members were hired to support the PD. Doctoral students with graduate research assistantships not paid for by the grant contributed to the research as well as a doctoral student engaged in an unpaid research internship and doctoral students who volunteered their time.

Participants

The participants in this study were from a large metropolitan area in the Mid-Atlantic United States and were chosen for their proximity to the researchers. They were all teachers and assistant teachers in three Head Start programs in the region. In one location, assistant teachers were more functioning as paraprofessionals, who worked with a high level of guidance from the teacher; in the second they were co-teachers, who worked with the teacher; and in the third they were defined as teacher assistants, who worked with some guidance from the teachers. Nevertheless, they all had direct responsibilities for small groups of children in the classroom, and they all spent a considerable amount of time interacting with children. As part of the larger study, teachers and assistant teachers in the three locations were randomly assigned to either the experimental group or the control group. Those assigned to the experimental group participated in the PD model described above. For this qualitative study, only those who participated in the PD were included in the focus group discussions and the interviews.

Twenty-seven teachers (a total of 13) and assistant teachers (a total of 14) participated in this study. They were diverse with a majority of non-white (non-Caucasian) teachers and assistant teachers in year one and white teachers and assistant teachers in year two. The majority in both years spoke English only. The education levels of teachers and assistant teachers varied, with a majority of participants in the first year having a high school diploma or associate's degree and a bachelor's degree or higher in the second year. Most participants majored in early childhood education and had taught for three or more years. Table 1 provides demographic information on the participants in both years of the PD study.

As mentioned earlier, the teachers and assistant teachers were engaged in different forms of interactions in groups and as individuals. Table 2 provides information on the amount of time spent in each mentoring year. To accommodate their after-school schedules, on-site community meetings and large-group institute days were shortened in the second year. Therefore, participants received more hours in institute days and on-site community meetings in the first year, but more in-classroom mentoring in the second year. Also, it is notable that assistant teachers in both years received less mentoring hours because they chose not to or were unable to stay beyond their contract hours during in-classroom mentoring days and on-site community meetings.

Interview procedures

We conducted interviews to examine teachers' and teacher assistants' views in regard to their varied mentoring experiences. In both years, doctoral students (three females and one male with three minority ethnic groups and one majority ethnic group) not familiar to the participants conducted interviews at the end of the intervention period. Doctoral students not involved in the implementation of the study conducted the interviews to provide a safe and comfortable space for participants to express their views and opinions (Bloor *et al.* 2001). A qualitative approach was chosen because it provided the opportunity to ask in-depth questions and receive detailed teacher evaluation of the model (Hatch 2002, de Marrais 2004). In interviewing, we investigated levels of satisfaction with the content, processes and structure of the mentoring and how teachers implemented new knowledge. Teachers shared their perceptions of important components, helpful materials and further

THE PROFESSIONAL DEVELOPMENT OF EARLY YEARS EDUCATORS

Table 1. Teacher information.

	Year 1		Year 2	
Characteristic	Teachers ($n = 4$)	Teacher assistants ($n = 5$)	Teachers ($n = 9$)	Teacher assistants ($n = 9$)
Race or ethnicity				
White	0	0	7	2
African-American	4	4	2	3
Spanish/Hispanic/Latin origin	0	1	0	3
African-American and White	0	0	0	1
Fluent languages				
English only	4	2	9	5
English and Spanish	0	1	0	3
English and Arabic	0	2	0	1
Highest degree				
High school diploma	2	3	1	6
AA degree	1	0	1	1
BA degree	1	2	4	2
Master's degree	0	0	3	0
Major of highest degree				
Early childhood	2	2	3	7
Elementary	0	0	1	0
Other	1	2	2	0
N/A	1	1	3	2
Teaching experience				
2 years or less	0	2	0	2
3–10 years	1	3	3	4
11+ years	3	0	6	3

Table 2. Mentoring activities: average hours and minutes.

	Institute mentoring days	On-site community meetings	In-classroom mentoring
Year 1			
Teachers ($n = 4$)	31 h 30 m	18 h	4 h
Teacher assistants ($n = 5$)	31 h 30 m	17 h	5 h
Year 2			
Teachers ($n = 9$)	22 h 20 m	7 h	7 h
Teacher assistants ($n = 9$)	21 h	5 h 28 m	6 h 31 m

needs. One of the interviewers was involved in both the focus groups and the individual interviews to maintain consistency.

In year one, focus groups were used to identify the main themes that were important to participants for further exploration (Patton 2002) and PD development. Also, based on recommendations for focus group research (Krueger and Casey

2009), they included two groups for 90 minutes each with one for the five teachers and one for the four assistant teachers. The five teachers and four assistant teachers met in separate groups to prevent bias from power differentials (Merton 1987), but were diverse enough within groups to have some diversity in their experiences (Jarrell 2000). Two moderators and an assistant kept track of the equipment for audio-taping and video-taping and facilitated the focus groups. Both moderators were unknown to the participants and were recruited because they share the same cultural and linguistic backgrounds as the teachers and assistant teachers. Stewart *et al.* (2006) examined the role of the moderator in focus group research and recommend training to limit interviewer bias and increase the opportunity to learn from participants. The moderators attended a three-hour training prior to the interviews, on the goals and procedures for conducting focus groups, including ways to probe responses, questions to avoid, allowing time for all participants to voice their opinions and encouraging all to take part in the interview, especially those who were less talkative. Onwuegbuzie *et al.* (2010) recommend immediate debriefing of moderators so taped debriefing sessions were conducted afterwards to obtain immediate feedback from moderators.

In year two, individual interviews were used to gain more depth on the topics of interest to researchers (Museus 2007). Two research assistants conducted the interviews with the teachers and assistant teachers. The two researchers were also trained to conduct individual interviews and elicit information from participants. Interviews lasted from 25 to 30 minutes and were recorded.

Data analysis procedures

Transcripts of focus group and individual interviews were the main data source for analysis of teachers' and assistant teachers' responses. We conducted a 'key concepts' analysis of the transcripts (Krueger 1998, Krueger and Casey 2009), in addition to the word-by-word transcription of the conversations and notations of non-verbal behaviors recorded by a note-taker (pauses, silence, laughter, etc.). Three researchers analyzed the transcripts and followed the protocol for qualitative data analyses in which each rater read through transcripts, gathered responses under each one of the questions asked and individually conducted open coding of emerging themes. The raters then generated a list of themes independently, discussed with a second rater, and decided on a list of common themes. Each conducted a second reading of transcripts to apply the common codes for themes, listed the frequency of emerging themes and compared with the other rater. Any codes that differed were discussed in depth until consensus was reached.

Findings

Our in-depth examination of written transcripts revealed overall satisfaction with the PD model and specifically with three of the model's components: the institute days, community meetings and in-classroom mentoring. When analyzing the discussions of what teachers and assistant teachers found most meaningful about the PD model, three themes emerged: the focus on usable knowledge; the opportunities for networking with colleagues within and across sites; and mentors' positive interactions that supported their learning. Three themes also emerged in the discussions of what was least meaningful about the PD model and their suggested changes to the model. Participants questioned the selection process, the benefit of the model across all PD participants and the clarity of the expectations for their involvement in the PD. They also provided suggestions on ways to better use technology to support their learning.

Overall satisfaction

In the interviews, all teachers and all but one assistant teacher shared their perceptions of what were the most and least meaningful aspects of each of the components and what they gained from their involvement in the PD.[1] Overall, both the teachers and assistant teachers expressed high satisfaction with the PD model and the key elements of its implementation. For example, one assistant teacher remarked: 'I think it's been good for me personally. Other than that, I don't have anything – nothing against. [To] the contrary, I think it's been very beneficial.' One teacher admitted that she 'dreaded' the thought of participating in the PD. But then they said: 'I come and I am like okay. It was cool, and it was beneficial, and I got this. I learned stuff, you know.' Although some seemed to feel ambivalent about their involvement at times, once engaged in the process most viewed the PD as a positive experience. However, one assistant teacher had no positive comments to make about any aspect of the PD. At the beginning of her interview, she stated: 'I just don't know what the point of this whole thing [the PD] was. I don't feel like I learned anything.' It seems that for this particular assistant teacher there was no point or benefit in attending PD not mandated by Head Start. For her, anything above and beyond the job description was understandably a waste of time and effort.

When asked specifically about the institute days, community meetings and in-classroom mentoring, all but the one assistant teacher shared positive outcomes from each of these ways PD was delivered. They believed all three elements gave them access to usable knowledge that could be enacted in their classrooms and that their learning was enhanced by networking with colleagues during the institute days and community meetings. They also talked about the important role in-classroom mentoring played in their learning and discussed the way in-classroom mentoring provided support as they enacted what they learned from the institute days and community meetings in their own classrooms. In addition, they noted the vital role that the guidance, modeling and feedback during in-classroom mentoring played in their development, which is consistent with the literature on individual mentoring aspects of PD.

Less successful, in their opinion, were the attempts at using technology to support their professional growth, a fourth component of the model. Although some made use of technology (e.g. Blackboard software, email, telephone calls, etc.), three of the teachers indicated that they did not use the technology-based supports effectively. They cited lack of knowledge and time as reasons they did not use some of the online support. Some, like this teacher, indicated that they preferred face-to-face interactions: 'I don't want to communicate that [online] way.' She wanted interactions that would allow her to communicate using her hands. Two additional teachers appeared to be concerned about others' perceptions based on what they wrote online. One teacher explained: 'The problem for me with chat rooms is that you don't want everybody else to think you're stupid. So, people who might feel that way about asking a question might not participate.' However, that same teacher mentioned that she made use of and benefited from emailing one-on-one with her mentor. Others also noted the value of the technology-based supports and mentioned supports such as using the Blackboard site to access valuable resources. Overall, there appeared to be resistance to using technology to support PD partly due to lack of proficiency in communicating using a variety of technologies and partly because of a preference for face-to-face interactions.

Usable knowledge

One theme prevalent throughout the focus group discussions and across the interviews was the teachers' and assistant teachers' appreciation of the focus on sharing knowledge that is usable and applicable immediately in their classroom. All teachers and all but one assistant teacher (i.e. specifically the one mentioned above who had no positive comments) indicated that one of the most meaningful elements of the PD was the focus on learning new knowledge that could be enacted in the classroom. In their discussions, they addressed the importance of providing applicable reading materials and resources, focusing on lesson planning ideas and formats, and sharing proven strategies that were tested and suggested in the research.

The one assistant teacher mentioned above who was not satisfied with the PD believed that usable knowledge was important, but indicated that no usable knowledge had been shared during the PD. She suggested that an improvement to the PD would be to 'have stuff that teachers could actually use in the classroom.' She explained: 'I didn't learn anything I haven't already learned from the classes I've been taking to get my degree.' Although the others were generally pleased with the new information they learned, several of the more experienced teachers commented that some of the material was a review of information that they already knew.

Reading materials and resources

Teachers and assistant teachers indicated that the reading materials (three teachers mentioned reading articles) and other resources (12 teachers referred to resources) shared throughout the PD provided valuable knowledge they could apply in their classrooms.[2] For example, one teacher noted that the 'articles read ... were thoughtful and thought provoking,' while another did not find the reading materials useful. She indicated that there was no information in the articles that she would be able to implement in her classroom. Eight also commented on the usefulness of the videos shared that provided information and examples of teachers implementing strategies in their classrooms, while four suggested that additional use of videos may have been helpful.

Lesson planning strategies

A theme more prevalent with the teachers than the assistant teachers was the focus on lesson planning strategies. For example, one teacher stated that what she found most beneficial was the 'lesson plan.' The teachers shared that they thought the format was helpful because it encouraged them to think about what they need to do for the individual children in their classrooms. For example, one teacher noted: 'The format of [the mentor's] lesson plan was great and even for the children with special needs it had an area there where I guess I can individualize for the areas

THE PROFESSIONAL DEVELOPMENT OF EARLY YEARS EDUCATORS

that I need to really work on.' Another explained that it was beneficial because: 'it made me look at the kids a little different as far as who needed what – less support or more support. And it just made me break down my lesson plan even more.' Another teacher's comments focused more on how what she learned prompted her to think about her lesson plans in a different way: 'It gave me basically a way to look at my lesson plans more critically because I was able to individualize work for certain children in the classroom and basic things – some things I may have been missing.' For the most part, they seemed to value the knowledge the mentors shared and the way the mentors empowered them to apply it in the classroom, which are integral to the LEARN framework of PD.

Evidence-based strategies

The theme most often discussed was the emphasis on evidence-based strategies that could be applied immediately in classrooms. They discussed evidence-based strategies within the framework of intentional teaching, including its components such as culturally responsive practice and including all children as well as specific content strategies focused on reading, science and mathematics. In these discussions, they focused on activities that involved high engagement and ones they thought were easily enacted in their classrooms. Teachers also had specific feedback about activities promoting intentional teaching and cultural responsiveness.

Eight elaborated on how the focus on intentional teaching was meaningful to them. One assistant teacher explained:

> You learn how to be intentional and plan your classroom. When we concentrate and try to plan it, we are intentionally doing it. You learn step by step. You learn how to observe first, to assess our kids, and see how and plan for their level or their abilities and the interest. So, we set our goals first and then plan our activities to get to their goals.

Participants specifically discussed the benefit of learning strategies to implement culturally responsive practices in their classrooms, including all children, and using assessment to guide instruction. For example, a culturally responsive practice activity that was implemented in year one sparked more interest in the topic amongst participants, and as a result was developed in more depth for the second year of PD. This activity, where the mentor provided instruction in a different language, was very popular amongst teachers. Eight in the second year named this as the most meaningful activity in the program. One participant described the activity:

> The mentor did a lesson where we were like the ESL students. She spoke the whole lesson in her language, Hindi. I have half the class speaking Spanish and so you know – never ever experiencing what they experience. That was huge for me. Being more aware of some things I can do to help reach those kids.

Another added:

> Actually the whole thing was helpful about how to be intentional like anything that we teach has to have a purpose. It's not just simple, to teach the children something. And I think that influenced me a little more because it's not just to cover a subject and to finish what we were gonna do during the day.

Teachers and teacher assistants also discussed content area strategies. For example, when asked about the most beneficial aspects of the model, eight responded that the science and mathematics activities were one of the most beneficial aspects. One assistant teacher explained: 'In these areas, especially science where we learn how to include the science into our curriculum into the classroom – like use science from around you, from the environment outside and use them to plan activities.' Other teachers mentioned reading strategies, especially dialogic reading, as another opportunity for learning new information. It was apparent that the teachers and assistant teachers valued the fact that knowledge gained was applicable and usable in their environments.

Mentor interactions and support

In both years, teachers and assistant teachers addressed the gains from mentoring indicating that mentors were resourceful, flexible and used multiple means of communication. Teachers agreed on certain qualities that made the mentoring relationship positive and helpful. They named characteristics such as 'mentor was knowledgeable,' 'positive and likeable' and not judgmental or critical as important components of a successful mentoring relationship. Teachers also valued that mentors brought additional resources and materials to use and learn about. One participant explained:

> I had a student who had a speech problem. I felt bad because he kept talking to me and I had no idea what he was talking about. My mentor told me that you have to listen to him, and now he got better and I can understand him. She told me to use visuals for science and stuff like that. I was trying not to use science because he was already adapting to that and he wanted to point instead of talking and I didn't want him to do that. But she said start it off like that and then graduate up to the words. So she helped out with that.

Debriefing one-on-one or with the mentors' team was embedded in the on-site community meetings forum available in the model. Participants found that the mentors' attempts to follow-up and simplify PD materials and content were very helpful. An assistant teacher said:

> The mentor discussed with us, and if you don't understand she would tell you again and again. And if you still need more after the meeting, she would stay with you to see what you don't understand and after that she confirms that we feel comfortable again.

In addition, participants valued the fact that mentors modeled certain practices addressed in the PD during the in-classroom mentoring activities (this quality of mentoring was mentioned 29 times in interviews and focus groups). They also gave very specific feedback related to the concepts enacted in the classroom (e.g. feedback on working with children who are dual-language learners). They appreciated the mentors' ability to share professional knowledge on alternative strategies and provide new perspectives on classroom issues and the opportunity to discuss the in-classroom mentoring interactions. One teacher noted:

THE PROFESSIONAL DEVELOPMENT OF EARLY YEARS EDUCATORS

> For me, the most meaningful experiences were when I got to sit down with my mentor and actually talk about specific children and get her feedback on what she saw during the classroom and the tips that she gave me to help me out with certain children. That to me was the biggest benefit for me from the program.

Eleven participants mentioned how important it was that the mentoring is conducted in a non-threatening manner and that they as teachers were not evaluated. This quality was mentioned in interviews and focus groups. One remarked:

> I never felt judged; I felt supported, which is how it's supposed to be I would think. But it was a valuable thing because it was in a classroom. That's a huge meaningful thing for somebody to come in your classroom on the spot, live action, and be able to help. That was wonderful.

Another added:

> I like the fact that it was a very nonthreatening situation. When you are observed, it puts you on edge because you know you are getting evaluated or you know something of that nature. And I didn't feel that stress. She was there to help us if we needed help and we could ask her questions and she participated in activities with the children.

It was evident the teachers and assistant teachers appreciated the individualized support they received from their mentors and that they found the knowledge, modeling and feedback especially beneficial. The way mentors were able to identify useful resources and make adaptations also appeared to foster a sense of learning.

Networking with colleagues

The teachers and assistant teachers also indicated that they appreciated the networking opportunities with colleagues from their own and different sites that took place as a result of their participation in the institute days and on-site community meetings. In their discussions, 16 participants indicated that the institute days, on-site community meetings or both were beneficial because of the networking opportunities they afforded. For example, one assistant teacher said:

> I liked the big group meetings [referring to institute days] and getting different ideas. They would split us up and so we'd be working with other schools and we'd get so wrapped up just talking and having a good time about the situations so I really enjoyed that.

Participants also compared practices such as assessments used, student needs and management issues. A teacher participant expressed her appreciation of the space to converse with colleagues in the following:

> I always feel like I am in an enclosed capsule in my classroom. I have no idea how other people do circle time, or whatever. So, the fact that other people at my center shared what they were doing ... that gave me a good eye into what was going on that I may not have done very well ... and it's nice to find out that other people were having the same problems you're having. Like I said, we are so isolated trying to keep our own heads above water you don't get to talk with other staff members like you should.

Teachers and assistant teachers had favorable views of the on-site community meeting forums and the networking opportunities provided with their peers at the same schools in addition to the chance to understand teachers' practices and reasoning behind their decisions. They pointed out the lack of these types of opportunities during the school day and in their own PD days. One mentioned the value of meeting both in large groups and with your peers. She said: 'We had the most insight when we shared with each other [besides] sharing with the group that you are already with that you see all the time. Sometimes teachers don't have the opportunity to network with their own team.'

Concerns and suggestions

We also asked about what was least meaningful in the PD experience and areas for improvement of the model. Some expressed concerns and provided suggestions to improve the experience. Areas of improvement focused on the following themes: selection criteria, benefits of model to all and clarity of expectations.

Selection criteria

Teachers and assistant teachers brought up the issue of the criteria used for selecting PD participants. Several indicated that those participating should decide on joining and not the director.[3] One teacher elaborated:

> The way that people were picked I understand was random, completely random. I can understand that you need a completely random base to do a study, but there were people in my school who would've fought to do this [the PD]. They really, really wanted to do it. And some of the people, who were picked to do it, hated it. They felt like it was a big fat waste of time. They were very resentful. They did not do their share of what they were supposed to do. So to me, they were useless in what you were trying to do.

Benefits of model across participants

Another concern was the benefit of the model across teachers and assistant teachers. Three of the lead teachers suggested that the model works best for novice teachers and assistant teachers. One teacher said, 'Some activities were repetitive and not needed for veteran teachers.' Another added that the institute days provided more of a refresher on topics that she could have taught herself because she had been teaching for a long time. One teacher explained:

> I think probably newer teachers to the profession would benefit a great deal more from this program than perhaps those of us who have been doing it for a significant amount of time. I think it would be incredibly beneficial for them.

Clarity of expectations

Participants also suggested that expectations be stated more clearly. For example, one teacher stated:

> We were very unclear about the whole picture of the program: what it was about, what it was gonna be, how were we involved, how much did we need to – just the whole picture of what this was … We really didn't have a clear understanding of the expectations.

Others, like this teacher, suggested ways to make expectations clearer:

> Maybe to clarify the in-classroom support and the forms. That aspect of it so teachers can really benefit from it. I think just to have a clearer understanding of the component. Because I don't feel like I utilized it to its fullest potential just because I didn't have the total understanding.

Use of technology to support learning

We also asked specifically for thoughts about the online mentoring component of the model. Online mentoring was proposed and presented to the group but was only partially implemented using email and electronic discussion boards. There was a general agreement (19 participants) that some type of online component was helpful, especially having access to the mentor and resources, but there was a lack of enthusiasm about using more advanced methods of online mentoring such as chat rooms, video chatting and Skyping (mentioned by seven participants). It was clear that participants perceived they needed more support and training for online mentoring to be successful. One teacher said: 'Yes, chat would be cool. Message, yah all that stuff sounds like great ideas. I would also like to see more videos showing strategies.' Another teacher added: 'I am the last person to ask because I have been very reluctant to even deal with computers. I don't want to communicate this way… It wouldn't be as helpful for me, to really get good mentoring.'

Discussion

This study, with its emphasis on teachers' and assistant teachers' perspectives and evaluation of a PD model, contributes to our understanding of ways to develop effective and sustainable pedagogy based on principles of adult learners. The use of a PD system where teachers learned the knowledge, enacted it in their classrooms with the support of a mentor, and assessed and reflected on their practice (Snow et al. 2005) by networking with colleagues and a mentor without punitive and evaluative aspects (LEARN) allowed teachers to learn from the mentoring relationship. The networking opportunities also proved to be significant for participants in this study. The study suggests three major findings that emerged from interviews: the importance of providing usable knowledge in PD, the critical role that mentors play in promoting change in skills and practices through supportive interactions and, finally, the benefits of providing opportunities for Head Start teachers to network and exchange ideas with colleagues from the same program and others.

Usable knowledge

Our study supports the literature on the importance of ensuring that the PD content is applicable and usable in the classroom. It also supports the suggested benefits of targeted workshops. In particular, our study supports the conclusions of Domitrovich et al. (2009), who suggested that focusing on usable content first made teachers more interested in learning and mentoring. In addition, our study found support for the assertion that providing usable and applicable knowledge ensured that teachers understood and implemented the material (Diamond and Powell 2011,

Van Driel and Berry 2012). In-classroom mentoring allowed us to model and reinforce the content addressed in the daylong PDs and, as a result, advocate for the relevance of the content offered in the large-group setting.

Mentor's support and interactions

There are also certain characteristics that make mentoring more successful, especially when implemented one on one. When mentoring is individualized and actively engages the learner, it is more welcome and attractive to teachers, especially when mentors provide non-evaluative feedback. This finding supports lessons learned from previous studies about the importance of making mentoring a trusted relationship and not an evaluative one. As suggested by Mattern and Scott (1999), when mentoring was added to the PD, teachers began to implement it because they got immediate feedback to try new strategies. In their study, teachers reported that the mentor should be someone to be 'admired, prepared, wise, wonderful, friendly, enthusiastic, motivating, and never judgmental' (1999, p. 16). More recently, Bagnato (2011) suggested that mentoring and coaching that is separate from the Head Start evaluation system works best because it allows teachers to change in non-threatening manners. In research by Landry *et al.* (2009), the most effective mentoring was one that allowed for feedback. According to these authors: 'Not only was the most comprehensive professional development effective in improving the quality of teaching and classroom environments, but it was also effective in promoting children's learning' (2009, p. 462). In this study, we learned that the nature of the interaction with the mentor and the characteristics of the mentor including the support they provide in one-on-one situations make a difference in the applicability of the PD model.

Networking

It is clear from our findings that most Head Start teachers and assistant teachers valued the networking opportunities provided with colleagues from the same program and others. A majority of the participants named the multiple networking opportunities as an important benefit of the PD. The teachers and the assistant teachers worked in small groups and one-on-one in all forms of the mentoring model (institute days, on-site community meeting and in-classroom mentoring). The institute days themselves provided multiple small-group and large-group activities across the sites. The on-site community meetings and in-classroom mentoring included interactions with mentors and colleagues from the same site. This finding is aligned with recent literature and supports the assertion made by Han (2012) that continuous PD intervention with multiple avenues for interactions with peers and more experienced mentors meets teachers' needs for developing skills and pedagogy. In the study conducted by Hofman and Dijkstra (2010) where they compared two different PD programs, the authors found the most effective program was one where teachers worked with each other to build a network and focus on specific content.

In addition to the conclusions discussed above, teachers' concerns about 'clarity of expectations' need to be addressed. Teachers who were resistant to join this PD remained so throughout the span of the project, and colleagues noted their attitude and the importance of 'buy in' and clear expectations. Teachers and assistant

THE PROFESSIONAL DEVELOPMENT OF EARLY YEARS EDUCATORS

teachers in this study were assigned to participate by their administrators. While we hoped their attitudes would change as the program progressed, one assistant teacher's comment that none of the content was beneficial suggests a consistent level of resistance to this PD. This concern brings up the question of choice and whether teachers or administrators should determine PD needs.

This study brings up further questions in regard to effective mentor–mentee relationships and the major ingredients necessary to develop trusting relationships that allow for change in teacher behaviors. Further research is necessary to determine whether the skills taught and enacted in the classrooms as a result of the mentoring are sustained and for how long. Additionally, the components and characteristics of a successful PD are critical to develop successful mentor–mentee relationships. The further development of this PD model should include implementation in additional Head Start programs to evaluate the effect of this comprehensive PD on teachers' and assistant teachers' knowledge, skills and attitudes, but also on knowledge about research-based teacher development initiatives.

Lastly, in this study we found that assistant teachers were more positive about the overall model than teachers. Questions remain about whether or not this PD model targeted foundational skills that met the needs of assistant teachers more than the needs of the teachers. Consideration of who decides on the content of the PD activities and what roles mentees, administrators and university partners play needs further study. The evaluation data collected from assistant teachers will assist professionals working with preschool teachers to plan effective strategies and PD that develop skills specific to working with young children and improving early childhood outcomes. These data highlight the importance of including teachers and assistant teachers in PD and the planning of activities with teachers' and assistant teachers' input in mind.

Implications

Although limited by the reliance on Head Start teachers' and assistant teachers' perceptions from one geographic area in addition to the small sample size, these findings provide insight into what early childhood educators perceive is important to their PD. It is apparent that early childhood education administrators and staff developers should make it a priority to implement a LEARN framework of PD that takes into account the importance of providing opportunities for teachers and assistant teachers to gain usable knowledge within a PD model that is sustained over time, offers opportunities for new knowledge to be enacted in the classroom with the support of a mentor, and engages participants in networking opportunities that allow them to learn from their peers as well as an expert mentor. Within the LEARN framework, the words of these participants also highlight the importance of providing choice in PD activities and sharing clear expectations when expecting participants to engage in required PD. Additionally, their comments illustrate the need to examine more carefully the role of online learning and PD participants' skills related to and attitudes toward using distance-learning technologies to enhance their learning.

In addition, further research is needed to delve more deeply into the components of the PD model (i.e. large-group institutes, in-classroom mentoring, small-group community meetings and online support) to determine the effects of these professional learning opportunities on classroom instruction and, ultimately, on children's growth and learning. Specifically, we encourage researchers to examine more deeply the role in-classroom mentoring plays in teachers' professional growth and its impact on children. Research suggests that in-classroom mentoring positively influences teachers' instructional practices, which can in turn enhance children's learning (Diamond *et al.* 2013). However, the words of these participants leave us wondering about the optimal intensity and duration of in-classroom mentoring opportunities, the importance and nature of the relationship between mentor and mentee, and the way in-classroom mentoring interacts with the other components of the PD.

Also of interest is research that examines PD models including teachers and assistant teachers. The teachers and assistant teachers in our study raised issues about meeting the needs of a wide range of abilities and experiences. It makes sense to provide PD to all adults in the classroom. However, the question of how to individualize to build upon strengths and meet varying interests and needs warrants further attention.

Conclusion

It is clear that, overall, the Head Start teachers and assistant teachers found this LEARN framework of PD that involves learning new knowledge, enacting it in the classroom, assessing the enactment and reflecting on the outcomes while networking with peers and expert mentors to be beneficial to their learning. The relationships formed with the faculty, staff and doctoral students who served as mentors and the networking opportunities provided between mentors and mentees and among mentees emerged as key elements influencing teachers' and assistant teachers' perceptions of the value of the PD experience across the various components. As researchers who served as mentors and developed our own relationships with the teachers and assistant teachers, we were not surprised to discover the important role our interactions appeared to play in the participants' satisfaction and perceptions of their own learning. Through our interactions with the teachers and assistant teachers, we also engaged in a process of learning, enacting, assessing and reflecting that was influenced by the networking that occurred throughout all components of the LEARN framework of PD.

Funding

This research was supported by the Administration for Children and Families, US Department of Health and Human Services.

Notes

1. Teachers and teacher assistants are combined unless otherwise stated.
2. Numbers are out of total of 27 teachers and assistant teachers.
3. Because the mentoring was part of a research study, random assignments were used to select participants.

References

Anders, P., Hoffman, J., and Duffy, G., 2000. Teaching teachers to teach reading: paradigm shifts, persistent problems, and challenges. *In*: M.L. Kamil, *et al.*, eds. *Handbook of reading research*. Vol. III. Mahwah, NJ: Lawrence Erlbaum, 719–742.

Assel, M., *et al.*, 2007. An evaluation of curriculum, setting, and mentoring on the performance of children enrolled in pre-kindergarten. *Reading and writing*, 20 (5), 463–494. doi: 10.1007/s11145-006-9039-5.

Ayling, D., Owen, H., and Flagg, E., 2012. Thinking, researching and living in virtual professional development community of practice [online]. Paper presented at ASCILITE 2012, Future Challenges | Sustainable Futures, 25–28 November, Wellington, New Zealand. Available from: http://www.ascilite.org.au/conferences/wellington12/2012/images/custom/ayling,_diana_-_thinking.pdf [Accessed 4 October 2013].

Bagnato, S., 2011. Identifying instructional targets for early childhood via authentic assessment: alignment of professional standards and practice-based evidence. *Journal of early intervention*, 33 (4), 243–253.

Birman, B.F., *et al.*, 2000. Designing professional development that works. *Educational leadership*, 57 (8), 28–33.

Blank, R., 2010. A better way to measure: new survey tool gives educators a clear picture of professional learning's impact. *Journal of staff development*, 31 (4), 56–60.

Bloor, M., *et al.*, 2001. *Focus groups in social research*. London: Sage.

Bredekamp, S. and Copple, C., eds., 2009. *Developmentally appropriate practice in early childhood programs serving children from birth through age 8*. 3rd ed. Washington, DC: National Association for the Education of Young Children.

Brouwer, P., *et al.*, 2012. Community development in the school workplace. *International journal of educational management*, 26 (4), 403–418. doi: 10.1108/09513541211227809.

Burns, M.S., *et al.*, 2012. An interaction, a conversation, often in the context of play: constructing intentional teaching in early childhood education. *NHSA dialog: a research-to-practice journal for the early childhood field*, 15 (3), 272–285.

Bybee, R., 1997. *Achieving scientific literacy: from purposes to practices*. Portsmouth, NH: Heinemann.

Cummins, L., 2004. The pot of gold at the end of the rainbow: mentoring in early childhood education. *Childhood education*, 80 (5), 254–257. doi: 10.1080/00094056.2004.10522809.

De Marrais, K., 2004. Qualitative interview studies: learning through experience. *In*: K.B. de Marrais and S.D. Lapan, eds. *Foundations for research: methods of inquiry in education and the social sciences*. Mahwah, NJ: Lawrence Erlbaum, 54–68.

Diamond, K. and Powell, D., 2011. An iterative approach to the development of a professional development intervention for Head Start teachers. *Journal of early intervention*, 33 (1), 75–93. doi: 10.1177/1053815111400416.

Diamond, K.E., *et al.*, 2013. *Synthesis of IES research on early intervention and early childhood education (NCSER 2013–3001)*. Washington, DC: National Center for Special Education Research, Institute of Education Sciences, US Department of Education. Available from: http://ies.ed.gov/.

Domitrovich, C., *et al.*, 2009. Fostering high-quality teaching with an enriched curriculum and professional development support: the Head Start REDI program. *American educational research journal*, 46 (2), 567–597. doi: 10.3102/0002831208328089.

Donovan, M.S., Bransford, J.D., and Pellegrino, J.W., eds., 1999. *How people learn: bridging research and practice*. Washington, DC: National Academies Press.

Epstein, A., 2007. *The intentional teacher: choosing the best strategies for young children's learning*. Washington, DC: National Association for the Education of Young Children.

Evans-Andris, M., Kyle, D., and Carini, R., 2006. Is mentoring enough? An examination of the mentoring relationship in the pilot two year Kentucky teacher internship program. *The new educator*, 2 (4), 289–309. doi: 10.1080/15476880600974867.

Hammerness, K., *et al.*, 2005. How teachers learn and develop. *In*: L. Darling-Hammond and J. Bransford, eds. *Preparing teachers for a changing world: what teachers should learn and be able to do*. San Francisco, CA: Jossey-Bass, 358–389.

Han, S.H., 2012. Professional development that works: shifting preschool teachers' beliefs and use of instructional strategies to promote children's peer social competence. *Journal of early childhood teacher education*, 33 (3), 251–268.

Hatch, J.A., 2002. *Doing qualitative research in education settings*. 1st ed. New York, NY: State University of New York Press.

Hofman, R. and Dijkstra, B., 2010. Effective teacher professionalization in networks? *Teaching and teacher education*, 26 (4), 1031–1040.

Holland, H., 2005. Teaching teachers: professional development to improve student achievement. *American educational research association research points*, 3 (1), 1–4.

Jarrell, M. 2000. Focusing on focus group use in educational research. Presented at *annual meeting of Mid-South Educational Research Association*, 15–17 November, Bowling Green, KY.

Joyce, B. and Showers, B., 2002. Improving inservice training: the messages of research. *Educational leadership*, 37 (5), 379–386.

Krueger, R., 1998. *Analyzing and reporting focus group results*. Thousand Oaks, CA: Sage.

Krueger, R. and Casey, A.M., 2009. *Focus groups: a practical guide for applied research*. 4th ed. Thousand Oaks, CA: Sage.

Kuh, L.P., 2012. Promoting communities of practice and parallel process in early childhood settings. *Journal of early childhood teacher education*, 33 (1), 19–37. doi: 10.1080/10901027.2011.650787.

Landry, S., *et al.*, 2009. Effectiveness of comprehensive professional development for teachers of at-risk preschoolers. *Journal of educational psychology*, 101 (2), 448–465. doi: 10.1037/a0013842.

Loucks-Horsley, S., *et al.*, 2010. *Designing professional development for teachers of science and mathematics*. Thousand Oaks, CA: Sage.

Mattern, V. and Scott, B., 1999. Mentoring means higher quality of care for children. *Dimensions of early childhood education*, 27 (4), 11–19.

Merton, R., 1987. The focused interview and focus groups: continuities and discontinuities. *Public opinion quarterly*, 51 (4), 550–557. doi: 10.1086/269057.

Museus, S., 2007. Using qualitative methods to assess diverse institutional cultures. *New directions for institutional research*, 136, 29–35. doi: 10.1002/ir.229.

National Association for the Education of Young Children, 2011. *Early childhood education professional development: training and technical assistance glossary*. Washington, DC: NAEYC.

Onchwari, G. and Keengwi, J., 2008. Teacher mentoring and early literacy learning: a case study of a mentor-coach initiative. *Early childhood education journal*, 37 (4), 311–317.

Onwuegbuzie, A., Leech, N., and Collins, K., 2010. Innovative data collection strategies in qualitative research. *The qualitative report*, 15 (3), 696–726.

Patton, M., 2002. *Qualitative research & evaluation methods*. 3rd ed. Thousand Oaks, CA: Sage.

Puig, V.I. and Recchia, S.L., 2008. The early childhood professional mentoring group: a forum for parallel learning. *Journal of early childhood teacher education*, 29 (4), 340–354. doi: 10.1080/10901020802470168.

Simon, S., *et al.*, 2011. Characteristics of effective professional development for early career science teachers. *Research in science & technological education*, 29 (1), 5–23. doi: 10.1080/02635143.2011.543798.

Snow, C.E., Griffin, P., and Burns, M.S., eds., 2005. *Knowledge to support the teaching of reading: preparing teachers for a changing world*. Indianapolis, IN: Jossey-Bass.

Stella, A. and Gnanam, A., 2004. Quality assurance in distance education: the challenges to be addressed. *Journal of higher education*, 47 (2), 143–160.

Stewart, D., Rook, D., and Shamdasani, P., 2006. *Focus groups: theory and practice*. Thousand Oaks, CA: Sage.

US Department of Health and Human Services, Administration for Children and Families, Office of Head Start. 2009. *Head Start program performance standards and other regulations* [online]. (45 CFR Chapter XIII 10-1-09 Ed.). Available from: http://eclkc.ohs.acf.hhs.gov/hslc/standards/Head%20Start%20Requirements/45%20CFR%20Chapter%20XIII/45%20CFR%20Chap%20XIII_ENG.pdf [Accessed 4 October 2013].

Van Driel, J. and Berry, A., 2012. Teacher professional development focusing on pedagogical content knowledge. *Educational researcher*, 41 (1), 26–28.

Wei, R., Darling-Hammond, L., and Adamson, F., 2010. *Professional development in the United States: trends and challenges. Phase II of a three part study*. Dallas, TX: National Staff Development Council.

Wenger, E. and Snyder, W., 2000. Communities of practice: the organizational frontier. *Harvard business review*, 78 (1), 139–145.

Whitebook, M. and Bellm, D., 1996. Mentoring for early childhood teachers and providers: building upon and extending tradition. *Young children*, 52 (1), 59–64.

Wong, A. and Premkumar, K., 2007. An introduction to mentoring principles, processes, and strategies for facilitating mentoring relationships at a distance [online]. Available from: http://www.life-slc.org/learningprinciples/Mentoring_Principles.pdf.

Zaslow, M., *et al.*, 2010. *Towards the identification of features of effective professional development for early childhood educators.* Policy and Program Studies Service, Office of Planning, Evaluation and Policy Development Publication. Washington, DC: US Department of Education.

Zigler, E. and Styfco, S., 2010. *The hidden history of Head Start.* Oxford, UK: Oxford University Press.

Educators' expectations and aspirations around young children's mathematical knowledge

Bob Perry and Amy MacDonald

Let's Count is a mathematics professional learning programme for preschool educators in Australia, managed by a prominent non-government organisation and sponsored by industry. It has been implemented in both face-to-face and online modes over 2013/14. Let's Count is based on the constructs that all young children are powerful mathematicians and that children should be given opportunities to access mathematical ideas through play and interactions with peers and adults, including family members. In this paper, we report on an evaluation of the impact of Let's Count on the educators' beliefs, expectations, aspirations and practices around preschool mathematics education. The evaluation utilises a mixed-methods approach in which educators have responded to brief written surveys as well as email and telephone interviews. The main findings from this research are demonstrable shifts in educators' beliefs and attitudes about, expectations of and aspirations for the mathematical learning of young children. These shifts have resulted in rich mathematical learning opportunities for children and conversations with both children and adult family members in preschool settings. Findings from this research suggest that Let's Count, in both of its modes, has had a positive impact on the children's mathematical learning as well as the educators' beliefs and practices.

Introduction

Mathematics in early childhood

There has been some reluctance amongst early childhood educators in the past to include mathematics as part of the early childhood curriculum (Sarama and Clements 2002, Anthony and Walshaw 2007, Perry and Dockett 2008). However, as Lee and Ginsburg (2007) have argued, there is a large body of research which shows that children are more competent mathematicians than previously assumed. There has been a significant shift in thinking, with young children now celebrated as capable mathematical thinkers and learners (Clements and Sarama 2002, Sarama and Clements 2002, Balfanz *et al.* 2003, Lee and Ginsburg 2007). This perspective is reflected in national statements on mathematics learning in early childhood (National Association for the Education of Young Children and National Council for Teachers of Mathematics 2002, Australian Association of Mathematics Teachers and Early Childhood Australia 2006).

In a recent survey of early childhood educators in four states of Australia (Hunting *et al.* 2008, 2012), there was overwhelming agreement by the educators that young children were capable of mathematical activity and thought well before they started school. This result has been echoed in many other Australasian studies, with the general agreement that all children in their early childhood years are capable of accessing powerful mathematical ideas and that they should be given the opportunity to access these ideas through high-quality child-centred activities in their homes, communities and prior-to-school settings (Anthony and Walshaw 2007, Faragher *et al.* 2008, Perry and Dockett 2008, MacDonald 2012).

What children learn about mathematics in the early years can be important in their transition to learning at school. For example, Duncan *et al.* (2007) performed a coordinated analysis of six longitudinal data-sets relating changes in early skills to later teacher ratings and test scores of school reading and mathematics achievement. They found that school-entry mathematics, reading and attention skills were associated with later achievement, and noted that the predictive power of early mathematics skills was particularly impressive. However, Duncan *et al.* (2007) also cautioned that their findings did not support the adoption of 'drill-and-practice' curricula, and argued that play-based curricula designed with the developmental needs of children in mind can easily foster the development of academic and attention skills in ways that are engaging and fun.

Play and investigation

Much has been written about the importance of children's play in their learning (for example, Dockett and Fleer 1999, Brock *et al.* 2009, Department of Education, Employment, and Workplace Relations [DEEWR] 2009, 2010, Dockett 2011). Indeed, Australia's national early childhood curriculum framework, *Belonging, Being, Becoming: The Early Years Learning Framework for Australia* (DEEWR 2009), emphasises the importance of play in young children's learning.

There is much evidence to indicate that children can have many mathematical experiences during play (Ginsburg 2000, 2002, Seo 2003, Wolfgang *et al.* 2003, Perry and Dockett 2008). However, this potential can only be realised if the mathematics in children's play is noticed, explored and talked about. The role of the 'knowing adult' is important here, and it is crucial that educators, parents and other family members have the knowledge and confidence to notice, explore and talk about the mathematics in children's play (Anthony and Walshaw 2007, Hunting *et al.* 2013, MacDonald 2015, Carruthers 2015).

Educators (including parents and teachers) who are effective in promoting their children's learning through play often adopt the role of *provocateur* (Edwards *et al.* 1993), through which they observe and assess the understandings demonstrated by individual children and then generate situations that challenge these. This may involve asking questions, introducing elements of surprise, requiring the children to explain their position to others and working with children to consider the logical consequences of the positions they adopt. Through such provocation, children are stimulated to investigate the challenges set by the situations generated and to work with the mathematics arising from these.

Partnerships with families

It is quite clear that families are important contexts for young children and that they do have a significant impact on the learning opportunities provided to these children. In their extensive review of the field, Henderson and Mapp note 'a positive and convincing relationship between family involvement and benefits for students, including improved academic achievement. This relationship holds across families of all economic, racial/ethnic, and educational backgrounds and for students of all ages' (2002, p. 64).

Children's experiences within their families can influence their learning and their dispositions to learning. Resources provided to the child by the family (Kiernan and Mensah 2011), home routines and environment strongly predict educational and behavioural outcomes for children well into the primary years (Melhuish *et al.* 2008).

While the development of positive, fruitful and collaborative partnerships with families can be quite time-consuming for early childhood educators, they are of great importance in children's learning and underpin *Belong, Being, Becoming: The Early Years Learning Framework for Australia* (DEEWR 2009). In particular, the Partnerships principle states the following:

> Learning outcomes are most likely to be achieved when early childhood educators work in partnership with families. Educators recognise that families are children's first and most influential teachers. They create a welcoming environment where all children and families are respected and actively encouraged to collaborate with educators about curriculum decisions in order to ensure that learning experiences are meaningful.
>
> Partnerships are based on the foundations of understanding each other's expectations and attitudes, and build on the strength of each others' knowledge.
>
> In genuine partnerships, families and early childhood educators:
>
> - value each other's knowledge of each child
> - value each other's contributions to and roles in each child's life
> - trust each other
> - communicate freely and respectfully with each other
> - share insights and perspectives about each child
> - engage in shared decision-making. (DEEWR 2009, p. 12)

The professional development of early childhood educators

The professional development of educators generally has received much attention. However, the professional development of early childhood educators, specifically, has attracted relatively little research (Lieber *et al.* 2009). Those studies which have been conducted focus largely on global indicators of quality, with evidence to suggest that the development of specialised knowledge in key domains such as literacy may enhance quality practices (Koh and Neuman 2009). Indeed, literacy as a knowledge domain is widely represented in the professional development literature (for example, Justice *et al.* 2008, Koh and Neuman 2009), with numeracy receiving much less attention. Most instances of numeracy-focused professional development have occurred within primary school contexts (for example, Polly 2012), rather than focusing on the numeracy development opportunities within early childhood settings. However, one recent example of mathematics professional development in early childhood settings is that of Simpson and Linder (2014), who explored the preparedness of early childhood educators to develop mathematical knowledge in children aged birth to five years, and found that existing professional learning opportunities were seen by the educators to be inadequate. This is consistent with the findings of a major Australian study of early childhood mathematics education by Hunting *et al.* (2013). Simpson and Linder (2014) have called for future research studies to inform and improve the current professional development practices in mathematics for early childhood educators. With this in mind, scrutiny of the Let's Count professional development programme seems warranted.

A key issue identified in the research literature is the context of the professional development, with most studies to date focusing on events occurring within early childhood rooms (Brown *et al.* 2009). However, taking an ecological view of early childhood education encourages the consideration of broader contextual factors impacting upon teacher practices and children's learning, such as relationships with parents and other caregivers, parental engagement in the early childhood education service, teacher characteristics and children's approaches to learning (Brown *et al.* 2009, Downer *et al.* 2009).

As well as both the content and context of professional development programmes, varying approaches to the delivery of professional development for early childhood educators have been considered. Professional development programmes typically use a combination of group-focused supports such as workshops and resources, along with individualised supports such as coaching or mentoring (Lieber *et al.* 2009). The coaching model has been positioned as a highly promising approach to professional development (Domitrovich *et al.* 2009, Lieber *et al.* 2009). A coaching model requires the crafting of new skills and practices to fit the personal styles and values of early childhood educators in their applied settings (Sheridan *et al.* 2009). Coaching models are built on mutual trust between coaches and educators, rather than the coach taking on an evaluative or supervisory role (Polly 2012). It is argued by Koh and Neuman (2009) that, to be most effective, professional development should be based on both knowledge and its application to practice in context – an approach, they argue, which is befitting a coaching model of professional development. Based on their review of the literature, Koh and Neuman (2009, pp. 543–544) describe the development of a coaching model with the following general features:

- onsite – coaches model practices in the contexts of the educators;
- balanced and sustained – coaches provide ongoing education rather than one-off activities;
- facilitative of reflection – coaches observe, listen and support rather than dictate;
- collaborative – coaches establish rapport, build trust, develop mutual respect and interact extensively;
- corrective feedback – coaches provide descriptive rather than evaluative or judgemental feedback; and
- prioritising – coaches assist educators in identifying priorities and developing action plans.

This is consistent with Domitrovich *et al.*'s (2009) review of effective professional development training processes that identified some emerging 'best practices', namely training which:

> is specific and targeted (Guskey 2003); involves opportunities for practice with feedback in naturalistic contexts (Elmore 2002, Putnam and Borko 2000); and provides teachers with adequate time to reflect on their own practices, set goals, and self-evaluate (Bowman, Donovan and Burns 2001). (Domitrovich *et al.* 2009, p. 404)

Another emerging area of early childhood professional development that is demonstrating great potential is the delivery of professional development programmes in online forms. Downer *et al.* (2009) identify specific areas of potential, such as the delivery of more dynamic professional development experiences, scalability of programmes and sustained consultation. While only a few examples exist in the literature at present, these examples demonstrate that this is an approach to professional development which appears to be having some success. For example, Landry *et al.* (2009) implemented small-group online training to enhance language and literacy practices in a range of early childhood education programmes serving low-income families, and found this approach to have positive gains in terms of children's outcomes and teachers' instructional practices. Downer *et al.* (2009) found that implementation of the My Teaching Partner Consultancy online professional development programme was an effective means of improving preschool teachers' interactions with children; although there was some variation in the extent to which teachers demonstrated responsiveness to participation in various aspects of the programme. Downer *et al.* suggest that further study of online professional development programmes is warranted so as to enhance educator responsiveness and exposure to this form of professional development.

Noticing, discussing and exploring mathematics: Let's Count

'The Smith Family is a children's charity helping disadvantaged Australian children to get the most out of their education, so they can create better futures for themselves' (The Smith Family 2013). Let's Count is a new early mathematics programme that has been designed by The Smith Family and mathematics education researchers to assist educators in early childhood contexts to work in partnership with parents and other family members to promote positive mathematical experiences for young children (three to five years). The programme aims to foster opportunities for children to engage with the mathematics encountered as part of their everyday lives, and talk about it, document it and explore it in ways that are fun and relevant to them.

Let's Count involves early childhood educators in the role of partners with the parents and family members of the children in their care about ways they can notice, discuss and explore mathematics with their children. Let's Count includes a professional learning programme for educators to assist them in this critical role and to help them consider their own pedagogical approaches in mathematics and add to their repertoire of successful practices.

Let's Count aligns with the first national early years curriculum framework in Australia (DEEWR 2009) through its use of play and investigation as its key pedagogical approaches and through its contribution to Learning Outcome 5: Children are effective communicators.

In summary, Let's Count has the following characteristics:

- partnerships among early childhood educators and families;
- play and investigation for all;
- recognition of all as potentially powerful mathematicians;
- realisation that mathematics learning can be fun for all when it is undertaken in a relevant and meaningful context;
- advising of families by early childhood educators;
- meaningful documentation of learning; and
- strong links to the theoretical and practical bases of the Early Years Learning Framework for Australia.

Professional development of early childhood educators

Educators implementing Let's Count have undertaken professional development in one of two quite different modes. The first mode involves face-to-face workshops run by facilitators trained by the authors of the programme. The second mode involves educators enrolling in an online university subject, and implementing the learning experiences and assessment requirements for that subject.

Mode 1: face-to-face learning

Let's Count has been implemented through a programme of professional development consisting of two full days of professional learning with approximately one month's self-monitored field-based learning between them. To the end of 2013, 134 educators undertook this mode of Let's Count professional development. The first component of the professional learning provided information about the programme and its theoretical and practical bases. Discussions, workshops and activities aimed to prepare the educators to work with parents and other family members from their settings. These involved play, investigation and intentional teaching approaches. After the first professional learning module, educators were able to prepare and undertake the following activities with their families:

- discussions with family members that outline the Let's Count programme and set the foundations for activities in the family aimed at the enhancement of young children's mathematical learning;
- planning to encourage families to report on the various mathematical activities in which their young children were engaged with the family, either at home or in other venues;
- assistance for the families in documenting these mathematical activities and recognising the mathematical learning that is being experienced by the young children and their families; and
- celebration of the mathematical learning that has been experienced.

These activities were undertaken in the one-month period between the first and second professional learning modules and beyond. Also during this period, the early childhood educators completed the following activities, along with others that they suggested during the first professional learning module:

- make a photographic and/or video record of the mathematics being experienced by children in their setting;
- keep a journal of the ways in which children in the setting use mathematics;
- note interactions with parents and other family members around mathematics in the families;
- collate their families' documentation of mathematical experiences outside the setting so that they may be presented as part of the second professional learning module; and
- write a learning story about their experience of Let's Count.

The second professional learning module of Let's Count provided opportunities for the early childhood educators to show their colleagues, and the Let's Count facilitators, what they had achieved since the initial Let's Count session. In particular, they were encouraged to share:

- a summary of what they, their children and their families did in terms of mathematical activity and learning;
- an analysis of what this means for the educator's programme and for the relationships built with the families;
- what they think would be useful to have happen into the future; and
- how such a plan might be sustained.

Mode 2: online learning

The Let's Count professional development programme has also been delivered in an online mode, in the form of a 12-week distance education subject offered through Charles Sturt University. The development of an online distance education mode provided a means of sustaining the Let's Count initiative as well as achieving a wider impact on the early childhood community – beyond what might be possible in a face-to-face workshop mode. To date, the online offering has been completed by 184 educators.

The online mode of Let's Count is consistent with a 'coaching' model of professional development, whereby participants work through the professional learning materials under the guidance of a university educator with specific expertise in early childhood mathematics. In keeping with Koh and Neuman's (2009) characteristics of a coaching model, the online mode of Let's Count was designed to be both collaborative and sustained, with participants regularly interacting with the university educator through communication methods such as synchronous chat rooms and asynchronous forums. These communication methods allowed the participants to receive ongoing professional support and guidance from the university educator, but also allowed the university educator to become familiar with the participants and the contexts in which they worked.

The subject required early childhood educators to complete six online modules and associated tasks, as well as submit two items for assessment. The modules consisted of reading materials and learning activities expanding on the original Let's Count materials used in the face-to-face mode, which explore the following topics:

THE PROFESSIONAL DEVELOPMENT OF EARLY YEARS EDUCATORS

- early childhood and learning;
- play and investigation;
- the role of families in young children's learning;
- learning mathematics in the early years;
- attitudes, culture and language in children's mathematics learning;
- examples of mathematics in young children's lives;
- games, children's literature and music;
- using prior-to-school opportunities to inspire families; and
- ideas to help families notice, explore and talk about mathematics.

As a means of 'enacting' the Let's Count principles and practices, the online mode requires early childhood educators to engage with two key pedagogical approaches – family gatherings and learning stories.

Family gatherings

Consistent with the face-to-face mode of Let's Count, early childhood educators participating in the online mode were required to engage with the children, parents and other caregivers in their setting. In the online mode, this was accomplished through the implementation of 'family gatherings', which are essentially workshops designed to allow early childhood educators to have conversations about mathematics with parents, and to assist parents to help their children learn mathematics. Key to the family gatherings is a focus on the 'everydayness' of mathematics and the use of everyday activities and resources. Family gatherings are also used in Let's Count as a way of developing positive relationships between educators and families within early childhood settings. These gatherings take many forms: for example, Let's Count educators have brought together a small group of families for a face-to-face workshop; they have worked individually with a small selection of families; they have gathered both physically and virtually, capitalising upon the potential of online social networks; and they have held brief meetings over a period of time, or have met for one or more extended blocks of time.

The design, implementation and evaluation of a family gathering constitute the first assessable component of the online mode of Let's Count. Educators are required to produce a *PowerPoint* presentation in which they document their planning process, communication with families, implementation and outcomes of their family gathering, and the impact of the gathering on their own practices and those of the families involved. Throughout the process, educators were encouraged to think creatively about how they might 'gather' families around the topic of early mathematics development, in ways that best suited the interests and needs of the families. The main thing educators were encouraged to remember – and emphasise to families – was that family gatherings are an opportunity for early childhood educators and parents to work together to explore the mathematics in children's lives.

Learning stories

A second pedagogical approach employed in Let's Count was the writing of mathematical learning stories (Carr 2001, Carr and Lee 2012), and it was this activity which constituted the second assessable component of the online mode. Participants in Let's Count were asked to use learning stories to document the mathematical learning of children who participated in the family gathering. Additionally, educators were asked to write a short personal statement reflecting on the potential of learning stories for assessing mathematical learning and discussing this learning with children, families and colleagues. While no set format for the learning stories was given, the educators were encouraged to include three key features in their stories:

- description of the context and what happened;
- analysis of the child's mathematical learning; and
- suggestions for how this learning might be further developed (with a focus on what families can do).

This approach was designed to assist early childhood educators in noticing, naming and explaining mathematical development in the early childhood years. Educators were encouraged to attend more closely to the potential for mathematical development in children's play and investigation, and in doing so to enhance their skills in communicating children's mathematical learning to others. Furthermore, the learning stories provided an opportunity to discuss children's mathematical learning with families, as well as to identify possibilities for how they might explore mathematics at home with their child.

Early childhood educators' beliefs and attitudes about, expectations of and aspirations for the mathematical learning of young children

Both approaches to the implementation of Let's Count have been evaluated using a number of data collection methods that varied across the two modes of professional development.

For the face-to-face mode educators, data were gathered from a series of three interviews across the year of implementation of Let's Count. The data drawn for this paper came from 37 completed sets of three interviews. (Data were also gathered from children and family members who participated, but these are reported elsewhere; Gervasoni and Perry 2015). Interviews were conducted by trained interviewers under the supervision of one of the authors. Each interview was transcribed and the content analysed by the interviewers, who independently and then collaboratively established emergent coding frames using constructivist grounded theory approaches (Charmaz 2006). From this analysis, six themes emerged. For the online mode, data reported here were generated from email interviews (Eviews) (Fenton 2012). Analysis of the online Eview data used the six themes derived from the analysis of the face-to-face data. The match with the six themes was very strong. Both authors independently ratified the categorisation of these data into the themes.

Each of these themes indicates that Let's Count has had an impact on educators' pedagogical practice, while also highlighting the challenges educators face as they navigate how the programme can work in their individual settings. The six themes are as follows:

(1) engaging families with mathematical learning and Let's Count;
(2) continuity of mathematical learning between the early childhood setting and home;
(3) impact of Let's Count on educator confidence, professional identity and pedagogical practice;

THE PROFESSIONAL DEVELOPMENT OF EARLY YEARS EDUCATORS

(4) awareness of the potential of everyday tasks for prompting mathematics discussion;

(5) sustainability of Let's Count over time; and

(6) children's engagement with mathematical learning and mathematical concepts.

Illustrative interview and Eview excerpts for each of these themes are provided below. Comments from educators who undertook the face-to-face mode of professional learning are designated 'F/F' while those from educators who undertook the online mode of professional learning are denoted 'On'.

Engaging families with mathematical learning and Let's Count

Educators from both groups used a range of strategies to get families involved in Let's Count. These ranged from hands-on, one-off events and sending home mathematics resources, to more day-to-day strategies incorporating mathematical learning into their everyday dialogue with families. One-off events were initially really successful, but sustained dialogue with families about their children's mathematical learning was a challenge for a number of educators:

> I think the main difference that it made was the way we engaged the parents in it and we didn't do a lot, it was just little things like putting notices out, putting little newsletters out about it and also we had a board out the front where we just put a little maths problem on there and the parents could sort of get involved. It was just something they could do on the way home or something they could do on the way in. ... And that sort of got the parents really interested and talking about maths a lot more. (F/F)

> There were lots of highlights over this subject. I loved the fact that parents actually realised that they were doing these great things with children already but didn't actually know it or understand the benefits of it. I also loved the fact that parents were into it just as much as the children ... the positive feedback I got from them was very inspiring. (On)

> Well I guess honestly, there hasn't been an awful lot of interest from the parents, to be perfectly frank. When we first started looking at it and we put out lots of information for the families, lots of requests to have those sort of conversations, there's probably a core of say five parents who were really keen to know about it at the beginning and have discussed it with us during the year. But it's certainly ... I think that one of the thought processes was that we were enabling the parents to feel that they could go home and really spearhead the mathematical kind of education for their children but for the most part I feel that it's actually empowered us to feel that we're better educators. (F/F)

> I think it helped to promote parents' understanding of how important and valuable their role is in the education of their child. It also promotes how effective relationships with their child's educator can assist their child's learning and development. (On)

Continuity of mathematical learning between the early childhood setting and home

Many of the interviews and Eviews discussed continuity of mathematical learning between home and school and the importance of established communication strategies among educators and parents:

> If I can give parents some key pieces of information and ideas I think I can really encourage other parents to also do things at home with their children and enhance their

child's learning in the home environment or at least be aware of what they are doing and the benefits of doing what they are already doing. (On)

Cooking is a big one and we do a lot of that here as well. But the children often comment on what they've made at home. So that we think that has a lot of maths in it. Because we've been talking about things like water displacement at preschool I know that they're now jumping in and out of their baths and watching the water go up and down and things like that. (F/F)

I have noticed an improvement in some of the children's recognition of numbers. I've been concentrating on that. And some of them actually come from home and say 'Miss XXXX we did ...' (F/F)

From engaging in this project I learned that maths really is part of everyday learning at home for the children. It is just not labelled as such in many instances. Parents were doing things with their children that they normally did, just were more aware of the mathematical process in these activities. (On)

Impact of Let's Count on educator confidence, professional identity and pedagogical practice

Many of the educators in both modes of professional learning expressed the feeling that Let's Count had impacted on their confidence and practice. Equally, educators commented on the growth in confidence and competence around mathematics of many of their colleagues and of parents:

It's just been overwhelming how staff once they get that concept in their head how they're looking for it everywhere. It's been really beneficial to enlighten staff who might not have actually thought of activities in that way before. So it's been really fantastic in that respect. And XXX and I are always looking for new ways to invent, both outside and inside, to create that maths in our kinder environment. (F/F)

I'm not confident with maths but after undertaking the course I felt I benefitted as well as the children. It gave me the confidence to implement more 'maths' type activities and to talk confidently about maths. (On)

How do I feel about maths? ... I used to think of maths as sums. You know, when you think of maths you think of sums, like sitting at a high school desk trying to do these sums that you can't work out. But having now looking at maths in a different way I kind of see that it is everywhere and we do use it every day. So I'm starting to feel a bit more confident with that. (F/F)

My confidence in communicating about maths with others is much stronger. ... I am now more interested in seeking the mathematics in life for myself. I see maths as something that can be approached and tackled rather than avoided. ... I think our conversation may have increased the parents' confidence in their child's mathematics abilities, in the months before starting school. (On)

Awareness of the potential of everyday tasks for prompting mathematics discussion

The notion that there is mathematics in everything has clearly been accepted by many of the educators. While the depth of the mathematics being noticed is not great, the very fact that it is being noticed is a positive aspect that educators bring from their experiences with Let's Count:

Whatever we're involved in, even with the gardening outside, we look at how many plants we have planted, we look at the pictures of them when their fruits develop, what shape is it. Colours and everything, whatever we do we're attempting to incorporate maths throughout. (F/F)

I think just like the parents involved in this project it has actually made me more aware of how much maths is in everyday things and how we can incorporate maths into just about everything. It is really like that 'light bulb' moment when you finally just 'get it'. (On)

I actually silently mention to myself at certain times 'That was maths you just used. See, you did need it when you grew up'. (On)

And straight away the staff were almost like whatever situation we were doing, it wasn't just about the book, it was also about the maths concept in it. It wasn't just about group time, suddenly it was also about maths concepts sort of thing. So it became more of our day to day language whereas previously it had really been biased towards literacy. (F/F)

Sustainability of Let's Count over time

The sustainability of programmes like Let's Count depends not only on the quality of the initial professional learning but on the continued enthusiasm and drive of the participants and the quality of the programme. Many challenges need to be faced, particularly around the mobility of the early childhood education workforce in Australia (Productivity Commission 2011). Some of the educators interviewed were very keen to see a sustainable future for Let's Count in their settings:

I just think it has been a good thing for us to do and particularly I like the way the parents are really involved and it's more about them, because that will hopefully continue on for the rest of their child's schooling and for other children that they may have in their family as well. (F/F)

I think with the current staff we have got it will continue very well but again, if that staff changes it would depend on the abilities and the interests of those staff I suppose. It would be certainly something that I would like for anyone to continue but it would just really depend on how that kindergarten teacher wanted to work and their own knowledge of those things. And usually you find when a program is introduced like this it works really well but when the momentum stops so does the program. (F/F)

I intend to regularly revisit the Let's Count learning resources to help me to remember the many facets of mathematics that are observable and extendable in children's work and play. I have made myself a little revision document summarising some of the mathematical concepts, processes and ideas. I also intend to create some posters with examples of children playing with maths to inspire myself and other to continue seeking and providing for mathematics learning. (On)

We're actually looking forward to doing it again next year, just so that we can move on and further … Because although it's mainly for our ones going off to school our younger ones have been involved in it too so just to see where we can take them after two years of doing it. So we're just sort of looking forward to what they're going to come up with, having been involved in it twice, to see basically what they're going to get out of it and what other concepts we can do and what challenges lie ahead really. (F/F)

Children's engagement with mathematical learning and mathematical concepts

So much of educators' knowledge of what children are capable of doing, how they engage with activities and how they are disposed to this learning comes from their observations of the children in play and other, perhaps more structured, contexts.

The Let's Count educators often described their awareness of the advances in children's mathematics learning that they have noticed. In some circumstances, these advances have been quite dramatic (these educator observations have been confirmed through child assessment; Gervasoni and Perry 2015):

> So far I think it's fantastic. I'm really seeing the children ... Just their knowledge is just blown me away, of what concepts they're understanding. Their understanding of like symmetry and patterns. And now it's starting to be more about adding. Last week we worked out that 10 x 3 is 30 and that was from a story book that was '10 Red Apples' from Dr Seuss. ... And the book was actually from a little girl as well. So they just have been absorbing the maths and really extending them further with just like the slightest bit of encouragement which is fantastic. (F/F)

> I can see the way the children engage with activities or staff in relation to maths. The more exposure the child has had at home is reflected in how knowledgeable they are in the activity or interested in extending on this. (On)

> The children are more interested in learning about maths now so instead of me doing structured maths activities we are doing this all the time so the children have created their own positive dispositions for learning. (On)

> Before 'Let's Count' children only participate in maths activity when they're asked to but now they have built interest in maths and we need to extend their skills in deeper maths concepts such as counting, sorting, and classifying. (On)

Discussion

While the two modes of professional learning undertaken by the Let's Count educators are quite different in their structure, duration and characteristics, both seem to have made a positive difference to the educators, families and children in terms of the ways in which they interact with mathematics. The face-to-face mode of professional learning in Let's Count has many of the characteristics criticised by current professional learning researchers. However, it does meet Domitrovich *et al.*'s (2009, p. 404) requirements of being 'specific and targeted'; and providing 'teachers with adequate time to reflect on their own practices', even though early childhood settings in Australia are very busy places. Because many of the early childhood settings sent more than one staff member to the first Let's Count workshop, there was the potential for Domitrovich *et al.*'s (2009, p. 404) third requirement – 'involves opportunities for practice with feedback in naturalistic contexts' – to be met through peer feedback. However, the opportunity for feedback to be given by a mathematics education expert was generally not available to face-to-face Let's Count participants as it was for the online mode.

Participants in the online mode of professional learning for Let's Count clearly experienced all of Domitrovich *et al.*'s requirements for effective professional development. Also, the online mode demonstrates almost all of the characteristics of the coaching model as described by Koh and Neuman (2009). The one characteristic listed by Koh and Neuman not met by the online mode is that the professional learning in a coaching model should be in the educator's contexts. This is clearly impossible in a distance education subject. However, the quality of the interface available at the university and the use of chat rooms and forums seem to have overcome this apparent deficiency.

Both approaches to professional learning used in the Let's Count programme seem to have had a positive impact on the early childhood educators' beliefs and attitudes about, expectations of and aspirations for the mathematical learning of young children, and their implementation of the programme. Let's Count is having a significant impact on young children's learning (Gervasoni and Perry 2015) and this has been a continuing encouragement for educators to continue enthusiastically in the programme. Some of the enthusiasm for the programme can be seen in the excerpts presented in this paper. Perhaps the strength of the programme itself means that either of the carefully devised professional learning modes for Let's Count will be successful.

Conclusion

One of the key themes identified in the analysis of the Let's Count educator responses highlights the impact of Let's Count on educator confidence, professional identity and pedagogical practice. Many of the educators have commented on how they feel much more knowledgeable and confident both in their own mathematics but also in understanding how their mathematical education practice can be improved. This is consistent with international research highlighting the important relationship between educator confidence and their mathematics education practices (Anthony and Walshaw 2007, Hunting *et al.* 2013, MacDonald 2015, Carruthers 2015). The data presented in this paper suggest that this increase in educator knowledge and confidence, and the resultant impact on practice, is the case whichever of the modes of professional learning has been undertaken. This is an important finding given the success of Let's Count in the enhancement of young children's mathematical knowledge and skills (Gervasoni and Perry 2015). It means that the programme is more sustainable as educators will be able to choose the mode of professional learning that better meets their needs.

These positive trends in educators' knowledge, interest and confidence in mathematics learning and teaching are reinforced through many of the interview quotes recorded in this report. It seems clear that participation in Let's Count has made a difference in this regard.

Disclosure statement

No potential conflict of interest was reported by the authors.

References

Anthony, G. and Walshaw, M., 2007. *Effective pedagogy in mathematics/pāngarau.* Wellington, NZ: Ministry of Education.

Australian Association of Mathematics Teachers and Early Childhood Australia (AAMT/ECA), 2006. *Position paper on early childhood mathematics.* Available from: http://www.aamt.edu.au/about/policy/earlymaths_a3.pdf

Balfanz, R., Ginsburg, H., and Greenes, C., 2003. The big maths for little kids early childhood mathematics program. *Teaching children mathematics*, 9 (5), 264–269.

Bowman, B.T., Donovan, S., and Burns, M.S., eds., 2001. *Eager to learn: educating our preschoolers.* Washington, DC: National Academy Press.

Brock, A., *et al.,* 2009. *Perspectives on play: learning for life.* Harlow, UK: Pearson Education.

Brown, J.R., *et al.,* 2009. Professional development to support parent engagement: a case study of early childhood practitioners. *Early education and development*, 20 (3), 482–506.

Carr, M., 2001. *Assessment in early childhood settings: learning stories.* London: Paul Chapman.

Carr, M. and Lee, W., 2012. *Learning stories: constructing learner identities in early education*. London: Sage.

Carruthers, E., 2015. Listening to children's mathematics in school. *In*: B. Perry, A. MacDonald, and A. Gervasoni, eds. *Mathematics and transitions to school: international perspectives*. Dordrecht: Springer.

Charmaz, K., 2006. *Constructing grounded theory: a practical guide through qualitative analysis*. London: Sage.

Clements, D. and Sarama, J., 2002. Mathematics curricula in early childhood. *Teaching children mathematics*, 9 (3), 163–168.

Department of Education, Employment and Workplace Relations (DEEWR), 2009. *Belonging, being and becoming: the early years learning framework for Australia*. Canberra: Commonwealth of Australia. Available from: http://www.deewr.gov.au/earlychildhood/policy_agenda/quality/pages/earlyyearslearningframework.aspx

Department of Education, Employment and Workplace Relations (DEEWR), 2010. *Educators belonging, being and becoming: educators' guide to the early years learning framework for Australia*. Canberra: Commonwealth of Australia.

Dockett, S., 2011. The challenge of play for early childhood educators. *In*: S. Rogers, ed. *Rethinking play and pedagogy in early childhood education: concepts, contexts and cultures*. London: Routledge, 32–47.

Dockett, S. and Fleer, M., 1999. *Play and pedagogy in early childhood: bending the rules*. Sydney: Harcourt Brace.

Domitrovich, C.E., *et al.*, 2009. Individual factors associated with professional development training outcomes of the Head Start REDI program. *Early education and development*, 20 (3), 402–430.

Downer, J.T., Kraft-Sayre, M.E., and Pianta, R.C., 2009. Ongoing, web-mediated professional development focused on teacher-child interactions: early childhood educators' usage rates and self-reported satisfaction. *Early education and development*, 20 (2), 321–345.

Downer, J.T., *et al.*, 2009. Teacher characteristics associated with responsiveness and exposure to consultation and online professional development resources. *Early education and development*, 20 (3), 431–455.

Duncan, G.J., *et al.*, 2007. School readiness and later achievement. *Developmental psychology*, 43 (6), 1428–1446.

Edwards, C., Gandini, L.G., and Forman, G., eds., 1993. *The hundred languages of children: the Reggio Emilia approach to early childhood education*. Norwood, NJ: Ablex.

Elmore, R.F., 2002. *Bridging the gap between standards and achievement: the imperative for professional development in education*. Washington, DC: Albert Shanker Institute.

Faragher, R., *et al.*, 2008. Children with Down syndrome learning mathematics: can they do it? Yes they can! *Australian primary mathematics classroom*, 13 (4), 10–15.

Fenton, A., 2012. Using a strengths approach to early childhood teacher preparation in child protection using work-integrated education. *Asia-Pacific journal of cooperative education*, 14 (3), 157–169.

Gervasoni, A. and Perry, B., 2015. Children's mathematical knowledge prior to starting school and implications for transition. In: B. Perry, A. MacDonald, and A. Gervasoni, eds. *Mathematics and transition to school: international perspectives*. Dordrecht: Springer.

Ginsburg, H.P., 2000. Children's minds and developmentally appropriate goals of preschool mathematics education. Paper presented at the *annual meeting of the American Educational Research Association,* New Orleans, LA, April.

Ginsburg, H.P., 2002. Little children, big mathematics: learning and teaching in the pre-school. *In*: A.D. Cockburn and E. Nardi, eds. *Proceedings of the 26th Annual Conference of the International Group for the Psychology of Mathematics Education*. Norwich, UK: PME, 3–14.

Guskey, T.R., 2003. What makes professional development effective? *Phi delta kappan*, 84 (10), 748–750.

Henderson, A.T. and Mapp, K.L., 2002. *A new wave of evidence: the impact of school, family and community connections on student achievement* [online]. Austin, TX: National Center for Family and Community Connections with Schools. Available from: http://www.sedl.org/connections/resources/evidence.pdf [Accessed 23 February 2015].

Hunting, R., *et al.*, 2008. *Mathematical thinking of preschool children in rural and regional Australia: research and practice*. Bendigo, VIC: LaTrobe University.

Hunting, R., Mousley, J., and Perry, B., 2012. *Young children learning mathematics: a guide for educators and families*. Melbourne: Australian Council for Educational Research.

Hunting, R., *et al.*, 2013. *Mathematical thinking of preschool children in rural and regional Australia: research and practice*. Camberwell, VIC: ACER Press.

Justice, L.M., *et al.*, 2008. Quality of language and literacy instruction in preschool classrooms serving at-risk pupils. *Early childhood research quarterly*, 23 (1), 51–68.

Kiernan, K.E. and Mensah, F.K., 2011. Poverty, family resources and children's early educational attainment: the mediating role of parenting. *British educational research journal*, 37 (2), 317–336.

Koh, S. and Neuman, S.B., 2009. The impact of professional development in family child care: a practice-based approach. *Early education and development*, 20 (3), 537–562.

Landry, S.H., *et al.*, 2009. Effectiveness of comprehensive professional development for teachers of at-risk preschoolers. *Journal of educational psychology*, 101 (2), 448–465.

Lee, J. and Ginsburg, H., 2007. What is appropriate mathematics education for four-year-olds? Pre-kindergarten teachers' beliefs. *Journal of early childhood research*, 5 (1), 2–31.

Lieber, J., *et al.*, 2009. Factors that influence the implementation of a new preschool curriculum: implications for professional development. *Early education and development*, 20 (3), 456–481.

MacDonald, A., 2012. Young children's photographs of measurement in the home. *Early years*, 32 (1), 71–85.

MacDonald, A., 2015. *Let's count*: early childhood educators and families working in partnership to support young children's transitions in mathematics education. *In*: B. Perry, A. MacDonald, and A. Gervasoni, eds. *Mathematics and transition to school: international perspectives*. Dordrecht: Springer.

Melhuish, E.C., *et al.*, 2008. Effects of the home learning environment and preschool center experience upon literacy and numeracy development in early primary school. *Journal of social issues*, 64 (1), 95–114.

National Association for the Education of Young Children (NAEYC) and National Council for Teachers of Mathematics (NCTM), 2002. *Early childhood mathematics: promoting good beginnings: a joint position statement* [online]. Available from: http://www.naeyc. org/about/positions/psmath.asp

Perry, B. and Dockett, S., 2008. Young children's access to powerful mathematical ideas. *In*: L.D. English, ed. *Handbook of international research in mathematics education*. 2nd ed. New York, NY: Routledge, 75–108.

Polly, D., 2012. Supporting mathematics instruction with an expert coaching model. *Mathematics teacher education and development*, 14 (1), 78–93.

Productivity Commission, 2011. *Education and training workforce: early childhood development*. Research report. Canberra: Author.

Putnam, R.T. and Borko, H., 2000. What do new views of knowledge and thinking have to say about research on teacher learning? *Educational researcher*, 21 (1), 4–15.

Sarama, J. and Clements, D., 2002. Building blocks for young children's mathematical development. *Journal of educational computing research*, 27 (1), 93–110.

Seo, K.-H., 2003. What children's play tells us about teaching mathematics. *Young children*, 58 (1), 28–34.

Sheridan, S.M., *et al.*, 2009. Professional development in early childhood programs: process issues and research needs. *Early education and development*, 20 (3), 377–401.

Simpson, A. and Linder, S.M., 2014. An examination of mathematics professional development opportunities in early childhood settings. *Early childhood education journal*, 42 (5), 335–342.

The Smith Family, 2013. *Who we are* [online]. Available from: http://www.thesmithfamily. com.au/

Wolfgang, C.H., Stannard, L.L., and Jones, I., 2003. Advanced constructional play with LEGOs among preschoolers as a predictor of later school achievement in mathematics. *Early child development and care*, 173 (5), 467–475.

'The exchange of ideas was mutual, I have to say': negotiating researcher and teacher 'roles' in an early years educators' professional development programme on inquiry-based mathematics and science learning

Stavroula Philippou, Chrystalla Papademetri-Kachrimani and Loucas Louca

This paper explores the experiences of 14 early years educators who participated in a continuing professional development (CPD) programme coordinated by two of the paper's authors. The programme was part of a three-year research project, which aimed at introducing early childhood educators to an inquiry-based approach to mathematics and science education and involved participants as teacher-researchers and curriculum-makers in cycles of action research. From this CPD experience, teachers appeared to reconceptualize traditional teacher and researcher 'roles' in more fluid and equitable ways, leading us to explore characteristics of the programme conducive to this shift. The main data source comprised teacher interviews, supplemented by video-recordings of group meetings, classroom enactment of activities and the facilitators' field notes. Findings suggest that the shift was encouraged by the gradual formation of a community of practice; a reconceptualization of the 'practical'; and the epistemology-oriented approach adopted in mathematics and science education. The discussion highlights the implications of these findings for early years educators' professional development, and the problems of the 'theory–practice' divide in such development. Furthermore, the discussion stresses the importance of the socio-cultural context in which such projects take place, particularly as these often draw heavily upon international literature.

Introduction

This paper reports on a reflective study, which explores the experiences of 14 early years educators who participated in a continuing professional development (CPD) programme coordinated by two of the paper's authors (referred to as facilitators). As such, the article can be viewed as a conversational paper, which aims at sharing these experiences in a reflective manner (for example, Avgitidou 2009, Banegas 2011). The CPD programme was designed and implemented in the second year of a three-year research project entitled 'Integrated Mathematics and Science Literacy

Framework' (the project acronym in Greek is PLEGMA which means 'net'). This took place in Cyprus and lasted from 2011 to 2014. The project aimed at introducing early childhood teachers to an inquiry-based learning approach to mathematics and science education. Contrary to prior experiences of in-service training models prevailing in the Greek-Cypriot context, the 14 teachers were now involved in CPD as a group of teacher-researchers through cycles of action research (AR) and a process curriculum development model. The analysis described here indicated that the participants' experience challenged a number of their original expectations prior to the project, especially how they perceived and talked about their own role as teachers, in addition to that of the facilitators as researchers-academics. In this paper we aim to describe these shifts and to interpret them in relation to certain characteristics of the CPD programme, which seemed to have brought them about. The paper comprises four parts; firstly the notions of AR, teacher CPD in 'communities of practice' and curriculum development are explored to indicate how they were intertwined in the design of the PLEGMA programme in the context of mathematics and science inquiry-based learning. In the second and third parts, the research methods and findings of the study are presented respectively. Finally, the findings are discussed in a reflective manner as we engage with the issues most significant for implications for our practice as teacher educators.

Locating PLEGMA theoretically: designing continuing professional development for early childhood educators in mathematics and science

The programme from which the data for this paper were collected was mainly designed as AR, drawing upon Stenhouse's idea of the teacher-researcher to whom 'curriculum research and development ought to belong' (1975, p. 142) and Elliott's (1991) support of collaborative (rather than individual) AR. AR may be restricted to technical or even practical rationales, but would ideally be emancipatory: by linking critical social science with educational research, emancipatory AR aims at transforming education and empowering teachers through a better understanding of their workplace (Carr and Kemmis 1986, Grundy 1987). We found Denscombe's (1998) definition particularly useful in the design of this study as he defines AR by referring to four main characteristics. Firstly, AR deals with *practical* issues, comprising issues and problems, concerns and needs, arising as a routine part of activity in the 'real world'. Secondly, AR is geared to *changing* matters, where research takes place not just to understand but to alter concerns as part of the research process, by bringing together theory and practice. Thirdly, AR is committed to a process of research in which the application of findings and evaluation of their impact on practice become a part of the *cycle of research*. Fourthly, AR involves those affected by the design and implementation of the research, encouraging them to *participate as collaborators* in the research rather than being subjects of it, as opposed to traditional research (see, for example, Carr and Kemmis 1986, Anderson 2002). This fourth characteristic regarding the balance between researcher and teacher roles has attracted considerable attention in the literature (cf. Bevins and Price 2014), since challenging the theory–practice divide is difficult to achieve within both the context of traditional educational research and the historical experience of teachers being unable to make their knowledge public (Cochran-Smith and Lytle 1993). Kelly differentiates the teacher-researcher model, in which teachers' perspective must be central, from simultaneous-integrated AR where teachers must be active collaborators in the research, 'but they need not be the initiators [...], nor passive recipients of it. Where teacher-researcher AR "takes" teachers' problems as its subject matter, simultaneous-integrated action research starts by "making" a social issue [...] problematic for teachers' (1985, p. 140).

By considering AR as an approach for curriculum development, we gravitated towards process approaches to curriculum and the concept of teachers as curriculum-makers. From this perspective, curriculum is not viewed 'simply as a document or a programme of study external to teachers', but rather as 'a complex phenomenon that takes shape in the throes of teachers' and students' pedagogical relationships' (Craig 2009, p. 606). Such a conceptualization of curriculum regards teachers as relatively autonomous and their role as significant. This significance, however, is not drawn from a 'fidelity perspective', which restricts the teacher role to that of an applier of others' knowledge/decisions/curricula developed by 'experts/academics'. Neither is it drawn from a 'mutual adaptation perspective', which expects teachers to negotiate with 'experts' in order to implement a 'mutually adapted' curriculum to a particular context. Rather, the significance stems from the conceptualization of curriculum as an enactment: a process of interaction between teachers, pupils, materials and the official context. Thus, the curriculum is the construction of personal meaning by the participants to this process (see Snyder *et al.* 1992). Consequently, we regarded curriculum development as a process, as opposed to goal-oriented or product-oriented curriculum development. In this case, goals become procedure principles used to highlight knowledge such as the development of inquiry, research and reflective capacities amongst pupils, or helping pupils examine and speculate on their sources (Lovat and Smith 1995). This was also conducive to the mathematics and science education approach adopted in this project, which aimed at developing such epistemological processes amongst learners, as explained later in the paper.

Against this background of AR as a process approach to curriculum development, we use the term 'continuing professional development' to suggest the value of continuing development during teachers' professional lives within formal (including initial teacher education), informal and non-formal settings. This distinguishes it from '(in-service) training', proposing more complex, dynamic and interactive processes of learning, and construes the teacher professional as a researcher working within a community, rather than, for example, a technician (see, for example Villegas-Reimers 2003, Day and Sachs 2004, Day *et al.* 2006, Yuen 2012, Dadds 2014). To reflect further on the roles of researchers and teachers, we considered whether 'the fundamental purpose of the CPD [is] to provide a means of transmission or to facilitate transformative practice' (Kennedy 2014, p. 348). Kennedy (2014) uses this question to outline a spectrum of nine CPD models. At one end is an understanding of CPD as having the purpose of preparing teachers to implement reform prepared by others (transmission view). At the opposite end lies an understanding of CPD as supporting teachers in shaping, contributing and even critiquing education policy and practice (transformative view). Between these two ends lies a 'transitional view' of CPD. This includes models that may be shaped to support both the transmission and the transformative views. Increasing teacher autonomy implied by movement from one end of the spectrum to the other is difficult to achieve, even within the transformative view on which this CPD was based. This made the need to explore teachers' perceptions of their CPD experience essential. Furthermore, it positions this study amongst reportedly much-needed research on teachers' beliefs and practices during professional development (PD) (Tam 2015) and context-sensitive approaches, looking at the complexity of teacher learning during PD as opposed to studies causally linking PD to pupil outcomes (King 2014). Much research on teachers has focused on processes which have rendered PD more or less successful (for example, Avgitidou 2009). In this study, having explored the impact of the PD programme on teachers by comparing their mathematics and science teaching practice before and during the programme as an outcome (Papademetri-Kachrimani and Louca 2013), we search for those characteristics of the CPD 'process' that were identified and linked by teachers to their re-conceptualization of roles.

Finally, the programme was designed so that teachers worked in a group because this has been highlighted in the literature on teacher PD which draws on 'communities of practice' and 'professional learning communities'. Stoll *et al.* note that learning within professional learning communities, 'involves active deconstruction of knowledge through reflection and analysis, and its reconstruction through action in a particular context, as well as co-construction (of knowledge) through collaborative learning with peers' (2006, pp. 233–234). Such professional learning can only be envisioned when teachers interact in a group; however, we were also aware that a gathering of individuals does not 'guarantee' that they become a community. In Wenger *et al.*'s words, a community of practice comprises people who:

> become informally bound by the value that they find in learning together. This value is not merely instrumental for their work. It also accrues in the personal satisfaction of knowing colleagues who understand each other's perspectives and of belonging to an interesting group of people. Over time, they develop a unique perspective on their topic as well as a body of common knowledge, practices and approaches. They may also develop personal relationships and established ways of interacting. (2002, pp. 4–5)

In designing the CPD programme we tried to create opportunities for such 'personal satisfaction'. These opportunities arose as sustained contact and communication of the whole group was pursued and as the CPD programme was built on constructionist approaches to mathematics and science education that emphasize inquiry-based learning and the involvement of learners in activities. Such approaches do not simply aim at science and mathematics knowledge acquisition and understanding, but also at understanding the processes by which scientists study the natural world (Lotter *et al.* 2007, 2009), at teaching children how to think as mathematicians (Papert 1972). Learning was therefore seen as a socio-cognitive process, resembling that used by scientists in scientific communities, to pose questions and problems, formulate hypotheses, design, collect and analyse data, experiences and observations, formulate conclusions and construct or reconstruct theories. Within inquiry-based learning, emphasis may be placed on processes of investigation (for example, Gott and Duggan 1995, Etkina and Van Heuvelen 2007), problem-solving (for example, Blum and Niss 1991, Erickson 1999, Lubienski 1999) and modelling (for example, Constantinou 1999, English 2003, Lesh and Lehrer 2003, Louca and Zacharia 2012) as a means for supporting children to construct nuanced meanings of the world that surrounds them.

Enacting PLEGMA in practice: outlining the project and its context

The CPD programme aimed at supporting teachers to experience such learning in mathematics and science for themselves, to reflect upon this way of learning and their existing teaching practices and, finally, to proceed with designing and enacting activities following a cyclical process of action and reflection. Even though inquiry-based learning, as a generic epistemological basis, informed the broader project and the CPD programme, at no point did the facilitators impose this idea on the participants. This idea came about, on the one hand, through the teachers' involvement in the programme and, on the other, through the data collection and analysis by both the teachers and the facilitators during the three-year research project. Thus, the generic epistemological bases gradually developed into a process-based curriculum where certain processes (problem-solving, modelling, investigation) emerged as structured, cohesive procedures that constituted a dynamic web of developing scientific method skills, developing attitudes towards learning, acquiring experiences and constructing conceptual understanding in a way that makes learning meaningful for the learner and has an epistemological dimension (cf. Papademetri-Kachrimani and Louca 2014).

During the programme, teachers were separated into two groups: science and mathematics. We adopted a learner-centred/modelling PD model in which teachers first experience what they are later expected to enact with their pupils. Thus, at first, each group participated in authentic (designed especially for adults) constructivist, inquiry-based activities in science and mathematics respectively, and had the opportunity to reflect upon this experience. After the completion of this first part of the programme (comprising five three-hour meetings over two and a half months) the two groups participated in a joint meeting where they were asked to compare their experiences. To do so, they inevitably had to describe the activities in which they were involved to the members of the other group. As a result of this activity, teachers concluded that 'doing mathematics and science' was approached epistemologically in a similar way, the main difference being the content. The teachers themselves constructed the idea of a joint mathematics and science curriculum and articulated in their own words the characteristics of inquiry-based learning. In the two meetings that followed, the teachers presented and reflected upon data including videotaped activities, children's representations or constructions and personal reflective notes that they had collected from their practice at the start of the CPD programme. These were chosen as representative of their practice at that point in time. Their reflections helped them articulate, with the support of the group, what they now wanted to change in their practice when teaching mathematics or science, a process that was framed by the epistemological approach they had experienced in the first part of the programme. In light of this discussion, the teachers began designing, enacting and video-recording activities in their school classes, a process which was supported by the group. In each of the seven meetings that followed and completed the programme, the teachers presented and analysed data collected from the enactment of these activities, reflected upon them and moved on with a new cycle of curriculum development. Throughout this time the teachers worked with each other and the facilitators in ways that challenged both parties' initial conceptualisation of their role. Consequently, we decided to further explore this matter in an effort to understand why or how this came about.

This was deemed especially important in the context of Cyprus where early year educators enjoy lower status compared with primary and secondary school teachers, as perception of their work is often 'reduced' to a matter of care rather than education (cf. Diakidou and Phtiaka 1998) or merely preparation for primary schooling (Loizou 2008). The latter is also implied in the widespread use of the term 'pre-primary' (*προδημοτική*) rather than first or early childhood education in the Greek language. Notably, although official curricula for primary education have been adopted since the nineteenth century, an official curriculum for pre-primary education first appeared as a short chapter/section in the 1981 and again in the 1994 official state curricula for primary education. A separate, official curriculum for early childhood education was first introduced in 2011. When compared with other sectors of education, early childhood educators enjoy much more autonomy and flexibility, as beyond this official curriculum there have been no state pupil textbooks or teacher manuals or examinations to be followed, like in primary and secondary education.

Methods and data sources

As we were concerned with focusing on meaning, we adopted an interpretative approach to explore the 14 teachers' experiences of the programme and drew on them for our reflection. Interpretative studies 'are framed by descriptions of, explanations for, or meanings given to phenomena by *both* the researcher and the study participants rather than by the definitions and interpretations of the researcher alone' (LeCompte and Preissle 1993, pp. 31–32; authors' emphasis). Such an approach suggests that social research should capitalize upon the researchers' 'personhood' (Stanley and Wise 1983) and 'reflexivity' as 'the human capacity for participant observation. We act in the social world and yet are able to reflect upon ourselves and our actions as objects in that world' (Hammersley and Atkinson 1995, p. 21). As the programme came to a close, our experience as its facilitators fuelled questions regarding our own and the teachers' role, which we did not originally have in mind.

The main data source analysed in the study we report in this paper is semi-structured individual one-hour interviews with all 14 early years educators who volunteered to participate in the CPD programme during the second year of the project. The group of volunteers was formed after an open call was sent to all public and private kindergarten schools; 29 teachers initially responded, but some were rejected because they were kindergarten principals while others withdrew their interest for personal reasons. All remaining 14 were women, who came from three different districts and whose professional experience ranged between one and nine years. They were all leading a class during the year of the CPD programme with children from ages three to six. Three of them (referred to as Teachers 3.1–3.3 in the findings section) had also participated in the first year of the project. The other 11 teachers had only participated during the second year, six in the mathematics group (referred to as Teachers 1.1–1.6) and five in the science group (referred to as Teachers 2.1–2.5). The interviews were conducted and transcribed in Greek; the quotes presented in the paper are our translations into English. Participants were informed of the reflective aim of the study and that the data would be available to the authors (including the two facilitators) for analysis and reflection. During the interview, teachers were asked to narrate the course of their participation in the programme, from volunteering to participate to the whole process of experimenting in their classroom and interacting with the teacher group. They also expanded on their views on curriculum change, PD and teacher professionalism. Additional data used as supplementary data sources in this paper included video-recordings by the teachers of their enactment of science or mathematics activities in their classroom, video-recordings of the CPD meetings and the facilitators' field notes.

Adopting a grounded approach and moving between productive and inductive analytical techniques, we conducted open coding and later axial and selective coding, as we first identified concepts and codes, and then reduced them to categories and themes (Creswell 2007). We then focused on those themes that referred to different 'roles' taken up by the teachers and facilitators, with an eye on unpacking and untangling the ways in which the teachers created meanings regarding these roles. The findings below are organized around three characteristics of the CPD most closely related to this problematization of 'roles': shifts in teachers' initial understandings of the meaning of 'practical'; the gradual transformation of the group into a community of practice; and a re-construction of what 'doing mathematics and science' meant for them.

Re-conceptualizing the programme as being 'practical'

At the beginning of their interviews, teachers reported joining the programme because the programme brochure emphasized that it would be a 'practical' and 'experiential program', providing the opportunity 'to implement activities and receive feedback'. Some of them referred to originally joining the programme 'to learn new things' and 'move away from stereotypes', whereas others due to curiosity, 'because it was something new' and this made them 'wonder whether this new way [of doing mathematics/science] is feasible'. Both of the programme's facilitators reported in their personal field notes that some of the participants in the first meeting were explicitly asking for reassurance 'that they would learn something new' and that 'what they would learn can be implemented in their practice'. Teachers thus seemed to join the programme believing that it would follow a 'transmission view' and that the facilitators, as 'experts', had already developed a new body of knowledge that would be transferred to them. However, they were also somewhat suspicious towards this body of knowledge because they anticipated it to be 'theoretical' and distant from the reality of their practice. None of the teachers mentioned that they anticipated playing a role in constructing new knowledge nor participating in the process of designing activities, in order to provide feedback to the facilitators for the construction of this new knowledge. So the teachers seemed to expect that they would be given 'practical' activities to implement, in order to receive feedback as to whether, and in what ways, the implementation was considered successful or not by the 'experts'.

However, even though processes of activity development and feedback were indeed included in the programme, these were of a different nature. As one teacher, who had noted how she expected 'to implement activities and receive feedback', added to this statement immediately after, 'we had something else in mind and we came across something else' (Teacher 1.1). More particularly, teachers named two different dimensions of the programme as practical. Firstly, while explaining why she considered this programme successful, one of the teachers stated that it was because 'we were working in parallel to the children' (Teacher 1.1). Another teacher reported that 'I felt like a student learning and that then I had to implement what I had learned' (Teacher 1.2). Similarly, another teacher described that 'it wasn't just the theory, it was the practice, that we participated ourselves and had the opportunity to stand in the children's place and feel what it's like to go through these processes and learn in this way' (Teacher 1.5). Secondly, in almost all of the interviews the teachers reported that what made them believe in this new way of doing mathematics/science was that they had the opportunity to 'see things actually happen and become aware of things ourselves' (Teacher 1.1). Teacher 1.4 stated that, 'what made me revise my practice was the way my students responded and the interest they showed in this new way of learning', and added 'because it's different to listen about theories and it's different to see it in practice'. So, on the one hand, the teachers referred to the programme as being practical in the sense that they had the opportunity to experience learning in this new way themselves (thus describing the learner-centred dimension of the programme), while at the same time having the opportunity to try it in their practice and explore how it worked (thus referring to the AR dimension of the programme).

Teachers thus made special reference to the first part of the programme, where they had the opportunity to participate in authentic mathematics/science activities designed by the facilitators in ways which involved teachers in epistemological processes of doing mathematics and science. Teacher 2.2 emphasized that during this process she had the opportunity to reflect upon her existing practice and compare the activities she was currently enacting in her own classroom with what she was experiencing within the programme. In comparing this CPD with others, another teacher stated that 'it's one thing to be involved in the process yourself and a completely different thing to sit on a chair and just listen' (Teacher 1.6). She concluded that 'I'm convinced [in this approach] because through the implementation of activities I saw the children doing mathematics; I saw many concepts develop/being constructed' (Teacher 1.6). It is as if the phrase 'doing mathematics/science' gradually acquired a new meaning, an issue we will return to later on. In this first part of the programme, the facilitators played a leading role in initiating and directing the teachers towards inquiry-based learning. However, this was not pursued in a manner that interfered with the teachers feeling that they had constructed meaning for themselves as opposed to having such meaning imposed on them. The teachers explicitly referred to this aspect of the facilitators' role during the interviews. Some teachers reported that the facilitators 'knew but didn't tell'. One teacher reported that 'they would let us see for ourselves' (Teacher 1.1) and another that:

> we felt a little insecure because we didn't know from the beginning what would happen in the end, but I think the facilitator knew exactly where she wanted to take us, and even though we felt insecure, when you trust your teacher [facilitator] you feel more safe and are willing to continue even if you don't know where you are going. (Teacher 1.6)

In comparing this programme with another programme she had participated in, one of the teachers stated that even though the ideas seemed to be pretty much the same, the programme was very different because the other one was short in duration, each meeting was content-based (e.g. there was one meeting for geometry, one for numbers, one for probability, etc.) and it was not practical but theoretical, because 'the instructors would simply describe some activities that they [designed and] implemented themselves' (Teacher 1.1). Supporting our point on re-conceptualizing 'practical', this instance demonstrates how a teacher regarded a programme, where they were given 'practical' ideas for activities that had already been tested by the instructors, as not practical: the fact that the programme was content based and that the instructors expected teachers to implement their activities were seen as negative features of that programme. Additionally, she stressed the duration of the PLEGMA programme, a feature to which most teachers referred as positive. It was this

THE PROFESSIONAL DEVELOPMENT OF EARLY YEARS EDUCATORS

long-term duration and frequency (two meetings per month) that gave teachers the time to experience and explore their practice, reflect upon that trial in cycles of action and then reflect upon that action; such recognition pointed towards the value of AR as a form of CPD for them.

The emotional journey of knowledge in communities: becoming worth it

Despite the excitement, the interest and the positive feelings at the end, the teachers reported having a variety of negative feelings especially at the beginning of the programme, such as insecurity and stress. Gradually these began to disappear or were simply acknowledged as an important and constructive part of the process, especially once the shared knowledge and equitable relationships gradually built up. As reported in the interviews, one of the reasons for feeling stressed was the fact that teachers were expected to videotape themselves in their classroom; this anxiety was soon overcome, when they realized its significance for the process of reflecting upon their work, as well as for collecting and analysing data. One teacher also reported that she was stressed because she gradually realized she held various stereotypes which she could not easily reject (e.g. that there is one correct answer when doing mathematics and that the aim of an activity is to make the children give that answer). She added:

> but when we had the opportunity to talk to each other during the meetings we realised that this [finding it difficult to make a shift in their practice] was part of the process, we would find ways to overcome the difficulties, talk about our experiences and see that there were commonalities between us so we would move on. (Teacher 1.1)

As reported by some of the teachers, another reason for feeling insecure was that they were facing the unknown and that they did not know beforehand where the journey would lead them, even though they trusted that the facilitators knew. So even though the teachers referred to feelings of insecurity and stress, when they talked about what was happening during the meetings they described a very safe environment where they had a lot of support, not only from the facilitators but also from the other teachers in the group. They described an environment that helped them manage and overcome their stress and insecurity in a productive way.

Teachers connected this safe environment to the roles that they and the facilitators took up during the meetings. They stated that their role was active during the meetings, that they felt equally valued members of the group and that they had not one person but many people to lean on. They repeatedly stated that the facilitators were willing to help them at all times, even outside meeting times:

> The facilitators were there to help us during every difficulty, because I faced some difficulties during the process, but I knew exactly what to do next following the meeting. We would design; yes we would design the activities that we would implement next so this was very helpful. (Teacher 1.2)

The teachers also noted that they felt free and comfortable to express their opinion even if this was different from the facilitator's opinion:

> I wouldn't hesitate to say my opinion, and there were times when I would express an opinion that was different from the one expressed by the facilitator. I was never afraid to talk about anything. (Teacher 2.1)

THE PROFESSIONAL DEVELOPMENT OF EARLY YEARS EDUCATORS

> We would say this bit, they would say another bit or say try this and because we were working ..., they would also see and get enthusiastic about the things we were saying, so the exchange of ideas was mutual, I have to say. (Teacher 3.2)

Indicative of the importance the group acquired is that Teacher 1.2 (as quoted above) first talked about the facilitator as the person who would help her overcome the problems, but then used a verb in the first person plural to refer to processes that were taking place within the group. Further on in the interview, she stated that 'we would explain, talk to each other, move forward together, discuss, find ways together, share our experiences, revise our activities and collaborate in order to find ways to make our activities better'. Virtually these exact words were repeatedly used by all of the teachers during the interviews when they were trying to describe what was happening during the meetings:

> I felt myself as part of a team that implemented activities and had to bring back some results that we would talk about, we would build and continue together, it was a progressive process, I was not a passive receiver. I had my own opinion and we would build together and move on. [...]. We bonded. Knowledge brought us together. [...]. Now if I am facing a problem and I want to call someone, I will not call my best friend who is also a kindergarten teacher. I will call one of the teachers from the group who knows the philosophy. (Teacher 1.6)

During the interviews the teachers often referred to the ways in which this programme brought them together and made them feel like being part of a community, with common beliefs and philosophy, a community in which all teacher-members were experts and could support each other in processes of development and reflection. Thus, when wanting feedback from someone, teachers would not contact the facilitators but one of the other participants, even though they repeatedly mentioned that they felt comfortable to contact them at any time. One of the teachers described that when teachers of the group attended other seminars and heard something that was not compatible with what they were experiencing within the programme, they (teachers of the group) would (just) look at each other and know exactly what each other was thinking. She further commented how, during other PD seminars, the teachers of the group felt that they were different because they had learned 'about another way of thinking' (Teacher 3.1). On some occasions, they would even feel empowered to stand up to school inspectors, when the latter pushed them towards pedagogically opposite directions. Or they would show inspectors 'what was expected/wanted' during class inspections, but would continue with their own ideas at all other times.

When reflecting on the way the programme created new expectations in relation to their PD, the teachers reported that now they wanted to learn new things but not by simply sitting down and listening. In answering the question 'What would make you participate in other PD programs?', one teacher stated:

> I would mmm ..., I would like to know in advan ..., not know in advance. I would want to know that this process is going to bring some change to my practice and help me move away from stereotypes that I have in my mind. I want to manage to detach .... This is why most preschool teachers go from seminar to seminar, because they want the change, ... (Teacher 1.6)

On completion of the programme, the teachers identified and commented on this 'not knowing in advance', but rather discovering, constructing meaning and understanding

THE PROFESSIONAL DEVELOPMENT OF EARLY YEARS EDUCATORS

in the process were seen as significant. Now they expected PD programmes not only to talk about change, but to help them achieve change in their practice.

Re-constructing understandings of roles in PD and of 'doing mathematics/ science': two sides of the same coin

In responding to the question of how they perceived their role as teachers, they referred to themselves as teacher-researchers in both explicit and implicit ways:

> I don't feel that I have managed to totally grasp this new way, I still need a lot of work. It's a continuous search, we see, we try out and see and when you get a feeling that what you did was actually mathematics, you get feedback that what you are doing is right. I think I need time, I need to do more activities and acquire more experiences of this new way, with my children, in my classroom so that I can expand … I need to offer the children the best, search and constantly question myself. (Teacher 1.6)

It is noteworthy that even though this teacher thought she had not 'totally grasped' inquiry-based learning, she did not see this as a negative aspect of the programme, since she had learned that constructing understanding is an ongoing process in which her role is active and primary. Another teacher, who also referred to the importance of the teacher constantly searching and researching, added that this cannot be achieved if teachers work alone, 'if they search alone' (Teacher 1.4), emphasizing the need for belonging and having access to a group. This idea of seeing/ observing, collecting data and researching was something that came up in many of the interviews. One of the teachers, after stating that now she felt the need to observe and search, added 'I have also put the children in this position, every time we are going to do something new, we will investigate and search' (Teacher 1.4). So the way the teachers constructed an understanding of their role as teacher-researchers was reflected in the way their practice with children was transformed. From delivering pre-determined content/knowledge, teachers adopted strategies/approaches of enabling the construction of knowledge-as-process. As children were now expected to engage with mathematics and science inquiry in epistemologically similar ways to those used by scientists, so were teachers engaged in this process, by inquiring and researching their own practice. This seemed to be strongly associated with a change in how they viewed children and teaching. The teachers expressed their amazement at having the opportunity to 'actually see [their children] learn without being instructed/taught' (Teacher 1.4):

> Now I am more open. Before I was more stereotypical. Now let's say I will give the children a problem and through their answers and their representations I will collect data in order to plan the next step. While before I would simply give them the problem and the process would end there. (Teacher 1.1)

In reflecting upon the ways in which their practice changed, the teachers very explicitly stated that they had become more open and flexible. They no longer planned activities with a pre-determined end, simply applying them and then moving on to something new. This is exactly what the facilitators had planned and what the teachers had experienced as learners during the programme. The teachers stated that they now planned activities to create dynamic opportunities for learning: they reported that they were now closely observing what the children were doing, valued the children's perspectives and capitalized on them to dynamically expand the activities:

I have stopped teaching the numbers separately one by one. This is totally erased from my practice. I do more experiential things with my children, we investigate situations that lead us to concepts, everything results through processes of investigation. We get out of the school and look for things and connect everything with the real world. I look for real objects to bring into the classroom and I try so that learning and even what will be learned will result from the children. This was also a change that resulted from my participation in the program. (Teacher 1.4)

For me, learning no longer means that someone tells me and I understand. Learning is something that results from my experiences, my problems and questions, my mistakes. [...] the aim is no longer to learn things that they will probably forget. The aim is to look around them and try to make sense of what is happening and to be able to reach conclusions themselves. (Teacher 1.2)

In all of these quotations it is not always clear whether the teachers are talking about themselves or the children learning, since in either case they are talking about constructing meaning in the same way. Such occurrences were also frequent during the meetings. For example, in one of the science meetings (Meeting 9) during which teachers brought data from their classrooms (videos, photographs, children's drawings/work), one of the teachers (Teacher 2.3) brought in all the materials that she had used during the activity and the children had produced, providing also a short description of the lesson enactment. Then she paused at a child's drawing, indicating that she was unsure whether the drawing was presenting scientifically an idea about light or not. The facilitator then suggested that the answer would depend on what each of the participants understood as scientific (re)presentation of an idea. This sparked a discussion in which participant teachers debated the definition of scientific, slowly reaching a consensus that directed the definition towards including a sense of how things happen or what causes them. When the facilitator summarized this conversation, Teacher 2.3 wondered how to proceed in the next lesson. This was a familiar situation in the group: a teacher summarizing a previous lesson and opening up the discussion within the group on ideas for the next. By the end of the meeting, the group had reached two possible scenarios negotiated by the facilitator and the teachers; as the teacher would later enact them in her class, she would also collect data and analyse them to share with both teachers and facilitator to ponder on their next steps.

Discussion

The analysis indicated that traditional teacher and facilitator 'roles' were challenged and negotiated during the programme. In trying to interpret why this transformation was possible, we focused on the points that seemed most important from the teachers' perspective and discuss them in this last part of the paper in a reflective way, with an eye on exploring implications for our future practice as teacher educators. As noted in the description of the programme, drawing upon the traditions of AR, CPD in communities of practice and process curriculum development ideally provided the theoretical foundations for challenging boundaries between traditional 'roles' and attendant hierarchies derived from the academic versus practical knowledge binary. However, these foundations do not guarantee the questioning of roles. Even in the Anglo-Saxon contexts where these traditions emerged, facilitated by particular socio-historical circumstances and conceptualizations of teachers as autonomous, teacher–researcher collaboration has been a complex matter. One could argue that this complexity has been amplified by changing circumstances in these original contexts and that teacher autonomy has come under threat from national curricula or standards (see, for example, MacDonald 2003, Goodson 2007). Even though these traditions have since become dominant in (academic) teacher education internationally, if and how they become relevant in contexts where different conceptualizations of teachers as professionals prevail become questions for research. As Villegas-Reimers warns:

> even when teachers and their societies have the intention of promoting the role of teachers as researchers, the long-existing perception of teachers as being mere interpreters of the knowledge handed down to them by experts is a tough barrier to overcome before it is possible to revolutionalise the expectations and practices related to teachers and teaching. (2003, p. 109)

Indeed the Cypriot context has been a centralized context where teachers, as public servants, have historically had their autonomy undermined through state produced and inspected formal curricula (see, for example, Philippou 2014). One also needs to note the prevalence of more traditional PD provision, which usually takes the form of 'experts' delivering information at 'off-site' meetings (Karagiorgi and Lymbouridou 2009) and is individual and voluntary (Karagiorgi and Symeou 2006). Although there have been calls for AR (for example, Koutselini 2007, Karagiorgi *et al.* 2008), systemic support for reflection, self-study and feedback on teaching is rather weak (Karagiorgi and Nicolaidou 2009). Against these odds, this study seems to point towards possibilities of challenging teacher and researcher roles amongst early childhood educators, and what follows is a discussion of how the findings suggest this became possible.

Firstly, a condition conducive to reformulating roles was that a 'community of practice' seemed to have been created: teachers' accounts of their experience pointed towards definitions of a community of practice as a group of people 'who share a concern, a set of problems, or a passion about a topic, and who deepen their knowledge and expertise in this area by interacting on an ongoing basis' (Wenger *et al.* 2002, p. 4). More particularly, in Wenger's (1998) terms, such a community is characterized by three features, which the data suggest also characterized this particular group of teachers. Regarding 'community', participants interacted regularly and with commitment and indeed looked forward to the meetings; with regards to 'domain', participants shared similar aims and interests, despite their working in different schools and with different age groups; and finally, with regards to 'practice', discussions focused on real-life situations participants were experiencing in their classrooms and which were shared and discussed in a safe environment, especially through the use of video-recorded episodes from their teaching. What resonates especially with the teachers' emotional accounts of their experience is that despite difficulties in finding the time for the meetings, the additional workload to prepare before the meetings, the stress of enacting dynamic activities in their classroom and video-recording them all paled into comparative insignificance when put next to what they thought they gained, in terms of both knowledge and their personal relationships. This 'gain' did not take material form, for there were no 'materials' of ready-made activities or finalized lesson plans and manuals produced. Gain was mostly perceived as non-material. Calling each other up to discuss issues at any time, constantly trying to enact and reflect upon activities in their classroom, 'staring' at each other and feeling part of a different group sharing something

THE PROFESSIONAL DEVELOPMENT OF EARLY YEARS EDUCATORS

'special' during other PD programmes resonate with how communities of practice 'do not reduce knowledge to an object. They make it an integral part of their activities and interactions, and they serve as a living repository for that knowledge' (Wenger *et al.* 2002, p. 9). The teachers developed a certain way of knowing and being, taking the time to interact with both facilitators and peers to co-construct knowledge through dialogue; to question, challenge or negotiate their views with the facilitators; and to sustain discussions within the community without expecting 'answers' from the facilitators, even if they thought the facilitators already knew (as one teacher commented). This, however, was not entirely true, since despite the facilitators' knowledge of the inquiry-based approach to mathematics and science, there was no rigidly pre-determined content for the CPD (rather, this emerged in relation to what teachers brought in as experiences, concerns and questions) and there was no pre-determined structure of a joint mathematics and science curriculum or even the idea of this prior to the programme. The community thus seemed to fulfil the 'promise for altering the linear relationships through which information is handed down from those who discover the professional knowledge to those who provide and receive educational services' (Buysse *et al.* 2003, p. 265). Teachers' participation in such a community seemed to facilitate their challenging of such established 'linear relationships' which would anticipate facilitators taking a position above them in a hierarchy, in valuing their 'inner expertise' (as opposed to underestimating it; see Dadds 2014), and in becoming both users and producers of knowledge (Edwards *et al.* 2002). Although not dismissing the different expertise that the facilitators brought to the group and although teachers still sought facilitators' guidance, the community experience seemed to create 'openings' for re-envisioning their own role as professionals. They focused especially on the research and inquiry dimensions of their profession that they would continuously seek 'non-stop', even after the completion of the programme, as they noted. This came hand in hand with their view of facilitators as collaborators and supporters in this research process, rather than as expert leaders.

Secondly, and relatedly, the programme also seemed to create openings for redefining the 'practical'. When asked to unpack their expectations on joining the programme, participants stressed expecting guidance or 'how to' knowledge in a technical form; that is, one that would be easily applied in their classroom. This was juxtaposed to the theoretical as the out-of-touch-with-their-realities knowledge they usually received during PD. Gradually, however, 'practical' came to mean their active involvement in challenging their own assumptions and re-constructing knowledge through and during their experiential explorations in their own classroom and during the group meetings. This meant not requesting ready-made materials but rather being able to critique the existing formal ones to enact curriculum in ways which would be meaningful from their new perspective and in their own contexts, thus alluding to a contextualist epistemology (see Ellis 2007). In their review of communities of practice and professional learning communities, Enthoven and de Bruijn (2010) identify two main aims: the PD of their members; and the sharing and creation of knowledge. Our concern here with our findings is that even though the first aim was addressed since the teachers developed considerable knowledge in inquiry-based science and mathematics education (Papademetri-Kachrimani and Louca 2013), and despite their re-conceptualization of the practical as argued in this paper, they did not articulate either in an analytical/theoretical language during the interviews. When describing their experience of both the meetings and their classroom enactment, the main principles of inquiry-based learning were mentioned tacitly or embodied respectively. This led us to deliberate over the distinction between practice-based knowledge and formal, scientific knowledge. The first has practical value and is dependent upon both context and use. The second has value in reference to requirements for codification, what Gibbons *et al.* (1994) have called Mode 2 (practice-based) and Mode 1 (formal, scientific) knowledge production, respectively. Although Mode 1 results in generic, public knowledge, disseminating Mode 2 knowledge originating from practitioner research remains an issue (Enthoven and de Bruijn 2010). We also share this experience as we support these teachers in rendering their practical-as-contextual but not relativist knowledge available publicly in a theoretical language by writing chapters (see Papademetri-Kachrimani and Louca in preparation) and presenting their experiences at conferences (Papademetri-Kachrimani 2014).

Thirdly, we need to note the role of video in the creation of this community, in the blurring of traditional 'roles' and in the re-conceptualization of the practical. The value of video in terms of making more classroom context available for observation and discussion than would be otherwise possible has been extensively documented. This includes its potential to link theory to practice (see Marsh and Mitchell 2014). The video becomes a 'window to practice' (Zhang *et al.* 2011) and to a classroom context in which the teacher is more knowledgeable but in a manner recognizable by the group. During the CPD programme it thus seemed to further enable the challenging of researcher and teacher roles. As teachers came to understand themselves as learners researching and reflecting upon their practice with an eye for enacting (as in creating) curriculum with their pupils, the video became a means for their becoming 'strangers' (Greene 1973), for seeing the world of the classroom with a sense of wonder as opposed to the world of the classroom as routine, predictable and manageable, as a 'stable state' (Schön 1971). This mainly drew upon seeing their pupils through 'new eyes': listening to and observing the children more closely and, consequently, enacting activities more dynamically rather than worrying over what they had planned; valuing children's knowledge and potential; facilitating children through the use of space, time and materials to articulate their views. These are just some of the 'realizations' teachers mentioned during the interviews as having when repeatedly watching their video-recordings at home.

Finally, the findings suggest that the fact the CPD programme was conducted on inquiry-based learning for mathematics and science with early childhood educators was also conducive to this challenging of 'roles'. As noted earlier in the paper, early childhood educators in Cyprus enjoy much more autonomy over curriculum and teaching. This provided the necessary 'space' for experimenting with dynamic curriculum development in the teachers' classrooms. Despite control by inspectors, the absence of textbooks and examinations in early childhood education seemed to have created the circumstances for teachers to pursue and eventually truly engage with the CPD programme. The question of whether such a programme would have a similar effect on primary or secondary teachers remains open for future research. Similarly, the question of whether such an effect would be possible if the CPD focused on other subject areas is also worthwhile for future research. Our findings in this paper and elsewhere (Papademetri-Kachrimani and Louca 2013), however, suggest that inquiry-based learning, which has been highly connected to mathematics and science, was critical. As noted in the third section of the findings, time and again teachers referred to how this CPD was 'practical' because the epistemological approach to mathematics and science they had experienced as learners they would later enact in their own classrooms. Thus learning through inquiry-based learning in mathematics and science (as learners) about inquiry-based learning (as teacher-researchers) seemed to play a pivotal role.

Conclusion

These teachers seemed to be veering between, on the one hand, their request for guidance by the facilitators ('experts'/academics) as bearers of a different kind of knowledge to their own and, on the other hand, their expectations of 'practical' knowledge as readily applicable to their classroom practice when joining the programme. While reporting that their expectations were largely met, we realized that they ascribed different meanings to 'practical' and, by extension, to their and our own roles. This helped us think beyond the 'theory' versus 'practice' binary. In a programme constantly moving between the two, borders between roles were blurred, a process facilitated by how teachers constructed knowledge safely shared within a group that gradually became a community of practice. The 'practical' was reconceptualized from receiving recipes, materials and how-to guidelines, to participating in a contextual, constructivist process of socio-cultural immersion, to a community that produced rather than consumed knowledge. However, the kind of knowledge produced remains a point of concern for us, as its descriptive articulation during the interviews rendered it rather tacit. This is indeed an issue to which we need to return in future analyses of these data: What types of knowledge were at interplay in teacher–facilitator interactions during the meetings and in teachers' classrooms? Could this further support us in understanding how teachers challenged stereotypical roles? Weaving together AR, CPD, process curriculum development and inquiry-based learning in mathematics/science created a community of practice that facilitated certain 'openings'. These help us, as teacher educators, to reflect upon 'roles' and to further support teachers to challenge these in the future, achieved by becoming aware ourselves of the complexities and risks at stake. Ultimately, this is no more than what we challenged teachers to do in this project.

Acknowledgements

The authors would like to thank Maria Santis for her feedback on the article.

Disclosure statement

No potential conflict of interest was reported by the authors.

Funding

The PLEGMA project was supported by the Cyprus Research Promotion Foundation Grant [#ΑΝΘΡΩΠΙΣΤΙΚΕΣ/ΠΑΙΔΙ/0609(ΒΕ)/14]. The host organization for the project was the EUC Research Center.

References

Anderson, G.L., 2002. Reflecting on research for doctoral students in education. *Educational researcher*, 31 (7), 22–25.
Avgitidou, S., 2009. Participation, roles and processes in a collaborative action research project: a reflexive account of the facilitator. *Educational action research*, 17 (4), 585–600.

Banegas, D.L., 2011. Teachers as 'reform-doers': developing a participatory curriculum to teach English as a foreign language. *Educational action research*, 19 (4), 417–432.

Bevins, S. and Price, G., 2014. Collaboration between academics and teachers: a complex relationship. *Educational action research*, 22 (2), 270–284. doi:10.1080/09650792.2013.869181.

Blum, W. and Niss, M., 1991. Applied mathematical problem solving, modelling, applications, and links to other subjects – state, trends and issues in mathematical instruction. *Educational studies in mathematics*, 22 (1), 37–68.

Buysse, V., Sparkman, K.L., and Wesley, P.W., 2003. Communities of practice: connecting what we know with what we do. *Exceptional children*, 69 (3), 263–277.

Carr, W. and Kemmis, S., 1986. *Becoming critical: education, knowledge and action research*. Lewes: Falmer.

Cochran-Smith, M. and Lytle, S.L., 1993. *Inside/outside: teacher research and knowledge*. New York, NY: Teachers College.

Constantinou, C.P., 1999. The Cocoa microworld as an environment for modeling physical phenomena. *International journal of continuing education and life-long learning*, 8 (2), 65–83.

Craig, C.J., 2009. Flights from the field and the plight of teacher education: a personal perspective. *Journal of curriculum studies*, 41 (5), 605–624.

Creswell, J.W., 2007. *Qualitative inquiry and research design: choosing among five approaches*. 2nd ed. London: Sage.

Dadds, M., 2014. Continuing professional development: nurturing the expert within. *Professional development in education*, 40 (1), 9–16.

Day, C. and Sachs, J., 2004. Professionalism, performativity and empowerment: discourses in the politics, policies and purposes of continuing professional development. *In*: C. Day and J. Sachs, eds. *International handbook on the continuing professional development of teachers*. Maidenhead, UK: Open University Press, 3–32.

Day, C., *et al.*, 2006. The personal and professional selves of teachers: stable and unstable identities. *British educational research journal*, 32 (4), 601–616.

Denscombe, M., 1998. *The good research guide for small-scale social research projects*. Buckingham: Open University Press.

Diakidou, E.A. and Phtiaka, E., 1998. Νηπιακή εκπαίδευση ή φροντίδα; Ένα παιδαγωγικό δίλημμα [Early childhood education or care? A pedagogical dilemma]. *Παιδαγωγική Επιθεώρηση [Pedagogical review]*, 27, 7–30.

Edwards, A., Gilroy, P., and Hartley, D., 2002. *Rethinking teacher education: collaborative responses to uncertainty*. London: RoutledgeFalmer.

Elliott, J., 1991. *Action research for educational change*. Buckingham: Open University Press.

Ellis, V., 2007. Taking subject knowledge seriously: from professional knowledge recipes to complex conceptualizations of teacher development. *Curriculum journal*, 18 (4), 447–462.

English, L.D., 2003. Reconciling theory, research, and practice: a models and modeling perspective. *Educational studies in mathematics*, 54 (2/3), 225–248.

Enthoven, M. and de Bruijn, E., 2010. Beyond locality: the creation of public practice-based knowledge through practitioner research in professional learning communities and communities of practice. A review of three books on practitioner research and professional communities. *Educational action research*, 18 (2), 289–298.

Erickson, D.K., 1999. A problem-based approach to mathematics instruction. *Mathematics teacher*, 92 (6), 516–521.

Etkina, E. and Van Heuvelen, A., 2007. Investigative Science Learning Environment – a science process approach to learning physics. *In:* E.F. Redish and P. Cooney, eds. *PER-based reforms in calculus-based physics*. College Park, MD: American Association of Physics Teachers, vol. 1, 1–48.

Gibbons, M., *et al.*, 1994. *The new production of knowledge. The dynamics of science and research in contemporary societies*. London: Sage.

Goodson, I., 2007. Socio-historical processes of curriculum change. *In:* A. Benavot and C. Braslavsky, eds., in collaboration with N. Truong. *School knowledge in comparative and historical perspective; changing curricula in primary and secondary education*. CERC Studies in Comparative Education, vol. 18. Dordrecht: Springer, 211–220.

THE PROFESSIONAL DEVELOPMENT OF EARLY YEARS EDUCATORS

Gott, R. and Duggan, S., 1995. *Investigative work in the science curriculum*. Buckingham: Open University Press.

Greene, M., 1973. *Teacher as stranger*. Belmont, CA: Wadsworth.

Grundy, S., 1987. *Curriculum: product or praxis*. London: Falmer Press.

Hammersley, M. and Atkinson, P., 1995. *Ethnography; principles in practice*. 2nd ed. London: Routledge.

Karagiorgi, Y. and Lymbouridou, C., 2009. The story of an online teacher community in Cyprus. *Professional development in education*, 35 (1), 119–138.

Karagiorgi, Y. and Nicolaidou, M., 2009. Elementary school leaders' approaches towards staff development in Cyprus schools. *International studies in educational administration*, 37 (3), 71–83.

Karagiorgi, Y. and Symeou, L., 2006. Teacher professional development in Cyprus: reflections on current trends and challenges in policy and practices. *Journal of in-service education*, 32 (1), 47–61.

Karagiorgi, Y., *et al.*, 2008. Underpinnings of adult learning in formal teacher professional development in Cyprus. *Journal of in-service education*, 34 (2), 125–146.

Kelly, A., 1985. Action research: what is it and what can it do? *In*: R.C. Burgess, ed. *Issues in educational research; qualitative methods*. London: Falmer Press, 129–151.

Kennedy, A., 2014. Models of Continuing Professional Development: a framework for analysis. *Professional development in education*, 40 (3), 336–351.

King, F., 2014. Evaluating the impact of teacher professional development: an evidence-based framework. *Professional development in education*, 40 (1), 89–111.

Koutselini, M., 2007. Participatory teacher development at schools: processes and issues. *Action research*, 5 (4), 443–462.

LeCompte, M.D. and Preissle, J., 1993. *Ethnography and qualitative design in educational research*. 2nd ed. San Diego, CA: Academic Press.

Lesh, R. and Lehrer, R., 2003. Models and modeling perspectives on the development of students and teachers. *Mathematical thinking and learning*, 5 (2–3), 109–129.

Loizou, E., 2008. Το μέλλον ως αποτέλεσμα του παρόντος: Η νηπιοσχολική εκπαίδευση στην Κύπρο [The future as a result of the present: early childhood education in Cyprus]. *Σύγχρονο Νηπιαγωγείο [Contemporary kindergarten]*, 61, 90–92.

Lotter, C., Harwood, W., and Bonner, J., 2007. The influence of core teaching conceptions on teachers' use of inquiry teaching practices. *Journal of research in science teaching*, 44 (9), 1318–1347. doi:10.1002/tea.20191.

Lotter, C., Singer, J., and Godley, J., 2009. The influence of repeated teaching and reflection on preservice teachers' views of inquiry and nature of science. *Journal of science teacher education*, 20 (6), 553–582.

Louca, L.T. and Zacharia, Z.C., 2012. Modeling-based learning in science education: a review. *Educational review*, 64 (4), 471–492.

Lovat, T.J. and Smith, D.L., 1995. *Curriculum: action on reflection revisited*. 3rd ed. Katoomba, Australia: Social Science Press.

Lubienski, S.T., 1999. Problem-centered mathematics teaching. *Mathematics teaching in the middle school*, 5 (4), 250–255.

Macdonald, D., 2003. Curriculum change and the post-modern world: is the school curriculum-reform movement an anachronism? *Journal of curriculum studies*, 35 (2), 139–149.

Marsh, B. and Mitchell, N., 2014. The role of video in teacher professional development. *Teacher development: an international journal of teachers' professional development*, 18 (3), 403–417.

Papademetri-Kachrimani, C., 2014. *Οικοδόμηση Μαθηματικών εννοιών μέσω της μοντελοποίησης: παραδείγματα εφαρμογών σε διάφορα μαθησιακά περιβάλλοντα με μικρά παιδιά* [Developing conceptual understanding in mathematics through modeling: examples from various contexts with young children]. Symposium organized at the 5th Hellenic Conference of ENEDIM, Florina, Greece, 14–16 March.

Papademetri-Kachrimani, C. and Louca, T.L., 2013. Learning with and about modeling as a tool for teaching through modeling: sustainable professional development in science and mathematics pre-school education in Cyprus. Paper presented at the *European Science Education Research Association (ESERA) conference*, University of Cyprus, Nicosia, Cyprus, 2–7 September.

THE PROFESSIONAL DEVELOPMENT OF EARLY YEARS EDUCATORS

Papademetri-Kachrimani, C. and Louca, T.L., 2014. Η ανάπτυξη ενός ενιαίου πλαισίου Γραμματισμού για τα μαθηματικά και τις φυσικές επιστήμες στο νηπιαγωγείο: Η μετάβαση από ένα πρόγραμμα δεξιοτήτων επιστημονικής μεθόδου, σε ένα πρόγραμμα διεργασιών [The development of a combined framework for mathematical and scientific literacy for pre-school: from a skills-based to a process-based curriculum]. *In*: P. Kariotoglou and P. Papadopoulou, eds. *Τόμος επιλεγμένων εργασιών του 7ου Πανελληνίου Συνεδρίου Οι Φυσικές Επιστήμες στο Νηπιαγωγείο* [Proceedings Volume of Selected Papers of the 7th Hellenic Conference of Science Education in Pre-school]. Athens: Gutenberg, 99–112.

Papademetri-Kachrimani, C. and Louca, T.L., eds., in preparation. Ενιαίο πλαίσιο γραμματισμού για τα μαθηματικά και τις φυσικές επιστήμες στο νηπιαγωγείο: Μελέτες πρακτικών εφαρμογών [A combined framework for mathematical and scientific literacy for pre-school: case studies of enactments].

Papert, S., 1972. Teaching children to be mathematicians versus teaching children about mathematics. *In*: A. Floyd, ed. *Developing mathematical thinking*. London: Addison-Wesley, 235–245.

Philippou, S., 2014. 'Curriculum Studies' in Cyprus: a research agenda for curriculum, bildung and didaktik as challenges of translation and re-contextualisation. *European journal of curriculum studies*, 1 (1), 83–99.

Schön, D., 1971. *Beyond the stable state*. London: Temple Smith.

Snyder, J., Bolin, F., and Zumwalt, K., 1992. Curriculum implementation. *In*: P. Jackson, ed. *Handbook of research on curriculum*. New York, NY: Macmillan, 402–435.

Stanley, L. and Wise, S., 1983. *Breaking out: feminist theory and feminist research*. London: Routledge.

Stenhouse, L., 1975. *An introduction to curriculum research and development*. London: Heinemann.

Stoll, L., *et al.*, 2006. Professional learning communities: a review of literature. *Journal of educational change*, 7 (4), 221–258.

Tam, A.C.F., 2015. The role of a professional learning community in teacher change: a perspective from beliefs and practices. *Teachers and teaching: theory and practice*, 21 (1), 22–43. doi:10.1080/13540602.2014.928122.

Villegas-Reimers, E., 2003. *Teacher professional development: an international review of the literature* [online]. Available from: http://www.unesco.org/iiep [Accessed 12 April 2012].

Wenger, E., 1998. *Communities of practice: learning, meaning, and identity*. Cambridge: Cambridge University Press.

Wenger, E., McDermott, R., and Snyder, W.M., 2002. *Cultivating communities of practice: a guide to managing knowledge*. Boston, MA: Harvard Business School Press.

Yuen, L.H., 2012. The impact of continuing professional development on a novice teacher. *Teacher development*, 16 (3), 387–398.

Zhang, M., *et al.*, 2011. Understanding affordances and challenges of three types of video for professional development. *Teaching and teacher education*, 27 (2), 454–462.

The professional identity of early years educators in England: implications for a transformative approach to continuing professional development

Sarah Lightfoot and David Frost

This article examines the professional identity of nine early years educators currently working in the early years sector of education in England. These educators include teachers, teaching assistants, nursery practitioners and nursery nurses working with children three to five years old in the Early Years Foundation Stage in state-maintained schools. The article arises from a doctoral research study that gives voice to the professional identities of these early years educators. The policy background and particular context in which the research is carried out are outlined. The article reports on an exploration of these educators' storied perceptions of their professionality, which is multi-dimensional, complex and cannot be reduced to a list of personal characteristics, responsibilities and duties. The educators' experiences of continuing professional development are considered and an alternative approach is suggested in light of these educators' needs in terms of being valued, having connections and making a difference in their work contexts.

Introduction

The stimulus for this research was prompted by conversations with early years educators (EYEs) in England. Some EYEs seemed enthusiastic about recent policy innovations; keen to enrol on programmes that confer professional status or inspired by recent in-service training to make changes to classroom environments. Others appeared confused about the rate of change within the sector and what appear to be increasingly intensified working conditions. They described a range of feelings including disillusionment with their role, a sense of a loss of control over their daily practice and anxiety at a perceived downward pressure to prepare children for the next stage of more 'formal' schooling. It seemed important to consider how their differing experiences and emotional responses related to their perceptions of themselves as educators of young children. These conversations prompted an exploration of the notion of professional identity and the ways in which it might be construed, negotiated, sustained and contested.

The exploratory study outlined in this article focused upon the experiences of nine EYEs who work with three to five year olds in the Early Years Foundation

Stage (EYFS) in maintained primary and nursery schools in England. Its overarching aim is to explore and understand how these particular members of the workforce who have a multiplicity of qualifications, titles, roles and responsibilities and widely differing contracts, pay and working conditions negotiate and perceive their professional identities. This initial study seeks to build a conceptual model of professional identity in early childhood education that can inform further research. This entails exploring the types of development opportunities which might contribute to the growth of a particular form of professionality for all those who work with the youngest children.

We begin with an attempt to clarify what is meant by professional identity and how this relates to those working in the EYFS in England. We then offer a framework for understanding EYEs' sense of professional selves arising from their own perspectives, noting the role of the landscape in which they work in terms of their institutional context, current policy directives and other influences that affect the ways and the extent to which the early years workforce are characterised as 'professional'. We then discuss the implications of these findings for the role of continuing professional development (CPD) programmes that might contribute to influencing, enhancing or transforming professional identity.

We use the term 'early years educators' throughout the article.[1] When using this term we are referring to all adults working in EYFS classrooms irrespective of their role, job title or qualifications.

Conceptualising early childhood educator professional identity

A first step was to explore the concept of professional identity as it pertains to the work of EYEs in England in nursery and reception classes in maintained schools. The concept of professional identity is not straightforward: our brief exploration can be summarised by saying that it is inextricably linked to personal identity; it is not fixed but dynamic; it is multi-faceted; and changes in professional identity are linked to the concept of human agency. These dimensions are discussed in brief below.

The notion of professional identity cannot be separated from that of personal identity. Professional identity is not simply a matter of a role being adopted for instrumental reasons in the context of an occupation. It is not the sum total of attributes, beliefs and values used to define people in specialised, skill-based and education-based occupations or vocations (Benveniste 1987, Ibarra 1999). In short, it is about who we are rather than the part we are playing. A person's professional identity is bound to be unique on the grounds that there are many antecedent and contributory factors. It has long been argued that identity is always bound to be a 'work in progress' rather than a fixed state (Erikson 1975). Thus we can come to the idea of a process of 'identification' which implies that human beings are continuously engaged in the enterprise of identifying themselves (Brubaker and Cooper 2000). A comprehensive review of the literature on teachers' professional identity supports this idea of identification being an ongoing process of interpretation and reinterpretation of experiences (Beijaard *et al.* 2004).

Using the idea of identification immediately raises the question of the influences on that process, which is where the concept of socialisation comes into play. Social identity theory tells us that we identify ourselves through membership of social groups (Tajfel 1982, Jenkins 2008). Stryker and Burke (2000, p. 285) précis Mead's (1934) work on identity as 'society shapes self shapes social behaviour'. Identity is

THE PROFESSIONAL DEVELOPMENT OF EARLY YEARS EDUCATORS

then malleable and dynamic. It affects our behaviour and is affected by the experiences we have. Inevitably there are dilemmas and tensions involved in the construction and reconstruction of professional identity. Coldron and Smith (1999) found that teachers' professional identity, while being unique, nevertheless reflects the educational context or landscape that he or she is part of and it is in classroom practice where this becomes visible. Similarly, Connelly and Clandinin (1999) argued that professional identity changes owing to shifts in this landscape; for example, through policy change. These changes can be emotionally fraught as teachers attempt to maintain their 'story to live by'; a narrative thread that educators draw on to make sense of themselves and their practice.

Not only is professional identification a dynamic process but it also features sub-identities that may be more or less harmonised (Beijaard *et al.* 2004). For some writers there is an emphasis on the struggle to define yourself when circumstances may appear to be demanding a different identity construction (MacLure 1993). This may be linked to Eric Hoyle's (2008) discussion about the idea of teachers having a 'samizdat professionalism' as a strategy for being true to their values while satisfying externally generated requirements that might be at odds with these values. The idea that practitioners might be engaged in some kind of struggle for their identity suggests that a crucial variable here is human agency.

Agency is identified by Beijaard *et al.* (2004) as being an important element of teacher professional identity. The idea of identity being a self-constructed phenomenon suggests that individuals have some capacity for agency. Bruner talked about agency as a defining characteristic of humankind and how it is second nature for us to engage in reflection and the construction of narratives about our 'agential encounters with the world' (Bruner 1996, p. 36). From a sociological perspective, Giddens' (1984) structuration theory offers an explanation of the process by which social structures shape identity but are in turn shaped by the agency of individuals. This account is supported from a psychological perspective, especially in Bandura's (1989) extensive work in which he talks about agency being effected through 'reflective and regulative thought'. Reflection emerges as having a key role to play in enabling individuals to construct their identities and keep them under review, so to speak.

These themes are also apparent in the more recently emerged area of research concerning professional identity of EYEs. Although the research aims and methodologies employed differ, studies indicate that professional identity is dynamic rather than stable and fixed in biology and emphasise the social and discursive nature of these constructs (Davies 1989, MacNaughton 2000). Some do not provide a clear definition of the concept but highlight its close connection to a number of other features of professionalism which may be internal or external to the individual. These include discussions of:

- the interplay between personal and professional identities (Harwood *et al.* 2013);
- practitioner gender and class (Osgood 2006);
- the role of reflection in identity construction (Bleach 2014);
- the influence of national policy on EYE professional identity (Woodrow and Busch 2008); and
- the media's portrayal of the EYE workforce (McGillivray 2008).

Various groups of practitioners have been the focus of research, including student pre-school teachers (Egan 2004), nursery workers in private, voluntary, independent and state nurseries (Osgood 2010), nannies, nursery nurses and childminders (McGillivray 2008) and those with the more recent professional designations of Senior Practitioners and Early Years Professionals (Miller 2008). What is evident from these differently emphasised studies is that the notion of a single or blended definition of professional identity in the sector is problematic.

The professionalisation agenda in early years education

Early childhood education and care in England has been subject to unprecedented attention and relentless change in the last 15 years; some of this designed to eliminate the pervading split between the maintained state sector and the non-maintained private, voluntary and independent sector in terms of the diversity of settings and the provision they offer. This is compounded by a deep, historical institutional divide between early years education in maintained nursery and primary schools and the provision of care for babies and toddlers; for example, by childminders and at day nurseries. There has existed a tension between members of the workforce deemed to be maternal and caring as opposed to those who are degree educated and highly trained. Pay, status and conditions for employees in the private, voluntary and independent sector were and are still generally inferior compared with those in the education sector who are perceived to have more favourable pay, longer holidays and a shorter working day. Within an EYFS classroom in a primary or nursery school, similar tensions may also exist between colleagues. Policy stipulates that a 'school teacher' must be appointed to any reception or nursery class (Department for Education 2014, Department for Education and Skills 2003). However, the team may include others with various roles, responsibilities, qualifications and conditions of employment and traditionally viewed as teacher aides.

Policy integration in 2008 (Department for Children, Schools and Families 2008) sought to address the split between care and education by focusing on one of the key findings of the EPPE project (Sylva *et al*. 2004) that educational outcomes for young children were best in those settings which successfully united cognitive and social development. The EYFS guidance was further revised following the Tickell (2011) review. Despite the new framework apparently favouring a child-focused approach to early years teaching and learning and an insistence in the non-statutory guidance that children progress at different rates and at different ages, EYEs are nevertheless required to implement a curriculum that emphasises specific learning goals and statutory outcomes for the end of the key stage. The framework is explicit that the adults' overarching goal is ensuring young children are 'ready' for the work of Year 1. As such, this document seems to imply a particular role and identity for those working in this area, one which might involve a model of technical practice and be tightly regulated and subject to judgements in terms of performance. Other characterisations of EYEs have arisen from government policy and initiatives around the nature and purpose of early childhood provision. Those that see early years education as a means of social remediation (Department for Education and Skills 2003) cast the workforce as redemptive; others view them as parent substitutes at once providing a close, intimate relationship with the children in their charge and enabling parents to return to work themselves (Department for Education and Employment 1998).

THE PROFESSIONAL DEVELOPMENT OF EARLY YEARS EDUCATORS

The last decade has seen a wider policy drive to professionalise the workforce. New Labour's reform during 2005–2010 was driven by a not good enough workforce discourse (Osgood 2006) that involved the creation of an integrated qualifications framework (Children's Workforce Development Council 2006) intended to promote skills acquisition and career progression. Early Years Professional status was conferred after candidates met 39 competency standards with the intention to raise the quality and status of the workforce. Nevertheless, the Nutbrown (2012) review commissioned by the Coalition Government recommended a strengthening of qualifications so that educators might have the essential depth and breadth of knowledge and experience to meet the challenges their job entails. Qualifications introduced 'to move decisively away from the idea that teaching young children is somehow less important or inferior to teaching school age children' (National College for Teaching & Leadership 2013, p. 6) are the 'Early Years Educator' Level 3 role and Early Years Teachers (Graduate) roles that replace the Early Years Professional status. These new roles and qualifications have produced some unrest within the early childhood education and care community, particularly as the Early Years Teacher role does not confer Qualified Teacher Status. The Association for the Professional Development of Early Years Educators (TACTYC 2013) fear this new qualification will result in graduates who are paid less, have different terms and conditions of employment and fewer career opportunities than primary school colleagues. This newly introduced status then looks likely to promulgate the two-tier system already evident in the sector. The range and variety of qualifications and the type and level of training required to work with young children in England remain confusing, and according to some critics the ramifications of such training and qualifications are the creation of an environment where EYEs are increasingly regulated by government and teaching and learning is reduced to measurable technical outcomes measured through a competency framework (Moss 2006, Osgood 2006, Miller 2008). This raises questions about what being a professional means in the EYFS in England.

Reflecting on the conversations with practitioners referred to earlier, it seems plausible that the differences between these professionals' stories were perhaps related to the individuals' sense of agency as discussed above. Some practitioners were not as inhibited as others by regulatory changes and expectations. These individuals were active in pursuing their interests and talked about themselves and their work context in a positive manner. Why these differences were so pronounced in certain individuals and what enabled them to act as they did requires consideration. Perhaps by 'listening to the separate voices and trying to hear their stories' (Penn 1998, p. 14) it would be possible to explore the respondents' professional identities and begin to understand the types and forms of development opportunities that might support practitioners in making a difference in their work with young children.

The study

As explained earlier, this study recounts an exploratory project in preparation for a doctoral study arising from professional and personal interactions with EYEs. The aim was to ascertain EYEs' own perceptions, with accounts created on their own terms. It contributes to McGillivray's call for, 'future research to seek the views of practitioners themselves in order to explore the complexity of factors that contribute to professional identity' in the early years (2008, p. 252). Consequently the task of eliciting EYEs' thinking about their professional identity was not approached with a theoretical perspective set prior to data collection. Instead, the researcher (Sarah) was influenced by the work of Nias (1989), who pioneered the use of verbatim interview evidence gathered from a loosely framed set of questions to encourage long, discursive replies. Brock (2012) notes how crucial the researcher role is in this type of study, not only in terms of eliciting a depth of thinking from the participants but also in understanding the context from which the responses are drawn. The researcher's 20 years' experience as a Key Stage 1 and EYFS classroom teacher, including time spent as a school leader, permeates this project in terms of its focus, the methodological choices made, the researcher's interactions with the participants in the study and the sense she made of their responses. In addition there were established working relationships with many of the participants. Previous interactions with some of the participants, particularly those involved with the network group, had involved wide discussions and sometimes frank exchanges about dilemmas and decisions such as those faced on a daily basis by EYEs in terms of their practice and relationships with other colleagues, parents and children. Consequently it was assumed with some confidence that the participants would come to the interviews ready to share their experiences and opinions.

In keeping with its aims, the methodology for this small-scale study was interpretative and qualitative in nature (Creswell 2007). This approach is appropriate because of its potential to generate rich data about the subjective, unique and changeable nature of educators' professional identities. It would also be descriptive, presenting a multi-layered picture of relationships, settings and situations. Interpretivist research focuses on experiences, actions and perspectives of those involved and requires flexibility and responsiveness from the researcher. In order to enable her to facilitate shared understandings, the researcher would need to maximise those relationships already built with participants through dialogue and negotiation, practising those mentoring and consultancy skills described by Rhodes and Beneicke (2002).

To give voice to the subjective identities and experiences of the EYEs a small range of qualitative methods were used, including semi-structured interviews and follow-up conversations by telephone and email. All but one interview was conducted on a one-to-one basis. The other was a paired interview with two co-workers. This gave rise to some animated discussion. Some telephone and email contact was made after the interviews for further clarification of a small number of points. Some of the practitioners also participated in an earlier focus group discussion that was carried out in an informal network meeting. Brock (2012) indicates that a supportive environment is key for stimulating the types of fruitful discussions sought. Interviews took place in a variety of locations according to participants' preferences, including a staffroom, classrooms, an external courtyard and a local café. Some were during the school day and others after children had gone home. One took place during a weekend. Each interview took approximately 60 minutes, although the shortest was 30 minutes in length and the longest was two hours in duration. The interviews were digitally recorded and partly transcribed. Notes were also made throughout, reflecting on the context of each interview. Informed consent was acquired from all interviewees and a guarantee of confidentiality and anonymity was provided – all names used subsequently are pseudonyms.

The loosely structured interviews began with an invitation to 'tell me about your role here?' Detailed responses followed and so we can say that the initial direction of the discussion was set by the EYEs. By not imposing too stringent a schedule of

THE PROFESSIONAL DEVELOPMENT OF EARLY YEARS EDUCATORS

questions, it was possible to attend to the participants' perspectives about their professional identities. The questions asked varied from interview to interview as the researcher helped respondents to unpick the detail of their stories and sought to uncover the factors that enabled or hindered them in their work as EYEs.

The participants

The EYEs (five early years practitioners and four teachers) who participated in this initial study work within five maintained settings in south-east England. Many of the participants were already known to the researcher. Some belong to an informal network that, according to Marianne, one of the participants, meets regularly in order to: 'share ideas, talk about practice, have a cup of tea and let off a bit of steam'. Other participants are members of schools where the researcher has a connection through previous employment.

There was a disparate mix in terms of age and ethnicity; however, all nine participants in the convenience sample were female, reflecting the broader composition of the workforce. The participants occupied various positions and roles within their settings and had equally variable years of experience and qualifications; all worked with children aged three to five years at the later end of the EYFS. One female primary school head teacher also participated.

Analysing the data

The interviews were transcribed and the sorting, coding and analysis focused on exploring what was important for those EYEs who participated. Initially, reading and re-reading the transcriptions provided an increasing familiarity with the data. Highlighting themes, making notes and simple concept mapping helped to determine aspects of professional identity identified by the participants. This led to the formulation of 45 codes, which began to generate greater insight into the EYEs' perceptions of their professional identities and how they might be shaped by their values, beliefs and experiences, their immediate working context and the wider national policy context. Further reading helped to make connections between these codes and these were grouped accordingly.

Eight major themes emerged from the data, including:

- attraction and commitment to the role;
- experiences of being a professional;
- values held;
- types of knowledge and understanding required;
- degree of agency experienced;
- need for support from the early childhood community;
- influence of school contexts; and
- importance of training and qualifications.

These themes relate well to the literature about professional identity, particularly Brock's (2012) seven dimensions of early years professionalism. Identification of these themes enabled a better conceptualisation of the professional identity of early years practitioners. A next step was to focus on a smaller number of expressed needs common to the respondents regardless of differences in nomenclature, qualifications, personal biography and workplace:

- being valued;
- having connections; and
- making a difference.

These seemed to capture more adequately the complexity of professional identity as described by the EYEs. Each of these dimensions is now explained and illustrated with examples from the interviews to help demonstrate how they relate to EYEs' professional identities.

Early years educators' perceptions of professional identity

The three overarching dimensions are now used as an organising framework for a discussion of findings.

Being valued

The sense of being valued and its importance to the development and maintenance of a positive sense of professional identity runs like a golden thread throughout the interview stories. No matter what the participants' role or status, the educators' stories all indicate their need for recognition; for their expertise; their personal qualities; that they do a worthwhile job; and their aspirations for themselves and the children whom they educate and care for. Some of these aspects are outlined next.

This need to be valued is perhaps indicative of how those who care for and educate young children have been viewed historically. Their work has been likened to that of 'baby sitters', a low-status role mirroring the low status of children in society (Cohen *et al.* 2004). Such a view reinforces the stereotype that the education and care of young children is women's work; poorly qualified and poorly paid women at that. Unfortunately this image is still perhaps compounded by the fact that education for those under five is non-statutory. This is illustrated by Lisa's comment:

> Nursery is viewed as just a bit of playing … there's no real education going on. We are just kind, smiling ladies playing with little children. They should see my professional development targets …

Lisa highlights the conflict here between the type of dispositions often described as essential for the role, such as 'caring', 'approachable', 'loving' and 'reliable', and hints at the ways in which such maternal qualities are often exploited or denigrated in the more technicist approaches currently used to demonstrate professional competence (Osgood 2010).

What is evident from the data, however, is the way in which educators have come to make these aspects of the role their own. It does seem that the educators in this study do value these types of personal qualities and appear to invest heavily in the production of a 'caring self' (Skeggs 2003). For Eleni this construct of what it means to be an EYE influenced her career choice:

> You have to be patient and understanding. I understand children. I can empathise with them. That's what makes me suitable for the job. That's why I became a foundation stage teacher.

THE PROFESSIONAL DEVELOPMENT OF EARLY YEARS EDUCATORS

Eleni's professional identity appears to be robust. She appears assured of her role and status and encapsulates this in the use of her title of 'foundation stage teacher'. The other teachers who participated in this study also described themselves in terms of the age group taught, either as a 'foundation stage' teacher or a 'nursery teacher'. All explained their route to Qualified Teacher Status and mentioned the age range they had qualified to teach. There is a sense that they deserve their professional status and identity (Maloney 2010), although as Sadie notes:

> I have met people who think I get paid less than secondary school teachers because I work with the youngest children in education system.

Those who participated in the study who are not qualified teachers use a greater number of terms to describe their role and position at their school, although they are employed on similar conditions and contracts as a 'keyworker' for a number of children. Some role names derived from their initial training to work with children: for example, 'nursery nurse' or 'teaching assistant'. Others mentioned the job title on their contract: for example, 'early years assistant' and 'early years practitioner'. The range of terminology employed even in this small-scale study demonstrates some of the complexity of knowing who the workforce is and how they should be known. Cameron (2004) makes the case for a unifying title to refer to those working with young children. However, this is a concern for a number of reasons for two of the educators interviewed, as relayed in the following discussion:

> Lisa: I never call myself a practitioner. I always call myself a nursery nurse in a school ... Practitioner ... what a dry word. It sounds like it's nothing to do with children.
>
> Nina: I still class myself as a nursery nurse, not an early years professional either.
>
> Lisa: I feel like my identity has really been watered down ... now you can do an NVQ in 6 weeks and have the same status as us.
>
> Nina: There are so many qualifications now ... no-one knows what any of them mean ... or what they're worth. I worked really hard for my NNEB. It was a full-time two-year course.
>
> Lisa: No-one uses the nursery nurse title any more though. It used to be really something once to say you were a nursery nurse. You had trained and specialised to work with babies and children to seven. You were seen as a professional. But now ... It's become obsolete ... people think we are all the same ... I think we'll have to take more qualifications soon.

Breadth in current nomenclature has given way to uncertainty and ambiguity for these two educators. For them, the term 'nursery nurse' was important. They saw it as linked to a worthwhile qualification; it signified a certain status and involved particular knowledge and understanding of young children. This title and their identification with the role are far removed from the 'unfashionable' term noted by McGillivray with its 'connotations of a role that demanded no more than an ability to wash pots' (2008, p. 248). Lisa and Nina went on to discuss how they feel their role has been demeaned and diminished in recent years due to the training and qualifications structure currently in place. They felt that the role and title had been devalued, which impacted negatively on their sense of being valued professionally in schools and in the wider community.

Clare, a recently appointed primary head teacher who participated in the study, noted the importance of names. She had found similar feelings of disillusionment among members of her support staff throughout the school, although none were nursery nurses. They confided that some of this dissatisfaction came from the different role titles in use and the perceived differences in status and role. Clare took a novel approach to dealing with the situation by altering their job title to 'assistant teacher'. This was positively received by her staff. Clare observed immediate changes in individuals:

> Just something simple like changing their titles. It's made a complete difference to the way they feel about themselves and their jobs. The atmosphere in school changed overnight. Now we can begin to develop practice with a positive mind-set.

By making these initial changes with her staff, Clare demonstrates her awareness that developing professionals who are committed to working with young children requires an inclusive and coherent identity (Adams 2005).

Making connections

This is concerned with relational aspects of their experiences and how these shape professional identity. EYEs emphasise their connections with children and families, and with other members of the early years workforce in particular. Some participants also explored the extent to which their personal lives and characteristics are entwined with their sense of professional self.

In expressing their professional identity, all participants drew attention to the emotional content of their work. In common with Egan's findings, 'the language of care permeates their responses' (2004, p. 28). They talked of their 'passion' for their role and the need to be 'patient' and 'love for children and their families'. Hargreaves (2000) similarly observes that the younger the children involved, the greater the emotional intensity. However, a number of authors note how being perceived as and perceiving themselves to be caring and maternal in their work has contributed to the struggle EYEs have to be recognised as professionals (Moss 2006). Eleni's comments reflect how she is overcoming 'advice' given during her Postgraduate Certificate in Education training that was perhaps given with this in mind:

> At university they explicitly encouraged us not to get attached to the children. It wasn't seen to be being professional. I spent the first few weeks of my NQT year trying to be distant from these tiny children, trying to follow this advice. It just didn't work. It wasn't me and it certainly wasn't helping the children. I realised in fact I needed to be patient, to understand, to empathise … to be authentic. To show it, to use it. (Eleni)

Here she is engaged in the process of 'reclaim[ing emotion] as vital and credible in ECEC [early childhood education and care] practice' (Osgood 2010, p. 130). Similarly, a number of those interviewed were keen to point out that for them there is no paradox between care and education. They do not appear 'preoccupied with a regulatory gaze that denies them the use of their emotions to inflect professional practice' (2010, p. 130). They do not seem to have to struggle as Osgood (2010) fears to find opportunities to interact with children and their families that demonstrate their professional purpose as emotionally reflective educators. Instead they deliberately make use of their personal characteristics as a means of connecting to children and families:

> They are leaving their most precious thing in the world with you. You have got to show them that you care. (Nina)

THE PROFESSIONAL DEVELOPMENT OF EARLY YEARS EDUCATORS

For educators like Nina, making highly involved connections between children and their families is essential to their roles as educators. Emotional intelligence appears to these educators not only to be a desirable aspect of their professional identity, but it is recognised as an inherent part of the teaching and learning process (Hargreaves 2000). Such a high level of involvement is seen to be necessary in order to ascertain a child's needs and difficulties so that learning can take place:

> Being professional in the early years is absolutely about being attached and in tune with the children. Otherwise how will they learn? (Eleni)

So, as with the participants in Harwood *et al.*'s (2013, p. 10) study, these EYEs appear to be 'resistant to dichotomised ideas of care (ideal mother) and education (techno-rationalist)'. Furthermore, some educators' responses appeared to give glimpses of identities and perceived roles that go far beyond the care versus education debate:

> You need to be connected and have a nurturing relationship with children. It's important that you are the children's consistency – you let them know to trust you and then you can help. You've got to have that consistency then they start talking. If you have empathy and listen you can help them. I listen and then something…my brain erupts … I see something I can use. You have to show them it's ok to be a different colour, it's ok if you can't find the words … we need to prepare them to be resilient for the world. (Amelie)

Expending oneself in this way can be costly. Osgood (2010) notes the need for support for EYEs to sustain and nourish this aspect of professional identity. The participants in this study draw attention to this, noting how they often feel 'mentally not just physically tired' and 'vulnerable after giving so much every day'. They demonstrate their awareness of how the networks of colleagues to which they belong can help in these circumstances. The networks take various forms: the foundation stage team of colleagues within the school; cluster groups that meet on a regular basis; and online membership of early childhood education forums. These connections and their impact upon the professional self are described in various ways. For Eleni, the opinions of her team members have affected views of herself as an educator:

> My teaching assistant has really helped with my confidence. Just little things she says like, 'the way you speak to parents is spot on … you'd never guess you were in your NQT year'. She mentioned how my planning is really clear … I can just feel myself grow.

This feeling of validation also runs through Marianne's interview. Although she is a more experienced educator, she admits to having times when she feels uncertain about a newly introduced initiative or in the face of an impending Ofsted visit:

> What I like is the backup, the feeling of solidarity and being with others with a shared ethos. I prefer the group input and the support of the network is brilliant. (Marianne)

As hinted at by Marianne, the groups not only provide emotional sustenance. When prompted to explain what she meant by support, Marianne added:

> I think with our cluster meetings with other early years colleagues that I learn the most. Our discussions are great and I always get new ideas. The clusters are a smaller group, we have input and influence the theme and so you get more out of it. We have a laugh or even a cry …

253

These networks give educators an opportunity to compare stories of their current experiences, to reflect on practice that works and practice that is unhelpful. For some, their developing professional identity is related to their membership of a community where they can interact with one another and recognise each other as participants (Wenger 1998). Spirited debates take place about local and national policy. For example, during a discussion about documenting children's progress:

> Highlighting those sheets … It's so ridiculous. The development matters booklet wasn't meant to be for that … There's got to be a better way … (Sadie)

According to Sachs (2003) these types of communities can be forces to be reckoned with but the EYEs are content to focus on their daily work:

> I like the reassurance from the group to know I'm on the right track with journals, type of observations. Using that knowledge I can make changes and bring what we do in line with others. (Eleni)

There seems to be untapped potential indicated here, with glimpses of what Sachs (2003) calls the activist professional and which relates to the third theme, 'making a difference'.

Making a difference

This dimension highlights the importance that all of the EYEs, irrespective of their status or role, attached to a sense that they were able to make a difference to the education of young children in their settings; to the families with whom they worked; to practice in their settings and within local communities. The EYEs offered many examples of the ways in which they were actively making a difference and so actively shaping their professional identity as individuals who matter to others.

Kayla, an early years assistant, recounted a story of how she had worked intensively with one little boy over an academic year:

> At first he just couldn't socialise and really couldn't cope with lunch time. I sat next to him every day … encouraging him, modelling what to do. Now he's so different – eats a variety of foods, joins in activities. I saw him and his family in the town recently. So rewarding … seeing a family happy. I really like that part of the job.

What appears to be significant is that not only were they able to make a difference, but they were able to do this in a way that satisfied their personal and professional values. Sadie explains:

> I like teaching in the foundation stage because although you have the framework you can be creative. There's lots of flexibility and you can make decisions yourself about the curriculum, what you feel the children need, your learning environment, how you use the day …

Changes to EYFS policy, overdue Ofsted inspections and time-consuming assessment paperwork were all mentioned by the EYEs but they did not seem overly anxious about them. Marianne speaks for the majority when she says:

> Since 2006 there have been lots of changes. We are always having to move on and change and I'm really happy to do this. I feel there's always another way, something to explore or move on with. I'm really happy to have a go and go for it. Tracy [nursery

nurse] tears her hair out though! I don't see that you can ever stand still … always something new and if it benefits the children and makes a real difference to them, then I'm happy to go for it.

This comment echoes Brock's (2012) findings that EYEs were able to abide by their core values and beliefs whilst implementing policy and prescribed curricula. Sadie and Maria, both experienced teachers, managed to preserve their professional identity and professional practice as they negotiated imposed changes.

As explained earlier, this study was carried out in preparation for an action-based initiative linked to a doctoral research project. The premise is that those factors EYEs define as influencing professional identity have implications for the ways in which we would aspire to support them through CPD opportunities. The final sections of this article explore the current context for CPD in early years education. We then outline how we might go forward with an alternative approach that draws upon and nourishes their professional identities.

Continuing professional development in early years education

Although the sense of entitlement to CPD is welcome, the recently revised Department for Education statutory framework for the EYFS states the following:

A quality learning experience for children requires a quality workforce. A well-qualified, skilled staff strongly increases the potential of any individual setting to deliver the best possible outcomes for children. (Department for Education 2014, p. 10)

Providers must support staff to undertake appropriate training and professional development opportunities to ensure they offer quality learning and development experiences for children that continually improves. (Department for Education 2014, p. 20)

Disappointingly there is no explicit definition of what constitutes 'quality' and the nature of the training and professional development is not specified further in this statutory document. The focus here is CPD as a key strategy for the implementation of policy. The message about what it is to be a professional in the EYFS in England is implicit but clear. Not only are EYEs expected to provide quality learning experiences, they are charged with ensuring children achieve predetermined, assessable outcomes outlined in the framework. They are construed as technicians. Nina succinctly sums up her position in respect to national and institutional expectations:

I'm not a professional in most people's eyes … but I have to act like a professional and I have a professional job to do. I have to make sure my 'key' children make their expected progress by the end of the year. I'm accountable.

Professional knowledge and related practices for some appear to be something that can simply be transmitted and put into action with positive effect. The professionality privileged here has an individualistic focus, the orientation is one of compliant implementation and the drivers are standards, rules and outcomes (Frost 2014). There is no sense of EYEs as active and reflexive agents, no mention of the professional identities they bring with them in terms of their 'individual dispositions and emotions, day-to-day lives and relationships, training and education' (McGillivray 2008, p. 246). This multi-faceted professional identity seems to be at risk.

Reclaiming and reconstructing continuing professional development

We are interested, then, in finding alternative constructions of support for professional development. Some writers describe how the current climate poses challenges and dilemmas for providers of professional development opportunities for the early years workforce (Miller 2008, Ingleby and Hedges 2012). Following our preliminary exploration of early years practitioners' professional identity and their experience of CPD hitherto, we want to identify the features of programmes in which participants would experience being valued, having connections and making a difference. This is echoed in Moyles' statement below:

> If we want professionals, then professional understanding itself needs to be nurtured, to be allowed time to develop and opportunity to be applied. Educational improvement depends upon practitioners feeling they WANT to make a difference; upon them feeling empowered and professional. (Moyles 2001, p. 89)

Each of the EYE's stories demonstrates a commitment to making a difference, but their reflections also reveal a sense of frustration with some forms of CPD that they have accessed in the past:

> Courses can be a bit hit and miss. I'm not keen on this type of training. It's ok for keeping you current with initiatives or regulations – Letters and Sounds or safeguarding training...but for anything else ... there's very little impact to show. (Colette)

> Day courses just depend on the individual trainer. I've become more discerning now ... I don't want a wasted morning. (Marianne)

This sense of frustration is compounded by some educators' sense that aspects of their professional development do not seem to be currently addressed:

> What I really want now is some sort of leadership course. I'm leading a team of five. I want something with an Early Years focus. I'm not a born leader and need some input ... (Marianne)

> It's the dynamics of the relationships between the team that's hard sometimes. I try hard to articulate and share my understandings and expectations. I'm not always sure how to go about it. (Eleni)

> I try to work on impact – bringing ideas back to the setting and working with the whole team to get the initiative on board. The real challenge ... the question for me is how do I get this message across to others when they are busy and I don't want this to be an add on? (Sandra)

These educators are trying to engage with a particular aspect of professionality, namely leadership, which is frequently disregarded or perceived as an optional extra in the early years education sector (Rodd 1998, Moyles 2001).

Professional development approaches in which the concept of leadership is central are uncommon. Examples in the United States are highlighted in the literature on teacher leadership. One such is the National Writing Project in which teachers empower other teachers to develop their practice, which is firmly focused on 'building capacity to engage in transformation' (Lieberman and Miller 2004, p. 13). Closer to home, the HertsCam Network also embraces the idea of teacher leadership, but the approach adopted there rests on the assumption that it is possible to enable all educators to develop their leadership capacity in ways which suit their circumstances and professional concerns, irrespective of job title or designated role. This non-positional and inclusive approach has enabled many educators to lead innovation, build professional knowledge, develop their leadership capacity and influence colleagues and practice in their schools, enhancing their professional identity (Frost 2012). In light of the findings of this study, we believe that this approach is an entirely appropriate method for nurturing EYEs' professional identities no matter what their role and supporting them to make a difference to children and families, their colleagues and beyond their own setting.

Our vision is for EYEs to develop an enhanced professionality in complete contrast to that suggested by the revised framework; one where the focus is collegial and each is a member of a learning community; where the orientation is towards innovation and agential activity; where the drivers are EYEs' principles and moral purposes (Frost 2014). However, the mobilisation of EYEs' enormous potential requires specific support, in terms of planned intervention and dedicated structures, activities and tools to inspire them and enable them to develop this prospective aspect of their professional identities.

Towards transformative professional development

The exploratory study reported here informs the planning of an action-based initiative that will be effective in terms of valuing educators, helping them to forge and make the most of connections with others and supporting them as they make a difference to the lives of children and their families. We recognise the importance of elements such as the following (based on Cordingley *et al.* 2003, Frost 2012):

- belonging to a setting-based group;
- using external expertise linked to school-based activity;
- scope for EYEs to identify their own professional learning focus;
- using tools for reflection and planning and experimentation;
- emphasising peer support;
- processes to encourage, extend and structure professional dialogue;
- processes for sustaining the professional learning over time to enable teachers to embed the practices in their own settings;
- recognition of individual educators' starting points;
- certification through a portfolio of evidence;
- internal support from senior leadership; and
- membership of a wider network of like-minded individuals.

Perhaps this approach would satisfy the needs of EYEs like Sadie, who says:

> In an ideal world I would like more head space ... a mentor to talk to ... time to plan, make changes, reflect, think with colleagues and with specialist advice when I need it. Then there would be excitement. CPD wouldn't be an onerous task!

Sadie's comments resonate with our vision for innovation and agential activity. The EYEs here seek professional learning that will empower them not only to transform themselves but to transform their contexts too. We want to support them.

Disclosure statement

No potential conflict of interest was reported by the authors.

Note

1. Our use of the term is not to be confused with the recent introduction of the national use of 'early years educator' to signify a level 3 qualification meeting specified criteria.

References

Adams, K., 2005. What's in a name? Paper presented at the *fifteenth annual conference of the European early childhood educational research association*, 13 September, Dublin, Ireland.

Bandura, A., 1989. Human agency in social cognitive theory. *American psychologist*, 44 (9), 1175–1184.

Beijaard, D., Meijer, P.C., and Verloop, N., 2004. Reconsidering research on teachers' professional identity. *Teaching and teacher education*, 20 (2), 107–128.

Benveniste, G., 1987. *Professionalizing the organization: reducing bureaucracy to enhance effectiveness*. San Francisco, CA: Jossey-Bass.

Bleach, J., 2014. Developing professionalism through reflective practice and ongoing professional development. *European early childhood education research journal*, 22 (2), 185–197.

Brock, A., 2012. Building a model of early years professionalism from practitioners' perspective. *Journal of early childhood research*, 11 (1), 27–44.

Brubaker, R. and Cooper, F., 2000. Beyond identity. *Theory and society*, 29 (1), 1–47.

Bruner, J., 1996. *The culture of education*. Cambridge, MA: Harvard University Press.

Cameron, C., 2004. *Building an integrated workforce for a long-term vision of universal early education and care*. London: Daycare Trust Policy Paper no. 3.

Children's Workforce Development Council (CWDC), 2006. *Early years professional prospectus*. Leeds: CWDC.

Cohen, B., *et al.*, 2004. *A new deal for children?* Bristol: The Policy Press.

Coldron, J. and Smith, R., 1999. Active location in teachers' construction of their professional identities. *Journal of curriculum studies*, 31 (6), 711–726.

Connelly, M.F. and Clandinin, D.J., 1999. *Shaping a professional identity: stories of education practice*. London, ON: Althouse Press.

Cordingley, P., Bell, M., and Thomasen, S., 2003. *The impact of collaborative CPD on classroom teaching and learning*. London: Institute of Education, University of London.

Creswell, J.W., 2007. *Qualitative inquiry and research design: choosing among five approaches*. London: Sage.

Davies, B., 1989. *Frogs and snails and feminist tales*. Sydney: Allen & Unwin.

Department for Children, Schools and Families (DCSF), 2008. *Statutory framework for the early years foundation stage* [online]. Nottingham: DCSF Publications.

Department for Education (DfE), 2014. *Statutory framework for the early years foundation stage* [online]. Available from: https://www.gov.uk/government/uploads/system/uploads/attachment_data/file/335504/EYFS_framework_from_1_September_2014__with_clarificat ion_note.pdf [Accessed 14 August 2014].

Department for Education and Employment (DfEE), 1998. *Meeting the childcare challenge*. Green paper. London: HMSO.

Department for Education and Skills (DfES), 2003. *Every child matters: presented to Parliament by the Chief Secretary to the treasury by command of her Majesty, September 2003*. London: The Stationery Office.

Egan, B., 2004. Constructing a professional identity: some preliminary findings from early years students. *European early childhood education research journal*, 12 (2), 21–32.

Erikson, E., 1975. Identity crisis in autobiographic perspective. *In*: E. Erikson, ed. *Life history and the historical moment*. New York: Norton, 17–47.

Frost, D., 2012. From professional development to system change: teacher leadership and innovation. *Professional development in education*, 38 (2), 205–227.

Frost, D., 2014. Keynote address given at the *teacher education advancement annual conference*, 16 May, Birmingham.

Giddens, A., 1984. *The constitution of society*. Cambridge: Polity Press.

THE PROFESSIONAL DEVELOPMENT OF EARLY YEARS EDUCATORS

Hargreaves, A., 2000. Four ages of professionalism and professional learning. *Teachers and teaching: theory and practice*, 6 (2), 151–182.

Harwood, D., *et al.*, 2013. 'It's more than care': early childhood educators' concepts of professionalism. *Early years*, 33 (1), 4–17.

Hoyle, E., 2008. Changing conceptions of teaching as a profession: personal reflections. *In*: D. Johnson and R. Maclean, eds. *Teaching; professionalisation, development and leadership*. London: Springer, 285–304.

Ibarra, H., 1999. Provisional selves: 'experimenting with image and identity in professional adaptation' [online]. *Harvard business school archive*. Available from: http://hbswk.hbs.edu/archive/1275.html [Accessed 30 July 2014].

Ingleby, E. and Hedges, C., 2012. Exploring the continuing professional development needs of pedagogical practitioners in early years in England. *Professional development in education*, 38 (4), 533–549.

Jenkins, R., 2008. *Social identity*. 3rd ed. London: Routledge.

Lieberman, A. and Miller, L., 2004. *Teacher leadership*. San Francisco, CA: Jossey-Bass.

MacLure, M., 1993. Arguing for your self: identity as an organising principle in teachers' jobs and lives. *British educational research journal*, 19 (4), 311–322.

MacNaughton, G., 2000. *Rethinking gender in early childhood education*. Sydney: Allen & Unwin.

Maloney, M., 2010. Professional identity in early childhood care and education: perspectives of pre-school and infant teachers. *Irish educational studies*, 29 (2), 167–187.

McGillivray, G., 2008. Nannies, nursery nurses and early years professionals: constructions of professional identity in the early years workforce in England. *European early childhood education research journal*, 16 (2), 242–254.

Mead, G.H., 1934. *Mind, self and society*. Chicago, IL: University of Chicago Press.

Miller, L., 2008. Developing professionalism within a regulatory framework in England: challenges and possibilities. *European early childhood education research journal*, 16 (2), 255–268.

Moss, P., 2006. Structures, understandings and discourses: possibilities for re-envisioning the early childhood worker. *Contemporary issues in early childhood*, 7 (1), 30–41.

Moyles, J., 2001. Passion, paradox and professionalism in early years education. *Early years: an international research journal*, 21 (2), 81–95.

National College for Teaching & Leadership, 2013. *Standards for early years teachers: government response to the consultation on teachers' standards (early years)* [online]. Available from: https://www.education.gov.uk/consultations/downloadableDocs/EYTS%20Gov%20Response%20Accessible%20FINAL%20v1%200%201007131.pdf [Accessed 18 February 2015].

Nias, J., 1989. *Primary teachers talking: a study of teaching as work*. London: Routledge.

Nutbrown, C., 2012. *Foundations for quality: the independent review of early education and childcare qualifications (Nutbrown Review)* [online]. Available from: https://www.gov.uk/government/uploads/system/uploads/attachment_data/file/175463/Nutbrown-Review.pdf [Accessed 18 February 2015].

Osgood, J., 2006. Deconstructing professionalism in early childhood education: resisting the regulatory gaze. *Contemporary issues in early childhood*, 7 (1), 5–14.

Osgood, J., 2010. Reconstructing professionalism in ECEC: the case for the 'critically reflective emotional professional'. *Early years: an international research journal*, 30 (2), 119–133.

Penn, H., 1998. Comparative research: a way forward? *In*: T. David, ed. *Researching early childhood education: European perspectives*. London: Paul Chapman, 7–24.

Rhodes, C. and Beneicke, S., 2002. Coaching, mentoring and peer-networking: challenges for the management of teacher professional development in schools. *Journal of in-service education*, 28 (2), 297–310.

Rodd, J., 1998. *Leadership in early childhood*. 2nd ed. Maidenhead: Open University Press.

Sachs, J., 2003. *The activist teaching profession*. Maidenhead: Open University Press.

Skeggs, B., 2003. *Class, self, culture*. London: Routledge.

Stryker, S. and Burke, P., 2000. The past, present, and future of an identity theory. *Social psychology quarterly*, 63 (4), 284–297.

Sylva, K., *et al.*, 2004. *The Effective Provision of Pre-School Education (EPPE) project: final report: a longitudinal study funded by the DfES 1997–2004* [online]. Available from: http://eprints.ioe.ac.uk/5309/1/sylva2004EPPEfinal.pdf [Accessed 18 February 2015].

TACTYC, 2013. *TACTYC response to the teachers' standards (early years)* [online]. Available from: http://tactyc.org.uk/pdfs/Teacher's%20Standards.pdf [Accessed 18 February 2015].

Tajfel, H., 1982. Social psychology of intergroup relations. *Annual review of psychology*, 33, 1–39.

Tickell, Dame C., 2011. *The early years foundation stage (EYFS) review. Report on the evidence* [online]. Available from: http://www.education.gov.uk/tickellreview [Accessed 18 February 2015].

Wenger, E., 1998. *Communities of practice: learning, meaning and identity.* London: Cambridge University Press.

Woodrow, C. and Busch, G., 2008. Repositioning early childhood leadership as action and activism. *European early childhood education research journal*, 16 (1), 83–93.

Evaluative decision-making for high-quality professional development: cultivating an evaluative stance

Jennifer Sumsion, Joanne Lunn Brownlee, Sharon Ryan, Kerryann Walsh, Ann Farrell, Susan Irvine, Gerry Mulhearn and Donna Berthelsen

Unprecedented policy attention to early childhood education internationally has highlighted the crucial need for a skilled early years workforce. Consequently, professional development of early years educators has become a global policy imperative. At the same time, many maintain that professional development research has reached an impasse. In this paper, we offer a new approach to addressing this impasse. In contrast to calls for a redesign of comparative studies of professional development programmes, or for the refinement of researcher-constructed professional development evaluation frameworks, we argue the need to cultivate what we refer to as an 'evaluative stance' amongst all involved in making decisions about professional development in the early years – from senior bureaucrats with responsibilities for funding professional development programmes to individual educators with choices about which professional development opportunities to take up. Drawing on three bodies of literature – evaluation capacity-building, personal epistemology and co-production – that, for the most part, have been overlooked with respect to early years professional learning, this paper proposes a conceptual framework to explain why cultivating an evaluative stance in professional development decision-making has rich possibilities for systemic, sustainable and transformative change in early years education.

Introduction

Unprecedented policy attention to early childhood education internationally has highlighted the crucial need for a skilled early years workforce. Consequently, the professional development of early years educators has become a global policy imperative (Organisation for Economic Co-operation and Development 2012). How to best address this imperative, however, is far from clear. Indeed, Hill *et al.* (2013) contend that what appeared to be an emerging consensus about the characteristics of effective professional development programmes (see, for example, Mayer and Lloyd 2011) has been contested by disappointing findings from several recent randomised trials in the USA, even though these programmes incorporated design elements widely assumed to maximise teachers' learning in the compulsory school sector, such as a focus on content, active learning and collective participation. It therefore seems that research into effective approaches to professional development has reached an impasse (Hill *et al.* 2013).

As discussed in relation to the school sector, the apparent impasse arises primarily from the challenges of establishing meaningful and nuanced causal, rather than correlational, links between professional development, teacher learning and student outcomes, given multiple and complex mediating factors operating in 'real-world' settings (King 2014). Exacerbating these challenges, according to many commentators, are conceptual and/or methodological weaknesses evident in many studies of professional development. Commentators refer variously, for example, to lack of conceptual clarity or, conversely, overly narrow conceptual framing; limited attention to processes of professional learning, as opposed to the content, pedagogical approaches and mode of delivery of professional development programmes; inadequate information about the policy, workplace and other contexts in which studies are situated; insufficient detail concerning sampling strategies, participants and methods; and an overreliance on self-reporting and participant perceptions (Hill *et al.* 2013, Lauer *et al.* 2013, Waitoller and Artiles 2013). Similar concerns have been expressed about research into professional development in the early childhood education and care (ECEC) sector (Fukkink and Lont 2007, Klein and Gomby 2008, Sheridan *et al.* 2009, Zaslow *et al.* 2010); a sector characterised by additional complexities, including fragmentation of service provision, extensive variation in the education and qualification levels of early childhood educators, as well as a lack of attention to the development of leaders who can implement and sustain professional development initiatives aimed at programme improvement (Ryan and Whitebook 2012). Across both the ECEC and school sectors, therefore, there is a need for innovative, conceptually and methodologically robust ways to advance research into professional development – and thus to better address policy imperatives, improve pedagogical practices and learning outcomes, and achieve greater returns on public investment in teacher development.

In this article, and with particular reference to ECEC, we propose a new approach to investigating professional development. In contrast to calls for a tighter focus on establishing causal relationships (Wayne *et al.* 2008), the redesign of comparative studies of professional development programmes (Hill *et al.* 2013) and the refinement of researcher-constructed professional development evaluation frameworks (Desimone 2009, King 2014), we argue for the importance of studying systemic change within ECEC organisations. Our particular interest is in change in professional learning at the individual and organisational levels that we anticipate could arise from cultivating an 'evaluative stance' in relation to decision-making about professional development. The specific purpose of this article is to present our conceptualisation of an evaluative stance as a key aspect of professional learning and its possible affordances for advancing professional development research and practice.

We begin by explaining the current policy 'moment' in Australia that has intensified the need for well-informed and careful decision-making in the face of rapidly proliferating professional development offerings. We then outline the conceptual

THE PROFESSIONAL DEVELOPMENT OF EARLY YEARS EDUCATORS

underpinning to our notion of an evaluative stance. In doing so, we draw on and connect three bodies of literature that, for the most part, have been overlooked in research on professional learning: namely literature related to evaluation capacity-building (ECB), personal epistemology and co-production. In concluding, we refer briefly to our plans to 'test' our conceptualisation empirically.

The Australian context and current policy 'moment'

In Australia, the election of the Rudd-Gillard federal Labor Government (2007–2013) heralded a period of significant investment in ECEC. This investment took place under the auspices of the Council of Australian Governments' national reform agenda. Encompassing many social and economic policy portfolios, the reform agenda aimed to improve national productivity through achieving greater consistency (e.g. in policy and regulations) across all jurisdictions. Australia is a federated nation with eight states and two mainland territories, along with a federal jurisdiction, so this was an ambitious undertaking. As we have explained in more detail elsewhere, ECEC figured prominently in the national reform agenda (Sumsion *et al* 2009). Governance of ECEC is situated within State and Territory Departments of Education and Australian Government Departments of Social Services and of Education. Amongst the ECEC initiatives have been the development of National Early Childhood Development Strategy National Laws and Agreements (Sims *et al.* in press), a National Quality Framework and National Quality Standard (Irvine and Price 2014), a national Early Years Learning Framework (Sumsion *et al.* 2009) and a national Early Years Workforce Strategy (Cumming *et al.* in press). For greater detail, see Appendix 1.

Policy changes foreshadowed by the conservative federal Liberal–National Coalition Government following its election in 2013 suggest that aspects of these initiatives may now be under threat (Sumsion *et al.* 2014). Nevertheless, in 2014 the Australian (i.e. federal) Government introduced the Long Day Care Professional Development Programme (LDCPD), with funding redirected from what was known as the Early Years Quality Fund, established by the previous Labor government. The LDCPD Programme represents an unprecedented three-year (2014–2016) investment of AUS$200 million to support the professional development of the approximately 76,000 educators working in long-day-care centres (The Social Research Centre 2014). These centres generally open for a minimum of eight hours per day, for at least 48 weeks of the year, and provide education and care programmes for children, in some cases from six weeks of age through to children aged five and six years. In Australia, 'educator' is used as a generic term to refer to anyone, regardless of qualification, who works directly with children in an early childhood setting.

The explicit purpose of the LDCPD funding[1] is to support educators in addressing the requirements of the National Quality Standard and in implementing the Early Years Learning Framework (Australian Government Department of Education 2014), both of which place substantial expectations on educators. Those in leadership roles, for example, are expected to build a professional learning community that supports ongoing individual and organisational learning as the basis for continuous quality improvement. Every educator is also expected to engage in reflective practice (Australian Children's Education and Care Quality Authority [ACECQA] n.d.). In addition, there is an expectation regarding the involvement of all educators in the development and ongoing refinement of a centre-specific Quality Improvement Plan, which involves a self-report audit against each of seven quality areas to identify where to focus improvements. The Quality Improvement Plan is central to the external quality assessment and ratings process undertaken under the auspices of the ACECQA. Because the context and environment of every early childhood centre is different, there is a need to develop knowledge of and skills in decision-making for professional development that can be applied to specific contexts. Making effective use of the Quality Improvement Plan is regularly identified as an area requiring further work in the quarterly reports released by ACECQA (see, for example, ACECQA 2014). Collectively, these expectations and requirements highlight the importance of focusing on professional learning, not only of educators who often are the targets of professional development but also of those charged with dispersing funds for professional learning. Given that many leaders in the early years sector are not required to have specialised qualifications in early childhood education or leadership, the capacity to take an 'evaluative stance' (a concept we will explain presently) in everyday practice and in relation to decisions about professional development and learning is central to ensuring quality improvement.

Consistent with the emphasis on contextual differences in ECEC, a key feature of the LDCPD is the high degree of flexibility it affords leaders in identifying the professional development needs of their staff and deciding upon which professional development strategies, options and providers would best meet those needs (Australian Government Department of Education 2014). Extensive consultations with senior policy-makers, early childhood service providers and other key groups in the ECEC sector recently undertaken in our capacity as members of the Excellence in Research in Early Years Education Collaborative Research Network (an Australian government-funded early years research capacity-building initiative) (Mulhearn and Sumsion 2014) have highlighted their acute awareness of the ethical imperative of investing this professional development funding 'windfall' wisely. These consultations have also highlighted leaders' concerns about the potential for poor decisions and poor returns on investment in professional development. Such concerns are particularly evident in the face of escalating marketing campaigns from commercial providers of professional development offerings and initiatives of sometimes dubious quality. The present policy moment in Australia, therefore, creates urgency for research that can inform decision-making around professional development. It has also heightened our interest in professional learning possibilities that might arise from working with leaders to cultivate an 'evaluative stance'.

An evaluative stance: conceptual underpinnings

Evaluation is typically thought of as the systematic collection of data to investigate the implementation and effectiveness of programmes, policies or practices (Patton 2008). With regards to professional development, evaluation is usually some kind of assessment about what teachers and others learn from participating in a learning opportunity and how the learning programme might be improved. Instead of focusing research on the professional development programme and its impacts, however, we are arguing here for a focus on cultivating the capacities of individuals in educational settings to take an evaluative stance towards choosing professional development opportunities, and investigating how they apply an evaluative stance to their professional learning.

We use the term 'evaluative stance' to refer to a mindset (evaluative thinking and beliefs) and skill set (e.g. critical thinking skills), while acknowledging that these can be inextricably interconnected. In the context of professional learning, we suggest that evaluative mind sets and skill sets are geared towards analysing evidence to guide decision-making in the selection and implementation of professional development activities and initiatives, to ensure that intended outcomes are reached and programme improvements ensue. Our interest in, and conceptualisation of, an evaluative stance has its genesis in intersecting ideas from the literature concerned with ECB, personal epistemology and co-production. For ease of explanation, we discuss each of these three concepts in turn, while emphasising their interconnectedness. We also make links to existing literature about professional development that draws on, or gestures to, these or similar notions.

Evaluation capacity-building

ECB is a process by which strategies are designed and implemented to assist individuals, groups and organisations in the process of conducting effective, useful and professional evaluations (Preskill and Boyle 2008). ECB is widely considered more effective when embedded and ongoing within organisations (Stockdill *et al.* 2002), and when it is seen as more than a primarily individual capacity. Preskill indicates that ECB is about 'learning to think evaluatively' and involves 'evaluative thinking and practice' (2014, p. 117). A few theoretical models of ECB have been developed (Preskill and Boyle 2008) but we refer to two that appear to have strong potential to inform professional development research: the multidisciplinary model proposed by Preskill and Boyle (2008) and the integrated ECB model (Labin *et al.* 2012, Labin 2014).

The multidisciplinary model of ECB

Preskill and Boyle's (2008) multidisciplinary model of ECB draws on three research fields: evaluation; organisational learning and change; and adult and workplace learning. The model has two domains. The first describes motivations, assumptions and expectations as well as strategies for ECB. Motivations may include a range of intrinsic and extrinsic factors; for example, the need for an organisation to demonstrate accountability. Assumptions relate to issues such as the extent to which individuals within an organisation believe that: evaluation is important for decision-making; there is a need to make learning explicit (intentional); and taking an evaluative stance can promote programme effectiveness. Preskill and Boyle propose that individuals within an organisation must have a common set of beliefs and assumptions for effective ECB. Motivations and assumptions then lead to a range of expectations about ECB; for example, that an organisation will become more effective and develop its capacity for learning. Accordingly, motivation, assumptions and expectations determine the nature and implementation of ECB strategies; for instance, through internships, meetings, training, mentoring and engagement in communities of practice (Preskill and Boyle 2008).

The second domain of the model is the development of sustainable practice, through the transfer of learning about ECB; specifically, the transfer of knowledge, skills and attitudes. According to Preskill and Boyle (2008), transfer takes place within broader organisational contexts. The organisational systems and structures, along with its communication channels, leadership and culture, influence the organisation's learning capacity. In this respect, the multidisciplinary model of ECB (Preskill and Boyle 2008) bears some resemblance to the integrated ECB model (Labin *et al.* 2012, Labin 2014) described next.

The integrative ECB model

The integrative ECB model (Labin *et al.* 2012), which seemingly without explanation later became known as the integrated ECB model (Labin 2014), builds upon the conceptual work underpinning the multidisciplinary model (Preskill and Boyle 2008) to also provide an empirical overlay. Developed initially from the findings of a systematic broad-based research synthesis (Labin *et al.* 2012), and subsequently through factor analysis (Labin 2014), the integrative ECB model identifies constructs from existing ECB measurement tools and incorporates these into a heuristic representation. The high degree of consistency between the concepts identified in the conceptual literature and those identified in empirical studies suggests that the integrative ECB model has considerable construct validity. Thus it can be used 'to test the relationships hypothesized in ... models' of ECB (Labin 2014, p. 113). The integrative ECB model has three phases. First, there is the identification of needs or reasons why members of an organisation should engage in ECB. Next, stakeholders identify the activities they will engage in to develop their evaluation capacities such as professional development and data collection focused on examining aspects of an organisation. In the final and third phase, key stakeholders identify outcomes of their ECB at the individual, organisational and programme levels.

Within each of these phases there is considerable synergy with the concepts and constructs in the multidisciplinary model. Both models, for example, refer to what could be described as presage factors, both personal (individual) and situational (organisational) presage factors. Personal presage factors are individual needs (Labin 2014), attitudes, motivations and assumptions (Preskill and Boyle 2008). Situational presage factors, described in both models, are influencing factors at broader contextual levels such as the organisational leadership, culture, communication, systems and structures (Preskill and Boyle 2008), and mediating factors such as organisational capacity (Labin 2014). Both models acknowledge that personal and situational factors influence the implementation of ECB strategies or processes that, in turn, lead to individual and organisational outcomes, such as sustainable evaluation practices (Preskill and Boyle 2008, Labin 2014). Both models also recognise the significance of the role of adult learning and that ECB is essentially related to evaluation for learning. A key focus in ECB models, therefore, is how leaders within organisations can support professional learning using ECB.

Importantly, however, the multidisciplinary model (Preskill and Boyle 2008) and the integrative ECB model (Labin *et al.* 2012) vary in one crucial aspect: the latter emphasises the primacy of participatory and collaborative processes. Describing these processes as 'an essential thread in the fabric of ECB efforts', Labin *et al.* (2012, p. 324) eloquently argue the indispensable nature of participatory and collaborative approaches that actively engage all stakeholders in evaluation processes. Noting similarities to 'collaborative reflective practice', they refer to building a culture where stakeholders are 'sharing ideas, information and action, thinking and working in an evaluative way' (2012, p. 18). Whether collaboration is indeed essential to ECB, however, is contested (Clinton 2014).

THE PROFESSIONAL DEVELOPMENT OF EARLY YEARS EDUCATORS

As a research team, we are interested in examining professional learning in ECB in more detail. ECB is focused on organisational change by actors working together or individually to learn how to evaluate various aspects of the organisation. However, the focus is primarily on evaluation of the organisation, rather than on developing the ability of individuals within the organisation to use an evaluation approach that may lead to programme improvement. Similarly, the collective approach to ECB of the integrative model emphasises participatory decision-making of individuals in evaluation processes, but not necessarily how a collaborative approach might lead to new forms of professional learning. Accordingly, we turn to the literature on personal epistemology as an innovative theoretical framework, and to the co-production literature for a generative methodology.

Personal epistemology and professional learning

While the ECB models present a clear focus on personal and situational presage factors and the significance of professional learning, missing from these models is theorising on learning. A personal presage factor that may be considered in relationship to professional learning for ECB is personal epistemology. Personal epistemology refers to the beliefs individuals hold about the nature of knowing and knowledge. Utilising theory and research in the area of personal epistemology offers a way to better understand learning (Kang 2008) generally, and professional learning for ECB in particular. Although a substantial body of research has investigated the relationship between personal epistemologies and learning across a range of disciplines and contexts such as science and education, there appears to have been no such research in ECB.

Much of the personal epistemology research to date has examined how education contexts influence the development of personal epistemology (Hofer 2004). In germinal research, Perry (1970) and King and Kitchener (1994) showed that individuals may move from simple, 'black and white' views of knowledge through to complex, evidence-informed ways of knowing as a result of their participation in a class or programme of learning. A considerable body of recent evidence has mirrored these earlier findings. For example, researchers have described movement in personal epistemologies from absolutist (i.e. an absolute view of knowledge), to subjectivist (i.e. personal opinions count) to evaluativist (i.e. tentative, evidence-based evaluations of knowledge) (see Feucht [2010] for a review that builds on the work of Kuhn and Weinstock [2002]). Individuals with absolutist personal epistemologies view knowledge as right or wrong, and so see little need to be reflective or to evaluate knowledge. As individuals begin to understand that knowledge is tentative, they may conceive of knowledge and knowing as personal or subjective constructions. Subjectivist beliefs may lead to a view that personal opinions count, but knowledge still remains largely unexamined. Individuals with an evaluativist personal epistemology, however, understand that knowledge is subjectively constructed, but also recognise that some knowledge is 'better' than another. This means that knowledge claims are made on the basis of evaluating a range of perspectives and then coming to the 'best' evidence-informed response. From this perspective, knowledge is tentative, perspectival and constructed. In reflecting the potential range or development of personal epistemologies, research within the area commonly uses the terms 'naïve' and 'sophisticated' to depict opposite ends of a continuum of personal epistemologies (Pintrich 2002).

Personal epistemologies are activated during the process of learning and influence the extent to which we make meaning and engage in complex problem-solving (Hofer 2002). This suggests that personal epistemology belief systems may filter how ECEC professionals make decisions and how they engage in, and apply what they experience in, professional development (cf. Many *et al.* 2002, Muis 2004, Peng and Fitzgerald 2006, Yadav and Koehler 2007). Some research also suggests that evaluativist (or sophisticated) personal epistemologies are related to a greater capacity to engage in critical thinking (Braten and Stromso 2006). This is of crucial importance when we consider that the learning processes associated with taking an evaluative stance involve evaluating a range of perspectives/inputs and managing complex environments with multiple stakeholders. We theorise that policy-makers, leaders and educators in ECEC organisations who enact evaluativist personal epistemologies are more likely to engage in critical thinking and analysis based on evidence for a 'best' solution. While we have strong evidence to show that an individual's personal epistemology influences learning strategies and learning outcomes (Muis 2004), we know little about this in the context of ECB.

Given the clear focus on professional learning in the ECB research, we argue that an innovative theoretical approach is to focus on personal epistemology as a personal presage factor in addition to the attitudes, motivations and assumptions described by Preskill and Boyle (2008). To date, personal epistemology research has shown clear links between sophisticated personal epistemologies (mindsets) and critical thinking (skill sets). We argue, therefore, that a focus on encouraging evaluativist mindsets and critical thinking skill sets has the potential to provide a new way to both conceptualise and promote an evaluative stance in ECB.

Recent research also points to the importance of understanding more about the role of social contexts in the construction of personal epistemologies (for a review, see Brownlee *et al.* 2011). Hofer (2010), for example, noted that we still do not understand enough about how contexts influence personal epistemologies: 'These contextual influences may influence how teachers view the role of authority in knowledge building, the certainty of knowledge and how knowledge is justified' (Brownlee *et al.* 2011, p. 4). We also contend that a focus on social contexts through the use of co-production, as a form of collaboration, has the potential to engage stakeholders from across the early childhood sector in cultivating evaluativist mindsets with respect to professional learning in ways that could lead to systemic change.

Co-production

The term 'co-production' has been used mainly in health, human services and public administration literature to refer variously to collaboration between service providers and consumers of those services, or more broadly between state and citizen (Giddens 2003). Co-production provides a way of positioning citizens, consumers and service users as 'necessary, expert and generative co-participants' (Dunston *et al.* 2009, p. 40). Thus it involves a fundamental shift from 'doing *to* and doing *for*' to 'doing *with*' (2009, p. 41; original emphases). Further, and especially when the focus moves beyond the provider–client relationship common in welfare, co-production can be seen as offering a way of harnessing the productive and innovative capacities of different sectors (e.g. policy, academia, practice) in an endeavour to address complex and seemingly intransigent or 'wicked' (Rittel and Webber 1973) problems. In our case, the 'wicked' problem is how to promote evaluative

THE PROFESSIONAL DEVELOPMENT OF EARLY YEARS EDUCATORS

thinking and practice for the effective deployment of resources for professional development that leads to quality improvement.

With an emphasis on shared interests and learning partnerships, co-production can occur across all stages of service provision, from planning and design, to implementation, through to managing, monitoring and evaluation (Bovaird 2007, Dunston *et al.* 2009). Bovaird (2007), however, argues that its potential remains vastly underestimated, in part because of a paucity of 'detailed and situated analyses' about 'where and how increased levels of co-productive practices might be achieved' (Dunston *et al.* 2009, p. 44). Most analyses have focused on change initiated by individual practitioners and services, with little attention to its possibilities for bringing about systems-wide change (Dunston *et al.* 2009). To the best of our knowledge, to date, studies of co-production in the early childhood education sector have been confined to fostering greater parental involvement in early childhood services – see, for example, Pestoff (2006) and Pemberton and Mason (2009). Interestingly, these studies were undertaken respectively within the disciplines of public management and social policy, rather than the discipline of education – where, to our knowledge, the concept of co-production has not been taken up.

For us, then, questions have arisen as to whether it is a useful concept to import, given the existing emphasis on collaborative approaches to professional learning and development in much of the educational research literature (Kennedy 2005, Sheridan *et al.* 2009). What, if anything, might co-production contribute over and above, for example, the concepts of 'communities of practice' (Wenger 1998) or 'collaborative action research' as discussed by Kennedy (2005)? At this stage, our response is necessarily tentative for we are only just beginning to put the concept of co-production 'to work' in an empirical investigation. However, the explicit focus on joint decision-making about the effective deployment of publicly financed resources in many conceptualisations of co-production (Brandsen *et al.* 2012), including for the purpose for which we are intending to use it, seems to take it beyond the usual focus of many arguably similar concepts widely used in education. So, too, does the scope for systemic change through collaborative endeavour across sectors, rather than the more usual focus on change in a particular site.

Together, these three inter-disciplinary bodies of literature – ECB, personal epistemology and co-production – provide a conceptual framework for understanding and studying how the cultivation of an evaluative stance as part of professional development initiatives might lead to improving the learning of individuals and organisations as part of systemic change. That is, an integrative model of ECB provides insights into the kinds of skills and understandings needed to be able to critically evaluate the quality of programming in an educational setting and how well individuals within that programme are meeting the goals of an organisation. This then allows leaders to consider how they might target professional development efforts to improve instructional quality. Examining shifts in personal epistemologies permits the tracing of change both in the ways leaders approach their work as decision-makers and guiders of professional development while also permitting examination of how educators are changing their beliefs and practice in alignment with quality improvement efforts. By employing a co-production lens, the focus is extended beyond tracing the learning of individuals within an educational setting as a result of professional development to also consider how professional development can be shared and generative across educational settings through collaborations and partnerships.

Conclusion

Professional development is probably the most used means of improving instructional quality in education settings. Evaluation is typically a research design applied by those funding or leading professional development initiatives to ensure that the design of the programme leads to improvements in practice. Yet a number of scholars have documented that most professional development initiatives, even those based on adult learning principles and closely connected to the sites in which change is expected, often do not have their intended impact. While some argue that the problem lies in the limited ways professional development has been studied, we argue in this paper that what is needed is a reconceptualisation of the relations between evaluation research and professional development. Rather than evaluation being something used to examine professional development, we are suggesting that the cultivation of an evaluative stance be embodied within professional development initiatives as a means of ensuring professional learning opportunities are differentiated to particular educational programmes and the educators within them and also as a means to facilitate change across programmes.

The state of play in ECEC in Australia offers unique affordances for professional learning within its workforce. Our proposal of an 'evaluative stance' brings together three cognate bodies of scholarship – ECB, personal epistemology and co-production – to consider its possibilities for systemic, sustainable and transformative change to professional development in early years education. To test these ideas empirically, we are planning to undertake a three-year, mixed-method, multiphase, multisite study.

Joining us as collaborators are four organisations, including a government department, from four Australian states, with responsibilities for decision-making concerning professional development in the ECEC sector. Our collaborators will work with us as co-designers and co-evaluators in developing and testing (in other words, co-producing) a protocol for improving decision-making for high-quality professional development. While we have not begun the study, we have received enormous interest in the planned three-year project and its approach to thinking differently about professional development, and particularly about how wise decisions on investments in professional development might be made.

Much investment has therefore been, and continues to be, made in Australia and internationally in using professional development to build educator capacity with little attention to the deep shifts in epistemologies needed if educators are to change their practices. At the same time, focusing professional development primarily on improving the capacities of educators has prevented considerations of how professional development can contribute to the improvement of educational quality within and across settings. We believe that researching professional development, through the lenses of ECB, personal epistemologies and co-production, may provide a new way forward to not only ensure professional development is effective at one point in time but that professional development leads to ongoing improvements over time and across programmes. Although we have focused on the Australian context, our reading of international contexts – for example, as reported by the OECD (2012) – suggests that the need for systemic change of this kind is indeed a global imperative.

Acknowledgements

The authors would like to thank senior representatives from the following organisations for their encouragement to pursue the ideas articulated in this article: Gowrie South Australia,

THE PROFESSIONAL DEVELOPMENT OF EARLY YEARS EDUCATORS

the Health and Community Services Workforce Council, KU Children's Services and the Victorian Department of Education and Early Childhood Development. They also acknowledge the invaluable assistance of Dr Deanne Armstrong.

Disclosure statement

No potential conflict of interest was reported by the authors.

Funding

The preparation of this article was supported by the Excellence in Research in Early Years Education Collaborative Research Network, an initiative funded through the Australian Government's Collaborative Research Networks programme.

Note

1. https://www.education.gov.au/long-day-care-professional-development-programme.

References

Australian Children's Education and Care Quality Authority (ACECQA), 2014. *NQF snapshot Q2 2014*. Sydney, Australia: ACECQA.

Australian Children's Education and Care Quality Authority (ACECQA), n.d. *The national quality standard* [online]. Available from: http://www.acecqa.gov.au/national-quality-framework/the-national-quality-standard [Accessed 4 September 2014].

Australian Government Department of Education, 2014. *Long day care professional development programme* [online]. Available from: http://docs.education.gov.au/system/files/doc/other/ldcpdp_funding_guidelines_2.pdf [Accessed 4 September 2014].

Bovaird, T., 2007. Beyond engagement and participation: user and community coproduction of public services. *Public administration review*, 67 (5), 846–860.

Brandsen, T., Pestoff, V., and Verschuere, B., 2012. Co-production as a maturing concept. *In*: V. Pestoff, T. Brandsen, and B. Verschuere, eds. *New public governance, the third sector, and co-production*. New York, NY: Routledge, 1–12.

Braten, I. and Stromso, H., 2006. Epistemological beliefs, interest, and gender as predictors of Internet-based learning activities. *Computers in human behaviour*, 22 (6), 1027–1042.

Brownlee, J., Schraw, G., and Berthelsen, D.C., eds., 2011. *Personal epistemology and teacher education*. Routledge research in education. New York, NY: Routledge.

Clinton, J., 2014. The true impact of evaluation: motivation for ECB. *American journal of evaluation*, 35 (1), 120–127.

Council of Australian Governments, 2009. *Investing in the early years—a national early childhood development strategy* [online]. Available from: https://www.coag.gov.au/sites/default/files/national_ECD_strategy.rtf [Accessed 18 February 2015].

Cumming, T., Sumsion, J., and Wong, S., in press. Rethinking early childhood workforce sustainability in the context of Australia's early childhood education and care reforms. *International journal of child care and education policy*.

Desimone, L.M., 2009. Improving impact studies of teachers' professional development: toward better conceptualizations and measures. *Educational researcher*, 38 (3), 181–199.

Dunston, L., *et al.*, 2009. Co-production and health system reform: from re-imagining to re-making. *The Australian journal of public administration*, 68 (1), 39–52.

Feucht, F.C., 2010. Epistemic climate in elementary classrooms. *In*: L.D. Bendixen and F.C. Feucht, eds. *Personal epistemology in the classroom: theory, research, and educational implications*. New York, NY: Cambridge University Press, 55–93.

Fukkink, R.G. and Lont, A., 2007. Does training matter? A meta-analysis and review of caregiver training studies. *Early childhood research quarterly*, 22 (3), 294–311.

Giddens, A., 2003. Introduction: neoprogressivism: a new agenda for social democracy. *In*: A. Giddens, ed. *The progressive manifesto: new ideas for the centre-left*. Cambridge: Polity Press, 1–34.

Hill, H.C., Beisiegel, M., and Jacob, R., 2013. Professional development research: consensus, crossroads, and challenges. *Educational researcher*, 42 (9), 476–487.

Hofer, B., 2002. Personal epistemology as a psychological and educational construct: an introduction. *In*: B. Hofer and P. Pintrich, eds. *Personal epistemology: the psychological beliefs about knowledge and knowing*. Mahwah, NJ: Lawrence Erlbaum, 3–14.

Hofer, B., 2004. Epistemological understanding as a metacognitive process: thinking aloud during online searching. *Educational psychologist*, 39 (1), 43–55.

Hofer, B., 2010. Personal epistemology in Asia: burgeoning research and future directions. *The Asia-Pacific education researcher*, 19 (1), 179–184.

Irvine, S. and Price, J., 2014. Professional conversations: a collaborative approach to support policy implementation, professional learning and practice change in ECEC. *Australasian journal of early childhood*, 39 (3), 85–93.

Kang, N., 2008. Learning to teach science: personal epistemologies, teaching goals, and practices of teaching. *Teaching and teacher education*, 24 (2), 478–498.

Kennedy, A., 2005. Models of continuing professional development: a framework for analysis. *Journal of in-service education*, 31 (2), 235–250.

King, F., 2014. Evaluating the impact of teacher professional development: an evidence-based framework. *Professional development in education*, 40 (1), 89–111.

King, P.M. and Kitchener, K.S., 1994. *Developing reflective judgment*. San Francisco, CA: Jossey-Bass.

Klein, L.G. and Gomby, D.S., 2008. Working paper prepared for a working meeting on recent school readiness research: guiding the synthesis of early childhood research. Appendix C: a synthesis of federally-funded studies on school readiness: what are we learning about professional development? 21–22 October, Washington, DC.

Kuhn, D. and Weinstock, M., 2002. What is epistemological thinking and why does it matter? *In*: B. Hofer and P. Pintrich, eds. *Personal epistemology: the psychological beliefs about knowledge and knowing*. Mahwah, NJ: Lawrence Erlbaum, 123–146.

Labin, S.N., 2014. Developing common measures in evaluation capacity building: an iterative science and practice process. *American journal of evaluation*, 35 (1), 107–115.

Labin, S.N., *et al.*, 2012. A research synthesis of the evaluation capacity building literature. *American journal of evaluation*, 33 (3), 307–338.

Lauer, P.A., *et al.*, 2013. The impact of short-term professional development on participant outcomes: a review of the literature. *Professional development in education*, 40 (2), 207–227.

Many, J., Howard, F., and Hoge, P., 2002. Epistemology and preservice teacher education: how do beliefs about knowledge affect our students' experiences? *English education*, 34 (4), 302–322.

Mayer, D. and Lloyd, M., 2011. *Professional learning: an introduction to the research literature*. Melbourne: The Australian Institute for Teaching and School Leadership.

Muis, K., 2004. Personal epistemology and mathematics: a critical review and synthesis of research. *Review of educational research*, 74 (3), 317–377.

Mulhearn, G. and Sumsion, J., 2014. Research partnerships: joint pathways to quality? *Paper presented at the European Early Childhood Education Research Association conference*, September, Crete.

Organisation for Economic Co-operation and Development, 2012. *Starting strong III: a quality tool box for early childhood education and care*. Paris: OECD.

Patton, M.Q., 2008. *Utilized focused evaluation*. 4th ed. Thousand Oaks, CA: Sage.

Pemberton, S. and Mason, J., 2009. Co-production and Sure Start children's centres: reflecting upon users', perspectives and implications for service delivery, planning and evaluation. *Social policy and society*, 8 (1), 13–24.

Peng, H. and Fitzgerald, G., 2006. Relationships between teacher education students' epistemological beliefs and their learning outcomes in a case-based hypermedia learning environment. *Journal of technology and teacher education*, 14 (2), 255–285.

Perry, W.G., 1970. *Forms of intellectual and ethical development in the college years*. New York, NY: Holt, Rinehart and Winston.

Pestoff, V., 2006. Citizens and co-production of welfare services. *Public management review*, 8 (4), 503–519.

THE PROFESSIONAL DEVELOPMENT OF EARLY YEARS EDUCATORS

Pintrich, P., 2002. Future challenges and directions for theory. *In*: B. Hofer and P. Pintrich, eds. *Personal epistemology: the psychological beliefs about knowledge and knowing*. Mahwah, NJ: Lawrence Erlbaum, 389–414.

Preskill, H., 2014. Now for the hard stuff: next steps in ECB research and practice. *American journal of evaluation*, 35 (1), 116–119.

Preskill, H. and Boyle, S., 2008. A multidisciplinary model of evaluation capacity building. *American journal of evaluation*, 29 (4), 443–459.

Rittel, H.J. and Webber, M., 1973. Dilemmas in a general theory of planning. *Policy sciences*, 4 (2), 155–169.

Ryan, S. and Whitebook, M., 2012. More than teachers: the early care and education workforce. *In*: B. Pianta, ed. *Handbook of early education*. New York, NY: Guilford Press, 92–110.

Sheridan, S.M., *et al.*, 2009. Professional development in early childhood programs: process issues and research needs. *Early education & development*, 20 (3), 377–401.

Sims, M., *et al.*, in press. *Australian national ECEC reforms, with a focus on the National Quality Framework and the National Quality Standard*. Munich: Deutsches Jugendinstitute.

The Social Research Centre, 2014. *2013 National early childhood education and care workforce census*. Melbourne: Department of Education.

Stockdill, S.H., Baizerman, M., and Compton, D.W., 2002. *Toward a definition of the ECB process: a conversation with the ECB literature* (New Directions for Evaluation, no. 93). San Francisco, CA: Jossey-Bass.

Standing Council of School Education and Early Childhood (SCSEEC), 2012. *Early years workforce strategy: the early childhood education and care workforce strategy for Australia 2012–2016* [online]. Available from: http://www.cccav.org.au/component/docman/doc_down load/121-early-years-workforce-strategy-2012-2016 [Accessed 4 September 2014].

Sumsion, J., *et al.*, 2009. Insider perspectives on developing belonging, being & becoming: the early years learning framework for Australia. *Australasian journal of early childhood*, 34 (4), 4–13.

Sumsion, J., *et al.*, 2014. The 'state of play' in Australia: early childhood educators and play-based learning. *Australasian journal of early childhood*, 39 (3), 4–13.

Waitoller, F.R. and Artiles, A.J., 2013. A decade of professional development research for inclusive education: a critical review and notes for a research program. *Review of educational research*, 83 (3), 319–356.

Wayne, A.J., *et al.*, 2008. Experimenting with teacher professional development: motives and methods. *Educational researcher*, 37 (8), 469–479.

Wenger, E., 1998. *Communities of practice: learning, meaning, and identity*. Cambridge: Cambridge University Press.

Yadav, A. and Koehler, M., 2007. The role of epistemological beliefs in preservice teachers' interpretation of video cases of early-grade literacy instruction. *Journal of technology and teacher education*, 15 (3), 335–361.

Zaslow, M., *et al.*, 2010. *Toward the identification of features of effective professional development for early childhood educators: literature review*. Washington, DC: US Department of Education Office of Planning.

Appendix 1. A sample of Australian ECEC initiatives that include a focus on professional development

- National Early Childhood Reform Agenda – focuses on supporting increased access to higher-quality ECEC for individual and national benefit.
- National Early Childhood Development Strategy – makes links between quality service provision, the qualifications and quality of the ECEC workforce, and positive outcomes for children, families and society: 'The early childhood workforce is central to delivering early childhood development services and bringing about fundamental cultural change required for responsive service delivery' (Council of Australian Governments 2009, p. 20).

- National Quality Framework – in Quality Area 7 of the National Quality Standard, Leadership and Service Management, emphasis is placed on leaders building a professional learning community that supports individual and organisational professional learning as the basis for continuous quality improvement. In addition, related learning frameworks and the National Quality Framework Assessment and Ratings process place emphasis on reflective practice and ongoing learning to improve professional practice.
- Early Years Workforce Strategy: The Early Childhood Education and Care Workforce Strategy for Australia 2012–2016 – focuses on building a sustainable highly qualified and professional workforce able to deliver responsive and integrative service delivery. The Strategy is based on the premise that Australia needs a skilled workforce to realise current policy goals, and that access to effective professional development opportunities is integral to achieving a skilled workforce. The Strategy recognises that work of educators 'is complex and requires enhanced qualifications and ongoing professional development' (Standing Council of School Education and Early Childhood [SCSEEC] 2012, p. 2). The first goal is 'A professional workforce'; key success indicators include 'Increased participation by the sector in professional development and leadership activities, with a focus on professional educational practice, programme design and delivery and leadership'; and 'the ECEC sector has access to quality professional development' (SCSEEC 2012, p. 5).
- Professional Teaching Standards, Codes of Ethics and related Industrial Awards all include requirements and expectations for engagement in professional development.

Index

Note: Page numbers in *italic* type refer to figures
Page numbers in **bold** type refer to tables
Page numbers followed by 'n' refer to notes

abilities 145, 204
accessibility 23
accountability 20, 144, 145, 147, 187
action research 32, 56, 156
active involvement 148
active learning 135
adaptation 67
adaptive approach 50
additional needs 171, 196
administration 48, 49
administrative support 146
adult learning 187, 189, 201, 266
affect 70–74
affective forces 68
agency 245
alignment 5–6
analytical process 121
anxiety 70, 232
application 211; immediate 196
application software 69
applications 87, 88, 89
applied settings 211
articulation 24
arts 103
aspirations 216–221
assessment 17, 20, 41, 140, 215, 220, 264; self- 140
associate degree programs 15
assumptions 106, 265
attendance 80
attitudes 90, 97, 202–203, 216–221
Australia 7, 8, 29–43, 45–60, 171–184, 208–221, 262–271
authenticity 118–119
authority 51
autism 73
autonomy 52, 226, 229, 236, 238
awareness, self- 6, 119, 124, 125, 144

babysitters 13, 250

bachelor degree programs 16
balance 211
behavior 244; social 244
behavioral norms 154, 164
beliefs 216–220, 226, 233, 265
benefits 195
best practices 212
Bethelsen, D., *et al.* 261–274
bias 194
bicultural practices 160
blogs 88
boundaries 235
Brownlee, J.L., *et al.* 261–274
budgets 24
Burns, M.S., *et al.* 186–207
buy in 202

Campbell, T., *et al.* 186–207
care 80, 228, 246, 253
career progression 247
caring self 250
Cartmel, J., *et al.* 171–185
Casley, M., *et al.* 171–185
categories 137
celebration 146, 213
center leader 6
challenges 2, 5, 23–25, 41, 57, 184, 262; generating 209; implementation 146
change 3, 5, 46, 49, 171–184; Circles model 7, 174, 175, 180, 182; imposed 254–255; individual 160; leading 51–52; measurable 133; models 155, 174, 175; resisting 53; systemic 268, 269; timescales 165, 167
change mechanisms model 137, *137*
Charles Sturt University (Australia) 214
chat rooms 195, 201, 214, 220
check-ins 142–143
Cherrington, S., and Thornton, K. 152–170
Child Care and Development Fund Block Grant 22

INDEX

Child Development Associate 17
childcare workers 13
childminders 246
children: observing 219–220, 238; perceptions of 145, 234; priority 171
Circles of Change 7, 174, 175, 180, 182
citizens 268
citizenship 79
classroom: environment 138, 238; knowledge 144
co-teaching 190
coaching 7, 22, 214; model 211, 220
codes 51, 137, 194, 230, 249
cohesion 179
collaboration 42, 49, 53–55, 56, 103–104, 107, 165, 188, 214
collaborative learning 227
collaborative partnership 143–144
collaborative reflective practice 266
collaborators 225, 270
colleagues 32
collective decision-making 161
collective teaching 47–48
Colmer, K., Waniganayake, M. and Field, L. 45–63
common sense 65
communication 6, 53, 80, 81, 91, 214; strategies 217–218
communities 48, 81, 92, 233, 254; learning 190; online 191; of practice 190, 227, 236; professional 1
community meetings 187, 199, 202
compensation 14
competence 53, 80; digital 90; social 164
competency framework 247
competency-based credentials 16–18
complacency 41
complex system 149
complexity 47
compliance 41, 255
concepts 262
conceptual framework 269
conferences 40, 53, 88
confidence 32, 218, 221
confidentiality 84
conflict 161, 182
confusion 243, 247
connections 252
conscientization 98
consciousness-raising 75
consensus 161
constructionism 136
constructionist approaches 227
consultancy 34
consultation 98, 105, 106
consumers 268
contact 89
content 237; knowledge 187

content area strategies 198
context 11, 12–14, 47, 83, 128, 138, *138*; educational 245, 267; educator 211; policy 263–264; social 268
contextual factors 153, 210
continuity 217–218
continuum 55–57, **56**, 60
contradictions 67, 70–74
control 52, 177, **177**, 181
controversies 68
conversations 39, 55, 189, 243
cooking 218
costs 133
creativity 254
credentialing body 16
credibility 144
critical reflection 39, 48, 53, 57, 163
criticality 167
critique 92
crystallizing 101
cultural practices 67
culturally responsive practice 197
culture 34, 39, 49, 55, 57; contemporary 74–75; diverse 183; learning 154; popular 71; school 155; team 164
current approaches 5
curriculum 64–75, 79–80, 208
Cyprus 8, 224–239

data 20, 23, 103, 136, 147; analysis 36, 51, 121, 136, 157, 175, 194, 249; collection 23, 121, 157, **159**, 168, 264; review 51
database 23
day-to-day work 46
debates 55, 67, 93, 164
debriefing 198
decision-making 59, 98, 261–271; collective 161; participatory 267
decision-making power 51–52
definitions 66, 67
degree programs, associate 15; bachelor 16
degrees, online 23
delivery, mixed 12, 13
demands 175, **176**, 181, 184
democracy 97
dialogue 48, 53, 54, 57, 59; sustaining 217; transdisciplinary 178, 179–180
diary 39
difference, making a 254
digital competence 90
digital representation 86
digital technologies 6, 78–93
directors 48, 51, 55, 57, 58, 59
disagreements 164
discovery 233
discussion 50, 104, 160, 163, 174, 213; groups 80–88, 91, 93; prompts 218–219
dissonance 47

INDEX

distance education 214, 220
distributed learning 191
diversity 13, 24, 161, 162, 194
documentation 213, 214
downloading 101, 105
drawing 235
durability 24

early childhood education and care 3
early childhood education centers 48, 51, 57
early years 3
Early Years Learning Framework (Australia) 30, 45, 209, 263
ecological system 149
ecological view 211
editors 2
education, pre-primary 228
Education Review Office (New Zealand) 167, 169n4
Edwards, S., *et al.* 64–77
emails 142, 143, 196
emancipation 98, 102, 215
embedded instruction 133–134, 141
emotional intelligence 117–118, 253
emotional journey 232–234
emotional management 71
emotional responses 243
emotions 100, 105, 252
empathy 100, 108, 164
empirical studies 153
empowerment 108, 111, 173, 217
enactment 188, 190, 196, 215
encouragement 40
engagement 38, 202
England 116–117, 128–129, 243–257
enjoyment 180
enthusiasm 37, 70, 219, 221
entry requirements 14
environment 47, 57; classroom 138, 145–146, 238; enabling 49; home 210; inclusive 172; planned 58; safe 53, 232; school 146, 154; welcoming 210; work 22
environmental conditions 178, 179
environmental reinforcement 145
environmental system 148
equality 79, 124
equipment 147
equity 19
ethnography 82
evaluation 17, 31–32, 199, 215
evaluative stance 8, 9, 261–271
everyday learning 215, 218
everyday practice 59
everyday understanding 66
everydayness 215
evidence base 42, 49
evidence-based practice 148, 155, 167
evidence-based strategy 197

exchange 48
exemplar videos 141
expectations 200–201, 202, 216–221, 230
experience 18–19, 56, 89, 105, 122, 204, 235; childhood 105, 122, 123, **123**; community 237; familial 105, 210; interpreting 244; lived 97, **124**, **125**; reflective 117–119; sharing 224; work 175
experiential program 230
expertise 214; inner 237; shared 190
experts 8, 32, 38, 190, 230, 236; coaching 135; external 54, 145, 203; peer 233
exploration 215

face-to-face interaction 195, 196, 198, 202
face-to-face learning 213–214, 220
facilitation 57, 211
facilitator 156, 237
family: engagement 20, 217, 219; gatherings 215; partnerships 210, 213; relationships 105
farm set 69
Farrel, A., *et al.* 261–274
fear 143, 147
feedback 142, 143, 144, 164, 230; accessible 144–145; constructive 188; corrective 211; external 145; peer 220
feelings 100, 180, 232
Field, L., Colmer, K. and Waniganayake, M. 45–63
financing 19, 20, 21
flexibility 229, 234, 254, 264
focus 37; groups 51, 58, 69, 193
follow-up work 54, 55, 60
followers 84–85
forums, online 214, 220
Fox, E.A, Gomez, R.E. and Kagan, S.L. 11–28
fragmentation 25
Frost, D., and Lightfoot, S. 243–260
frustration 71, 256
funding 22, 66, 188, 264

gain 236
games 93
gardening 218
gender 13
global policy discourse 3
goals 68, 226; collective 190; shared 236
Gomez, R.E., Kagan, S.L. and Fox, E.A. 11–28
good intentions 147
governance 19, 20
government: intervention 46, 66; regulation 247; support 30
graduates 4, 13; degree programs 16
grant program 21
Grieshaber, S., *et al.* 64–77
ground rules 165
grounded theory 136, 175, 216

INDEX

group 227; discussion 80–88, 91, 93; dynamics 155, 165, 167; norms 165
growth 187; process 145
guidance 42, 59, 140, 141–142, 195, 214, 237

Hadley, F., Waniganayake, M. and Shepherd, W. 29–44
Head Start 187
heart 100
hierarchy 38, 235
high-quality teaching 13
higher education 15
history 11
holistic approach 38
horizontalization 121
human agency 245

ideas 81, 199, 235
identification 244
identity 8, 218, 221; professional 8
imagination 73, 74
impact analysis 48
implementation 255
in-house training 38
in-service training 15, 225
incentives 33
inclusion 256
Inclusion Support Agencies 171
Inclusion Support Facilitators 172, 174
inclusiveness 171
inconsistency 18
independent sector 246
individualization 143, 188, 196, 202
individualized approaches 54, 56
influences 138
informal initiatives 93
information transmission models 46
information-sharing 89
informative posts 84, 85, 87, *88*, 91, 92
infrastructure 57, 149
initiatives, informal 93
innovation 21–23, 56, 91, 155
inquiry: cycle processes 155; thorough 178
insecurity 231, 232
insight 101–105
inspectors 233
inspiration 217
instruction 234; embedded 133–134, 141
instructional strategies 189
instrumentalism 66
intelligence, emotional 117–118, 253
intensive support 143, 148
intentional investigation 46
intentional learning 7
intentional teaching 189, 197, 213
intentions 144
interaction 116, 195, 196, 198, 202, 226, 236; social 136

interest 220
international variation 4
Internet 7, 81; habits 79; resources 87, 146–147
interpretation 56–57
interpretive approach 229, 248
interpretive research 156
interviews 35, 121, 192, 216, 229; verbatim evidence 248
investigation 46, 209, 212, 234, 235
investment 263
invitations 2
involvement, active 148
iPod 73
Irvine, S., *et al.* 261–274
isolation 139, 144, 147, 160, 199

job titles 251, 252
job-aids 135, 140
journals 38–39, 51, 157, 164
journey 181
judgment 199
justice, social 124

Kagan, S.L., Fox, E.A and Gomez, R.E. 11–28
key messages 8
keywords 1
Kidd, J.K., *et al.* 186–207
knowing adult 209
knowledge 32, 119, 127; acquired 56; applicable 189, 211; classroom 144; co-constructed 56; collective 190; construction 173, 234, 237, 239, 267; existing 47, 48; expert 236; gap 49; leadership 48–59; living 237; new 230; pedagogical 87, 89; practical 237, 239; practice-based 238; prior 188; scientific 238; specialist 49; subjective 267; transfer 265; transmission 46; usable 195, 196–198, 201–202
knowledge-as-process 234
knowledge-sharing 54, 81, 190, 214, 237

labels 145
labor 67–68
Lakhani, A., *et al.* 171–185
language 93, 197; non-verbal 50
laptop 73
Layen, S. 115–131
leaders 154, 263
leadership 6, 257; absent 165; cluster 162–163; distributive 154, 162, 166; issues 159; perceptions 162; positional 165; supportive 154; theory 5, 6
Learn, Enact, Assess, Reflect, and Network (LEARN) framework 189, 203
learner 8
learning 7; active 135; adult 187, 189, 201, 266; collaborative 227; communities 190,

INDEX

227; context 138, 147; continuity 217–218; culture 154; distributed 191; everyday 215, 218; face-to-face 213–214, 220; formats 188; frameworks 189; histories 147; online 214–215, 220; partnership 269; potential 216; process 127; professional 1, 3, 6, 7, 8; spheres of 29; stories 215–216
lesson planning 196–197
Let's Count 8, 212–213, 216–221
Lightfoot, S., and Frost, D. 243–260
listening 98, 106, 123, 179
literacy 210
Louca, L., Philippou, S. and Papademetri-Kachrimani, C. 224–242
lunchtime 161

MacDonald, A., and Perry, B. 208–223
Macfarlane, K., *et al.* 171–185
McLaughlin, T., Shannon, D. and Snyder, P. 132–151
McLeod, N. 96–114
mandatory training 36
Mantilla, A., *et al.* 64–77
marae 160, 169n3
marketing 88, 91
marketization 12, 91
Marklund, L. 78–95
materials 236; reading 36, 40, 106–107, 196, 214
maternal qualities 250
math 8
meaning 120, 122, 137, 229; constructing 226, 227, 231, 235
meaning-making 122, 128, 136
meeting time 166
mentor workshops 103
mentoring 22, 32, 38, 91, 93
methodology 262
mindsets 168
mistakes 235
mixed delivery 12, 13
mixed-methods approach 173
mobility 25
modeling 72–73, 188, 198, 202, 228
moderators 194
Moodle 157, 169n2
moral panic 68
Most Significant Change questions 173
motivation 144, 146, 148, 265
motive objects 64–75
Mulhearn, G., *et al.* 261–274

narrative 122, 126, 128
Nasser, I., *et al.* 186–207
National Board of Professional Teaching Standards (US) 17–18
National Quality Framework (Australia) 30
National Quality Standard (Australia) 263

National Writing Project (US) 256
netnography 82
network 146, 147
networking 38, 188, 199–200, 202
New Zealand 7, 152–168
nomenclature 251
norms: behavioral 154, 164; group 165
notes 142
novelty 89
novice 38, 165, 200
numeracy 210
nurseries 246, 250
nursery nurse 251
nurture 253
Nuttall, J., *et al.* 64–77

observation 144, 199, 219–220, 234
one-off events 46, 53–54, 188, 2017
online communities 81, 191
online degrees 23
online forums 214, 220
online learning 214–215, 220
online training 212
open-mindedness 178
opinions 160, 178, 183, 232
opportunities 234
organizational structures 57–58, 156
outcomes 68, 115, 138, 255; child-learning 145
outside 72
ownership, shared 154

Papademetri-Kachrimani, C., Louca, L. and Philippou, S. 224–242
parents 218
participation 98–99, 101, 106, 143–144; collective 188
participatory decision-making 267
partnership 35, 143–144, 145, 190, 212; collaborative 143–144; with families 210
partnerships principle 210
pay 246
pedagogical aid 86
pedagogical approaches 47
pedagogical knowledge 87, 89
pedagogical practice 46
peers 38, 187, 200, 203
Peppa Pig 69
perceptions 35, 204
performance reviews 54
performing 101, 108, 126
Perry, B., and MacDonald, A. 208–223
personal impacts 181
personal statement 216
personalization 142, 143, 188
personhood 229
perspectives 178, 181, 182
phenomena 120, 121

INDEX

Philippou, S., Papademetri-Kachrimani, C. and Louca, L. 224–242
photos 73, 214
Pīwakawaka (New Zealand) 159–161
planning 24, 143; lesson 196–197
play 64–75, 90, 93, 209, 212, 250; observing 219–220
PLEGMA 225, 227–229
policy: innovations 243; integration 246
policy-makers 2
popular culture 71
portfolio 17
positivity 195
potential 257
poverty 187
power 51–52, 99, 105; differentials 194; positional 167; relations 167
practical 237, 239; issues 215; program 230, 231; steps 109
practice 32, 67; changing 47; communities of 190, 227, 236; culturally responsive 197; de-privatized 154, 163; everyday 59; evidence-based 148, 155, 167; guides 141–142; reflective 42, 163–165, 266; review 162; shared 140, 154, 160; sustainable 265; theory 65; transformative 226
practitioner 246; inquiry 36, 37, 56; research 55, 56
pragmatism 1
praise 144
praxis 47, 56, 101
pre-primary education 228
pre-service training 14–15
preferences 145
preparation 12–14; professional 14–15, 17
presage factors 266
preschool 82; teachers 13
presencing 101
presentation 215, 228
prior-to-school settings 30
prioritization 211
priority children 171
privacy 84
private sector 246
problem-solving 108, 172
problems: speech 198; wicked 268
procedure principles 226
process 57, 58, 226, 227, 228
professional communities 1
professional development framework 7
professional identity 8
professional learning 1
professional learning communities 7
professional learning and development 3; critical evaluation 6; reclaiming 8
professional network 146, 147
professional preparation 14–15, 17

professional readings 36, 40, 106–107, 196, 214
Professional Support Coordinators 31
professionalization 30–31, 67, 71; agenda 246–247
profit-making 128–129
promotion 88, 91
prototyping 101
provocateur 209
punishment 147

qualifications 3–4, 31, *37*, 116, 192, 247; formal 39–40
quality 33, 255; assessments 41, 264; assurance 18; enhancement tools 19–20; indicators 210
questioning 100

race 13
Race to the Top – Early Learning Challenge Fund (US) 21
reaction 72
reading: circle 40; professional 36, 40, 106–107, 196, 214
real world 215, 235
reciprocity 24
recognition 250
reflection 39, 48, 53, 57, 163, 182, 211, 228; collaborative practice 266; critical 172, 173, 180, 181; self- 37, 39, 42, 48, 53, 57, 179
reflective capacity 6
reflective journals 38–39, 157, 164
reflective practice 42, 163–165, 266
reflective thought 245
reflexivity 229
refreshers 200
regulation 4, 22
reinforcement 145
relational conditions 154, 163, 166–167
relational issues 159
relationships 186, 188, 190; positive 215; trusting 202, 203
repetition 24
representation 2, 228
research 262; action 32, 56, 156; base 23; interpretive 156; journal 51; practitioner 55, 56; review 152; themes 5, 32
researcher 8, 226; engaged 156
resilience 48
resistance 202–203
resources 72, 87, 140, 175, **176**, 181; family 210; Internet 87, 146–147
resourcing 166
respect 53, 177, 178
responses, emotional 243
responsibility 51
return on investment 264
review 106, 152, 162; performance 54; self- 167

INDEX

Riroriro (New Zealand) 161–162
role titles 251–252
roles 229, 230, 232, 234–236, 238, 246, 247
romanticization 71–72
routines 161; home 210
rules 255
Ryan, S., *et al.* 261–274

safe environment 53
safe space 105, 178, 183
safety 105, 106, 139
samizdat professionalism 245
sample size 183
satisfaction 194, 195, 204, 227
school 154; reculturing 155; transition 209
science 198; education 8
searching 234
seeing 101
selection criteria 200
self 244; caring 250
self-assessments 140
self-awareness 6, 119, 124, 125, 144
self-concepts 119, 124, 125
self-confidence 32
self-direction 91–92
self-knowledge 119, 127
self-motivation 148
self-perspectives 179
self-reflection 37, 39, 42, 48, 53, 57, 179
self-review process 167
sense-making 235
sensing 101
sensitivity 48
service: ethic 155; providers 268
Shannon, D., Snyder, P. and McLaughlin, T. 132–151
sharing 214
Shepherd, W., Hadley, F. and Waniganayake, M. 29–44
short courses 46
simple things 71
situations: challenging 209; social 34, 55
skilled workforce 261
skills: evaluative 265; facilitation 57; foundational 203; interpersonal 59; professional 48; school-entry 209; technical 46, 53; technological 46, 65; transmission 46
Smith Family, The 212
Smith, K., *et al.* 171–185
Snyder, P., McLaughlin, T. and Shannon, D. 132–151
social behavior 244
social competence 164
social context 268
social interaction 136
social justice 124
social situations 34, 55

socialization 244
software 69, 147
spaces 99, 108, 238; safe 105, 178, 183
specialism 1
specialized training 13
speech problem 198
spheres of learning 29
spontaneity 191
stable state 238
staffing 30–31, 40, 163, 166
stakeholders 33
standardization 41
standards 18, 236, 255
state sector 246
status 19–20, 116–117, 228, 246, 247, 250
stereotypes 183, 232, 234, 239
stories 119, 120, 122, 247
strangers 238
strategic approach 40–41, 54
strengths 126
stress 7, 232
structural conditions 154, 156, 162, 163, 166–167
structuration theory 245
structure 48, 237
subject matter 86
suggestions 164, 177
Sumison, J., *et al.* 261–274
superficiality 46
support 139, 140, 142, 143, 146, 253; individualized 199; intensive 143, 148; online 195, 196; Professional Coordinators 31; roles 161
supportive conditions 154, 163, 166–167
Supportive Environmental Quality Underlying Adult Learning (SEQUAL) 22
surprise 209
sustainability 18, 211, 214, 219, 265
Sweden 78–93
symbolic interactionism 136
systemic approach 32, 33
systems thinking 5

targets 108, 212
teacher-researchers 225, 234
teachers 8; preschool 13; United States 12–14
teaching: collective 47–48; high-quality 13; intentional 189, 197, 213; materials 141–142; quality 12–13
team culture 164
teamwork 162, 164, 233; effective 166
technical assistance 22; centers 20
technical skills 46
technicians 255
technological knowledge 85–86, *85*, 89
Technological Pedagogical Content Knowledge framework 83, *83*
technological skills 46, 65

INDEX

technology 23, 146–147, 191, 195, 201; digital 6, 78–93
telling 235
tensions 67, 160, 246
terminology 3, 251
thematic analysis 157
themes 84, 194, 216–217, 249
theories 46, 47, 117–119, 230, 231, 237; pre-digital 75
theory-practice divide 225, 239
therapy 127
thinking 174; critical 268; differently 270; evaluative 265; otherwise 7, 178, 180, 181
Thomas the Tank Engine 69
Thornton, K., and Cherrington, S. 152–170
thought, reflective 245
time 40, 42, 81, 133, 165, 166, 231–232
tools 22–23, 68, 74
traditions 96, 235, 236
training 46; costs 40; defining 54; government 46; in-house 38; in-service 15, 225; mandatory 36; online 212; pre-service 14–15; specialized 13
transfer 265
transformation 7, 47, 48, 55, 56, 235, 256, 257
transitional view 226
transmission: models 46, 47, 57; view 230
trends 33
trouble-shooting 146
trust 53, 155, 164, 167, 178–179, 202; mutual 211
trust-building 160
turn-taking 164
turnover 42
two-tier system 247

understanding, everyday 66
uniqueness 145

United States (USA) 5, 7, 11–25, 123–149, 186–204; teachers 12–14
unthinkable 181

validation 253
value 1, 177, 204, 250
variety 21
video 196, 201, 214; cameras 141, 146; exemplar 141; recording 69, 228, 229, 232, 238
vision 5, 34, 66, 127; development 160; shared 147, 154, 163
vocational education 3, 4
volunteering 168

wages, hourly 14
Walsh, K., *et al.* 261–274
Waniganayake, M.: Field, L. and Colmer, K. 45–63; Shepherd, W. and Hadley, F. 29–44
web *see* Internet
whānau 155, 169n1
what works 23
will 100
wisdom 59
women 12
wonder 238
Wood, E., *et al.* 64–77
wooden train set 69
work: characteristics 174; environment 22; experience 175
workers, childcare 13
workforce 3; demographics 13–14, 35–36, 173, 192, **193**, 229; retention 36, 81; skilled 261; turnover 166; women in 12
working: conditions 14; hours 246
workshops 173, 213; one-shot 188; targeted 201